The Complete Book of Wills, Estates & Trusts

The Complete Book of Wills, Estates & Trusts

4TH EDITION

Advice That Can Save You Thousands of Dollars in Legal Fees and Taxes

Alexander A. Bove, Jr., Esq.
Melissa Langa, Esq.

ST. MARTIN'S GRIFFIN NEW YORK

First published in the United States by St. Martin's Griffin,
an imprint of St. Martin's Publishing Group

www.stmartins.com

Book design by Richard Oriolo

Library of Congress Cataloging-in-Publication Data

Names: Bove, Alexander A., Jr., 1938- author. | Langa, Melissa, 1954-author.
Title: The complete book of wills, estates & trusts : advice that can save you thousands of dollars in legal fees and taxes / Alexander A. Bove, Jr.; Melissa Langa.
Other titles: Wills, estates, and trusts
Description: Fourth edition. | New York : St. Martin's Griffin, 2021. | Prev. edition is classed under KF755.Z9.
Identifiers: LCCN 2020045305 | ISBN 9781250792747 (trade paperback) | ISBN 9781250792754 (ebook other)
Subjects: LCSH: Wills—United States—Popular works. | Executors and administrators—United States—Popular works. | Estate planning—United States—Popular works. | Probate law and practice—United States—Popular works. | Trusts and trustees—United States—Popular works.
Classification: LCC KF755 .B68 2021 | DDC 346.7305/6—dc23
LC record available at https://lccn.loc.gov/2020045305

Our books may be purchased in bulk for promotional, educational, or business use. Please contact your local bookseller or the Macmillan Corporate and Premium Sales Department at 1-800-221-7945, extension 5442, or by email at MacmillanSpecialMarkets@macmillan.com.

First Edition: 1991
Second Edition: 2000
Third Edition: 2005
Fourth Edition: 2021

10 9 8 7 6 5

Contents

5: Common Will Provisions

6: Uncommon Will Provisions—Controlling from the Grave

7: Spouses' and Children's Rights to an Estate

8: Estate Management

13: Probate, Trusts, and Taxes

14: Dealing with Lawyers

A Helpful Introduction

After several years and over 100,000 copies in print, we felt it was time to update *The Complete Book of Wills, Estates & Trusts.*

This new and revised fourth edition reflects changes to the relevant estate and gift tax laws since the last edition and adds some special new planning concepts, such as trust decanting and spousal lifetime access trusts. We have even expanded our glossary, adding dozens of terms commonly used in the field of trusts and estates.

For our new readers, whom we wholeheartedly welcome, you can look forward to a clear, often humorous discussion and plain-language explanation of virtually every aspect of settling an estate (subject, of course, to differences in state law), contesting a will or defending a will contest, and even selecting a lawyer to help settle an estate. (If things go wrong, we even tell you how to fire an estate lawyer.) And of course, there are discussions and explanations of just about every type of trust that is used in an estate plan, even including so-called "asset protection" trusts, onshore and offshore, as well as a brief review of the reporting requirements for offshore trusts. In addition to a discussion of each type of trust, our chapter 13 on probate, trusts, and taxes is (as are many of our topics) unique to this book and can save you time, trouble, and money in developing and understanding your own estate plan.

It should be clear when you do read the book, however, that it is NOT a substitute for expert professional advice. It is foolhardy to try to do your own estate plan using an online service where you can "zoom" in and out of technical documents drafted by lawyers (hopefully) who don't know you or your family and who don't personally discuss with you your objectives and options. As we say in chapter 12, it's like buying a cheap mail-order suit: you can't expect it to fit or be fit to wear, but at least you saved some money! Or so you might think. Unfortunately, your heirs will pay for it later.

Our aim in writing this book was to offer readers honest and clear discussions of all the issues covered based on our decades of practice and teaching in the trusts and estates field. Our earlier editions were rewarded with widespread acceptance by the readers who acquired the book, many of whom communicated with us about the content as well as related issues. This was and is extremely gratifying to us, and we continue to welcome questions and comments from our "old" and new readers alike.

Alexander A. Bove, Jr., and Melissa Langa

Special Note to Readers

The authors have attempted to explain complex legal topics in an understandable and often humorous fashion. To that end, we have taken some liberties with the facts of selected actual legal controversies and documents. The legal concepts they are meant to illustrate, however, are real.

Acknowledgments

The authors wish to acknowledge the invigorating support, inspiration, and limitless patience of their spouses, Catherine Bove and Jeff Wulfson, and the tireless efforts and constructive assistance of Kim McMahon, the Chief Operating Officer of the Bove & Langa law firm.

The Complete Book of Wills, Estates & Trusts

1

The World of Wills

I have nothing, I owe a great deal; the rest I give to the poor.

—the will of Rabelais, a fifteenth-century satirist

Was Rabelais serious, or was this just another example of his wonderful satire? Did this single sentence make a valid will? Whether it did or not, it certainly helped immortalize Rabelais, since it is hard to find a discussion of wills that does not make mention of his. Rabelais, no doubt, would have been immortalized regardless of his will, since he left the world so much more in the form of his literary works. But for those of us who leave little more than some money and a few greedy relatives, the fact is that a colorful or unusual will may offer some prospect of immortality that we would not have otherwise. Although the world of wills can be colorful, however, it can also be grim. A will can be a source of security to a family or it can bankrupt them, as we will see.

Your Own Nobel Prize

Most people know, or at least think they know, what a will is, and they generally treat a will with a certain degree of respect. After all, wills are almost universally regarded as a sort of permanent memorial, a person's final statement to the world, offering, in many cases, a touch of immortality. A perfect illustration of this is the will of Alfred Nobel, who truly immortalized himself through the provisions of his will. Just a year before his death in 1896, Nobel wrote out his will, which, despite its humble and relatively simple language, gave birth to one of the most widely known and respected memorials in the world—the Nobel Prize. This is what he wrote that formed the foundation for the prize:

> The whole of my remaining realizable estate shall be dealt with in the following way: the capital, invested in safe securities by my executors, shall constitute a fund, the interest on which shall be annually distributed in the form of prizes to those who, during the preceding year, shall have conferred the greatest benefit on mankind. The said interest shall be divided into five equal parts, which shall be apportioned as follows: one part to the person who shall have made the most important discovery or invention within the field of physics; one part to the person who shall have made the most important chemical discovery or improvement; one part to the person who shall have made the most important discovery within the domain of physiology or medicine; one part to the person who shall have produced in the field of literature the most outstanding work of an idealistic tendency; and one part to the person who shall have done the most or the best work for fraternity between nations, for the abolition or reduction of standing armies and for the holding and promotion of peace congresses. The prize for physics and chemistry shall be awarded by the Swedish Academy of Sciences; that for physiological or medical works by the Karolinska Institute in Stockholm; that for literature by the Academy in Stockholm, and that for champions of peace by a committee of five persons to

be elected by the Norwegian Storting. It is my express wish that in awarding the prizes no consideration whatever shall be given to the nationality of the candidates, but that the most worthy shall receive the prize, whether he be a Scandinavian or not.

Paris, November 27, 1895

Alfred Bernhard Nobel

Through this "simple" will, carefully handwritten by Nobel himself (as allowed in Sweden) in the Swedish language, Nobel thought, no doubt, that he had included all the necessary provisions to carry out his now-famous plan. Actually, Nobel's will was very poorly drafted (he disliked lawyers and, therefore, decided to write it himself) and resulted in protracted legal battles, requiring the court to clarify and interpret important issues relating to, among other things, the selection of candidates and awarding of the prizes. Nevertheless, after years of court proceedings in several different countries and about a half-million dollars (a respectable fortune in those days) in fees, legacies, and expenses, the remainder went to establish permanent immortality for Nobel.

Then there are other types of immortality—one that results when the deceased was a popular figure *before* his death, so there is a great deal of continuing public interest in how he left his estate, and another where there is a bitter and very public dispute over the provisions of a will, or both, such as in the case of the late Howard Hughes. Hughes, the eccentric Nevada billionaire, died in 1976, a bitter, emaciated, ninety-two-pound remainder of a man, and almost instantly the fights began over his estate. Over forty wills surfaced after his death, each claiming to be the billionaire's last will. The most famous of these was the "Mormon will," purportedly found on the desk of an official of the Mormon Church. The Mormon will, which appeared to be in Hughes's own handwriting, left one-sixteenth of his $4 billion estate to Melvin Dummar, a gas station operator who, as the story goes, picked up a poor old man on a deserted road and gave him a lift to Las Vegas and a quarter to make a phone call. The poor old man turned out to be Howard Hughes, who, in a gesture of generosity totally foreign to his reported character, left Dummar a princely chunk of his estate. Dummar's story was later recounted in the 1980 film *Melvin and Howard*.

The fairy tale would have been complete had the Mormon will been declared valid, but after a trial that took the better part of a year and several million dollars in legal fees, Dummar and the Mormons lost the case. Despite the appearance of forty wills, the courts finally decided that Hughes died without a will. All in all, it took more than thirty-four years to settle the estate, providing a comfortable annuity to the battalions of attorneys who represent the estate and its labyrinthine interests in oil wells, real estate, airlines, television stations, hotels, and casinos.

The estates of Hughes and Nobel were admittedly extremes. Still, some of us may achieve a touch of immortality by creating our own little "Nobel" prize in the form of a small scholarship fund or a research grant, while others may unwittingly achieve the same result as Hughes by leaving no will, a defective will, or several wills, or even a valid will that becomes the subject of a bitter dispute. Or perhaps we will express some wish or bequest so unique that it finds its way into newspaper articles and law books, such as that of Sandra West, late of California, whose will directed that she be buried "in my lace nightgown . . . in my Ferrari, with the seat slanted comfortably." Whatever the case, the fact remains that our wills will be governed by the same principles and applicable rules of law as those of Howard Hughes, Alfred Nobel, and Sandra West.

In the cases of Nobel and Hughes, it is interesting (and essential) to note, for instance, that both of these famous estates consisted almost entirely of *probate property,* and this is why their wills were so important. A person's will deals only with property or assets that are part of his *probate estate,* and the probate estate is governed by the local probate process. In this chapter, we will look at the power as well as the vulnerabilities of probate, and the complexities as well as the absurdities of the process. Technically, the probate process involves a "proving" of the deceased's last will (i.e., that it was a properly signed, valid will under the law and that it was the last one the decedent made). But as a practical matter, the probate courts also deal with disputes relating to the transfer of the property of a deceased person and claims against his estate. Therefore, if the deceased left a will, it is the job of the probate court (some states call it the surrogate's court, orphan's court, or chancery court) to decide whether the will was valid according to the laws of the applicable state, and if it is declared valid, the probate estate will be disposed of according to the will. If the will was not valid, or if the deceased left no will, then the probate court will order the deceased's property disposed of through the probate court according to state law.

If, in the meantime, there are any disputes relating to the estate or claims against the estate made by the decedent's creditors, employers, family members, or anyone else, or if there are bills to pay or anything else that could possibly interfere with the final settlement of the probate estate and payment of bequests to the beneficiaries, the probate court will deal with it all as part of the probate process. Here's how it all happens and why, step by step.

The Probate Process—Step by Step

In a civilized society, a legal mechanism for dealing with a deceased person's property is essential. Think of the chaos that would result if, when someone died, the law allowed anyone free access to take all or any part of the deceased person's property on a "first come" basis. Instead, we have developed a system that protects and sometimes directs the distribution of property on a person's death. Our laws recognize that some order must be maintained in the situation, and so they provide, among other things, for what is called the right of "freedom of testation" and a legal process to deal with those estates that have exercised that right, as well as those that have not.

Freedom of testation simply means the right to leave your property on your death in almost any manner you choose. Few people realize that this is not a "natural" right. It would be quite possible, for example (though it would certainly meet with resistance), for the government to rule that on a person's death, all of his property would belong to the government. Such an approach, however, would, among other things, discourage the acquisition of property and would soon undermine our capitalistic system. Therefore, we are "allowed" to freely acquire property during our lifetime, to keep it or dispose of it as we wish, and on our death, we are "allowed" to decide, subject to certain obligations to keep our spouse and children in mind, who will get what is left. These decisions, if you want them to be carried out, must be reflected in a valid will or some other legal disposition, as more thoroughly discussed in chapter 11; otherwise, the laws of the state will decide how your property will be divided. Whether or not you decide to exercise your "freedom of testation" and make a will, the dividing and transfer of the property that is part of your "probate estate" can only be done by the probate court.

When we talk of your "probate estate" (or "probate property") in this sense, we mean any type of property that stands in your name *alone* at the time of your death or that would require action on the part of your personal representative[1] or administrator to collect and administer under the terms of your will or under state law if you left no will. It would not include, for instance, jointly held property or assets held in a trust or assets that are payable to a named beneficiary at death, since those arrangements generally supersede provisions of a will. Probate property includes only property over which you *alone* would have control. From a "legal" perspective, therefore, if on death we wish to transfer any of our "probate" or "estate" property to someone who survives us, or if our estate is to be given to the spouse and children equally because we left no will, just how would this be accomplished? They could not simply "take" the property that stands in your name alone because they would not have legal ownership of it. And on what legal grounds could they support their ownership if they did take it? This is why we must have some orderly legal process if we are to recognize any rights to transfer property at death, and this is where the probate process comes in.

Whether you decide to write your own will or to have no will at all, whether you are a beneficiary of an estate or a creditor, and whether you think there will be no disputes or you can't wait to start one, it is very important for you to understand how the probate process works. This is because probate is the system that determines and governs the distribution of the probate estate to the heirs and beneficiaries, the payment of estate debts after death, the resolution of disputes and claims against the estate, and contests against the will.

STEP 1: FINDING THE WILL

When a person dies, the first thing that must be done concerning distribution of his property is to determine whether he left a will. In most cases, family members will know or have an idea that there was or was not a will left by the deceased. If not, a search of the deceased's papers and safe-deposit box may offer some leads. If the deceased had a lawyer or saw one before his death, the lawyer should be asked if he has any knowledge of a will.

In many states, it is a crime to conceal a will, and most states have laws requiring anyone in possession of the original will to submit it to the probate

---

[1] Historically the terms *executor* (male) and *executrix* (female) were used to identify the person who administered a will. The modern term, and the one we use throughout the book, is *personal representative*. This gender-neutral term includes all individuals of whatever gender identification, as well as banks and other entities who might serve in this role.

court within a certain period (often thirty days) after a person's death, with penalties for failure to do so.

Rather than conceal a will, however, if someone in possession of a will does not want it probated, he is more likely to simply destroy it. This is also a crime, but it is almost impossible to prove that a person has concealed or destroyed a will unless someone actually saw him do it. There are, unfortunately, a number of cases where there was a strong "commonsense" inference that a will had been destroyed but no way of proving it, and no copies or other evidence existed to show what it said. In one case, a man we'll call Irving notified his girlfriend, Rosie, who was his close companion for twelve years, that he had made out a will leaving everything to her. Before he met Rosie, Irving had a will in which he simply left his estate to his brother and sister, his only two relatives. On Irving's death, the will he told Rosie he made out could not be found. Several months later, Irving's brother "discovered" the old will among Irving's papers and submitted it for probate. Although she felt certain that Irving's brother had simply torn up the new will, Rosie had no standing to object to the old will and no proof, other than Irving's statement to her, that he had made a new one. There was nothing she could do to prevent the old will from being allowed.

STEP 2: STARTING THE PROBATE OF THE ESTATE

Once the will is located, it (the original) is sent to the probate court in the appropriate district of the state where the person was domiciled (had his permanent residence) at the time of his death. If the original is lost or destroyed, a verifiable copy may be submitted to the probate court, but the parties seeking to have the copy allowed must be prepared to satisfy the court that there was no funny business. Submitting the will to the probate court, by itself, does nothing other than to place the will on record with the court. In order for any action to be taken on the will, someone, usually the personal representative named under the will, must ask ("petition") the probate court to approve the will as the last will of the deceased. (The word "probate" is from the Latin *probare*, meaning to test and approve.) If for some reason the personal representative does not offer the will for probate, any interested party, even a creditor of the deceased, may do so. Under the "Uniform Probate Code," enacted in various forms by nineteen states as of this writing, there is a three-year window of opportunity to offer a will for probate—after that, special permission must be received by the court before the will is allowed to be processed.

If you want to see if your state has adopted the Uniform Probate Code, check out the Uniform Laws website at http://www.uniformlaws.org.

Petitions for the probate of a will are relatively simple forms available at the probate court for the district or county of the decedent's domicile. This is not to say that there are no complexities; states with the Uniform Probate Code offer four types of probate: voluntary (for very small estates), informal (often used in uncontested estates), formal (where a judge determines testacy, declares the will the last will, and determines heirs), and supervised (where the personal representative's actions are subject to ongoing court oversight). Therefore, the personal representative needs to select the process that best fits the estate, but once selected the request (petition) for probate itself is the easy part. In substance, it simply asks the court to allow the will that has been submitted to the court as the decedent's last will.

If there was no will, then the petition takes a different form. It suggests to the court that the decedent left no will and asks that a person (named in the petition, and more than one person may be named) be appointed as administrator to represent and administer the deceased's estate. If there is no will (referred to as "intestacy"), the deceased's probate property is distributed according to the laws of the state (as more particularly discussed in chapter 2). Whether or not there was a will, most states require that the petition include the names and addresses of all of the "heirs at law" (generally meaning those persons who the law says will inherit if there is no will). Usually this would be the spouse and children (and grandchildren if a child is deceased and has left descendants—the child's children or grandchildren), or the parents and siblings, and often one or more charities.

Whether there is a will or not, in both instances the clerk of the probate court is typically most helpful to any person trying to understand probate procedures and the appropriate forms to file. Don't hesitate to speak up and ask questions if you are going it alone without the help of a lawyer.

STEP 3: NOTICE TO HEIRS AND INTERESTED PARTIES—TIME TO CONTEST

In most states, after the petition for probate is filed, the probate court will order that notice of the petition be given to the heirs and other "interested" parties (those who may not be heirs but who may be named in the will) and, in some cases, that "publication" must be made. Publication is the placing of legal notice in the local newspaper to the effect that John Jinx has died and a petition has been submitted to the court asking that Jane Jinx be appointed as the personal representative (or administrator if there was no will) of his estate. The publication and notices will also suggest that if you wish to object to the allowance of the petition, you or your attorney should file an "appearance" on or before a certain date. In those states that require notice, this designated date (sometimes called the "return date") is very important, because if no objections to the petition are received by that date, the court will allow the petition. An "appearance" in this case is a written statement to the court stating that you (or your attorney on your behalf) object to the allowance of the will or the appointment of the person who asked to be appointed the personal representative. This does not mean if you miss the date or later discover that you should have objected that you cannot, but an objection filed after the date designated by the court as the "deadline" will be accepted by the court only if there was a good reason for the failure to file the objection within the allowed time. If adequate notice is not given as required by the state's laws, probate may not be allowed. Remember, as a general rule (exceptions are discussed later in the book), the probate assets do not include jointly held assets, assets payable to a named beneficiary other than the "estate," and assets in most trusts.

Some states take the reverse approach and immediately allow the petition for probate and appointment of a personal representative as soon as the will is filed, *without* notice to the beneficiaries. This does not mean, however, that no one can object. In fact, in those states that allow the will without notice, a person who wishes to contest the will or the appointment of a personal representative often has a much longer period within which to do so—usually until the estate is settled and the personal representative is discharged by the court.

In those states where notice and/or publication is required, the information in the newspaper publication will also be sent directly to you if you are an heir or an interested party in the estate. Obviously it must be sent to you sufficiently before the return date to give you adequate time to object to the allowance of the petition if you wish to do so.

The filing of an objection to either the allowance of the will or the appointment of the personal representative is surprisingly straightforward. All you (or your attorney) need to do to begin the contest is notify the court that you object. That's it. A brief letter to the appropriate court will suffice with proper reference to the court docket, reference, or file number, saying something such as, "I object to the allowance of the petition of Jane Jinx requesting that a certain document be allowed as John Jinx's will and that Jane Jinx be appointed as executrix," (signed) Jesse Jinx. Or, your attorney will file a similar notice stating, "Please enter my appearance on behalf of Lulu D'Amour in opposition to the allowance of the will of James Jinx." In either case, be aware that soon (from only a few days to sixty days in some states, much longer in others) you will be required to *specify* just what it is you object to and why, and the laws at this stage begin to be somewhat more complex, so it would be foolhardy to attempt to go much beyond this point without an experienced lawyer. Judges are generally not sympathetic to people who try to represent themselves in will contests.

STEP 4: APPOINTMENT OF THE PERSONAL REPRESENTATIVE OR ADMINISTRATOR

Note: While we discussed above that the party appointed to oversee the settlement of the estate where there is a will is called the personal representative, and that where there is no will the party is called an administrator, from here, we will use "personal representative" for convenience. If no one objects to the petition for the allowance of the will or (if there is no will) to the petition for administration of the estate without a will, then the court will usually appoint the personal representative named in the will (or the administrator named in the petition) to be the personal (legal) representative of the deceased's estate. Once formally appointed by the court, the personal representative will attempt to locate all assets in the deceased's name and will take legal title to all of the deceased's probate assets, so that estate property may be "dealt with" in the process of settling the estate. In other words, all of the deceased's individual bank accounts, securities, and other assets (real estate is subject to special rules in many states) that are a part of his probate estate will then be titled "Jane Jinx, Personal Representative, Estate of John Jinx."

The personal representative is the person responsible for all aspects of settling the estate, including paying debts and taxes, dealing with claims against the estate, filing necessary tax returns, and ultimately distributing the estate property to the beneficiaries. After receiving his appointment, however, one of the first things the personal representative must do is prepare and file an estate inventory.

STEP 5: FILING THE ESTATE INVENTORY

Within one to three months (depending on the particular state) after the personal representative has been appointed, he is required by law to file a "complete" inventory of the estate's assets. (This would include only the *probate* assets as further described below.) The inventory is submitted to the court and, like all other papers submitted to the court, becomes a matter of "public record," available to anyone who wants to look at it unless the court determines otherwise.

Briefly, there are two reasons for the filing of the inventory. First, the inventory indicates to the court the items of probate property for which the personal representative will later "account" (tell the court in detail what he did with all these items when the estate is settled). Second, it lets the beneficiaries, creditors, and all other interested parties know the contents of the deceased's probate estate. If the personal representative delays or refuses to file an inventory, any interested party may ask the court to order him to file one, although if there are no disputes or contests, personal representatives often file their inventories late.

The probate inventory will include *only* probate property, which is *any* type of property (stocks, bonds, real estate, furnishings, jewelry, copyrights, claims against others, etc.) that *belonged to the deceased* at the time of his death. Normally, this only includes property that stood in the deceased's name alone, but could very well also include property that was being held by someone else, including joint property, for example, that the personal representative believed should be a part of the deceased's probate estate. Otherwise, as noted earlier, nonprobate property, such as jointly held property, life insurance or retirement plan benefits payable to a named beneficiary, or assets in a living trust, generally will not be included in the probate inventory, except in specified cases discussed later.

STEP 6: PAYMENT OF CLAIMS

In order to facilitate an orderly settlement of the estate within a "reasonable" period of time, every state provides for specified time periods within which claims against the estate *must* be made; otherwise, they will not be collectible, no matter how valid. The period usually begins at a specified time, say on the date of death, or the date of the personal representative's appointment, or three months *after* the personal representative has been appointed or has given notice to creditors, and ends from six to twelve months after that. Unless the court for some reason allows an extension, it is *only within this period* that a creditor may make a formal claim against the estate, and state courts are fairly strict on this point. The personal representative, however, has an obligation to notify all known creditors and to make a reasonable effort to identify creditors, so that they will have the opportunity to file a claim within the special period. Since this period is specified as being "open" to creditors' claims against the estate, the personal representative must be careful not to prejudice creditors by distributing all or too much of the estate property to beneficiaries before the end of the specified period. If that happened, then the personal representative would be held *personally liable* for valid creditors' claims, and it is for this reason that personal representatives will not, as a rule, distribute estate property before the end of the special claims period.

This is not to say that claims may not be paid by the personal representative before or after this special time period, since the personal representative can pay valid, undisputed claims almost any time he wants, with the exception that federal government claims (such as unpaid income taxes) must under federal law be paid first when assets of estate are insufficient to pay all debts.

It is usually the disputed and particularly the unknown claims that worry the personal representative and apply to this special period. Once the period expires, the personal representative need worry only about known claims that he intends to pay, other valid expenses, taxes, and, finally, distribution to the beneficiaries.

STEP 7: PAYMENT OF DEBTS, FEES, EXPENSES, AND TAXES

Simultaneous with his assessment of what claims may be made against the estate, the personal representative will begin to determine the remaining debts, fees, and expenses that he is aware of (such as doctors' bills, utility bills, outstanding charge account balances, year of death income taxes, and of course legal, accounting, and personal representative fees), since all of these items will have a bearing upon the estate taxes that may be due in the estate. In fact, part of the personal representative's job is to file the income and estate tax return and see that the taxes are paid when due (estate taxes are usually due within nine months after the date of death, unless an extension is granted). Claims and expenses for which there is no dispute are usually paid by the personal representative within this nine-month period. Often overlooked is that the probate estate itself is a taxpayer, and the personal representative must file income tax returns where the probate estate consists of income-producing assets.

STEP 8: FILING THE ESTATE TAX RETURNS

Putting all this information together, the personal representative will prepare (or have a professional prepare) the deceased's estate tax returns showing all the property included in the estate (not just the probate property), reduced by allowable claims and deductions, to arrive at the tax due, if any. Filing of the estate tax returns does not mean the estate is settled. In fact, the federal and/or state governments may take several months to a year after filing to "accept" the returns or to respond by asking for more information or, in some cases, in deciding that the estate will be audited. Until the returns are accepted and the final tax liability (if any) is agreed upon and paid, the personal representative should not distribute all the assets of the estate. If he does and if there is not enough money left in the estate to pay the balance of the tax due, he will be *personally liable* for payment of the remaining tax on the probate estate.

Note that if the estate is "small" enough in size, it may not be necessary to file a federal estate tax return at all (called "form 706"). That is, if the value of all the property included on the deceased's federal estate tax return does not exceed the allowable "tax-free" amount, then no federal return is due. (See chapter 14 for a discussion of estate taxes.) This does not mean that the state in which the deceased lived or owned property would not require its own estate tax return or a separate estate tax, since state laws vary on this. You can go to the website of your state's department of revenue to determine if that state has an estate tax. Just type "estate tax" into the search window, and the results should give you the answer. Or, if you are shopping around for a state with no estate tax, you can do a web search of "states with no estate tax," and you may get your answer that way. But, as always with the web, verify!

In many states, even though no estate tax may be due, if the decedent owned real estate, it may be necessary to file a return or record a document in a registry of deeds where the real estate is located just to "prove" that no taxes are due so the beneficiaries can inherit the property without fear of a tax or a state lien on real property being discovered later. Once estate tax returns are filed and finally accepted, the federal government (if requested by the estate) and state government will normally give the personal representative a "closing letter" (typically without asking), stating that no further taxes are due in the deceased's estate. In most cases, receipt of the closing letter(s) is quickly followed by distributions to the beneficiaries and the closing of the estate itself.

STEP 9: GIVING THE BENEFICIARIES THEIR MONEY (FINALLY)

After all tax matters for the estate are settled and all bills and expenses paid or amounts set aside, the personal representative may then prepare to distribute what is left to the beneficiaries according to the terms of the deceased's will, or according to the laws of the state if the deceased left no will. If there was a contest and a negotiated settlement, the personal representative would prepare to make the full distributions required under the settlement. *Note:* if there are disputes or lawsuits still outstanding against the estate, it is unlikely that final distributions will be made until these are settled.

Before the personal representative will actually make payment or transfer property to beneficiaries, however, he should prepare a release for each beneficiary to sign, indicating that the beneficiary accepts the proposed distribution in full settlement of any claims or legacies he has in the estate and releases the personal representative from any further claims or personal liability. Together with the release, the beneficiaries may also receive a copy of the "final account" that the personal representative proposes to file with the probate court. This is a detailed financial report of all the assets of the probate estate; the income and expenses, disbursements, and other transactions made by the personal representative on behalf of the estate during estate administration; and the proposed final distribution of the remainder to the beneficiaries, leaving a balance of zero. The beneficiaries are usually asked to review and assent to the personal representative's account, but if they object, they may notify the personal representative or the court. An objection to the personal representative's proposed account will, of course, cause the personal representative to withhold final distribution to the beneficiaries until the objection is satisfactorily dealt with.

If you are a beneficiary of an estate, you should *not* sign a release until you have seen and are satisfied with the personal representative's account. Absent fraud, it will be difficult after you have signed the release to object to excess personal representative fees, or legal fees, or some other estate expense or distribution. (For more on this, see chapter 8.)

Once the beneficiaries sign the release and assent to the personal representative's final account, they can then expect to receive their inheritance from the estate (although, in many cases, if there is enough money in the estate and no disputes, they may have already received an advance on their inheritance). Happily, the beneficiary receives the inheritance free of income tax. Once the inheritance starts earning income, the beneficiary of course includes that income on his income tax return.

STEP 10: CLOSING THE ESTATE

When the personal representative has paid or settled all debts, fees, and taxes and has prepared the estate's final account, and assuming the personal representative has already obtained the assents and releases of the beneficiaries, the personal representative is faced with the decision of whether to close the estate. Generally, the options will include (1) keeping the estate open indefinitely (with the personal representative continually on the hook for claims against the estate), (2) closing the estate informally (with the personal representative off the hook typically within one year of the informal closing), or (3) closing the estate formally (with the probate court relieving the personal representative of all liability). Depending on the option that is used, the personal representative will submit his final account to the probate estate's beneficiaries, and often the probate court, asking that the account be "allowed." Allowance of the account by the probate court in a formal closing means that the beneficiaries and the court have accepted this report as a complete and accurate record of the settlement of the estate. When this happens, the estate may be closed and the personal representative discharged of all duties and liabilities.

If this is all there is to it, then why are estate settlements so confusing, time-consuming, and expensive, especially where probate is involved? Two reasons. First, if you review the above steps once again, you will see that each step takes time under the best of circumstances. Locating all of the deceased's assets, getting date of death valuations on each asset (necessary for the inventory and especially the estate tax returns), and changing them into the name of the personal representative can take months. And the second reason is that things seldom go according to plan. If there are minors who may inherit, for example, the court will usually take extra pains (and delays) to see that they are protected. If the deceased left property in more than one state, then you can be sure of substantial delays and additional legal costs. There may also be a dispute over claims, or over what belonged to the deceased and what didn't, or there may be difficulty in locating the beneficiaries and getting their assent, as in the case of the New York man who left specific bequests of $3,000 each to several cousins in Poland. By the time they were located and the necessary communications authenticated and certified by the proper authorities, more than two years had passed and a sum equal to the bequests had been expended. (Keep this in mind if you plan to leave something to people in other countries.)

Still another reason it can take so long to settle an estate, even *without* complications, is that each of the steps described above is vulnerable to interference by heirs, spouses, creditors, and the vagaries of the system. And as noted above, each step may be taken only in its due time. If, for example, bequests are paid before debts are settled or claims made, the personal representative could be personally liable for any shortfall, so he will be sure to wait the necessary time before payment. Similarly, taxes are almost never paid before the due date of nine months after death, since to do so would be depriving the estate of the use and interest on that money. And after the taxes *are* paid, the personal representative must then wait until told by the government that no further taxes are due before complete distribution of what is left can be made. For all these reasons, you should, in most cases, have a lawyer to help you out—but not just any lawyer.

Do You Really Need a Lawyer?

Something that Howard Hughes and Alfred Nobel had in common was that they both disliked lawyers, and each, therefore, wrote his own will. But had Hughes or Nobel anticipated the hundreds of thousands of dollars in legal fees (*millions* in Hughes's case) that would be generated by their stubbornness, they might have bitten the bullet and paid a lawyer to plan their estates properly.

As suggested above, in all but the smallest and simplest estates, it is a good idea to consult an attorney—but not just any attorney. Although the issues of hiring, paying, and firing (if necessary) an estate attorney are more thoroughly discussed in chapter 14, suffice it to say here that for preparing your will, you should find an attorney who is experienced in preparing wills (and other estate documents, such as trusts). For help in settling an estate, you should find an attorney who is experienced in settling estates and who will charge you on an *hourly* basis for her work, rather than a percentage of the estate. In some estate cases a premium over the hourly rate may be appropriate, but in most situations it is not called for. You should also ask for a written fee agreement to protect both of you (this is required in some states). Keep in mind that in settling an estate, your lawyer does not have to "take over" the entire estate. She can simply guide you in assembling the necessary information, obtaining appraisals, filing forms that she has completed, etc., so that you can, if you wish, do a good deal of the groundwork while she supplies the professional advice, thereby keeping the legal fees to a minimum. In fact, if she is a busy attorney, she will appreciate this arrangement, as it takes some of the time pressures and less productive tasks away from her. From your perspective, however, you have a professional to guide you through the complications of estate settlement, and if a mistake is made, she is responsible. By writing your own will or settling someone's estate on your own, *you* are assuming all of the responsibility for matters in which you are not trained or with which you are unfamiliar. If you try to do it yourself and mess it up, in addition to whatever penalties and *personal liability* you or the beneficiaries may face, you'll probably accomplish just what Hughes and Nobel accomplished—generating thousands of dollars in legal fees that could have been avoided.

Keep This in Mind

Every state has a process—the probate process—that must be followed to transfer any assets that were left in the deceased's name alone. That process can be streamlined, or it can be cumbersome and expensive. Either way, in every state it can be obstructed by a complaint or an outright contest. Things can be done to avoid such obstructions or even to avoid the probate process entirely, but there are right and wrong ways to go about them.

2

Do You Really Need a Will?

To my dear friend Mrs. George Hale, I give and bequeath the Satisfaction of being remembered in my will; and I leave my lawyer, Huber Lewis, the task of explaining *to* my relatives why they didn't get a million dollars apiece.

—from the will of Edwin O. Swain, who died penniless

Since Swain didn't have a dime, did he really need a will? Even if you do leave money or property, can't you just place everything into joint names or into a trust and forget about your will?

Actually, everyone has a will, whether she likes it or not. That is, every state provides laws that dispose of a person's estate if she did not make arrangements to dispose of it herself. Technically, of course, these laws do not constitute a "will," but they do accomplish the very thing that a will is designed to do—dispose of your property at death. They are called the laws of "intestacy" or the laws of "descent and distribution," and they attempt to divide the estate in a manner that follows the usual tendency of people to provide for their families. For instance, in many states, if a person dies "intestate" (without a will), his property will pass one-half to his surviving spouse and one-half to his children. In states that have adopted the Uniform Probate Code, the result may differ, with the spouse receiving the entire intestate estate if all the children of the decedent are also the children of the surviving spouse, less if there are children not of the marriage, such as children from the first marriage of the deceased spouse. This does not mean, however, that if such a division is satisfactory to a person she need not bother to make out a will. The laws of intestacy do not distinguish between adults and minors, for instance, so if the deceased died without a will and left minor children, the court would have to appoint a guardian (who controls the person), conservator (who controls the finances), or both (even though there may be a parent surviving), who would administer the funds for the minor until the age of majority (eighteen in *most* states). And if the child suffered from a disability, the guardianship and conservatorship could continue indefinitely. Most of us would rather determine for ourselves the terms and conditions for providing for our families, depending upon the individual family's circumstances, and the way to do that is by making out a will (often as part of a broader estate plan). In addition to these concerns, there are many other important factors, as we will see in this chapter, including an overview of the shares your relatives will take if you die without a will, what property they will divide and what property is beyond the reach of these laws, and the options offered to you through your will.

Heirs and Shares

Most of our laws of succession are derived from the early English laws, but fortunately they have been modernized. In old England, real estate was considered to be the most important and valuable family asset (as it often is today), and the law provided that a wife could *not* inherit real estate from her husband except for the right to live there if she survived him. Under the English law of primogeniture, ultimately all of the husband's real estate would pass first to the eldest son, or to that son's children, if any, otherwise to the next eldest son, etc., the males always being given preference. Fortunately, as I said, we now follow the modernized version of this law, which basically treats males and females equally and does not discriminate against wives.

Briefly, the order of inheritance where there is *no* will follows the general pattern outlined below, but be sure to keep in mind that specific state laws may differ, and the laws in the community property states (Arizona, California, Idaho, Louisiana, Nevada, New Mexico, Texas, Washington, and, for some purposes, Wisconsin) may differ substantially with respect to the share of a surviving spouse. Although the laws of intestacy are intended to favor the family, they can sometimes effect the opposite, and when that happens, there is no way to change the state-ordered distribution, no matter how unfair or unintended it may be.

It is not unusual, for instance, for a "divorced" spouse to inherit a surviving spouse's full share because death of the other spouse occurred before the divorce became legally final or before the proceedings were completed. In other cases, the spouses may simply be estranged for years, never having formally obtained a divorce, and the law allows such a surviving spouse to take a full share, since in the eyes of the law she is still a surviving spouse.

There is one option that intestate beneficiaries may employ to change the intestate share they are about to receive, which can give the family the opportunity to salvage some of the lost planning the deceased failed to do. That is for one party or another to "disclaim" all or a part of the prescribed share. A disclaimer is simply a rejection of all or any part of the expected share before it is received or used in any way. It must follow certain requirements and must generally be made within nine months of death (in this case). When accomplished, the share is treated as if the disclaiming person predeceased the deceased person. The big advantage is that the transfer of the disclaimed share is not subject to the federal gift tax. This might be desirable, for example, where the surviving spouse of the deceased was already wealthy and to accept more would only increase the taxes in her subsequent estate. She could disclaim her intestate share, and it would pass to the children or grandchildren, if a child was deceased.

With all this in mind, here is a brief outline of the usual distribution of a person's probate estate in the states where the Uniform Probate Code is not in effect, when there is no will, keeping in mind in each case that it applies to what is left *after* payment of estate debts, expenses, fees, and taxes, and that state laws may differ:

a. If the deceased left a spouse and children, the estate will pass one-half to the surviving spouse and one-half to the children. If a child is also deceased and left children of his own, those children (i.e., grandchildren of the person who died without a will) will divide the share of their parent. (In a number of states, instead of fifty-fifty, the shares are one-third to the surviving spouse and two-thirds to the children, or child, if only one. Furthermore, some states differentiate the shares of real estate and other types of property.) It should be easy to check the law of your state.

b. If the deceased left a spouse and no children or grandchildren, the estate will pass one-half to the surviving spouse and one-half to the "next of kin" (basically meaning blood relatives of the deceased). Many states provide that where there are no children or grandchildren, the surviving spouse will take the whole estate up to a certain amount, and the rest will be divided as stated above. (For example, the spouse may take the whole estate up to $200,000, but if it exceeds $200,000, then she will take $200,000 plus half the rest.)
c. If the deceased left children or grandchildren but no spouse, the whole estate would be divided equally among the children. (As explained above, if a child died before the deceased, leaving children of his own, those children would divide the share of their parent. For instance, if Jane died leaving two children, A and B, plus four grandchildren whose father was C, a deceased child of Jane, then the four grandchildren will divide C's one-third share of Jane's estate. This is often referred to as the right of representation.)
d. If the deceased left no spouse and no children or grandchildren, the whole estate would pass to the deceased's *next of kin.*

Where the Uniform Probate Code is in effect, the common intestacy scheme is:

a. All to the surviving spouse if the decedent has no living descendants or parents.
b. All to the surviving spouse if all the children of the decedent are also the children of the surviving spouse.
c. The surviving spouse receives $200,000 and three-quarters of the rest if there are no living descendants but there is a living parent.
d. The surviving spouse receives $100,000 and half of the rest if all the children of the decedent are also the children of the surviving spouse and the surviving spouse has at least one living descendant who is not a descendant of the decedent.

e. The surviving spouse receives $100,000 and half of the rest if one or more of the decedent's surviving descendants is not a descendant of the surviving spouse.

The portion, if any, of the intestate estate not passing to the surviving spouse passes, in this order, to the decedent's living descendants per capita (per person) at each generation; if none then to surviving parents; if none then to descendants of the parents per capita at each generation; and if none then to the next of kin.

Next of kin generally refers to surviving blood relatives if there are no lineal descendants (i.e., no children, grandchildren, great-grandchildren, etc.) of the deceased, and with respect to next of kin, there are "orders of preference" as to rights of inheritance. In most states, for example, if the deceased left parents and brothers or sisters, the deceased's parents will first inherit the estate. Next would come brothers and sisters equally (if the parents did not survive the deceased), then children of deceased brothers or sisters, then more distant relatives. In most states, "half bloods" are treated the same as "whole bloods"—meaning, for example, that a half sister who shares one parent is treated as a sibling of the decedent just as a full sister who shares both parents.

For example, say that Brewster dies without a will, survived by his ninety-two-year-old mother, a brother, and two nieces who are children of Brewster's deceased sister. In this case, Brewster's mother will inherit his entire estate. If she died before Brewster, then Brewster's estate would pass one-half to his brother and the other half to his two nieces equally. (The two nieces would take the share their mother—Brewster's sister—would have taken.)

The *spouses* of these persons in any of these categories, including spouses of children and grandchildren of the deceased, would almost never inherit under the laws of intestacy. For instance, say that Webster died without a will, survived by two of his three children. One child died before him, leaving a spouse, but no children of his own. Webster's estate will pass only to his two children. The spouse of Webster's deceased child will not inherit.

Similarly, *stepchildren* of the deceased and nephews and nieces of the deceased's spouse are never considered next of kin. If these persons are the *only* surviving "relatives" of the deceased, then the deceased's property will pass to the state. To illustrate, say that Stanley, a widower, dies without a will, leaving a stepson, and two nephews from his wife's side of the family. There are no other relatives. Stanley's estate will pass to the state where he had his principal residence at the time of his death.

A child of the deceased in gestation on the date of death but born after the deceased's death will inherit just as if he were born during the deceased's lifetime, with many states imposing a certain minimum time an after-born child must live—120 hours, for example. Adopted children are treated the same as natural children for inheritance purposes. Up until recently, illegitimate children in most states could inherit only from their mother, unless the father acknowledged the child as his during the father's lifetime. (A 1986 U.S. Supreme Court decision changed this, however, since it held that state laws could not discriminate against such children.)

And what of a child who is conceived posthumously by the use of stored genetic material, sometimes referred to as an "ART child," one whose life is in part produced by artificial reproductive technology? Science has come a long way since 1978's first test-tube baby, but the law has been slow to keep up. Very few have laws on this subject. Just eleven states have enacted the Uniform Parentage Act, which states:

> If an individual who consented in a record to be a parent by assisted reproduction dies before placement of eggs, sperm, or embryos, the deceased individual is not a parent of the resulting child unless the deceased spouse consented in a record that if assisted reproduction were to occur after death, the deceased individual would be a parent of the child.

Thus, in those states adopting the uniform act, there must be a prior written consent by the deceased before his ART child will be considered an heir under the intestacy law, and in many instances the ART child must be born within some specific time period after the deceased's date of death—California uses two years. Outside those few jurisdictions with a law on the books, families will have to look to the courts to decide if an ART child is a member of the family or not. Of course, you can decide for yourself by specifically including or excluding ART children in your estate plan documents.

Now that you have all this technical data under your belt, you must remember two critical points:

1. These rules apply *only* to inheritance where the deceased left *no will*; and
2. These rules apply *only* to property that passes through the deceased's *probate* estate.

Therefore, if the deceased left a will (and if the will is allowed by the probate court), *none* of these "intestacy" rules will apply, except for the rule relating to adopted children. Adopted children are treated as natural children unless the will specifies otherwise. If, on the other hand, the deceased had a will, but it was later lost or destroyed and is considered revoked, then these rules *will* apply, no matter how unfair their application may be. Similarly, if the deceased left no will but left all of his property in joint names with others (or in some other form of ownership that avoided probate), there will be no property to which the rules can apply (unless the joint ownership was successfully contested by the PR or a disgruntled heir)! Let's look at a couple of cases that illustrate these points.

Jack Dawson remarried a few years after he lost his first wife, Sally. His relationship with his second wife, Flora, seemed excellent, so he made out a new will leaving almost his entire estate to her and only small gifts to his three children. Subsequently, however, the relationship between Jack and Flora began to deteriorate. They argued constantly, and Flora was making Jack's life miserable. Jack became more and more upset until one day, while sitting in front of the fireplace in their living room, Jack decided to confront Flora with his anger. He waved his will in front of her face and told her he had decided to revoke it, whereupon he threw the will into the burning fire and stormed out of the room. Flora rushed to the fireplace and retrieved the will, which was singed but intact. A few months later Jack died.

When Flora offered the will for probate asking that the entire estate pass to her, Jack's children objected, as he had told them of the incident, thinking that his will had burned in the fire. He did not make out another one.

Under such circumstances, the court held that Jack's will was revoked. Since he did not make another, he died without a will, and his estate was divided half to Flora and half to his children, even though Jack wanted Flora to get nothing.

When Mary Trindle was widowed at age sixty-two, she moved in with her daughter, Angela. As Angela's family grew, their home became too small, so Mary bought a new home, in both her own name and Angela's name as joint tenants. Although Mary's other three children visited her regularly and remained on good terms with her, Angela was the one who took care of Mary. Because of this, Mary gradually placed all of her other assets in joint names with Angela, including bank accounts, securities, and even her government savings bonds, so that Angela could "get at" the money if anything happened to Mary. On Mary's death, the other children looked for their share of Mary's estate, since Mary died without a will and the state laws provided that the children would share Mary's estate equally in that case. Unfortunately, these laws only apply to "estate" (*probate*) property, and Mary's jointly held property passed automatically to Angela, *outside* Mary's probate estate. The other three children would split nothing equally, unless they could prove that Mary did not intend for Angela to receive the entire estate (more on this in chapter 11).

Probate Property vs. Nonprobate Property

The PR of the deceased's estate has a duty to collect all of the estate assets. Estate assets—more often called *probate assets,* or assets comprising the *probate estate*—include all of the property that the estate's PR is entitled to administer for the benefit of all parties "interested in the estate." Such parties include not only beneficiaries and heirs but also the deceased's creditors. It is very important, therefore, to distinguish probate property from nonprobate property, to separate just what is available to beneficiaries, heirs, and creditors from what is not. As explained earlier (and as I will repeat many more times throughout this book), the heirs, beneficiaries, and creditors of the estate are normally entitled only to the *probate* property (of course, there are exceptions), and property that avoids probate is likely to avoid the reach of these parties.

One way to approach the question is to ask exactly what property *belonged* to the deceased at his death. For the most part, this would include items that were held in the deceased's name *alone,* or if held with others, held in a manner that did not permit the other owners to take the deceased's share on his death. For instance, if the deceased had real estate under a "tenancy in common" with his brother, then the deceased's share would be a part of his probate estate and would not automatically pass to his brother. Note the difference between a tenancy in common and a joint tenancy: under a joint tenancy (discussed in more detail in chapter 11), the survivor takes all of the property without probate, whereas under a tenancy in common, the share of each tenant passes through his probate estate. The difference is normally revealed in how the title reads (although evidence to the contrary could change the result): "A and B" (without any additional words) and "A and B as tenants in common" generally indicate a *tenancy in common,* while "A *or* B," or "A and B *as joints tenants,*" or "A and B *jointly,*" or "A and B *jointly with right of survivorship*" would all indicate *a joint tenancy.*

In addition to the more common types of assets, such as real estate, securities, bank accounts, business interests, works of art, etc., that are regarded as probate property if they are in the deceased's name alone, here are other types of property interests that may be considered probate property:

Partnership or LLC share. If the deceased was a partner of a partnership, the remaining partners are required to account to his estate for the deceased's interests in the partnership (although it is possible to hold a partnership share in joint names or in a trust to avoid probate). A membership interest in a limited liability company (LLC) is generally treated the same as a partnership share for probate purposes, although it is possible for the membership or partnership agreement to provide for a beneficiary designation on the member's death.

Lawsuits. If the deceased had started a lawsuit against someone before his death and it is the type of action that survives his death (such as a contract action or other type of suit to recover property damages or a personal injury claim, or even a will contest), then his PR may continue the action, and any recovery will be a part of the probate estate. If the deceased's death was caused by someone's negligence, then most state laws provide that the PR may bring a "wrongful death" action, part of which may be subject to probate if "conscious pain and suffering" occurred.

Life insurance policies. If the deceased was the insured under a policy and if the policy proceeds were payable to the deceased's "estate" (usually a bad idea), then the proceeds will be probate property. If the deceased was the *owner* of a policy on someone else's life, then the policy *itself* (not the proceeds, since the insured person would still be alive) would be a part of the deceased's probate estate.

Gifts made just before death. If the deceased made "deathbed" gifts, and if, because of this, there is not enough money in his probate estate to pay his creditors, the gifts may be ordered back to the estate, to become probate property.

The estate is named as beneficiary or default beneficiary. For various reasons, including bad advice, a contractual arrangement, or just plain ignorance, a person's estate will be named as beneficiary of some benefits payable on the death of a decedent. For example, a company benefit plan may be payable "to the participant's surviving spouse, if any, otherwise to his estate." As a general rule, causing funds to be payable to the estate is a bad idea (see a bit more on this in the chapter 3 section "What Property Will Pass under Your Will?").

Once again, it is only the *probate* property that is disposed of by the will. Nonprobate property passes outside the probate estate and is not disposed of through the will. So if you have a nonprobate estate (where all the assets pass to others without the need of the will), why do you need a will?

Options Your Will Offers You

For one, you could make a statement similar to that of Edwin Swain at the outset of this chapter, simply "mentioning" people in your will but not leaving them anything, thereby enabling you to honestly say, "I want you to know I have mentioned you in my will." On the other hand, you could actually "leave" them bequests of the thousands of dollars you don't have, as Cora Johnson did.

Cora gave a great deal of thought as to how she wanted to leave her "fortune." She finally went to her lawyer in Boston and had him draw a will, enumerating several bequests and legacies to favorite friends and charities that amounted to about $700,000. The only problem was that Cora's entire estate was valued at less than $100. It seemed that Cora had been informed that she was about to inherit a fortune from the estate of a close friend of hers from New York. (According to Cora, after her friend made out her will, the friend subsequently became very ill and mentally incompetent, so Cora was confident that her friend's will could not later be changed.) Unfortunately, Cora never revealed the identity of her friend to anyone, and, according to the probate court records, Cora's estate never received the funds. In fact, Cora's will has mysteriously disappeared from the probate court records in Boston! Perhaps some of her "beneficiaries" stealthily removed it to use as a dartboard.

In addition to disposing of property that you don't yet have and, of course, property that you *do* have, here are other options that a will offers, some of which can be exercised *only* through your will.

NAMING A GUARDIAN AND CONSERVATOR FOR YOUR MINOR CHILDREN

In prior times, a court-appointed guardian would both take care of the minor child and manage the minor child's property. Now, those two jobs are divided. The *guardian* controls the day-to-day personal affairs of the minor child—the person of the child: where the child goes to school, selection of doctors, where the child lives, and the like. The *conservator* controls the financial affairs of the minor child. So, even if your spouse survives you, it may be necessary to name a conservator for your minor child or children. Although the surviving parent is the natural guardian of the child's *person,* she or he is not the natural guardian of the child's *property.* If the minor child receives any property through the estate, such property must be held by a conservator (or, in some cases, a custodian, as noted below). If no one is nominated (the will merely *nominates,* the court *appoints,* but the court is normally bound to honor the wishes of the deceased, unless inappropriate), then the court will make its own nomination and appointment. Furthermore, in your will, you can provide for a *successor* guardian. That is, you can say, "If my husband cannot serve as guardian of my minor children, then I nominate my brother and his wife, John and Jean Johnson, to be guardians of my minor children." While it is common to name spouses, John and Jean, it might be preferable to name the sibling only (John) in the event John and Jean divorce while the child is still a minor. Naming both John and Jean muddies the waters.

GIVING DIRECTION TO GUARDIANS AND CONSERVATORS

Few people (including attorneys) think of this. It is quite permissible to add in your will instructions to your guardians regarding the care, education, or domicile of your minor children in the event both parents are deceased. For instance, you might say, "In the event my spouse and I are both deceased, leaving minor children, I direct that my guardians see that they are provided with counseling to help them deal with the loss of their parents. I further direct my guardians to use their best efforts to place my minor children in schools (or private schools) of a caliber and reputation similar to those of the Newton public school system (or the Tom Brown private school, etc.), and if possible, I would like them to continue to live in the general area of Maintown, California."

Not all of these instructions may be carried out to the letter, but it would certainly be clear that the conservator would be authorized to make any reasonable expenditures to enable the guardian to carry out your wishes, and you have made it clear to your guardians just what your wishes are. For example, despite its importance to the mental well-being of the child, it is quite rare for the guardian to provide a child with counseling on the loss of his or her parents.

NAMING A CUSTODIAN

If you make bequests of money or property to a minor child, a conservator must normally be appointed, since a minor child cannot take title to property. Unless other provisions are made, the conservator, once appointed, must submit an annual account to the probate court and must ultimately make the property available to the child when the child reaches the age of majority (eighteen in most states). If instead you name a *custodian* to hold the property (generally, this is allowed for amounts up to $10,000), you will be dispensing with the need for a conservator (for *this* property only), and the custodian, in most states, is not required to file an annual account to the probate court. Furthermore, most states allow the custodian the option of holding the property until the child reaches age twenty-one, even though eighteen may be the age of majority. Another option is for the will to leave the minor child's inheritance to a statutory custodian under a Uniform Transfer to Minors Act. A "UTMA" account is not limited in size in most instances but, similar to the method above, has a "custodian" of the funds who holds and manages them on behalf of the child until the statutory age—typically eighteen or twenty-one.

UNBORN BENEFICIARIES

If a will provides that shares of the estate may be taken by a person born *after* a person's death (this is often done unintentionally), then there may be what are called "unborn" or "unascertained" beneficiaries. For instance, say that Bill leaves his estate three-fourths to his children, equally, and one-fourth to his grandchildren, equally. On Bill's death, one of his daughters is pregnant. The child-to-be is considered an unborn beneficiary on Bill's death, since he or she, as Bill's grandchild, will take a share of Bill's estate assuming a live birth. In order to see that such unborn beneficiaries are not shortchanged by the PR or the other beneficiaries, the probate court will often appoint a special guardian (usually a lawyer known to the court) to look over the actions of the PR and others on behalf of the unborn beneficiary. This special guardian is sometimes called a "guardian ad litem" or "GAL," and he is entitled to charge a fee for his services, which are often superfluous. Many states allow a testator to *dispense* with the appointment of a guardian ad litem by including instructions in the will to that effect, and doing so can save the estate considerable time and expense. Again, ART children bring additional complications into the administration of the estate. To date, no state has appointed a GAL for stored genetic material existing at a person's death, but what of the ART child born many years later? Unanswered questions abound in this area.

INSERTING A NONCONTEST CLAUSE

If you are making bequests under your will and have more than a nominal probate estate, you may want to consider a "noncontest" or "anticontest" (and sometimes called "in terrorem") provision. This is designed to discourage disgruntled beneficiaries, and basically provides that if they contest the will, they will lose their share. (Noncontest provisions are discussed in much greater detail in chapter 10.)

CHOOSING A PERSONAL REPRESENATIVE FOR YOUR ESTATE

Without a will, you cannot choose the person who will handle the settlement of your estate. In your will, you may not only name one or more personal representative (PR), but, as with guardianship, you may name successors if these individuals cannot serve. This can be extremely important, since an orderly and expeditious settlement of the estate can be enhanced by a properly selected PR. (This is discussed in much greater detail in chapter 9.)

SURVIVAL AND SIMULTANEOUS DEATH PROVISIONS

Although it does not happen often, family members do die in common disasters or within a few days or weeks of one another. The first situation relates to "simultaneous" death, where it is impossible to tell who died first. Under the laws of all states, you have a right to declare in your will who is considered to survive in this case. This can be important, especially in the case of jointly owned property, for instance, where, if you do not specify who is the survivor, then "each is considered to have survived the other." The *expensive* and awkward effect of this (without a declaration in your will) is to split the joint property and require one-half to pass through each estate.

There are also tax reasons for using a simultaneous death election. The spouse with the larger estate should normally declare that, in a common disaster, the other spouse is considered to have survived. In the typical estate plan, this has the effect of "equalizing" the estates and bringing both into a lower estate tax bracket.

The other "survival" provision deals with those cases where a beneficiary survives you by a few hours or a few days or weeks. This is quite different from a common disaster. In this case, it is clear who died first.

The problem is that you normally want a beneficiary to inherit and use the property for the rest of his life, not for a few days or weeks. The other problem in this situation is that the bequest would go from your probate estate to the *beneficiary's* probate estate (since he or she died just after you), causing *double* probate costs, delays, and legal fees. For these reasons, many lawyers add a standard provision that says, "In order for a person to be considered to have survived me under this will, she or he must have survived me by sixty days." (Sixty days is somewhat arbitrary but considered reasonable.) You should not make the "waiting period" more than several months, however, since the provision itself would then operate to hold up the probate process, as the PR is forced to wait to see who survives the prescribed period.

BUSINESS INTERESTS

If the probate estate includes business interests that are "personal" to the deceased, such as a sole proprietorship, it is very important that the will contain *specific* provisions authorizing the PR to carry on the business. If there are no such provisions and the PR continues the business without authority, he will be *personally liable* to the persons he deals with (in the business), and he will also be *personally liable* for any losses incurred by the business while he acts without authority. (If the provisions are not in the will, the PR would normally ask the probate court for the authority, but this would be an added expense.) See appendix II for a sample provision.

FUNERAL ARRANGEMENTS, LAST COMMENTS, AND BODY "DISPOSAL"

Your wishes regarding funeral arrangements or other special instructions will normally be carried out unless they are frivolous and wasteful. As to body disposal, you may be surprised to hear that after your death, you have no property rights to your body, and wishes that you express in this regard *may* be carried out, out of respect, but are not legally enforceable against your family or beneficiaries. Organ donations fall somewhere in between, as they are allowed by law in most states, but if, in fact, your family objects to your body being cut up and the parts sent to various institutions, the institutions will not contest it.

In your will you can also, of course, express personal wishes, make statements of observation or appreciation, or even express opinions about people, but most lawyers discourage this, as it often leads to trouble. If, for example, you want to finally tell someone what you really thought of him over the years, it could get your estate in trouble, or at least lead to additional expenses. There are a number of cases, for instance, where testators disinherited lineal descendants (children and grandchildren), stating that it was because they were illegitimate, and many of these cases resulted in lawsuits against the estate.

The more common of vituperous testators, however, simply express not-so-pleasant feelings about a spouse or a child or, of course, an in-law, as in the case of the father whose will left his son-in-law "fifty cents to buy a good stout rope with which to hang himself and thereby ridding mankind of a most infamous scoundrel." Rumor has it that upon hearing of this special bequest, the son-in-law responded, "Too bad my poor father-in-law did not live to enjoy the bequest for himself."

CONDITIONAL BEQUESTS

Conditional bequests, designed to "force" people to comply with otherwise unenforceable or nonbinding requests (such as marrying within a certain religion or carrying out special funeral arrangements) are also possible, but they must, of course, be within the law. For instance, you cannot make a bequest conditional upon the beneficiary committing a crime or doing something that is impossible to do or is against public policy. Other than that, however, you do have a great deal of leeway, since no matter how eccentric the condition, the beneficiary does have the right not to carry it out and refuse the bequest, as in the case of the California man who left his nephew $5,000 on the condition that the nephew, who was a professional gambler, "pledge himself to religion and become a man of the cloth." The nephew, to whom $5,000 was little more than a week's wages, graciously refused the bequest, finding the "paper" more attractive than the "cloth."

In short, there are many things you can do, some things you may do, and a few that you must and can only do in your will. And since you simply cannot know what your family and property circumstances will be at your death, what will be in your probate estate, or what will be the cause of your death, you'll always need a will.

Keep This in Mind

Even though you may think you don't need a will, because, for example, everything you own is in joint names with others, or in a trust, or because you have no "estate," it is impossible to predict what you will own or be entitled to at your death—and if you don't have a will, the state where you live will determine who gets your property. Further, it is in the will where you name a guardian for your minor children. So, as to the need for a will, to paraphrase a popular expression, "don't leave this world without one."

3

What Is a Will?

Dear Edward,
This letter leaves me in bed with high fever. I do not know whether I should live to see morning. You have from childhood always shown yourself to be a friend, now I am sick and have one more favor to ask—in case I die see that old Buffington has nothing of mine, not even a lock of my hair. Eliza did what she could for me and I want her to have our home in Yazoo City. Buffington has not given me a copper. I could say more but am too sick.
Truly yours, Mamie Buffington

Mamie wrote this letter on Christmas Day in 1898 and died a few short months later. Subsequently, Mamie's letter was offered for probate as her will. "Old Buffington" was Mamie's husband, who, for obvious reasons, objected to its allowance, claiming the letter was not a valid will. Was it? Doesn't a will have to be witnessed? Or notarized? But aren't handwritten wills an exception?

In most states, to be valid, a will must follow very strict requirements of signing and witnessing, and in some cases, notarizing as well. In others, however, a simple statement entirely in the handwriting of the deceased, and signed (and dated) by him or her, can be considered a valid, enforceable will if it is made with the intent that it be a will. Such wills are called "holographic" wills, meaning entirely handwritten by the person who signed it.

The case of Mamie Buffington took place in Mississippi, a state that recognizes holographic wills, and in fact, Mamie's letter was held to qualify as a valid will. (A holographic will need not be witnessed, but it must be completely handwritten, signed, and dated by the testator.) "Old Buffington," therefore, didn't get a "copper," or even a lock of Mamie's hair. Though the Buffington case is not a recent one, the law is still the same in those states that recognize the validity of a holographic will. And the disputes are still the same as well. In fact, many authorities feel that the continued allowance of holographic wills actually introduces disputes, since it encourages a person to attempt to make his own will simply by writing it out, even if it is just a "simple" letter! As seen in our previous chapter and in subsequent ones, there are many special and important provisions that should be contained in a will that are practically never in a holographic will. But even in those states that recognize the handwritten "holographic" will, all *wills,* whether handwritten or not, must meet certain requirements, and wills that are not handwritten must be signed with certain formalities to make them valid. In this chapter, we'll see just what is needed to make your will valid, whether handwritten or not.

Formalities of a Will

1. The will must be in writing. Except for special cases, such as holographic wills (and, in the case of certain life-and-death situations, oral, also called "noncupative," wills), ordinary wills *must be in writing, must be signed by the testator* (the person making the will), and *must be witnessed by two witnesses* (some states still require three witnesses).

Traditionally, unless a will meets *all* the necessary requirements, it will not be valid, *no matter how close it comes.* The modern trend, triggered by a seminal 1975 article by legal historian Professor John Langbein of Yale Law School, is to admit a will to probate if there is *substantial compliance* with the formalities of the applicable state law. If there is clear and convincing evidence that the deceased intended the document as a last will, and the will substantially complies with all the formalities, it should be admitted to probate to effectuate the intent of the deceased. In addition to substantial compliance, some states have adopted a *harmless error* approach, such as when there is some minor problem with the witnessing of the will. Finally, the

Uniform Probate Code opens a back door to probating a will that lacks formalities by permitting the petitioner to prove to the court by extrinsic evidence that the document was intended by the deceased to be a will.

But if the will does meet the necessary requirements, formally or by exception, it *will* be valid (unless disallowed on some other grounds, such as incompetence of the testator or undue influence exerted on the testator by others), even though some of its features are unusual.

For instance, the "writing" need not be in English. A will may be written in any language, even in a language the testator did not understand, so long as he understood the contents and *intended* that the document be his will. Of course, if it is in a foreign language, the will must be translated into the language of the court in which it is probated.

As to what material the will is written on, this has been the topic of many unusual court cases and interesting articles. The only requirements are that it be written or inscribed on a substance that results in a readable and reasonably permanent record. (A will written on a block of ice or scratched in the sand, therefore, would probably not be valid.) Records show that a number of wills were written on the backs of envelopes and train tickets, and one was scratched on the fender of a tractor by a dying man. But perhaps one of the more unusual is the famous "petticoat will" case of California. There, the testator, George Hazeltine of Los Angeles, was in a hospital, dying. He sought to make out his last will, but a piece of paper was nowhere to be found. Obligingly, one of Hazeltine's nurses lifted her dress and tore off a piece of her petticoat, on which Hazeltine wrote out his will. It was witnessed by two nurses and later actually offered for probate in the Los Angeles probate court. Because of the novel circumstances, the petticoat will enjoyed national attention. It was disallowed, *not* because it was written on a petticoat, but because one of the witnesses was also a beneficiary.

Photographs or tape recordings are not valid as wills as they are not considered "writings," nor are videotape recordings, convincing as they may be. Therefore, unless you want to go down in wills history as the person who chiseled his will on the outside of the fifty-second floor of a skyscraper or engraved it on the head of a pin, you'll probably be far better off if you just have it typed on paper, like the rest of us. After all, it's not what the will is written *on* but what it *says* that matters.

2. The will must be signed by the testator. With the exception of a "noncupative" will (one that is made orally in a life-and-death situation, such as a soldier in battle), this is a basic and very strict requirement for *every* type of will in *every* state. What constitutes a signature, however, may surprise you. For openers, it need not be legible. (When you think about it, however, this rule may be perfectly reasonable, since with the exception of English teachers, few people have legible signatures.) A misspelled signature is also valid, probably for the same reason illegibility is not fatal, the essential ingredient being that the testator *intended* the mark to authenticate the document as his will. In fact, any "mark" intended to act as authentication, such as a line, a dot, an "X," or even a fingerprint, could be sufficient. And a testator who is physically unable to sign is permitted to have *someone else* sign for him, as long as the testator understands the contents of the will and the other person signs the testator's name *in his presence* and *at his direction*. Without this provision, illiterate testators would not be able to make a will, nor would people who were paralyzed or simply too ill to sign. A good illustration of this is the will of Christopher Reeve, the actor who played Superman and who later became paralyzed from the neck down as the result of a horseback-riding accident. Reeve's will was actually signed by his wife, Dana, in his presence and at his direction. The will as signed by Dana (of course, she signed Christopher's name to the will) was duly admitted to probate in the Westchester County Surrogate's Court.

Those who *can* sign, however, need not necessarily sign their legal name—although it is silly not to, as this just increases the chance of litigation, as in the case of "Nannie" Rodgers. Mrs. Rodgers's will contained bequests of real estate and money and was very poorly written. To make matters worse, she signed it "Aunt Nannie." Of course, the heirs contesting the will claimed, among other things, that her signature was not valid. In upholding the will, the Kentucky court said, in effect, that the testatrix may sign her full name, or an abbreviated name, or even an assumed name, so long as there was no intent to deceive, and so long as it was her intent that the instrument operate as her will. Aunt Nannie's signature was valid, but the probate of her will was delayed by the contest.

On the other hand, if the testator does not *finish* signing, the signature will *not* be valid. For instance, say that a testator intends to write out his full name, such as "Grover Lambeck," but after writing only "Grov" or "Grover La" (or any part of the full name without completing the signature or the mark he *intended* to make), he suddenly drops dead or has a stroke or simply stops writing, then the partial mark or partially written name is *not* considered a signature. Of course, if what he wrote was all he *intended* to write, as in the case of Aunt Nannie above, then the partial signature would be valid.

Generally, the signature is only required once, and customarily it is placed *at the end* of the will. In many states the signature may be placed anywhere on the will, so long as the will was complete when the testator signed it, he knew of its contents, and he intended the signature to authenticate the entire will. It is foolish, however, to sign anywhere but at the end. If a bequest is written in *below* the testator's signature, for example, immediate and obvious questions arise as to its validity.

To ensure that no changes or additions are made after the will is signed, most attorneys will have the testator initial or sign each page of the will. While this may be good practice, it is not a legal requirement for the validity of the will.

3. The will must be witnessed. Most states require that there be at least two witnesses to the testator's signature. Note, however, that *the witnesses do not need to know the contents of the will.* The witnesses must be competent (legally able to testify that they witnessed the will), but in most states they need not necessarily be adults. The fact that they may later become incompetent or die before the testator does has no effect on the validity of the testator's will.

A witness should not be a person who is named as a beneficiary under the will, nor should he or she be the spouse of such a beneficiary. If this happens, the beneficiary may not be allowed to take his bequest under the will, although for all other purposes the will may still be valid. And it is only the witness or the spouse of a witness to which this rule applies. It does not affect a bequest to some other relative of a witness. For instance, Robert is a witness to the will of his brother Morris, and Morris's will leaves a $10,000 bequest to his nephew (Robert's son), George. The fact that Robert witnessed his brother Morris's will would not cause George's bequest to be disallowed.

Furthermore, qualification of the witness is important only *at the time the witness signs.* A subsequent "disqualification" will not matter. For example, Joe makes out his will leaving half of his estate to his niece, Priscilla. One of the witnesses to Joe's will later marries Priscilla. Priscilla will still be eligible to receive her bequest, since she was not the spouse of a witness at the time of the signing.

If a will has *more* than the required number of witnesses, it will still be valid, but if it has *fewer* than the prescribed number, it will not.

If a witness also happens to be named personal representative or trustee under the will, this has no effect on the will or on the appointment of the witness as personal representative or trustee, since neither of the appointments is considered to be a bequest or benefit under the will.

As to the actual signatures, the same rules as discussed above for the signature of the testator apply to those of the witnesses. That is, though it is preferable that they sign their full name, any mark or abbreviation will be sufficient so long as they intend it to operate as a witnessing to the testator's signature.

4. The testator must sign "in the presence of" the witnesses and the witnesses must sign "in the presence of" the testator and "in the presence of" each other. The testator must sign his will "in the presence of" the witnesses, but most states also allow the testator to *acknowledge* his signature in the presence of the witnesses. In other words, he could simply say to the witnesses, "This is my will; I signed it yesterday, and today I would like you to witness my signature." (This is considered the same as signing it again in their presence.) Their subsequent signatures as witnesses in his presence would then be valid.

If the testator is actually in the presence of the witnesses when he signs, that is also sufficient, even though the witnesses do not actually watch him sign. Similarly, the witnesses must sign in the presence of the testator, and he must be in a position to be able to see them sign, even though he does not actually watch them do so, or could not, as in the case of a blind testator. For these reasons, lawyers will usually gather the testators and all the witnesses in a room for the signing, allowing no one to leave until the signing and witnessing is completed. If, for example, the testator signed, then one *witness* signed and was called out of the room before the other witnesses signed, the validity of the will could easily be questioned in most states.

Signing Your Own Will at Home

If you haven't already noticed, the formalities of executing a will are quite rigid—"almost" is no good. That is, if you are one witness short, or if no one saw the testator sign, or if a witness was called out of the room before the signing was completed, the entire will could be held invalid. Therefore, if it is necessary for you to have your own will signed "at home" or somewhere other than your lawyer's office, here are some helpful hints.

The testator should read the will over to be sure it leaves his property as he wishes. Handwritten wills should be avoided wherever possible, except perhaps in cases of extreme emergency, even in those states that recognize "holographic" (handwritten) wills. If there are errors in the will, the will, or at least the corrected pages, should be retyped in full. Erasures, crossing out lines, and writing new provisions in the margins should be avoided whenever possible, as they raise obvious questions. If such changes must be made on the face of the will, the testator should sign his name in the margin beside *each* such change, and the witnesses should then sign or initial below the testator's mark to show that the changes were made to the will *prior* to its signing.

The will should be "integral." That is, each page should logically follow the one before it, and, preferably, each page should be signed or initialed by the testator. (Some attorneys also have the witnesses initial the pages as well.) Finally, the pages should be fastened together. These steps are *not* required by law but are an excellent idea to prevent a later questioning as to whether the document presented for probate was the *exact* document that the testator signed as his will.

Be sure that the witnesses are competent and that none of them is mentioned as a beneficiary in the will or is the spouse of such a beneficiary.

At the time of the actual signing, the testator and the required number of witnesses should be brought together in a room. If the testator is not known to the witnesses, they should be briefly introduced. The testator should then announce to the witnesses something along the lines of, "This is my will. I have carefully read it and I understand and approve of the contents. Now I would like you to witness my signature." The testator should proceed to initial each page, and then sign his name in full at the end of the will, in front of the witnesses. The witnesses should then sign, in front of the testator, and none of the witnesses should leave the room until everyone has signed. The witnesses should also write their addresses beside or below their respective names. If a witness's signature is not legible, his name should be printed below it. The date of the signing and witnessing should be included.

Many states also allow the addition of a "self-proving affidavit" to the will. This is a statement that is later offered as proof that the will was properly signed, and, if no one objects, the affidavit will avoid the necessity of bringing one or more of the witnesses before the court (after the testator's death) to testify as to the signing. If your will has a self-proving affidavit, then a notary public would also have to be present, since the affidavit must be notarized.

When signing is completed, the will is usually handed to the testator, and he decides where to keep it. Of course, it should be kept in a safe place. Some testators leave it with the attorney, and some states allow for depositing the will in the probate court for the district where the testator resides. This is for safekeeping only, and does not constitute legal action of any kind. (Later in this chapter, more details are given on where to keep your will.) Wherever it is stored, a copy of the signed will should be left with the testator's attorney for his files. If the original is lost, the availability of such a copy may prove extremely valuable. Note that only *one* will is signed. The only times a "second" will is signed are to amend the first will, to make a new one, or to simplify the distribution of foreign property in cases in which the testator has property in a different *country.*

Who May Make a Will?

Anyone having "testamentary capacity" may legally make a will. Do you remember hearing the phrase "of legal age and sound mind"? Basically, this is testamentary capacity.

Legal age is not necessarily the age of majority. Every state allows a person age eighteen or over to make a will, though in many of those states the age of majority is twenty-one or twenty or nineteen. Once "legal age" is reached, however, a person has the right to make a will, so long as he is of "sound mind," often a much more difficult question than that of legal age.

A person is of "sound mind," according to the law, when he or she can understand in a general way

- the nature and extent of his property;
- the people to whom he would "normally" leave such a property; and
- the manner in which he is leaving such property under his will.

This does not mean that only an intelligent person or one who is generally regarded as "normal" can make a will. The standard of capacity necessary for making a will is actually not very high, and a person meeting the requirements outlined above may at the same time be regarded as weird or eccentric by his peers. Such persons, as well as those who are not weird but merely "slow" or "dull," and even some who are under a guardianship or conservatorship for mental incapacity, could make a perfectly valid will if they are capable of the basic understanding stated above. It is the level of such understanding that is the test rather than the reasonableness of the will itself.

A person, therefore, need not be in "perfect" mental health or be totally aware of every facet of his financial and business situation to make a will. Rather, an essential issue is whether the testator knew to whom he wanted to leave his property and understood that his will would accomplish this. In this regard, it is not necessary that the testator be able to understand the meaning of the technical terms in his will, nor must he be able to comprehend the legal steps necessary to carry out his plan. Similarly, it is not necessary that the testator understand the intricacies or even the exact amount of the property or estate he presently owns.

All that is necessary is that the testator is *capable* of understanding them when he makes out his will. In other words, if the testator *thought* he had only two parcels of real estate but in fact had *five* parcels, a bequest of "all my real estate to B" would cause all five parcels to go to B, so long as the testator had the *capacity* to understand the nature and extent of his estate. *The fact that he did not realize what he had is not relevant.* This point is further illustrated in the case of the will of Nancy Shaw, who thought she was leaving only $500 to Campbell College but in fact left the school nearly $20,000!

After a number of communications with her attorney, Nancy had him make out a will that contained about forty specific bequests, which, she believed, practically exhausted all of her estate. Thinking that the balance would only amount to about $500, she wrote her attorney, "If there is any money left in my estate it may go to Campbell College," and this was incorporated into her will.

During the trial, evidence was offered that Nancy Shaw was somewhat eccentric, that on occasion she broke down without apparent reason, and that she thought her relatives were plotting to take her estate. There was also evidence showing that Nancy Shaw had never been to Campbell College (or to any other college for that matter), or that she even knew anything of the college, except that there had been a picture of the college hanging in the church she attended. Finally, there was evidence to show that if Nancy had known how much Campbell College would receive, she would have left it to her other heirs.

This belief, however, was not important to the validity of Nancy Shaw's will, the Kansas Supreme Court said. The essential issue was whether Nancy was capable of understanding the extent of her property. The evidence of the specific bequests and the bequest of "any money left" was itself enough to convince the court that she did have the capacity to understand, and Campbell College was allowed to receive the larger bequest.

It is interesting that although evidence of Nancy Shaw's eccentricities was brought forth in this case, it was not regarded as having a bearing on her capacity to make a will. Although extreme eccentricities, especially if evidenced by the provisions of the will itself, can at least *suggest* a certain lack of capacity (or, to put it another way, they would elicit the reaction that only a crazy person would include such a provision in his will), courts are reluctant to treat this, by itself, as conclusive of the testator's lack of capacity.

Take for example the case of James Kidd, a gold prospector who was declared dead by an Arizona court in 1963 after having mysteriously disappeared several years earlier. Kidd's will left the bulk of his estate "to go in a research or some scientific proof of a soul of the human body which leaves at death I think in time their [*sic*] can be a Photograph of [the] soul leaving the human at death, James Kidd."

Although Kidd's bequest could certainly be considered eccentric, it was not, by itself, an indication that he was mentally incompetent or did not have the capacity to make a will. In fact, in the Kidd case, after some "soul-searching" on the part of the probate court judge, Kidd's money was actually given to the American Society for Psychical Research in New York City to establish a fund to carry out, as near as possible, the search for evidence of the "soul" as provided in James Kidd's will.

Rather than pure eccentricities, therefore, there must be an actual lack of mental capacity to render the will invalid. The more common cases are those where the person is clearly mentally deficient, usually from a medical standpoint. The obvious persons in this group would include those who are mentally retarded or mentally disabled, who are unable to form and understand a testamentary plan. Another form of incapacity, however, is often more difficult to distinguish—that is, where a person is considered to be "mentally deranged."

A mentally deranged person may appear to be quite normal and able to understand very well the "natural objects of his bounty" and the extent of his estate, but because of his derangement, he is considered unable to make a rational testamentary plan. A person suffering from extreme paranoia, for example, thinking that his wife and children are plotting to kill him, may make a will leaving his estate to a casual friend whom he trusted. Such a person is said to be mentally deranged and suffering from, in the words of the law, an "insane delusion."

An insane delusion is a false belief that results from a diseased or deranged mind, a belief that operates against all facts and reason. A false belief by itself, however, is *not* a delusion. The fact, for instance, that a person disinherited a child because he falsely believed the child was not his is not an insane delusion and would *not* warrant a finding by a court that the testator did not have the necessary mental capacity on the basis that he was suffering from an insane delusion.

To suffer from an insane delusion, a person must believe in a state of facts that does not exist and that no rational person would believe to exist. This is, in part, why eccentricities are not considered to be insane delusions. They may constitute strange or queer behavior, but they often have no bearing on the testator's capacity or belief in making his will. And even where there is an insane delusion, as a general rule the insane delusion will only invalidate a will if it operates to cause the testator to make a disposition of his property that is clearly a *result* of the delusion and *contrary* to what he might otherwise have done. Accordingly, if the delusion, no matter how insane, did *not* affect the disposition of property, the will may be held valid, as illustrated in the case of Oren Eveleth Emery of Iowa. Oren believed his son was trying to kill him. Nevertheless, he made out a will leaving all his property to that son, even though he had other children. The other children contested Oren's will, arguing, among other things, that Oren was suffering from an insane delusion (that his son Emery was trying to kill him) and, therefore, the will should be set aside. The court observed that if this delusion had affected Oren in any way, it would have been to *omit* his son rather than leave the property to him, so although it was in fact an insane delusion, it did not invalidate the will.

In the case of Louisa Strittmocher, the court did overturn her will because of an insane delusion, although some might disagree with the court's conclusion. Evidence in that case showed that Louisa, who never married, had such an insane hatred of men that it affected her capacity to make a will.

Louisa apparently had a normal childhood and was quite devoted to her parents, yet she later wrote, "My father was a corrupt, vicious and unintelligent savage. Blast his wormstinking carcass and his whole damn breed." Additional evidence showed that she had a morbid aversion to men and that she "looked forward to the day when women would bear children without the aid of men and all male children would be put to death at birth." She became a member of the National Women's Party and began talking of leaving her estate to the party. Sure enough, she made out her will to that effect, and just a month later, she died.

Louisa's heirs contested the will, offering testimony from her physician, who stated that, in her opinion, Louisa suffered from severe paranoia. The New Jersey court agreed, holding that Louisa was suffering from an insane delusion and lacked the capacity to make a will. Accordingly, the will was held invalid and the money went to Louisa's heirs.

In summary, there are many factors that influence our ability to make a will, but anyone who has the "capacity" to make a will may make one. Capacity generally means the ability to understand what it means to own property, to understand in a general way what it is you own, to understand that there are people to whom you would "normally" leave your property (even though you decide not to leave it to them), and to understand that you can dispose of your property by making out a will.

You do not have to be in "perfect" health, either mentally or physically. You simply have to have the capacity. Persons under guardianships for mental weakness, for instance, can still make a will if they have the required understanding, even if only for the brief period in which they made the will. Likewise, persons who are extremely ill or very old, or who suffer from a severe handicap such as blindness or deafness, can make a will. Even persons who are otherwise healthy, however, may "lose" their capacity to make a will because of an insane delusion.

Wills Made in Another State

Regardless of where your will was made out, the laws require it to be probated in the place where you had your principal domicile (residence) at the time of your death, assuming it needs to be probated at all. (As discussed previously, if a person's estate consists entirely of nonprobate property, and if there is no other requirement or request that probate be initiated, then the will need not be probated.)

But what happens if you made out your will when you resided in Boston, Massachusetts, then moved to Charleston, South Carolina? Is your Massachusetts will still "good"? Must you rush to make out a new will? Does the Massachusetts will now cover *all* of your property, including that in Massachusetts, South Carolina, and in other states?

The general rule is that if your will was properly executed according to the laws of the state in which you executed it, then it will be valid in another state if you subsequently move, even though the laws of the new state are different. For instance, say that you reside in Massachusetts and you make out a will, under which only two witnesses are required. You later move to South Carolina, which requires three witnesses to a will. If you should die in South Carolina without having made a new will, your Massachusetts will would most likely be valid in South Carolina, as it was properly executed under Massachusetts law when you resided there. The question is, however, whether this "foreign" will has the necessary validity to dispose of your property in South Carolina, Massachusetts, and elsewhere. When a person dies leaving property in another state (in his own name), it becomes necessary to take out probate not only in the state in which he was domiciled (resided) at the time of his death but also in those other states where he left such property. This procedure is called "ancillary administration," which is a fancy term for additional probate, additional legal fees, and additional delays. (This is covered further in chapter 11.) Fortunately, the ancillary administration does not require the will to be proved all over again, but it does require proper certification of its proof in the domiciliary state (South Carolina, in our example above), so that the foreign state or states can see that it was held to be a valid will according to the probate court in the state of your residence. After certification of this proof is submitted to the satisfaction of the court in the "foreign" state, then ancillary probate will be allowed in the state where the property is situated.

If you do have property in other states, you should consider making arrangements that will preclude the need for ancillary administration on your death (or disability). The two principal ways of accomplishing this are through joint ownership and through a living trust; in my opinion, a trust is by far the more preferable method.

If property in a foreign state is held by the deceased and another as "joint tenants with rights of survivorship," then on the death of the deceased, the other joint tenant will own the foreign property without the need for probate or ancillary administration. The problem is that this will not apply to the need for probate due to mental incompetence (or guardianship, for instance) of one of the joint owners, nor does it provide for the contingency that the other joint owner might die first. For these reasons, a simple, living trust (as discussed in detail in chapter 12) is preferable, as it can provide for both of these contingencies, avoiding ancillary administration in each case.

Despite all this, it is very important to understand that each state has the absolute right to impose its own laws on all property situated within its boundaries, regardless of what a will provides and regardless of whether the property is held in a trust or under a joint tenancy. It is this principle that in part makes the issue of foreign wills unsettled. The state laws are not consistent, for example, as to the rights of a surviving spouse at death. Say that state X allows a spouse to take a "forced share" (the share she can take regardless of the provisions of the deceased spouse's will; see chapter 7) of one-third the estate and state Y allows her to take one-fourth the estate. And say that the deceased died a domiciliary of state X, also leaving property in state Y. His surviving spouse, if she elected to take her forced share, would take one-third the property in state X and one-fourth the property in state Y. In the same context, states can decide whether the spouse's share should include property held in joint names with another or held in a living trust. This does *not* mean, however, that a foreign state can extend a spouse's rights to property outside that state.

As a general rule, therefore, it is a good idea to have your will reviewed by a local estate attorney if you change domicile to another state. If you have property in states other than that in which you live (that is, in which you have your principal residence), you should definitely take steps to avoid the necessity of ancillary administration in the "foreign" states. And if you think your surviving spouse will attempt to disregard your will and take her forced share, plan ahead.

What Property Will Pass Under Your Will?

As briefly noted in chapter 2, the provisions of a will apply only to property held in the deceased's name alone or property that is held or payable in a way that it must pass through the deceased's *probate* estate. Ignorance of this essential fact has caused fights, bitterness, and disappointment in many a family.

Quite often, for example, a family is shocked to find that even though Dad's will left the home to his two children, they will not get it because it was held in joint names with his second wife. Since it was held jointly, the home did not pass through Dad's probate estate and, therefore, did not pass under the terms of his will. For this reason, anyone making a will *must also* review the titles and status of each asset and item of property that he or she has, to ensure that the specific property will pass under the terms of the will or bypass the will altogether. This is not to say that I recommend that all of your property pass through your will. I *do not.* I do recommend, however, if you are to have a will and if your will contains bequests of property, that you take the necessary steps to see that your wishes are carried out. To do this, you should review your assets to see just what will pass under your will (through your probate estate) and what will not.

Property or assets in *your name alone,* such as a home or a bank account or a stock certificate, must pass through your probate estate and, therefore, under the terms of your will. But as you will see in the discussion that follows, there can be many instances when the title to property is deceiving, or where there may be no "title" problem but an improper beneficiary designation, or where property you did not know you would have at your death comes into your probate estate.

Tenant in common. In cases where you are a tenant in common, the disposition of your share on your death is not so readily apparent. For instance, if you are a co-owner of property with someone else, the property or other asset is not in your name "alone," but your share may nevertheless be a part of your probate estate. The main difference between a tenancy in common and a joint tenancy is that the share of a deceased *joint* owner will pass to the surviving joint owner, thereby avoiding probate, while the share of a deceased tenant in common will pass to the deceased tenant's *probate* estate. Since it becomes part of your probate estate, it will pass under the terms of your will.

Unfortunately, it is not always easy to tell whether the property was owned under a tenancy in common or a joint tenancy, as people often confuse the two, assuming that if there are two (or more) names on the title, it is a joint tenancy. *This is not so.* Titles standing in the names of "A and B," for example, without any other words or designation, is a tenancy in common, and if A dies, his share (presumably one-half) will pass to his probate estate. Of course, if the title reads "A and B, as tenants in common," then it is even clearer.

Life insurance or other arrangements with named beneficiaries. In most cases, life insurance proceeds (or any other financial or benefit plan that allows funds to be paid to a beneficiary named by you) are payable directly to the named beneficiary (to a spouse, or to children, or to a trust, for example) on your death, without further legal action. Because of this, the funds will avoid probate and will not pass under the terms of your will. In certain cases, however, they can *become* probate assets because of a slipup in planning. For example, say that you are the owner of an insurance policy on your life, payable to your spouse as beneficiary. Your spouse dies *before* you and you never added another ("secondary" or "contingent") beneficiary. In this case, the proceeds would be payable to your *probate estate* and, therefore, would pass under the terms of your will.

Some advisors (*not* this one) actually recommend that your life insurance proceeds be payable to your estate. In other words, the beneficiary description would read, "The estate of the insured," or words to that effect. Unless there is some clearly compelling reason to do this, I would strongly recommend against this designation for the following reasons:

1. It will increase legal and administrative fees for settlement of the estate;
2. It will expose the insurance proceeds or other benefits to creditors of your estate;
3. It will expose funds to an estate tax (which may have otherwise been avoided); and
4. It will ensure a substantial delay before your beneficiaries can enjoy the money. Otherwise, it's a great idea!

Trusts. Creation of a "living" trust (which is discussed in more detail in chapters 11 and 12) naming yourself and/or your spouse as trustee and placing your assets into the trust during your lifetime has become a very popular method of avoiding probate. Some attorneys, however, draft such trusts to provide that on the death of the grantor (the person who created the trust), the assets remaining in the trust will be distributed "to the grantor's estate." This is sort of like building a lifeboat and then poking a large hole in it. I strongly advise against such trust arrangements; they carry the same hassles and headaches as life insurance policies designating the estate as beneficiary.

Lawsuits and inheritances. There may also be assets that must be probated and pass under the terms of your will whether you like it or not. These are usually assets that become "yours" *after* your death or *on account of* your death, such as damages recovered as a result of lawsuits brought for personal injuries that lead to your death, or inheritances from a person who died shortly before you, leaving you a share of her estate.

The first situation could arise, for example, where a person was injured in an auto accident and, after a period of suffering, died. The personal representative of that person's estate would sue the negligent party for personal injuries (on behalf of the deceased) as well as for causing the deceased's death. The portion of the recovery received by the personal representative that is attributable to the personal injuries will become part of the deceased's probate estate and will pass under the terms of the deceased's will. The other portion usually passes according to special state laws relating to the distribution of "wrongful death proceeds," in most cases going to the deceased's spouse and children.

The second situation would usually arise, for example, where Uncle Bill died and left $25,000 to his nephew Bob. Before Uncle Bill's estate was settled, however, nephew Bob died. The $25,000 bequest from Uncle Bill would have to be paid to nephew Bob's estate (i.e., to his personal representative) and would then be distributed under the terms of nephew Bob's will.

Probate of nonprobate property. It is sometimes possible for your personal representative to question transfers or arrangements you may have made during your lifetime to avoid probate on your death. If he is successful, this has the effect of turning nonprobate property (that would pass outside your will) into probate property (that will pass under the terms of your will). For the most part, this exposure normally lies with jointly held property. For instance, say that you opened a joint bank account with your daughter and placed half your savings into it. Meanwhile, your will leaves "everything" to your three children equally. Noting this inconsistency, your personal representative could easily argue that the joint bank account you had with your daughter should be part of your probate estate, that you added your daughter's name merely as a convenience, and that you never intended that she should get more than the others. If the personal representative were successful (which is quite possible if there were sufficient evidence to show your intentions), the bank account would pass to your *probate* estate, and the funds, therefore, would pass according to your will. (If you have such joint bank accounts and do not wish them probated, you should write out a statement to that effect, in your own words, indicating your wish and intention that the other joint tenant should own the balance in the account on your death, and send your written statement to the other joint tenant.)

In short, do *not* assume that your will takes care of all of the property you own at the time of your death. If you are like millions of others, you have some property that will pass under your will and some property that will not. The best estate plan considers and coordinates the best disposition of *all* of your property, probate and nonprobate, according to your wishes.

Joint Wills

A joint will is a *single* document signed by two testators, properly witnessed, and designed to act as a will for both of them. It is generally agreed by lawyers and other estate advisors that having a joint will is a bad idea and little better, if not worse, than having no will at all. The most perplexing issue is why anyone (or rather any two) would have a joint will in the first place.

In the typical joint will, husband and wife leave all of their property to each other, and on the death of the survivor, all of the property to their children. Since this is all in *one* will, complicated legal questions arise. For instance, can the survivor change her mind and make a *new* will? Some cases have held that she cannot, since the joint will could be considered irrevocable—after all, the first spouse died thinking that the surviving spouse would honor their agreement to leave their one will intact. But what if the surviving spouse decides that one of the children should be left out for some justifiable reason? Could the newly omitted child contest the new will on the basis that the joint will was irrevocable? Or could he sue the estate of the surviving spouse for breach of contract? A few cases have considered this possibility.

Then there is an estate tax problem with joint wills. If one spouse leaves property to another pursuant to a *contract* rather than voluntarily, then the amount left to the surviving spouse will *not* qualify for the tax-free marital deduction applicable to bequests to spouses (see chapters 12 and 13). If the joint will, therefore, is held to be a contract between the spouses, which it usually is, then the estate, depending on its size, could end up paying needless additional estate taxes just because of the joint will.

In short, there is *no* reason to have a joint will. If you want to lock in a bequest to certain beneficiaries after the death of the surviving spouse, you can do this through an irrevocable trust and still enjoy the tax-free marital deduction. If you desire to make a gesture of love for each other, stick to roses and holding hands instead of joint wills.

Where to Keep Your Will

Once your will is prepared and properly signed and witnessed, you should be careful to keep the original in a safe place. Most law firms have safety vaults for storage of original documents, such as wills and trusts, and this is one possibility. If you prefer more formal storage, the probate courts in most states will accept the will for safekeeping for a small fee. If you store it with the probate court, it is not released to anyone but you or your personal representative (guardian or conservator) until your death. A third alternative would be to place the will in your safe-deposit box. This introduces other questions, such as, Who else has access to the box? and Will there be a delay in getting into the box at your death? The laws of most states allow a search of the safe-deposit box after death to determine if it contains your original will. Finally, you could keep the will in your desk drawer or glove compartment, but these locations are clearly not advisable. Of the three "safe" locations—i.e., your lawyer, the probate court, or your safe-deposit box—I suggest either of the first two, to eliminate positively any chance of monkey business with the instrument.

Keep This in Mind

While there may be many interesting anecdotes about wills, such as one written on a matchbook cover or the side of a building, it is foolhardy to try to do it yourself, except in true emergency cases, or to think you're saving money by using an online form. This is like buying a mail-order suit and expecting it to fit. A will is a legally binding document designed to dispose of all the property in your probate estate. Get it done properly.

4

How to Cancel or Change Your Will

"The reason I asked you to come here and bring my will with you," Graham said to his daughter, "is that I want to revoke it. I intend to make a new will and reduce your share, as well as that of your brother." Graham was blind. He asked his daughter to hand him the sealed envelope that contained his will and she did so. After feeling the envelope with the seal he had previously placed on it and satisfying himself that it was the one that contained his will, he handed it back to his daughter and told her to throw it into the fire. Pretending to do so, she actually threw another piece of paper into the fire, calling her father's attention to the odor and the crackling of the burning paper, whereupon Graham was satisfied that his will was destroyed. Before he could make out another will, however, Graham died.

Was this an effective revocation of Graham's will? Should the daughter be prohibited from offering the will for probate since she interfered with her father's wishes that it be destroyed? What if the will was, in fact, destroyed? Could the children then offer a copy of the will for probate?

Or how about this second hypothetical scenario: Graham asks his daughter to open the envelope and hand him the will. After she does so, Graham asks her to identify the particular page that leaves a share of his estate to his son and daughter. She reads through the will and instead identifies the page *following* that bequest, whereupon Graham takes his pencil and draws lines through the entire page, adding at the bottom of the page the words: "I hereby reduce my son's and my daughter's shares to one-fourth my estate instead of one-half my estate." He then initials the page, which in fact contained some small monetary bequests to friends and charities, and hands the will back to his daughter, satisfied that his wishes will be carried out. Will they?

Was this a valid amendment to Graham's will? Would it have been a valid amendment if he had written on the correct page? Are the bequests to friends and charities revoked since he crossed them out and initialed the page? We will find out in this chapter.

The Formalities Required for Changing a Will

As explained in chapter 3, wills are serious business. They must be in writing and signed and, except for holographic (handwritten) wills, which are allowed in a number of states, witnessed with very strict formalities according to the laws of the state governing the validity of the will, unless one of the exceptions applies. This is because the law takes very seriously the disposition of a person's property after his death and wants to be absolutely sure that the person understands the terms of his will and that there is no (or little) room for doubt about his intentions—this makes sense, as the person will be deceased when the will is offered for probate and unable to speak for herself. In view of this, changing or revoking a will is of no less importance, since both similarly affect the disposition of a person's property after death. Therefore, any change or revocation of the will must also conform to the law; otherwise, they will not be honored.

Changing the terms of a will is normally (and best) done through a "codicil." A codicil is an amendment or change to a will, signed with the *same formalities* as a will (that is, with two or more witnesses, etc.), and has the added effect of "republishing" the original will that it amended (except insofar as it is changed by the codicil). Republishing is the same as restating the previous will (even though all of the provisions of the previous will are not actually repeated in the codicil). This means that a properly signed codicil can actually correct a deficiency in the signing of a previously signed will.

For instance, say that in his will, Charles left half his property to his sister, Charlotte, and the rest to charity. Charlotte's husband was a witness to Charles's will, the effect of which would be to negate the bequest to Charlotte, as explained in chapter 3. Later, Charles executes a codicil to his will, adding a $2,000 bequest to his favorite pub, and the codicil is witnessed by two new, independent witnesses. The effect of the codicil is not *only* to amend *Charles's* will to add the $2,000 bequest but *also* to republish (restate) his *entire* will (except as it is affected by the change) and "correct" the previous error in execution, so that his sister's share will then be valid.

Even the wording used in a typical codicil suggests the importance of the formality in language and execution. One might read, for instance:

> I, Graham Cracker, of Boston, Mass., having made my last will dated January 29, 1989, hereby make this codicil, amending said will as follows: I hereby delete Article III and substitute the following Article III in its place: . . .
>
> In all other respects (or, "Except as modified by this codicil"), I hereby ratify and confirm my said will in its entirety, signed (Graham Cracker), witnessed in his presence and in the presence of each other, (*Witness A*) and (*Witness B*).

Unfortunately, in changing their wills, many people would rather not pay an attorney to do it properly. They often prefer to do it themselves by marking up their original wills, writing in their own changes, crossing out bequests, and generally handling it in a fashion they think is proper, without regard to what the law requires—after all, it is *their* will.

As a general rule, this is about the riskiest way to do it. Although some states recognize "partial revocation," which is what happens when you simply cross something out of your will, to do so positively invites a will contest and litigation. Furthermore, if after crossing provisions out, you add some new provisions, such as a new beneficiary or a different bequest, then this constitutes a *change* (as opposed to a revocation) that can *only* be valid if it is made with the *same formalities* as the original will itself.

For instance, say that your will, in part, leaves $5,000 each to A, B, and C. You want to omit C, so you cross out his name on the will and initial the change. In *some* states, this could be treated as a partial revocation and operate to omit C's bequest. However, if you omit C and add D or reduce C's bequest from $5,000 to $500, simply by writing it in the margin of the will without following the necessary guidelines for executing a will, your proposed changes will be *useless,* having no effect at all. Furthermore, even in those states that might acknowledge your right to cross out C, the question arises as to what happens to the $5,000 that you originally left to C before you crossed him out. Since C does not now get the $5,000 (assuming your change is honored), then it must go to someone else or to the "residue," and this now has the possible effect of changing some other part of your will, which can only be done with the *same formalities* as executing the will itself.

Therefore, in our example above where Graham made his changes on the wrong page of the will, he neither reduced his children's shares nor changed the specific bequests to his friends and charities. All of these were *totally unaffected* by his markings on the will because the changes were not made with the same formalities required in making and signing the original will. For the same reason, it did not matter that he had made the attempted changes on the wrong page. It would have had no legal effect in this case (other than to stimulate a will contest).

In short, you should *never* try to amend your own will by crossing out pages or paragraphs and substituting the new provisions on your own. (Initialing or signing your name in the margin beside your change only confirms that you don't know what you're doing.) If you want to make a change that will have the intended legal effect, do it through a properly executed codicil and avoid the probability of a long and expensive will contest.

Changing Your Will (Intentionally or Unintentionally) by Disposing of Your Property

It is quite common for a will to be affected unintentionally by the testator selling, giving away, or otherwise disposing of an item of property that he has mentioned in his will. For instance, in his will, Rob leaves his collection of books to his son Jeremy. Later, Rob decides to donate his book collection to the New York Public Library, which he does. On Rob's death, his will still leaves the book collection to Jeremy, but there is no book collection for Jeremy to take. Must Rob's PR purchase a similar book collection to give to Jeremy? Can Jeremy sue the estate for an amount equal to the value of the book collection? Can the PR substitute some other item of equal value? Since Rob allowed the specific bequest to remain in his will, isn't this an indication that he wanted it to stand? If the books were stolen or destroyed before Rob's death rather than given away by Rob, would this change the result?

The answers to all of these questions would at first glance seem to hinge upon the issue of Rob's intention. That is, did he intend that his son, Jeremy, receive a book collection on his death, no matter what? Originally, the courts did look to the intention of the testator, but the law later evolved into the "simple" and sole question of whether the item of property is in the testator's estate at the time of his death. If it is not, the bequest is said to be *adeemed* and the beneficiary gets nothing, regardless of the circumstances leading to the ademption (disposal) of the property. This principle is clearly illustrated in the unsuccessful lawsuit brought by Maude Welch to force her husband's estate to give her the car her husband owned.

In his will, Maude's husband, M.C. Welch, left the following bequest: "I hereby give and bequeath to my wife, Maude Trickle Welch, twenty-five thousand dollars cash, my Packard automobile, and all my household goods, furniture, and jewelry." The rest of the estate was left to M.C.'s brother and sister. Just before his death, however, M.C. traded in the Packard automobile for a Lincoln, which he still owned when he died. Maude, of course, claimed the Lincoln should be hers, since M.C. clearly wanted her to have a car for her use. The fact that he didn't change his will was simply an oversight, Maude claimed. The estate countered with the argument that M.C. did not leave Maude a Lincoln but a Packard, specifically. Since he did not own a Packard, Maude should get nothing in this regard, as the bequest was "adeemed."

The court agreed with the estate. The will, they said, was plain and unambiguous. It read, "my Packard automobile," and to hold that this language should mean any other automobile that M.C. owned would be to change the law of wills. The court said,

> The rule is universal that, in order to make a specific legacy effective, the property bequeathed must be in existence and owned by the testator at the time of his death, and the nonexistence of property at the time of the death of a testator which has been specifically bequeathed by will is the familiar and almost typical form of ademption. This may result from a variety of causes, such as a gift during the lifetime of the testator of the particular article which was the subject-matter of the legacy, or its consumption, loss, or sale, and in each of such instances the courts have held that the legacy is adeemed. Where the testator

> substantially alters the form of the subject-matter of his bequest as by making wool into cloth, or a piece of cloth into a garment, the legacy is adeemed, because the subject-matter cannot be restored to its former state.

But supposing that, after buying the Lincoln, M.C. had purchased another Packard (not the one he first owned). Would the second Packard go to Maude under his will? It would, since the will operates as of the time of the testator's death, and it would be presumed that he wanted *this* Packard (i.e., the one he owned at the time of his death) to go to Maude. He would, in effect, have *restored* the "adeemed" property so the bequest could be carried out. A similar result would occur, for instance, in the case where Woody leaves his "beach house on Cape Cod" to his daughter, Wackie. Later, Woody sells the beach house, and still later he buys another beach house on Cape Cod. Wackie would get the second beach house, since it adequately satisfies the description in the will. If the second beach house were located somewhere else, however, a different result would occur.

This rule of ademption only applies to *specific* bequests or legacies (other than money). That is, those bequests addressing and identifying a specific item or items of property, even though in some cases the specificity itself may be general. For instance, "all my automobiles," or "my entire collection of books," or "all my household effects," or "the silver tea service that belonged to my grandmother." All of these are specific bequests of property, subject to ademption, to the extent that the described article or articles are not a part of the testator's estate at her death. Where a group of items is involved, the bequest could be adeemed in whole or in part, such as where only half the original book collection was left at the testator's death, or where only three pieces remained of grandmother's five-piece tea service, in which case, the beneficiary would receive the portion that remained. On occasion, however, the question of what remains can be confusing, as in the case of Mary de Garmendia.

Mary had two valuable strings of pearls, and in her will she left one to her friend Natalie and the other to Mrs. R., another friend. Just before Mary's death, however, she had the two sets of pearls combined to make a single string. Obviously this presented a problem, and Mary's PR took the position that Natalie's bequest had been adeemed, since there was now only one string of pearls.

In its opinion, the court noted that ademption could result not only through loss or destruction of the object but also from changes that cause a loss of its identity. For example, if the stones in a diamond bracelet were removed and placed in several other pieces of jewelry, a bequest of the diamond bracelet would be adeemed. In this case, however, neither of these (i.e., neither a disposition nor a loss of identity) had really occurred. The PR had one collection of pearls bequeathed to two persons, and this was no different than if the two beneficiaries were left a stack of books or a herd of cattle. The property could easily be divided by the owners, as it had not lost its identity nor was it destroyed, and the pearls were divided.

Of course, if the article or articles were destroyed, then the case of ademption (and therefore loss of the bequest) would be clear, right? The answer is an unequivocal maybe. Among other things, it depends upon *when* the articles were destroyed. An interesting case that illustrates this point is that of Anne Shymer, who died when the *Lusitania* sank. In her will, Anne left her clothing, jewelry, laces, and other personal articles to her mother. Most of these articles, however, went down with Anne and the *Lusitania.* As a result of insurance claims made for the lost articles, Anne's husband, as PR of her estate, received about $9,000 as reimbursement for the articles, and Anne's mother contended the funds should be paid to her, since they were a direct reimbursement for the articles that were left to her in Anne's will. Anne's husband, however, argued that the bequest was *adeemed,* since the articles were clearly lost, so the money should pass with the rest of the estate.

The court, on the other hand, noted that an ademption, to have the same effect of eliminating the bequest, must take place *during the lifetime of the deceased.* Here, there was no evidence that such was the case, and the reimbursement rightfully belonged to Anne's mother as reimbursement for articles otherwise bequeathed to her and lost *after* Anne's death.

What about the situation where the testator leaves a specific item to a beneficiary in his will and then decides to give the beneficiary that same item during his lifetime? Must the PR replace the item to satisfy the bequest? Of course not. When such an event occurs, the bequest is held to be adeemed (canceled) by extinction.

In sum, when the specifically bequeathed item of property is lost, destroyed, stolen, or otherwise disposed of *during the deceased's lifetime,* unless that item is given to the beneficiary during the testator's lifetime, the beneficiary loses out and generally has no recourse. But does the same rule apply to money?

Involuntary Changes in Your Will—When There Isn't Enough Money to Go Around

In his will Sal left $50,000 to his wife, Sally, and the rest of his estate went to his four children equally. As it turned out, Sal's entire estate after expenses amounted to about $50,000, just enough for the bequest to Sally. Does this mean his children will get nothing?

In another will, Sebastian left the following bequests: $10,000 to each of his two children; $30,000 to establish a scholarship fund in his name; the home he lived in (worth about $200,000) to his wife (for total bequests of $250,000); and the rest of the estate to his mother and sister equally.

After expenses, Sebastian's estate was about $400,000, more than enough to cover all of these bequests, but shortly after his death, a claim was made against his estate by a former business partner he had cheated years earlier. The partner sued Sebastian's estate, and the court awarded him $275,000. When the estate pays this amount (which takes priority over the bequests), what happens to the rest? Will the children get their shares? Will there be a scholarship in Sebastian's name? Will the wife get the home? Will the swallows come back to Capistrano?

These cases reflect the principle of "abatement" of bequests in a will. *Abatement* is the forced reduction of bequests or shares when the testator's estate does not contain sufficient assets to pay debts, expenses, and all the prescribed bequests in full. When this happens, the bequests are "abated" (reduced) according to certain rules, unless the will specifies otherwise.

As a general rule, the first bequest to suffer is the "residuary" bequest. This is the one that usually says, "I leave all the rest, remainder and residue of my estate to . . ." The residuary bequest is the "pot" from which all expenses and shortfalls are generally funded, before any reduction for specific bequests (i.e., bequests of specific sums of money or items of property). (Remember, the will can provide otherwise.)

Therefore, in Sal's case, Sally would receive her specific bequest and the children would receive nothing. And if there were not enough to provide for Sally's full $50,000 bequest, she would simply take whatever money there was to apply toward it. If there is not enough in such cases, the beneficiaries have no recourse, since there is no obligation (nor ability) on the part of the testator to leave more than he has.

In the case of Sebastian's estate, the same rules apply, but the situation is a bit more complicated, since there are specific bequests of both money and real estate, and the estate, even though valued in excess of the $275,000 judgment, does not have adequate cash to pay the judgment. The next question is: Is all the cash used up first and then the remaining items sold to raise the necessary additional cash? Or does everyone pay a proportionate share of the cost?

Unfortunately, the rules are not consistent from state to state. Many states follow the common-law rule, which favors the use of "personalty" (anything other than real estate) to pay the costs before ordering the sale of real estate, while others treat both realty and personalty alike for purposes of abatement. Once this preference or nonpreference is established, then the bequests will be abated (reduced) proportionately.

That is, say that in Sebastian's estate the abatement of realty and personalty were treated alike. The total estate was $400,000, less a judgment of $275,000. Specific bequests totaled $250,000, leaving a "residuary estate" of $150,000 before considering the judgment. As noted above, the residuary estate would be applied first, so that the $150,000 would be applied in full toward the $275,000 judgment, leaving a balance of $125,000 due on the judgment. There is $250,000 left in the estate (before payment of the bequests) ($400,000 less $150,000), of which $125,000 must be applied to pay the balance of the judgment. In other words, each of the specific legatees must pay a proportionate share of the $125,000 (by *reducing* the amount they get), but just how is it divided?

The rule of abatement provides for a proportional reduction based on the relationship a given share bears to all the shares. That is, if two equal beneficiaries had to abate their shares, they would each be reduced by the same amount. Similarly, if A was to get $10,000 and B was to get $20,000, A would abate his share by one-third the shortfall, and B would bear two-thirds the shortfall.

In Sebastian's estate, then, where the specific bequests totaled $250,000 and the shortfall was $125,000, and assuming that bequests of real estate and personal property are treated alike for abatement purposes, then each beneficiary would bear the following share of the $125,000 shortfall:

			(SHORTFALL)		(REDUCTION OF SHARE)
2 children ($10,000 each)	$20,000 $250,000	x	$125,000	=	$10,000 ($5,000 each child)
Scholarship ($30,000)	$30,000 $250,000	x	$125,000	=	$15,000
Wife ($200,000)	$200,000 $250,000	x	$125,000	=	$100,000

That is, instead of receiving $10,000 each, the children would receive only $5,000 each, and instead of $30,000, the scholarship would only be funded with $15,000.

Unfortunately, the wife's share is in the form of real estate, and in order for the abatement of her share to be carried out, the real estate would have to be sold. If she did not want this to happen, she would have to borrow against it and pay the $100,000 herself.

Abatements can produce harsh results, but fortunately they are not a common occurrence. If there is a question about there being enough funds to pay all debts, expenses, and specific bequests, you should try to deal with it ahead of time, but as we saw in Sebastian's case, it is not always foreseeable.

How to Revoke Your Will

In a sense, complete revocation of your will is much simpler than changing it because the revocation, when effective, is absolute and complete, and the ways a will can be revoked are fairly well defined in the law. For instance, if you tear up your will into pieces with the intention of revoking it, it is clear that you have legally revoked it. Despite the clarity of the legal requirements for revocation, however, people will still find ways of complicating and confusing the issues.

As a general rule, you can successfully revoke your will by:

1. Physical acts done to the will (i.e., tearing it up or burning it) either by the testator or by someone else at the testator's direction;
2. A subsequent writing (such as a new will) expressly revoking the previous will or revoking it by implication, in whole or in part, due to inconsistencies; or
3. Getting married after the will is made, unless the will was made in anticipation of the marriage. But if your state has enacted the

Uniform Probate Code, it may be (depending upon what was enacted) that the will remains valid, and the new spouse is entitled to a statutory share of the probate property, which may change how the property subject to the will is distributed.

1. REVOCATION BY PHYSICAL ACTS DONE TO THE WILL

Just about every state has specific laws providing that a will can be revoked by acts such as "burning, canceling, tearing, obliterating, destroying, mutilating, and cutting" the will, or one or more words to that effect.

As clear as such acts may appear at first glance, however, they are the subject of a great deal of litigation. There are many cases, for instance, very similar to that of Graham's, described at the very beginning of this chapter. Graham, who was blind, asked his daughter to throw his will into the fire. She pretended to do so, and Graham was left to believe that his will was revoked. Of course, it was not. Though he asked that it be destroyed, the will remained in good condition and was presented for probate at Graham's death. The fact that the daughter deceived Graham was a separate matter and did not cause the revocation of his will.

In a somewhat similar case, which illustrates the same principle but with a different result, Samuel decided to revoke his will, so he carefully took the large envelope that contained the will and tore it in half. Because the folded will was so much smaller than the envelope, however, only a corner of the will was torn, and none of the "writing" was damaged. Was Samuel's will revoked?

It is not necessary that the tearing, burning, mutilating, etc., be a complete physical destruction of the will beyond recognition. In fact, even the slightest charring or tearing is sufficient, so long as it is done with the *intent* of revoking the will. If the testator directs someone else to destroy the will, as in Graham's case, it *must* be done in his presence. If he is not present, the revocation is not effective even though he may have directed it.

Presence and *intent* of the testator, therefore, are essential ingredients in these cases, *along with the physical act itself.* For instance, say that Erin Gobrah has two wills and wants to revoke one of them. By mistake she tears up the wrong one. Is either will revoked? No. Neither will was revoked by the act of tearing, since there was *no intent* to revoke the one that was torn by mistake, and the one intended to be revoked was not torn.

In short, there must be some form of physical destruction done to the will either by the testator or by someone else in his presence and at his direction, done with the intent to revoke. The destruction need not be complete, but need only reflect the testator's wish to destroy or cancel the will. Although the testator himself can change his mind and recover the will before the destruction is complete, interference by someone else without the testator's authorization will not prevent a revocation if the other elements are present.

Therefore, in Graham's case, no revocation occurred, since even though he had the *intent* to revoke, nothing was done to the will. And in Samuel's case, there *was* a revocation, even though his wife retrieved the will, since he had the intention to revoke the will and the physical act of destruction, though not complete, was done to the will.

2. REVOCATION BY A SUBSEQUENT WRITING

If you are the nonviolent type, and burning, tearing, or obliterating things does not appeal to you, you may prefer to revoke your will by a safe, simple writing.

You may have noticed, for instance, that most wills begin with language such as, "I, Mildred Smith, make this my will, *hereby revoking all wills and codicils previously made by me.*" If properly signed and witnessed (or otherwise meeting the state's requirements for a valid will), this "writing" would operate to revoke all previous wills and codicils. The writing revoking a previous will need not itself be contained in a will, but it would be more than a little foolish to have nothing more than such a writing, unless you do not want a new will, or unless the new will accidentally omitted the standard revocation clause. If for some reason, such as those just mentioned, a bare writing solely to revoke the previous will becomes necessary, the writing itself must meet the *same formalities* as the will, that is, intent, competence, and all the required signatures.

Confusion occasionally arises as to whether a writing that revokes a codicil to a will or a direct destruction (revocation) of the codicil itself revokes the underlying will. The general rule of law in this case is that revocation of a codicil does *not* revoke the underlying will, only the codicil.

3. REVOCATION BY GETTING MARRIED AFTER THE WILL IS MADE

If a person marries after he makes his will, the old rule, still true in many states, is that the marriage will automatically *revoke* a will that he made prior to the marriage, unless the will was made "in anticipation of" the marriage. That is, a will made in such a case will actually state something such as, "Having in mind my forthcoming marriage to Ruth Roth, I hereby make my will." Or "I hereby intend for this will to be effective notwithstanding any subsequent marriage." The requirement of anticipating or contemplating the marriage in no way means that the new wife or husband must be a beneficiary under the will. She will have her rights in any event if you leave her out, as explained in chapter 7. As stated above, under the Uniform Probate Code, the will stays in effect, and the new spouse is granted certain rights to the deceased's property.

While marriage has long revoked a will that would not anticipate the marriage, traditionally a divorce or annulment generally did not. At one time, a divorce had no effect at all on a previously made will, but now most states provide that unless otherwise stated in the court order dissolving the marriage, a divorce will revoke the particular *bequests* made in the will to the ex-spouse, and often will similarly revoke the appointment of the ex-spouse as executrix of the will. In other respects, the will would remain valid after a divorce.

4. PARTIAL REVOCATION BY HOMICIDE

Most states have laws that prohibit a killer from inheriting from his victim's estate. Therefore, the bequest to the murderer will be revoked and the estate disposed as if the murderer predeceased the victim.

Reviving a Previously Revoked Will

Occasionally a testator will revoke his will because of a belief in a point of fact or law, which after his death is discovered to be mistaken. Is there anything the beneficiaries of the previous will can do? For instance, take the case of Domenica Lunedi, a widow who made a will leaving her entire estate to her only child, Domenic. While skiing with friends in the Alps, Domenic became lost, and after a number of intensive searches, he was given up for dead. Two years later, convinced that Domenic was gone, Domenica revoked her will by making a new will, expressing her love for Domenic and leaving her estate to various hospitals and universities in Domenic's *memory.* Shortly thereafter, Domenica died. As it happened, Domenic was lost and seriously injured, but not dead. By the time he made his way back home, however, his mother was dead, and he found himself left without a dime.

While a revocation, if properly executed, absolutely revokes the previous will, some revocations, such as Domenica's, could be viewed as *conditional* revocations that are dependent on the condition being true. In other words, if Domenica had known that Domenic was not deceased, she would clearly not have revoked her previous will, and her belief that he was in fact deceased was apparent by the gifts to the charities in "memory" of Domenic. In such cases, courts have held that the revocation was dependent on the condition and if it could be shown *on the face* of the revocation that there was a material mistake on which the revocation was based (here it was clear in the revocation that Domenica believed Domenic to be dead), then the revocation would not be effective and the previous will would stand.

The same rule can apply to individual bequests that are revoked by a subsequent codicil or by a new will. In one case, for example, where a man made a codicil that revoked some bequests to certain relatives, stating "they being all dead," the bequests were allowed to stand when it was discovered that the relatives were, in fact, alive.

But don't rush to the courts just because your uncle left you out of his will on the basis that he thought you were unemployed but, in fact, you had a job. If the court believes that your uncle would have left you out in any event and the mistaken belief was not the motivating and principal factor behind the change, the disinheritance will stand.

Keep This in Mind

Every state has a statute that dictates the formalities of signing and witnessing a will. If any of these formalities is missing or not properly followed, the will is not valid. How does this relate to changing a will? Because every change in a will is like a new "partial" will and must follow the same formalities as a will to be valid. So if you wish to make a change to your will, resist the impulse to cross out a line or tear out a part and write in the change. It will do far more harm than good, and it may end up affecting the validity of the entire will.

5

Common Will Provisions

A word is not a crystal, transparent and unchanged; it is the skin of a living thought and may vary greatly in color and content according to the circumstances and the time in which it is used.

—Justice Oliver Wendell Holmes

Few attorneys would disagree that most of the millions of will contests over the past two thousand years have turned solely upon the meaning of a word or phrase. After all, a will is no more than a collection of words. It is the meaning and intent of those words, however, that truly challenges the mind and the purse. But, as Justice Holmes tells us, meanings and intentions are not always clear. So where does that leave us?

Personally, and with the greatest respect for Justice Holmes, I think Humpty Dumpty put it considerably more succinctly when he said to Alice, "When I use a word, it means just what I choose it to mean, neither more nor less."

Just what words *should* go into your will? Aren't there parts of every will that are just about the same? So what's the big deal about "words"?

A Question of Words, and the Use of "Boilerplate" Language

Use of the "right" words can make or break a will. Many people feel, however, that lawyers who draft wills never think about the words they use; they simply pull a standard form off a shelf and—bingo!—they have a will. Such standard forms and provisions are called "boilerplate," because, like the interchangeable metal plates of cylindrical boilers, the very same language is to a certain extent interchangeable from one will to another, word for word. Use of such "boilerplate" forms and provisions causes many to believe that an attorney might not even be needed if one can get one's hands on the right forms.

Part of this is true. The fact is that we *do* have hundreds of different forms and standard provisions relating to wills, which can in fact be readily used, word for word, from one will to another. But it is *only* the competent and knowledgeable use of such forms and individual provisions that enables an attorney to produce a "good" will at a fair price.

It is *not* true that lawyers do not think about the words they use. (Of course, as with any business, trade, or profession, there are varying levels of competence, and some may be able to show exceptions to the previous statement.) But a competent attorney will never use a document that he has not read and does not understand. If your attorney cannot explain to you the reason for and meaning of each provision in the will (or trust) he has drafted for you, you should change attorneys.

What many fail to realize is that the use of standardized forms and provisions by an attorney is actually quite advantageous to the client. These forms usually represent suggestions and development by legal scholars and specialists as the result of many years of study of court decisions, changes in the law, and just plain, practical experience, and, if the right form is chosen, *you* are getting the benefit of all that. It would be nearly impossible and financially prohibitive for your attorney to spend the same amount of time researching and developing these provisions just for you on an individual basis. You wouldn't expect your doctor to personally mix the drugs and chemicals of every prescription he gave you. Somewhat similar to the physician with the medicine, the critical role of your attorney in this respect is to have the knowledge of the standardized forms and provisions that will best protect your interests and satisfy your objectives under the law.

Although many of the "standard" provisions are necessary and helpful, some are superfluous or useless, and still others can actually be harmful. Unfortunately, attorneys who do not pay attention to the "words" they are using, or unsuspecting testators who decide to save a few dollars by making their own will from a "form" book, frequently perpetuate such useless and potentially harmful provisions.

For instance, for many years (perhaps a hundred or more!), attorneys and many form books continued to use the standard will provision regarding debts. (In fact, I wouldn't be at all surprised if your own will has one.) It is usually somewhere near the beginning of the will and says something like this: "I direct my Personal Representative to pay all my just debts and expenses as soon as practical after my death, etc." This is a totally useless provision that in some cases could lead to the payment of claims that otherwise might not have been paid. *Of course* your personal representative has to pay your "just debts and expenses"! So why do you have to direct him to do so? You don't. Just because the provision is "standard" does not mean it should be used in every case.

This is not to say there is no individualization in a will. There are always special provisions or insertions that must be drafted for each particular family. But in most wills, the majority of the provisions are in fact boilerplate. Following is a list of those boilerplate provisions that you'll find in most wills, and *why* you should find them there.

Some Common but Necessary Will Provisions

1. Exordium clause. This is the opening phrase of your will stating that it is, in fact, your will. The usual language is something such as, "I, Grover Lambeck, of Brooklyn, New York, declare this to be my last will, revoking all prior wills and codicils made by me."

This is all the exordium needs to say. It is *not* necessary to begin, "In the name of God, amen," or "Being of sound mind and mindful of the vicissitudes of life," or, as in the case of an Olympian's will, "Being of sound mind and athletic body," and so on. (If you have to *tell* everyone you are of sound mind, maybe you have a problem.)

As to recital of domicile, it is neither absolutely necessary nor legally conclusive that you are in fact domiciled where you say you are, but it is a *good idea* to have it, because at least it offers evidence that this is where *you* declared your domicile to be at the time you signed the will.

As to the revocation of prior wills, in this global age it may be important not to automatically revoke prior wills, such as a will executed under French law that is intended to be used in France, which is limited to disposing of your Paris condo at your death.

2. Survival clause. For every bequest you make under your will, including the residuary bequest, you should consider whether you want the named beneficiary to receive the bequest *only if she or he survives you.* If this is the case, then you *must* add the words "if she (or he) survives me" after each such bequest. If you do not, then the bequest will automatically pass to the beneficiary's probate estate if she does not survive you.

Furthermore, as explained in chapter 2, you can actually specify (within reason) just how long a beneficiary must live after you in order to be considered as having survived you for purposes of your will. This provision can be very important when, for example, a beneficiary dies a few hours or a few days after you. In such a case, you probably would *not* want the bequest to take effect.

For instance, your will can state that "a beneficiary shall not be considered to have survived me or another, for purposes of this will, unless such beneficiary shall have survived me or such other for a period of thirty (30) days." Thirty days is arbitrary and is not the required number for any legal purpose. It could just as well be ten days or sixty days, but most experts agree it should not be more than six months, as this can create estate-settlement delays and uncertainties and, in the case of a surviving spouse, can cause a loss of certain estate tax savings.

If the beneficiary does not survive you, then the share he would have received will pass to your residuary estate and be distributed along with that. (The residuary estate is what is left over after payment of all bequests and all expenses, taxes, and claims.)

To illustrate how the survival clause might work, say that Quincy's will provides the following: "I leave the sum of $50,000 to my brother, Randolph, if he survives me." The will also contains a sixty-day survivorship clause, requiring a beneficiary to survive Quincy by at least sixty days if he or she is to take the bequest. While traveling together, Quincy and Randolph are in an accident and Quincy is killed. Randolph hangs on for a few days, then dies. Under Quincy's will, Randolph (or his estate) will inherit nothing, as he did not survive for the sixty-day period required under Quincy's will. Without that provision, Randolph's estate would have been entitled to the $50,000 bequest since Randolph survived Quincy, even though only for a few days. Thus, *after* Quincy's estate was settled, the $50,000 bequest would have to be paid to Randolph's estate (adding costs and delays) and would then be distributed according to Randolph's will, if he had one, and, if not, according to the laws of the state where Randolph resided.

3. Simultaneous death (common disaster) clause. Related to the survivorship clause just discussed, the simultaneous death clause is, in fact, somewhat different. All states have adopted what is called the Uniform Simultaneous Death Act, which provides that if the testator and a beneficiary die under circumstances where it is impossible to determine the order of death, then the *testator* is considered to have survived the beneficiary, unless the testator's will provides otherwise. It is not harmful to have both a simultaneous death clause *and* a survivorship clause in a will, especially where a spouse is involved. In such a case, the will frequently provides that the spouse is excepted from the survivorship clause, and in the event of a simultaneous death, the will declares that the spouse with the smaller estate will be considered to have survived, for the purpose of reducing the federal estate taxes. (See chapters 12 and 13 for a fuller discussion of this.)

4. Tangible personal property. Although the concept and handling of tangible personal property is discussed in greater detail later in this chapter, it is mentioned here only to point out that it should be separated, as a *specific bequest*, from the residue of the estate. For instance, "I leave all my tangible personal property to my wife, if she survives me. If not, I leave such tangible property to my three children equally, or all to the survivor(s) of them."

Tangible personal property normally consists of household furnishing, jewelry, clothing, automobiles, and other "moveable" personal effects, and frequently it is simply taken by the surviving spouse and children without any formalities. Because of the federal income tax laws dealing with the treatment of distributions from an estate, however, this innocent taking of such tangible personal items in some cases can actually be taxable as *income* to the recipients. An exception to such tax treatment applies to specific bequests under the will and, therefore, it should be separately bequeathed as suggested above.

5. Powers of personal representative. Generally, lawyers make much more of a personal representative's powers than is frequently necessary, especially in smaller estates, since a personal representative has certain inherent powers necessary to carry out his duties to settle the estate, whether or not stated in the will. But it does not hurt to provide more extensive powers so as to eliminate any question on the part of third parties dealing with the estate, and in larger estates where the extent of the personal representative's duties is occasionally unknown, greater powers are quite appropriate. Furthermore, there are certain powers that *must* be specifically stated, including the authority to continue the deceased's business and the power to deal with or sell the deceased's real estate, if necessary. Therefore, if you have a business or income-producing real estate, your will should contain the necessary powers to allow the personal representative to deal with these items. (These issues are discussed in greater detail in chapter 9.) Most states have "statutory" personal representative's powers, which may be incorporated in the will simply by referring to the applicable law of the state.

If a *trust* is created under the will (a *testamentary* trust), it is essential that the trustee's powers also be detailed. They may be similar to the personal representative's powers but are frequently more extensive because such trusts are generally designed to continue for many years.

6. Guardian and conservator appointment. If you have minor children, you want to be sure your will deals with the appointment of a guardian, conservator, or both for them, as well as a successor guardian if the initially named guardian can't serve. And remember, this is actually a nomination rather than an official appointment. (This is covered in greater detail in chapter 2.)

7. Personal representative (remember, this is the same as the old term "executor") appointment. As with the guardian and other "appointments" under your will, this is a *nomination* rather than an official appointment. The official appointment of a PR comes from the court if no one objects to your nomination. As with the guardians for minor children, you should nominate a successor PR in case the first one named cannot serve. (Personal representatives are discussed in detail in chapter 9.)

8. Bond. With only a *few* exceptions, every "fiduciary" (i.e., personal representative, administrator, trustee, and guardian) must give a bond to secure the faithful performance of his duties, although in a few states the bond can be avoided. A bond is basically the person's promise to make good if he causes a loss to the estate as a result of his negligence or wrongdoing in carrying out his duties. The bond can be a personal bond "without sureties," meaning that it is backed only by the personal representative's personal assets, or it can be *with* sureties (outside guarantees). The sureties can either be *personal* sureties (friends of the personal representative who agree to pay if he runs off with the estate's money) or *corporate* sureties (an insurance company that guarantees payment). This provision usually states, "I name Bob Blank as Personal Representative and direct that he be allowed to serve without bond, or if a bond is required by law, then he should serve without sureties on his bond."

It is argued that a bond with corporate sureties adds to the expense of administering the estate, and this can be true, but, in fact, the costs are usually very small in proportion to the amount of money that is covered. If the personal representative and the primary beneficiary are the same, however, there may hardly be a need for a bond, for if he takes the estate's money, he is taking it only from himself. But if they are not the same, you may want to consider at least a personal bond.

9. Tax apportionment clause. This important provision typically states that all inheritance and estate taxes are to be paid from the *residue* of the estate. The usual purpose of the provision is to leave specific bequests intact, on the assumption, for instance, that if Sam leaves $1,000 to each of his four sisters, he wants each of them to receive the full $1,000, and not $1,000 minus taxes and minus legal and personal representative's fees. The typical apportionment clause allows them to get the full amount, and the estate taxes on their shares will be paid from the residue. Most states (including those having adopted the Uniform Probate Code) have apportionment statutes providing that *unless* the will states otherwise (which is what the standard tax apportionment clause does), each beneficiary will bear his pro rata share of the taxes based on the amount he receives and taking into account tax exemptions and other allowances. In practical effect, therefore, the typical apportionment clause anticipates that the specific legatees (i.e., beneficiaries who receive specified sums or specified items of property and charitable beneficiaries), if any, will receive only nominal amounts and that the residuary legatees (those who receive the residue of the estate) will receive the bulk of the estate. In this case, it is acceptable that they should also pay the taxes.

Problems can arise, however, when the specific legatees, as well as beneficiaries who receive property *outside* the will (through joint ownership, for example), receive a disproportionately large part of the estate. If, in this case, the will has a "standard" tax apportionment clause providing that the residuary estate pays the tax, there will almost certainly be trouble, not to mention an unfair distribution of the estate.

For instance, say that Merriweather's will has the usual tax apportionment clause, and his total estate is $200,000. He leaves $50,000 to each of his three daughters and the rest to his son. State inheritance taxes amount to $16,000, and expenses and legal fees (which are normally paid out of the residue regardless of the apportionment clause) come to an additional $6,000. The son, who receives the residue, will therefore receive $50,000 less $16,000 in taxes and less an additional $6,000 in fees, or a net of $28,000, while the daughters will each receive the *full* $50,000! If the apportionment clause were omitted from Merriweather's will, it would have caused each of the daughters to pay her fair share of the tax (although his son would still have paid the expenses).

Therefore, before you approve of the "standard" tax apportionment clause, take a careful look at the specific and charitable bequests you have made, as well as the items of property that pass outside your will, and see if the burden of tax payment is where you want it.

10. Avoid "extra" guardians. Whenever there are minor children who may stand to inherit from the estate, or even the possibility that a child, *yet unborn,* could inherit under certain circumstances, many states, in an effort to "protect" the interests of such minor children, will require that a guardian ad litem (GAL) be appointed on behalf of the minor child. This will be done *even though* one of the spouses is already appointed as guardian under the will, on the basis that since the spouse herself is also a beneficiary, she cannot be totally disinterested when it comes to the child. Therefore, the court will appoint a GAL (who is usually an attorney known to the judge or to the clerk of court) to review the estate matters on behalf of the minor child.

Despite this, it is possible in most states to *dispense* with the necessity of such an appointment, provided you feel comfortable that the persons you have appointed will do an honest job. The dispensation clause usually says something like this:

> If any occasion shall arise during the administration of my estate, or in connection with any matter or procedure connected with my estate, calling for the appointment of a person to represent the interests of persons unborn or unascertained or the interests of any other person, I direct that such appointment shall be dispensed with, if permitted under the law of the applicable jurisdiction.

There are also modern laws such as the Uniform Probate Code, which permit one person to represent another's interests ("virtual representation") if their interests are aligned and there are not apparent conflicts of interest.

11. Defining Family Members. As discussed earlier, families take many forms these days: blended families, adopted families, same-sex families, opposite-sex families, families with ART children. Your will could define who you consider your family to be for purposes of inheritance.

Note that these are by no means all the provisions that should or will be in your will. No doubt there will be numerous others to carry out your special wishes and objectives. For instance, there may be a noncontest clause (discussed in chapter 10) or several conditional clauses (discussed in chapter 6), or you may even come up with some new ones on your own!

Understanding the Difference Between Real and Personal Property

What is "property"? The term *property* is often interpreted by the lay public to mean real estate. In fact, property, in the basic legal sense, means anything that is capable of ownership. In this regard, it could include everything from a theater ticket to a yacht, from a share of stock to a movie contract with MGM, and from an apartment lease to ownership of the Empire State Building. All involve a property right of some sort, and all property rights are divided into two basic categories of property: real and personal.

Real property is any property interest in *real estate*—that is, land. A property interest in real estate could include a lease or a mortgage, as well as a deed to the real estate itself. (When buildings are constructed on the land, they generally become a part of the underlying real estate and, with rare exception, are not regarded as separate items of property.)

Personal property is any property interest in anything *other than* real estate, and could include shares of stock, a promissory note, a piano, an automobile, or a copyright.

Personal property is divided, in turn, into two categories: *tangible* personal property and *intangible* personal property. Basically, *tangible* personal property includes things you can move and touch and that have some "inherent" value, such as furniture, jewelry, clothing, paintings, collectible coins, rugs, etc.

Intangible personal property includes things that in themselves have *no* value, but which represent the *right* to something else. For instance, a share of stock is, in itself, a valueless piece of paper, but it represents value in the right to dividends and a share of proceeds if the company is liquidated; a copyright represents the right of ownership in a book, a song, or a work of art; a royalty interest represents the right to a share of profits in some resource; or a promissory note represents the right to collect money from someone.

Most wills separate only *tangible* personal property from the rest of the estate, and, therefore, the rest of the estate normally includes *intangible* personal property plus all real estate interests. Quite often there are more problems associated with tangible items of nominal value (i.e., mother's engagement ring) than there are with other estate property of much more substantial value, as illustrated below.

Dealing with Oriental Rugs, the Coin Collection, and Heirloom Jewelry

These items, as you now know from the above discussion, are all considered tangible personal property. In most estates, the blanket provision leaving all tangible personal property to a spouse or children is usually *intended* to include only the normal household furniture, clothing, and other articles of nominal value. You should be aware, however, that this same blanket provision will automatically include *all* of your tangible property, whether valuable or not. If you have items that are of sufficient value that you feel should be separated, then do so; otherwise you could invite questions and possibly trouble, as did the famous artist Mark Rothko.

Rothko left his wife his New York town house and all the "tangible" personal property in the town house. As it was, the town house contained a few million dollars' worth of Rothko's paintings. Rothko's personal representatives sued his wife, contending that the paintings should not be included under the tangible property clause. The court held that the will was clear and that the widow was entitled to the paintings.

Similar problems arise when beneficiaries are given the choice of "an item" of tangible personal property. Just what is "an item"? Of course, one item might be a piano or a clock, but what about a sixty-piece service of silverware? Is that one item or sixty? Or how about a stamp collection? Is that one item or one thousand? The question is illustrated (and answered) in the case stemming from the estate of Blanche Marston.

Mrs. Marston was a wealthy woman from an affluent suburb of Boston.

In her will she provided for numerous friends and relatives, and the bulk of her estate, including the proceeds from the sale of tangible items not left to individuals, went to the Marstons' charitable foundation. The bequest in question was to one Michael Lonigro, who was given the choice of "any three items of tangible personal property." Lonigro chose, as *one* of the three items, Mrs. Marston's extensive stamp collection, worth about $11,000. Marston's personal representatives objected, of course, on the basis that this should not be considered as one item. The Massachusetts court held for Lonigro. It would be quite foolish, the court said, to treat this single collection as twenty thousand or thirty thousand individual items of personal property. Mrs. Marston, in other parts of her will, had already indicated that she regarded her silver collection as having a "unitary character," and the collection of stamps should be treated no differently.

This treatment of collections as a single item of personal property is generally accepted, but within reason. A "collection" of jewelry, for instance, is not consistent with this view unless it is truly in the nature of a collection that was accumulated more as a unit than simply as a series of pieces that have the same character. In any event, to avoid the problem you should be specific and state how *you* want any such valuable "items" to be distributed.

LEAVING A "MEMORANDUM"

A statement as to the disposition of your tangible personal property is safest in the will itself, but many people are reluctant to do this because it makes public the items you owned (a will is placed on file at the probate court for any interested party to view). An alternative used by some is a "memorandum" given to your personal representative, containing a list of items and the respective beneficiaries to receive those items. Such a "private" memorandum is perfectly legal and binding *if* it meets certain requirements. Traditionally, it must first be in writing and in existence at the time the will is signed; second, it must be identifiable as the paper referred to in the will; and third, the will must state that the memorandum is in existence. In other words, you must have it written and preferably signed and dated at or prior to the time the will is signed. If you do all this, the personal representative is bound to follow your instructions on the memorandum. But if you do meet these requirements, then the memorandum will become "public," because the memorandum would be regarded as part of the will. Under the modern Uniform Probate Code, the writing still must be signed, must be referred to in the will, and must define the tangible property with reasonable certainty, but now the memorandum may be prepared before or after the will is signed, and you may alter it from time to time.

Instead, most people regard such a memorandum as some sort of a tangible flexible will (as to their tangible property), allowing them to modify the memorandum from time to time as they see fit. Although it is permissible to do so, your personal representative is *not* legally bound to follow it. As a result, if you leave your tangible property to be distributed "according to a memorandum" you leave with your personal representative, and if the memo does not meet the above requirements, the personal representative may be able to do whatever he wants with those items, or, more likely, there will be a fight over them.

Of course, if the personal representative can be "trusted" to carry out your memorandum, then things should go as you wish. In fact, where children are involved, many attorneys (the authors included) recommend that you write a "letter" to your children—which really amounts to a memorandum in a sense—asking that they honor the wishes you express in the letter relating to distribution of your tangible personal property. Although it is *not* legally binding, it usually places considerable moral pressure on your children to carry it out.

Another caveat: if a child is named personal representative of your estate and the personal representative is given authority to divide your tangible personal property among all the children in "substantially equal shares," this could also lead to problems in some cases. If you think there could be such a problem, simply name an independent person, a "special personal representative or administrator" if necessary, solely for the purpose of making decisions on the equitable division of your tangible personal property. Another option we often use to help avoid disputes is to provide that each child will be able to select an "item" of property in turn, by seniority or by drawing straws, stating in the will that sets or collections are to be kept intact where practical. If you do have one or two items that are disproportionate in value to the rest (such as a stamp or coin collection, or a single valuable painting), you should deal with these *separately* and should *not* lump them in with other items of your tangible personal property.

Finally, if there are large items of tangible property or items that require special handling that are bequeathed to individuals, you may want to consider (though it is not necessary) having those individuals pay for freight, insurance, storage, or other special costs attributable to the distribution of those items; otherwise the estate will have to pay those costs.

Leaving Something to Charity

Believe it or not, not everyone wants to make their children rich. There are many who believe that their money will be put to much better use by leaving some or all of it to charity. As explained at the outset of this book, however, there is no inherent right to bequeath your property to anyone or any organization; it is only the good grace of the state that allows you to do so. At one time, however, there were a number of limitations and "safeguards" imposed on us by these laws. One of them was the limitation on charitable bequests.

In early England, so much property was being acquired by churches and monasteries that the Crown became fearful of the tremendous power that the Church could wield; in addition, it was regarded as contrary to the nation's economic growth. To counter this trend, a law was enacted that made it illegal to leave property to a charity. Although we have no such law in the United States, these concerns, together with the strong tendency to protect the family, led to laws in a number of states that either limit the amount you can leave to a charity or require that the will containing the charitable bequest be executed within a specified time before your death, or both. Over the years, however, such laws were held to be unconstitutional and were ultimately repealed, the last as recently as 1985.

The time limitation was intended to prevent a person facing death from being unduly influenced by a charity or by the idea that he might buy a way into heaven. The time limitation usually provided that the charitable bequest will be invalid unless the will is signed at least a specified number of days or months prior to the testator's death.

But the charitable limitations never applied if the deceased left no heirs. Nevertheless, where large estates were involved, it seemed there was always someone who felt their own cause was a "charitable" one. In one New York case, for example (under a now-repealed New York statute limiting charitable bequests), an eccentric spinster left almost all of her $40 million estate to charity. Before you could say "the root of all evil," over two thousand claims were filed contesting the charitable bequest and asking for a share of the $40 million. Relatives came out of the woodwork, and, of course, most had their own attorneys. There were so many contestants and attorneys that special arrangements had to be made for hearings because they could not all fit into the courtroom. One creative "relative," however, stood out above the rest. He testified that he was the son of the spinster's deceased brother (which would make him her only nephew) and, if true, this would also entitle him to the entire estate. As evidence, he offered a Bible in which was recorded the marriage certificate of his mother and the spinster's brother. Because of the massive size of the estate and the vigorous contest, the whole matter was widely publicized, and this new "heir" quickly made the headlines. Unfortunately, a simple inspection of the Bible by the court disclosed that it was published twenty years *after* the date of the marriage certificate it contained, and the "nephew" was dismissed as a fraud and subsequently sent to jail.

As to the rest of the two-thousand-plus relatives, only nine were recognized by the court, and they shared the estate with the charity (and the lawyers, of course).

Even though there are no longer any restrictions on charitable bequests, if the testator gave what the heirs feel was "too much" to a charity, you can be pretty sure there will be trouble, especially if the circumstances surrounding the charitable gift appear suspicious. A recent case illustrating what would appear to be "suspicious" circumstances is that of the famous and colorful pianist Liberace.

Only eleven days before his death, Liberace, in the terminal stages of his disease, signed a new will leaving the bulk of his $115 million estate to the Liberace Foundation for the Performing Arts, a private charitable foundation. The lawyer who drafted the will was named personal representative of the will and was also named as director of the foundation. As soon as Liberace's heirs and previous beneficiaries learned of this, they filed proceedings to contest his will, the outcome of which we probably will never know, since after a few years of private battle, the matter was apparently settled out of court.

Some Final Words About Words

Although there is certainly no question that a will is no more than a collection of words, there is the very serious question of *whose words are they?* You go to your lawyer and tell her, "I want to leave this to Jack, that to Jill, and the rest to Mrs. Hill," which you feel should take no more than two or three sentences. Later she sends you a "draft" of a ten-page document, containing thousands of words, considerably more than a simple disposition of "this, that, and the rest."

Later, after you have signed a document you never really understood, you meet an untimely death (death is almost always untimely), and a will contest arises over whether you meant "this" when you said "that," and what is included in "the rest." The lawyers each build a convincing argument over why *you* wrote the will the way *you* did, witnesses are brought to testify as to *your* intentions and whether or not these intentions were reflected in *your* will, and then the court launches into its basic rules in interpretation and construction of wills to decide, once and for all, what *you* meant in the words of *your* will, which, in fact, was entirely drafted by your lawyer.

"Words are given their plain meaning," begins the judge, "and the answers must be found within the four corners of the will." "But the words were not really those of the testator," a contesting lawyer responds. "His *lawyer* chose the words. And since it was a person skilled in the use of words, why should we give them their 'plain' meaning? They should be literally and technically construed, since we cannot now ask the testator what he meant!"

"All right," the judge says, "to determine the intent of the testator, perhaps we should consider outside evidence." "But if we open the door to outside evidence," says another lawyer, "doesn't this destroy the sanctity and security of the will, which was so carefully executed before witnesses and all, just for that purpose? If there was a mistake," she says, "it was the *lawyer's* mistake. She didn't say it right."

"But how do we determine that?" replies the judge. "What about the accepted legal doctrine that there is a presumption of a just and reasonable meaning to the will, that the will speaks for itself as of the moment of death, and that the latter of two inconsistent provisions should prevail?" And so it will go, on and on and on, usually until the parties settle.

Actually, all of the arguments and principles mentioned above are valid and have been the basis of many court decisions in will contests. As to the question of whose words they are—they really should be a combination of yours and the lawyer's. Given the complexities of the law and the many provisions that belong in a will, which would be nearly impossible for a layperson to draft and understand, it is a fact of life that you should engage a competent attorney to draft your will and that many, if not most, of the words will be the lawyer's and not yours. This does *not* mean, however, that you need not or should not read it over carefully and ask questions about any provisions that you do not understand.

Only by asking, for example, would you know what a tax apportionment clause is and then be able to see whether your estate is being divided as you have instructed. Actually, the dispositive provisions (those that dispose of your property) should at least be able to confirm that "this part, that part, and the rest" of your estate will be divided as you directed and that, although the very words may not be yours, the thoughts are.

Keep This in Mind

Don't ignore or discount the "boilerplate" (standard) provisions in your will. Each of these plays an important role and has evolved over time for its purpose. At the same time, give plenty of thought to clearly stating your wishes as to who gets what, but it is generally not a good idea to go on and on with expressions of gratitude or relationships or stories. These are more appropriately (and safely) included in a separate letter or statement from you, outside the will.

6

Uncommon Will Provisions—Controlling from the Grave

I leave to my banker, Mr. Hubert Pingrey, the sum of £1,000, provided that, within six months of my death, he walk the length of Bond Street, at midday and not on a Saturday or a Sunday, dressed as a circus clown, which should give him an inkling of the feelings to which he subjected me before advancing me a loan.

—from the will of a disgruntled client

This is what is known as a *conditional bequest.* In this particular case, the banker, Mr. Pingrey, declined to meet the condition, which is always an option of the beneficiary. Conditional bequests, as one would imagine, take all manner of shapes and forms, and they seem to offer a testator some assurance (if the condition is valid and accepted by the beneficiary) that his wishes will be carried out after his death, or in some cases, as we will see, a guarantee that if his wishes are not carried out *before* his death, the beneficiary will not inherit.

The condition attached to the banker's bequest above may seem somewhat silly or eccentric to some, quite poignant to others. A study of the history of wills reveals that such bequests are limited only by the imagination of the testator, provided they meet the requirements of the law. As the U.S. Supreme Court said in one case of a conditional bequest, "The right of a testator to attach to a gift in his will any lawful terms he sees fit, no matter how whimsical or capricious, is widely, if not universally, recognized." And we *will* see just how whimsical and capricious a testator can be.

The Requirements of a Conditional Bequest

1. THERE MUST BE A CONDITION

This requirement may sound obvious, but it is a fact of law that the courts will not impose a condition where there was none, or where it was not made *clear* that a condition existed. In interpreting the language of wills, there is a presumption in favor of *vesting*. That means there is a presumption that the bequest should go to the person named, with no strings attached, unless the will *clearly* states otherwise.

For example, language such as, "I would like it if Gerard were to use this bequest for such and such," is *not* a conditional bequest. Similarly, language like, "I leave my son, Alexander, $50,000, providing he will be generous to his sister, Andrea," does impose upon Alexander the condition that he must provide something for Andrea if he wants to keep the $50,000.

If a condition is to be imposed on a bequest, therefore, it must be clearly stated as a condition, as in the case of the bequest to Mr. Pingrey at the outset of this chapter, where it was clear what Pingrey had to do before he could receive his £1,000.

2. THE CONDITION MUST BE LEGAL AND NOT AGAINST PUBLIC POLICY

If Mike leaves an annual income to his brother Mack, "so long as he continues to deal in drugs," or "provided he beats his neighbor once a month," or "provided he uses the funds in a movement to overthrow the U.S. government," such conditions are clearly illegal and would be totally ignored by the court.

In such cases, where the condition is clearly illegal, or where the condition is unclear, or where it fails to meet any of the other legal requirements, the condition is void and the bequest generally passes directly to the beneficiary *free* of any condition.

If a condition is not illegal when it takes effect (at the time of death) but later becomes illegal, then once again it becomes void. For instance, Mr. Fields owns a liquor store on a popular street in Philadelphia. The store was in the family for generations, and Fields would like it to continue as such. In his will, therefore, Fields states, "I leave to my son, W.C., an annual income of $20,000 provided that he continues to operate our family liquor store on Thirteenth Street, Philadelphia," and W.C. does so. A few years later, however, the city zoning board makes it illegal to operate a liquor store on Thirteenth Street. In this case, since the condition *became* illegal, it also became void, and W.C. could continue to get the income even if he had to close the store.

Conditions that are against public policy are not as easy to determine. The rules of public policy are not written down anywhere and are always a matter of objective and reasonable judgment at any given time. What was against public policy fifty years ago may be perfectly well accepted today, and what is considered against public policy in one court may be considered acceptable in another, although the underlying principles on which it is based remain the same. On this point, one court said that a condition is against public policy if it "contravenes any established interest of society, or conflicts with the morals of the time, tends to injustice or oppression, restraint of liberty or legal rights."

This reference comes from a case where the testator, a Mr. Schmitz, left a sum of money in trust for four (of six) brothers and sisters, on the express condition that "no one [of the four] of them shall at any time after my death have any communication with [the other two] verbally or in writing, nor live under the same roof with them, for twenty years."

Of course, there is nothing at all illegal in this condition, but is it against public policy? "The family is the origin of all society and all government, and this condition is damaging to and encourages dissension in the family relationship," said the court, citing numerous other cases containing conditional bequests prohibiting children and grandchildren from speaking to the testator's ex-spouse, requiring children to attend schools that would separate them from their parents, and prohibiting an aunt from visiting or communicating with certain nieces and nephews. Clearly, they said, Schmitz's condition forbidding brothers and sisters to speak to one another is against public policy and was held void. (Conditions prohibiting marriage or having children, or encouraging divorce, are similarly against public policy, as discussed in greater detail later.)

If there is more than one condition, and one is illegal (or against public policy) while the other is valid, the court will ignore the invalid condition altogether but will enforce the valid condition. For instance, Jacob Hawke left his property in trust for ten years. If at the end of that time his son had "reformed his intemperate habits" *and* divorced himself from his wife, the son would receive the property. The court held that the condition to obtain a divorce was not enforceable, but the condition to reform was, and the son would have to satisfactorily perform under the second condition, within the prescribed period, before he could inherit the property.

3. THE CONDITION MUST BE POSSIBLE TO PERFORM

If the condition stated in the will is or becomes impossible for the beneficiary to perform, through no fault of the beneficiary, then the condition becomes void. For instance, Bradford leaves his estate to his son Brad on the condition that he take care of and support Bradford's wife for ten years after Bradford's death. Three years after Bradford's death, his wife dies. Brad is, of course, excused from the condition since it is now impossible to perform. Similarly, Atkinson leaves a parcel of land to Educatum University on the condition that the university construct a dormitory on the land within three years of his death. The town rules absolutely that such a building may not be constructed on the land. The university will receive the land free of the condition.

4. THE TIME FOR PERFORMANCE SHOULD BE CLEAR

Conditional bequests generally fall into two categories—condition *precedent* and condition *subsequent*. The bequest to our banker friend, Pingrey, at the outset of this chapter, was a condition precedent, meaning that *before* Pingrey could get his bequest, he must perform the condition of walking down Bond Street dressed as a circus clown. Mr. Schmitz's bequest, in which he placed funds in trust for his brothers and sisters on the condition that *thereafter* (for twenty years) they should not speak to another brother and sister, illustrates a condition subsequent. If they did so within the twenty-year period, the benefits they were receiving under Schmitz's will would stop. Under a condition *subsequent,* therefore, the bequest would be given to the beneficiary subject to the carrying out of the condition. If he did not carry it out, he would have to give the funds back; under a condition *precedent,* the bequest is not given until the condition is performed.

In both cases, the time for performance is critical to the condition. In the banker's case, he had six months; in the brothers and sisters' case, twenty years. The condition would not fail, however, just because *no* time is specified for performance. In such cases, the court would give the beneficiary a "reasonable" time to do whatever it is you have requested he do.

If no specific time is stated and the condition appears to last forever (such as, "$1,000 to Shirley, provided she never changes her name"), other practical problems are introduced, since the condition would require either the funds to be held until it was clear the beneficiary had performed (which would be a little ridiculous, since it may take a lifetime) or the beneficiary to give back the funds if she violated the condition. Because both of these alternatives are impractical, it is likely that the court would order the conditional bequest be held in trust, and the *use* of the funds offered to the beneficiary for the indefinite time period, subject to a loss of the use if the condition was breached. If the amount of the bequest was small enough so as not to warrant being held in trust (as in the case of a $1,000 bequest), the court could order the bequest paid outright to the beneficiary, since keeping it in trust would only result in additional, unnecessary costs to the estate.

5. THE CONDITION MUST BE CAPABLE OF BEING CARRIED OUT

To be enforceable, the condition must be *capable* of performance and *certain* as to the determination of performance. In one case, a wealthy banker left a large chunk of his estate to a nephew on the express condition "that he shall never, on any occasion, read a newspaper, his favorite occupation." What's wrong with this condition? It is certainly not illegal and probably not against public policy, but it is impossible to determine performance. How would anyone be able to tell whether the nephew continued to read newspapers, especially if he washed his hands regularly?

Referring again to the case of Mr. Schmitz, public policy was not the only issue. Even if it was held not to be against public policy for Schmitz to forbid his brothers and sisters to speak, how could it be monitored and enforced? Interestingly, Schmitz *did* contemplate this problem and authorized his trust to spend up to one-half the estate income to enforce these rules, including the authority to "pay any person" $100 for furnishing conclusive evidence that the brothers and sisters had spoken, and he also provided that the trustee would be the sole judge of the validity of such evidence. Nevertheless, the court felt that the condition was void on account of its *uncertainty* of performance. Trust funds would have to be used, probably without effectiveness, to "spy" on the brothers and sisters, and it would be a continuing waste of the court's time to decide, upon someone's appeal, whether, in fact, they spoke and thus breached the condition.

There are many other cases—perhaps hundreds—restricting modes of dress, prohibiting drinking, or requiring the living of a "clean life," all of which lead to the same problems of monitoring performance. Some clever testators seem to anticipate this and couch their conditions in different, more identifiable terms of performance, such as that of a wealthy Englishman named Sargeant, whose will provided his nephews with a substantial annual income, but only under certain conditions: "As my nephews are fond of indulging themselves in bed in the morning, I wish them to prove to the satisfaction of my personal representatives that they have got out of bed in the morning, and either employed themselves in business or taken exercise in the open air, from five to eight o'clock every morning from the fifth of April to the tenth of October, being three hours each day, and from seven to nine o'clock in the evening from the tenth of October to the fifth of April, being two hours every evening; this is to be done for some years, during the first seven years to the satisfaction of my executors, who may excuse them in case of illness, but the task must be made up when they are well, and if they will not do this, they shall not receive any share of my property. Temperance makes the faculties clear, and exercise makes them vigorous."

6. THERE MUST BE A PLAN FOR UNMET CONDITIONS

A critical element to a conditional bequest is called a "gift over," meaning that you must provide what will happen to the bequest in question if the beneficiary does not meet the condition. If you do not, the condition may be ignored. In other words, you might say, "I leave one-third of my estate to my son, Hotschott, on the condition that within one year of my death, he writes a five-thousand-word essay on why he thinks I was a great father. If he fails to do so to the satisfaction of my personal representative, then the said one-third of my estate shall pass to my English teacher, Geraldine Scripter, of Quincy, Massachusetts, or to her heirs if she does not survive."

Taking this strategy one step further, you might consider including a provision to the effect that if for some reason a court holds that the conditions you placed on the bequest were invalid and unenforceable, then the property would pass to your backup beneficiaries. This would be an extremely important provision to include if there is a question that your conditions may be considered against public policy.

Having in mind all of these requirements, you can now conjure up your most creative conditional bequests. But to get you started, here are some of the more typical ones.

Some Varieties of Conditional Bequests

1. PROHIBITIONS AGAINST MARRIAGE

Perhaps one of the most common conditions you will find is the attempt to restrain or prohibit the future marriage of a beneficiary. Closely aligned with this is the condition that a beneficiary must obtain a divorce to be eligible to receive a bequest. The condition encouraging divorce has been repeatedly struck down by the courts as being clearly against public policy. Conditions prohibiting or discouraging marriage or remarriage, however, are not as absolute. Generally (although there is at least one exception explained below), *total* restraints against marriage are considered against public policy and therefore void. *Partial* restraints, however, are another matter.

A total restraint against marriage would be where, for instance, Cabot leaves half his estate to his granddaughter, Buffy, provided she never marries. Such a condition would be void, and, barring certain other provisions in the will, the bequest would go to Buffy without conditions. Restraints against a remarriage, however, are often upheld (perhaps on the basis that this helps the beneficiary avoid making the same mistake twice?), and if the condition prohibits the remarriage of a spouse, it is almost always upheld if it is "fair and reasonable" under the circumstances. In other words, it is perfectly okay to provide, "I leave my estate in trust and the income is to be paid to my husband, Lothario, for his life, provided that if he remarries, then his income is to cease and all remaining funds are then to be given to St. Concetta's Convent."

Partial restraints on marriage are more difficult to pin down as being either legal or illegal. A partial restraint does not prohibit marriage altogether, but merely prohibits marriage under certain conditions. For example, "I leave $50,000 to my daughter, Candy, provided she does not marry before the age of twenty-two," or "provided she does not marry someone of Italian extraction," or "provided she obtains the consent of her aunt and uncle, if they are not deceased, prior to becoming married," or "provided she sign a prenuptial agreement prior to the marriage." Generally, a partial restraint will be held valid unless it is "unreasonable." But what is unreasonable? Presumably, a partial restraint would be unreasonable if, because of its terms, it virtually prohibited marriage under most circumstances or under reasonably foreseeable circumstances, such as when a man was prohibited from marrying any woman under six feet four inches tall, or when a person was prohibited from marrying before she reached the age of fifty. These conditions virtually prohibit marriage under reasonable circumstances, and therefore would be void.

Note that the question of reasonableness here does *not* mean logical, objective, unbiased, or unbigoted. There are many conditions upheld by the courts that are clearly "bigoted" in the common usage of the word. For instance, it is not unusual for a testator to leave funds to a child or grandchild provided she or he does not marry a person outside the Jewish faith, or the Catholic faith, or some other religious affiliation. Generally these restrictions have been upheld, but as stated above, changing mores may alter these previous results.

In one case, with a much more narrow restriction, funds were left to children on the condition that "if either one of my children should marry [a person from] T.W. Phillips' family, then I only give him or her the sum of three dollars, to be all that he or she is to receive under my will." As one might expect, the daughter married into the Phillips family. She contested the provision on the grounds that it was an unreasonable restraint against marriage. But clearly it was not, the court said. Given the broad range of "permissible" restraints under the law, restraints against marriage into a single family was not unreasonable. She got three dollars and Mr. Phillips was hopefully of the gas and oil Phillips family.

2. PROHIBITIONS AGAINST RELIGIOUS AFFILIATIONS

Although the courts are not totally consistent on this point, bequests that are subject to the condition that the beneficiary adhere to a particular religion, renounce it, or study it, or marry or refrain from marrying someone in a particular religion, all have been held to be valid and enforceable. In one case, funds were left to a priest on the condition that he withdraw from the priesthood and from any other order or society associated with the Roman Catholic Church. The condition was held to be valid. In another case where the condition was upheld, funds were left to a child on the condition that the child be educated or brought up in the Catholic faith. And still another upheld bequest left the funds on the condition that the child only marry a person of the "Hebrew faith."

Contentions that such conditions are against public policy on the basis that they are unconstitutional as a restraint against religious freedom have generally been overcome on the argument that individual actions or transactions (i.e., a bequest under a will) are not bound by state or federal guarantees of constitutional rights and that the right of the testator to use his funds to encourage or discourage the following or promotion of a particular religious belief is no less a right to religious freedom on *his* part. Unless the conditions were illegal or would injure someone or operate against public policy, they will be upheld, "no matter how specious, how intolerant, how narrow and prejudiced or dogmatic they may appear to others."

3. CONDITIONS PROHIBITING THE USE OF ALCOHOL, TOBACCO, GROWING MUSTACHES, ETC.

These conditions, sometimes called reformation or character-improvement conditions or incentives, are almost as common as the conditions frequently placed on marrying. The usual problem with the character-improvement conditions, however, is monitoring them. Aside from that, and aside from the possible embarrassment of the beneficiary when the world learns that he is "immoral" (according to the testator) because he is addicted to drink, smoking, or whatever, they are perfectly legal, and if they meet the necessary requirements of conditional bequests, they are generally upheld.

But to be upheld, the terms of the condition must be clear and definite. Conditions for character improvement may often appear clear, but they are usually very indefinite. It is easy to understand that "if Bart stops gambling for five years, he can have one-half of my estate." But how would we know what Bart does unless we assign a private detective to follow Bart around day and night for the next five years? And what do we mean by "gambling"? Does it include a Mega Millions lottery ticket?

Or how about a condition that dictates how a person should dress? Such as the condition in the will of a minister who left his daughter a substantial bequest under the following terms:

> Seeing that my daughter Anna has not availed herself of my advice touching the objectionable practice of going about with her arms bare up to the elbows, my will is that, should she continue after

> my death in this violation of the modesty of her sex, all the goods, chattels, moneys, land, and other that I have devised to her for the maintenance of her future life shall pass to the oldest of the sons of my sister Caroline.
>
> Should anyone take exception to this my wish as being too severe, I answer that license in dress in a woman is a mark of a depraved mind.

The minister's condition by itself may have been valid when written (probably not today), but, once again, there are problems with its definitiveness and practicality. Must we follow Anna around for the rest of her life hoping that at some unsuspecting moment on a hot day she will roll up her sleeves? Another, perhaps more serious, problem with this bequest (and most others like it) is *who is holding the money?*

The "legal" approach to such a bequest would be to give Anna the funds "subject to divestment" (taking them away) if she breached the condition. Meanwhile, she could presumably do with the funds as she pleased. If I were Caroline's oldest son (the bequest provides that he will take the money if Anna dresses "immodestly"), I would ask the court to have the money held in trust so that Anna could not give it all away and then roll up her sleeves in defiance of the condition! But for how long? This is another common problem with such bequests. The will says, "should she continue after my death"—again, for how long? Since there is no specified limitation, the answer would be for the rest of Anna's life! Such a vague and indefinite condition would definitely fail.

In addition to the monitoring aspect, however, remember that the condition must be clear. Many conditional bequests have failed because of confusion and uncertainty, such as the case where the testator left his estate to his two grandchildren "provided that they did that which was right." Well, you may know what he meant and we may know what he meant, but who is to judge? And (again) the question of for how long arises. Must they do "what is right" for just a while after Grandpa's death, or for the rest of their lives? Should they file some sort of reports on what they did, when, and with whom? In this particular case, the condition was disregarded and the grandchildren received the funds outright.

So, if you want to improve a person's character by encouraging the cessation of drinking, smoking, gambling, or fraternizing with lawyers, you should think out carefully just what it is you do want, consider the steps reasonably necessary to monitor the character improvement, and *spell them out* clearly in terms definite enough that it can be determined (by someone other than yourself) whether your condition is met. Then you should appoint someone to decide or provide a method of determining whether the condition has been carried out. If the condition is otherwise clear and determinable but no one has been designated to judge whether or not your condition has been met, *the court* will appoint someone to do so.

4. OTHER "INTERESTING" CONDITIONS

A valid condition bequest can be a great persuader, since the beneficiary stands to lose the bequest if he ignores the condition. As a result, testators have used conditional bequests to cause (or at least attempt to cause) beneficiaries to dress a certain way, follow a particular profession, adhere to or reject a particular religious belief, keep a particular family name, refrain from talking to certain other family members, or avoid marrying into a certain family, etc. Here is a reasonably typical example of one of these conditions, perhaps a bit out of the ordinary but nonetheless worthy of reporting (the names were changed just a little to protect the "innocent").

Ansel Emmernecker had a substantial estate that included an elegant farm and more than enough funds to support it. His wife had died some years before, and he was left with an only son, Gifford, who himself had two children. Emmernecker's will left his entire estate in trust for Gifford, provided that Gifford complied with the terms of his will. If Gifford refused to comply, the estate would be sold, Gifford would get nothing, and the funds would be held in trust for Gifford's children under the same condition, which was this: that Gifford and his children keep the family name of Emmernecker, and "whenever necessary in the course of his life to write or spell the name of Emmernecker, he shall spell it exactly as it was spelled in this instrument and was spelled by my ancestors."

For some reason, Gifford had thoughts of changing his name. Attorneys he consulted told him he could change it to something like Higgens Emmernecker, or Gunther Emmernecker, but if Gifford wanted to keep his father's bequest, he had to keep the surname, Emmernecker, and he even had to *spell* it that way. According to the records, however, Gifford had in mind something more American and less conspicuous, perhaps something like Engelbert Humperdinck. So Gifford asked his attorneys to take legal action to see if there was a way they could "break" the condition.

The attorneys then argued that the court should ignore the condition as it was unduly harsh and might even interfere with Gifford's acting career. In the event that, without thinking, Gifford made some innocent mistake, like signing an autograph as "The Giff" or "M.N. Ecker" or "The Necker," he could lose the entire bequest. Furthermore, it was not clear how the trustees could monitor use of the name, and Gifford's attorneys argued that if a condition is vague and uncertain, the law should not require it to be carried out.

The court was not sympathetic. The opinion, eloquently written by the well-known justice Arbus Plasikowski, stated that "the testator's purpose was to perpetuate the ancestral spelling of the surname he proudly bore and in furtherance of that end he required his beneficiaries carry on the use and spelling of that name if they wished to receive the annual income from the trust." Emmernecker's condition was held to be valid and enforceable, and the Giff kept his name.

5. BEQUESTS TO CATS, DOGS, AND CHICKENS

At first glance, it would appear that discussion of a bequest to a cat, a dog, or some other animal does not belong in the category of a "conditional" bequest. Upon further examination, however, you will see that, in fact, it is one way to carry out such a gift.

As noted very early on in this book, the right to leave property on your death is not a natural or inherent right but rather only a privilege permitted by law, and therefore compliance with the law in this regard is essential if you want your property to pass according to your wishes. One facet of the law regarding the right of passing property on death deals with the identity of the beneficiary. Generally speaking, except as noted below, a beneficiary must be a person or a legal entity capable of appearing in court and accepting the bequest. That is, you cannot leave your money to a bridge or a flagpole (though it may be possible to leave money in trust for the *maintenance* of a bridge or a flagpole—see "Special Purpose Trusts" in chapter 12).

In this context, you can readily see that a cat, a dog, or a bird falls into the same category. And the more you think about it, the more you can see this rule makes sense. After all, you couldn't very well expect a dog to have a bank account or a credit card or to own real estate, or an old chicken to be placed in a nursing home or make a will leaving its property to the rooster down the road. Unfortunately, this does not stop people from leaving their estates to a favorite pet. When this happens, however, unless the particular state law has adopted special rules, the bequest is usually disregarded, and the estate passes to the next person designated or, if there is none, to the deceased's "residuary" estate (as explained in chapter 5). Note, though, that many states (thirty-five in 2020) have enacted the Uniform Trust Code (UTC), which at section 408 specifically permits a trust to be created for the benefit of a pet. Each state has tailored its own law based upon that state's legislative policy, but in general all "pet trust" laws limit the time frame of the trust and limit the amount of funds that can be placed in the trust.

For instance, in a state that has not enacted the UTC, say that Old Mrs. Osborne leaves $50,000 outright to her two favorite chickens, Pick and Peck. All the rest of her estate is left to her nephew, Sylvester. In this case, Sylvester will get the entire estate, and Pick and Peck won't get so much as a grain of wheat.

More and more such testators, being aware of this problem and perhaps having the common sense to seek advice, realized that there is a way to provide for their pets without leaving them any funds directly, that is, through a conditional bequest or a special trust. Old Mrs. Osborne could have provided for Pick and Peck by stating in her will, "I leave $50,000 to my farmhand, Old MacDonald, on the condition that he takes care of my chickens, Pick and Peck, for the remainder of their lives." The conditional trust is valid regardless of whether or not the state had enacted the UTC.

Of course, Mrs. Osborne should include some simple means of having Old MacDonald show that he is complying with the provisions, such as an annual chicken checkup by a vet, with a report to the court or to the personal representative. Otherwise, there is always the temptation that Old MacDonald would put the chickens on the wrong side of the gravy, with no one the wiser and Old MacDonald $50,000 richer. Even with all the reporting, however, it may be that, depending on how the court decided to treat the conditional bequest, Old MacDonald would be given the funds, subject to his carrying out the condition. If this happened, he would be more or less free to use the money as he wished, subject to an order to return what was left if he mistreated the chickens. To be certain, it would be best if Mrs. Osborne had the funds placed in a trust for a period of years; otherwise, Old MacDonald could conceivably spend the money and then disregard the conditions of the bequest.

If a testator does not want to go to the trouble of forming a trust for the benefit of the pet, perhaps the best way would be to leave the sum to a charity whose function it was to provide for such animals, on the condition that the charity assume the care of the testator's animals after his death. You could even take this one step further and provide for the *creation* of such a charity on your death, if you have enough money. A case in point is that of Jonathan Jackson of Columbus, Ohio, whose will left a sum to be used for the construction and maintenance of an elaborate home for cats (his own cats included). Jackson's will contained detailed plans of a cat house that would include dormitories, conversation areas, exercise grounds, an auditorium where the cats could listen to "accordion music," and, of course, "rat holes" for their daily sport. He left out a cocktail lounge. (For more on trusts for pets, see "Special Purpose Trusts" in chapter 12.)

Conditions on Burials, Funerals, and Memorials

Generally, these conditions, or more accurately *instructions*, are governed by the same rules discussed above for conditional bequests. Primarily, they must be legal and must not be against public policy. Where special burial or memorial instructions are involved, however, it seems that the public policy issue is the one that must be dealt with more often than the "legal" questions. There is nothing inherently wrong, for instance, with being buried just about anywhere you choose, but it would certainly be against public policy to allow someone to be buried in the center of a busy highway or entombed in the wall of a shopping mall. Similarly, you can have your ashes scattered anywhere you want, but to ask that they be scattered over all the Caesar salads served in a popular restaurant might be met with objection.

In short, it is not always easy to tell what is or may be against public policy and what is not. In one case, for example, a Midwestern woman's will directed that she be buried with all her jewelry. The personal representative of her estate, however, refused to do so on the basis that it would be wasteful and therefore against public policy. The probate court judge agreed and disallowed the provision, ordering that the jewelry be sold and the proceeds distributed according to other provisions of the will. "If the practice is developed in our state," the judge said, "to foster the burying of valuables with the deceased, our cemeteries, like the tombs of the pharaohs, will be ravaged and violated."

On the other hand, the burial instructions under the will of Sandra West, which in principle were similar to the above case, were carried out without question. As mentioned earlier in the book, Mrs. West's will directed that she be buried "next to my husband, in my lace nightgown . . . in my Ferrari, with the seat slanted comfortably." The Ferrari in this case was worth much more than the jewelry in the other case, but apparently no one objected to carrying out the bequest, and the court would not take it upon itself to deny the condition.

Several years ago we actually had a client who wanted his ashes shot off into outer space. When we explained the cost of renting space on a spaceship and the regulations regarding the placing of objects into orbit, he discovered it was likely to cost more than the amount of his entire estate. He quickly reconsidered and settled for scattering them over the tomato plants in his backyard. Space permitting.

THE DEEP FREEZE—COMING BACK FROM THE DEAD

In more recent history, there has developed a special situation that raises all kinds of complicated legal questions and issues relating to wills and disposition of the body. Under the unproven theory that if a body is properly prepared and frozen (far beyond ice-cube level) shortly after death, it may be revived at some time in the future when, hopefully, a cure is found for the cause of the death. A good deal of public attention was focused on this concept when the famous Red Sox baseball slugger Ted Williams purportedly directed in a contract signed prior to his death that he (actually, just his head) be deep-frozen, despite the fact that his will directed the cremation of his body (a different type of appointment). Assuming the contract was valid (one of the central questions in the estate dispute), Williams apparently believed that it might be possible in the future to reverse the freezing process and restore life functions to his body or even just to his head. According to information from Alcor Life Extension Foundation, a company that will freeze and store your body after death, either the whole body could remain frozen, or they have a special, reduced price for just the head (what they euphemistically refer to as "neuro-suspension," something we authors frequently experience).

John Henry (no, not *that* John Henry) and Claudia, two of Williams's children (and thus some of his "next of kin"), believed that their father did want his body to be frozen, purportedly so that he might be reunited with them in the future. At the same time, however, Bobby Jo Williams Ferrell (another of Ted's next of kin but one left out in a different kind of cold) believed the will clearly reflected Williams's last wishes, directing that his body be cremated and the ashes sprinkled at sea, which, she argued, should be honored. Which of those wishes and legal documents to honor became the subject of a bitter legal dispute among Ted's children.

As noted, numerous legal issues arise when a person leaves such instructions, particularly pertaining to the question of whether Ted had the "right" to dispose of his body after death.

In general, whether it is your body or your ashes, reasonable requests you make that are not against public policy will be carried out, *provided* your spouse and/or children do not object. Believe it or not, as a general legal principle, you do *not* have an absolute property right in your body (or ashes) after your death. Although your wishes will be given the first preference, they can be thwarted, and, as clearly demonstrated in the Ted Williams case, can lead to serious family disputes and huge expenses. One way to help avoid this is to make your bequests *conditional* upon those wishes or instructions being carried out (assuming, once again, that they are not unreasonable, impractical, or against public policy). Although this is no guarantee, it will certainly make the beneficiary think twice before deciding to disregard your instructions.

Furthermore, in the case of a deep-frozen body, what if the "deceased" was in fact revived in the future? What rights would he have? Could he get his property back? (No court, at this time at least, would ever agree to suspend the disposition of property at death for such a reason.) Thus, anyone thinking of being deep-frozen may also want to think about setting up some sort of really long-term trust just in case.

MEMORIALS

Memorials (including memorial ceremonies that are to be repeated on a periodic basis after death in memory of the deceased) are really a separate category, as they do not, generally, need to be conditional, and they are designed to live on far beyond the death of the testator and, in many cases, his relatives. The two most common memorials, for instance, are the graveyard type—which include monuments and mausoleums—and those that are charitable in nature, such as scholarships, for instance, or medical or scientific research grants, or artistic endeavors. Graveyard monuments, etc., are fairly straightforward and usually involve a onetime expense shortly after death to erect the monument. If the expense is not outrageous in proportion to the estate, the instructions will usually be carried out. Charitable memorials are relatively easy to set up under a will and most can go on "forever" in the name of the testator. For example, say that Friswold leaves $100,000 to Boston University to establish a scholarship in her name. Usually, the terms are that the school will use only the *income* from the $100,000, meaning that the $100,000 will remain intact virtually forever, each year producing a scholarship grant in the Friswold name.

Then there are memorials that are *not* charitable, and the law provides that these cannot go on forever, although they can nevertheless continue for many years after the testator's death. Briefly, in most states, a noncharitable bequest that does not pass outright to a particular person or organization cannot continue any longer than twenty-one years after the death of some designated person (or persons) who was alive at the time of the testator's death. For instance, Snodgrass leaves two children and three grandchildren surviving him at his death. His will provides that the annual income from one-eighth of his estate is to be used for the rental of a billboard that can be seen from the perpetually packed Southeast Expressway in Boston, Massachusetts. The billboard sign is to display a large picture of Snodgrass, smiling, with the caption, in large letters:

Sherman Snodgrass, smiling at you
from that big expressway in the sky.
He'll never be stuck in traffic again.

Snodgrass could provide that his noncharitable memorial would continue each year (after his death) until twenty-one years after the death of the *last* survivor of his two children and three grandchildren. It wouldn't matter which one of them survived, but twenty-one years after the death of the last one, Snodgrass's billboard display would have to cease (assuming no one torched it before that). In the states (at least seventeen as of 2020) that have abolished or substantially modified this rule, noncharitable trusts can last forever (or almost forever).

"DRINKS ON THE HOUSE IN MEMORY OF WHATSISNAME"

One of the more imaginative and festive memorials was created by one of our clients. Ernie provided that a portion of his estate be set aside in a

"Memorial Trust," where each year, on Ernie's birthday, the income from the trust is to be used to provide free drinks to all of the patrons who happen to be in his favorite tavern on that evening, to raise at least one toast "in memory of Ernie." Unless the money was used up earlier, this liquid memorial could continue for about fifty years after Ernie's death, by which time the patrons will probably have long forgotten who he was but will no doubt toast him with fervency anyway.

If you're thinking of a special memorial such as this, you must be careful to cover every contingency; otherwise you will simply add to the cost of it, or perhaps risk losing it completely, on the basis that it is indefinite or uncertain and cannot be carried out. In Ernie's memorial, for instance, provisions had to be made in the event the named tavern ever closed down or moved, or in the event his birthday fell on a Sunday or a holiday when the tavern would be closed, or in the event of a storm or other minor catastrophe, and, of course, he provided for "reasonable" tips for the bartender and other servers. Here's looking at you, Ernie!

Defaming from the Grave—Having the Last Bad Word

For some testators, a will offers the opportunity to say things they were reluctant or afraid to say during their lives. Sometimes they were afraid to say it because they were afraid of the results it would bring, so they chose the coward's way out, hiding behind the will, where the victim could not reach. But is this so? Isn't it possible for the victim to sue the estate for libel?

Research into the question of defaming from the grave discloses a great number of angry, sarcastic, and slanderous statements left by testators who wanted to have the last bad word, most of them toward wives, husbands, or children (or those who, in the eyes of the testator, "pretended" to be children), and of course, toward in-laws. Here are just a few.

The Marquis d'Aligre said,

> to my son I leave the pleasure of earning a living. For twenty years he thought the pleasure was mine.

But perhaps one of the most vituperative epitaphs of all was that of a harried husband, who left

> to my wife, ANNA WALTERS PRESTON, one-third of my estate. It is my earnest desire and everlasting wish that the above-named adulteress and fiend in human form, to whose wiles I fell a victim while temporarily separated from my first wife, this harlot whose insidious lies, poured into my ear daily, caused me to take the step which made a reconciliation with my first wife impossible, this she-devil who, in an effort to ruin my good name, has for the last three years circulated the most damnable lies about me ever uttered by human tongue, this unnameable beast, who has made life for me a living hell for the last three years or more, and by whom I stand in daily fear of being murdered while asleep, I repeat, it is my everlasting wish that this woman, whom I am compelled by law to call my wife, shall not receive one cent more of my very modest estate than she is entitled to under the laws of the State of Pennsylvania.
>
> —*Harry Preston*

One gets the distinct impression that Harry and Anna didn't get along too well. Or at least that was the way Harry viewed it, so he really let her have it in his will. There is no evidence, however, that Harry ever spoke that way to Anna until his death. We'll never know.

What we do know, however, is that in certain cases such language can give rise to a lawsuit against the estate for libel. Even though the bulk of such suits are unsuccessful, it can cost the estate thousands of dollars just to defend against such a suit, without considering the cost of any settlement. Furthermore, chances are you won't even get the satisfaction of having your nasty words become public, since the modern trend is to simply *delete* the slanderous expressions from the will, so that the "public" sees the will without the damaging language. For example, if your will says, "I leave to my no-good, worthless failure of a son, Bummer, the sum of $1,000, provided he stops stealing change from the church collection box," the court is likely to delete what is called the "nondispositive" parts so that, as far as the public is concerned, your "will" reads, "I leave to my son, Bummer, the sum of $1,000."

If for some reason you feel absolutely compelled to have a few nasty last words, then, instead of putting them in your will, you might consider writing a personal letter to the one you so dislike. It will probably have a much more lasting effect.

Noncontest Provision

The noncontest or anticontest provision, also called an "in terrorem" provision, is also a form of conditional bequest. This is because it leaves a bequest to someone on the express condition that that person does not contest the will (or trust). This provision is covered in greater detail in chapter 10 on will contests.

Keep This in Mind

It is fairly common to make a conditional bequest, the most common being the "noncontest" bequest: "I leave $5,000 to my son, Shifty, which he will forfeit if he contests this will." But you must be careful to meet the requirements of an enforceable condition, otherwise the bequest goes condition-free. You must also be sure to say what happens to the bequest if the condition is violated or not carried out. Note that the condition must be legal, clearly stated, and capable of performance. Finally, beware of making a condition that could take years to carry out—it could keep your estate "open" all that time.

7

Spouses' and Children's Rights to an Estate

I leave to my husband, Dom Witte, the sum of Five Dollars,
to be given to him at the rate of ten cents a month,
because he was so good to me.

—from the will of Barbara Witte

Must Dom settle for this? As a surviving spouse, doesn't he have "special" rights, or can he be disinherited and left with "ten cents a month"? And what about children? Aren't we legally obliged to leave them something?

As to spouses, most testators do want to provide for them and do so in their wills. But then there are those like Harry Preston, mentioned in the previous chapter, who thoughtfully referred to his wife as a "she-devil" and a "fiend in human form." Interestingly enough, however, Harry had the presence of mind (or perhaps heeded professional advice) not to attempt to completely disinherit her, but rather he left her "not one cent more than she is entitled to under the laws of the State of Pennsylvania." In doing this, Harry acknowledged, as any testator in this situation must, that most states give a surviving spouse the right to a certain share of the estate (sometimes called a "forced share") regardless of the provisions of the will.

Children are an entirely different matter. Even though a parent has a natural as well as a legal obligation to provide for minor children, there is generally no legal requirement that a parent leave a part of his estate to a child, whether a minor or not. This is not to say that children never have rights to contest a will (such as a minor child contesting a will to obtain satisfaction of the deceased parent's support obligation) or take a share of a parent's estate, but, as we will see, these rights are far less direct than those of a surviving spouse.

Disinheriting a Spouse—With and Without a Will

When the deceased spouse leaves a will disinheriting the surviving spouse, most states (but not Georgia!) allow the surviving spouse to *ignore* (or "waive") the will and take a forced share. The laws of those states that allow a surviving spouse to take a forced share are very specific in the amount that the spouse may take, but this does not mean that questions do not arise. For instance, if state X says that a spouse can disregard the provisions of the deceased spouse's will and take one-third of the "estate," does this mean one-third of the estate that passes under the will? Or does it also include one-third of the life insurance, as well as one-third of the property in trust and one-third of the property held jointly with a third party?

It used to be that the surviving spouse's right to waive the will and take a forced share applied only to the deceased's *probate* estate, and in many states that is still the case. The modern trend, however, extends this right to what is called the "augmented" estate, which includes *nonprobate* property, such as property the deceased spouse placed in trust (depending on the extent of control and enjoyment the deceased spouse retained in the trust), certain jointly held property between the deceased and others, and, in some cases, gifts made by the deceased spouse within two or three years of death.

In those states where the surviving spouse's rights only extend to the deceased's *probate* estate, it would be a very simple matter for a spouse to disinherit the other spouse merely by creating a nonprobate estate, and, in fact, this is what the modern-day Harry Prestons are usually advised to do if they wish to disinherit their spouses.

For instance, if Harry placed all of his property in a living trust, Anna Preston's rights to waive the will would not extend to the trust, and she would receive nothing. This could still be the case in states where the spouse's rights extend only in the *probate* estate, but beware the modern trend in state laws to go beyond this.

Generally, the spouse's election to waive the will and take a forced share *must* be exercised within a certain time after the will is submitted to the probate court and the personal representative is appointed. Unless the will itself can be attacked on some other grounds, little can be done before that. Normally, this involves waiting until the will is submitted for probate and allowed (by the court) as the deceased's last will. When this happens, the executor is appointed to administer the estate. Thereafter, the spouse must, within the prescribed time, file the written election to take the share allowed by law despite what is provided in the will. This time requirement is usually very strict and must be carefully followed. For instance, if state Z allows the spouse to waive the will provided that the spouse files a waiver with the probate court within six months of the appointment of the personal representative, the spouse's election *must* be made within that period. If it is made a week or even a day late, it is likely to be lost, despite the fact that the spouse may have an excellent excuse for being late.

Many states require that the election can be made only if the surviving spouse lives long enough to make it, while others allow the election so long as the spouse survived the deceased at all. In the first case, if the election must be filed no later than six months after the death of the first spouse, then a surviving spouse who died within six months of her husband could not make the election. In the latter case, even though the surviving spouse died shortly after the first, the personal representative of the surviving spouse's estate, if appointed within the prescribed time period, could still make the election, on her behalf, to take a share of the first spouse's estate. That share, once received by the personal representative, would then pass to the surviving spouse's estate.

If the waiver is made effectively, the surviving spouse's share, according to the laws of the estate, will generally be given priority over other shares under the will, but *not* over the debts, expenses, and taxes of the estate. After those are accounted for, then the "net" estate is arrived at, which is the amount on which the spouse's forced share is based. Once the forced share is paid, the rest of the estate can be distributed according to the will (or other arrangements, if the forced share involved nonprobate property).

Although it depends to some extent upon the law of the particular state, the general rule is that unless the testator expresses a contrary intent in his will, the *residuary* estate will bear the cost of the forced share. Of course, if the residuary estate is insufficient to cover the forced share, it has to come from somewhere, so then the specific bequests would be ratably reduced to make up the difference.

Not every state has a complicated forced share. In fact, most states simply give the surviving spouse the right to take one-third or, in some cases, one-half the estate outright, but short of that there is very little consistency among the states. Some restrict the spouse's rights to real estate that the deceased spouse owned at his death; others include all of the deceased's property but limit the election to "probate" property. Still others, and this is becoming a trend, as discussed earlier in this chapter, allow a spouse to take a share of the "augmented" estate, which goes far beyond the probate estate and includes jointly held property, certain gifts made by the deceased before his death, and certain trusts created by the deceased during his lifetime.

Usually, if a state's forced share allows the surviving spouse to go beyond the probate estate, it also requires the spouse to "account" for nonprobate property that she received because of the death of her spouse. That is, the spouse would be required to take into consideration the value of *all* of the property she receives on account of the death of the other spouse, including property they held jointly, in trust, and other nonprobate assets that passed to the survivor.

As we noted, however, there is little consistency among the states, except for the fact that every state has some provision that prevents, or is designed to prevent, total disinheritance of a surviving spouse. In community property states, the spouse's protection is not in the form of a right to elect against the will. There is no need for such statutes because the community property laws themselves give the spouse a right to one-half of *all* the property acquired by the spouses during the marriage (the "community"). Since one-half the marital property already belongs to the surviving spouse, there is no way that the deceased spouse could leave it to someone else in his or her will. The traditional community property states are Arizona, California, Idaho, Louisiana, Nevada, New Mexico, Texas, Washington, and Wisconsin. Some states, like Alaska, permit spouses to choose the application of the community property law. It is also important to note that the surviving spouse's forced share does *not* qualify for the estate tax marital deduction (see chapter 13). Therefore, amounts that a spouse takes as her forced share will be fully subject to federal (and possibly state) estate tax, whereas amounts voluntarily given her by the deceased spouse will not, because of the marital deduction.

It is very common to confuse the spouse's right to a forced share of the estate with the share a surviving spouse would take if the other died *without* a will (intestate). Although in some states the two may bear a resemblance, *they are not the same*. In fact, except for those few states where the forced share is by law *equal* to the intestate share (Arkansas and Minnesota, for instance), the forced share is usually *less* than the share a spouse would take if the other died without a will.

As described in chapter 2, when a person dies without a will, his surviving spouse can take from one-third of his estate to all of it, depending on the particular state's laws, whether there are children, and, most important, the extent of the *probate* estate. Does this mean, then, that if a person wants to disinherit a spouse, it is done by simply placing all property in joint names with, say, the daughter and tearing up the will? In some states, yes, but in others, no.

As noted earlier, the trend in many states is to make it harder rather than easier to circumvent the rights of a surviving spouse. It is finally being realized that the intention behind such laws is to protect and honor the marital relationship and to respect, even after death, the rights acquired by marriage. If a spouse is to be given rights to the "estate" of a deceased spouse, therefore, such rights should encompass *all* of the property that he or she owned and enjoyed at the time of his death. It is ludicrous to strictly limit such rights to the *probate* estate of the deceased spouse, when in fact the bulk of his or her estate often avoids the probate process entirely, and it is even more ludicrous to allow such rights to hinge upon the existence of a will. Based on this reasoning, a number of states are allowing a spouse to take a forced share of the "augmented" estate (which, as explained, includes nonprobate property) regardless of the fact that the deceased spouse left no will. And for those states that do not yet recognize this trend, we suggest it is only a matter of time.

Well, then, exactly what do I do if I am the Harry Preston type, intent upon leaving my spouse the absolute minimum and preferably nothing?

Short of giving the property away, not very much, if the trend continues. In the meantime, however, in those states that have not yet adopted the augmented estate concept, you can create a living trust (discussed in greater detail in chapter 11), name yourself as trustee, and transfer all of your property to this trust. It can allow you to enjoy the property so long as you are alive and well, and on your death the trust can direct that all of the remaining trust assets be paid over to, say, your children, or anyone else you designate as a beneficiary in the trust. Since this arrangement would avoid probate, it would also, in those states that base the forced share on the probate estate, avoid the reach of your surviving spouse. Unfortunately, it is not something you can absolutely count on, since the state laws are changing rapidly.

There are also occasions where a "spouse" who is not a spouse may have rights on the death of a partner—the "common-law" marriage. In a number of states, if a couple lives together and holds themselves out as spouses for a specified number of years (usually seven), then in the eyes of the law of that state they can be considered married. In such cases, the surviving common-law spouse has the same rights as a "legally married" spouse, including the right to waive the will and take a forced share, as discussed above.

Since it is not uncommon today for couples to live together for extended periods of time without being married, the rights of common-law marriage are becoming a more frequent concern. Those who do not necessarily want to share their respective estates with each other may find that the death of one after having cohabited for the required period of time might very well produce rights to the surviving partner that were never anticipated. For instance, in New Hampshire, if a couple lives together *"as husband and wife"* for three years before the death of either, they acknowledge that they live together as spouses, and the community believes them to be husband and wife, then the survivor has rights to the estate of the deceased partner similar to those of a surviving spouse.

To avoid this problem as well as other complications, such as the disruption of the estate by the surviving spouse of a "legal" marriage, couples should consider entering into an agreement that fixes their respective rights on death, as discussed later in this chapter.

Rights of Divorced or Separated Spouses Under a Will

Generally, once a divorce becomes final, the divorced spouse has no legal claim to the estate of his or her ex-spouse, unless, of course, the terms of the divorce decree call for some sort of payment on death. (It is not uncommon, for example, for a decree to provide for a lump-sum payment to the surviving ex-spouse in lieu of alimony.) Other than in such cases, no liabilities or responsibilities exist for ex-spouses. However, problems frequently arise during that period of time during which the spouses are "ex" in each other's eyes but not in the eyes of the law.

Just about every state allows for or requires a "cooling off" period after the initial divorce decree during which the spouses are still legally married. It usually takes anywhere from one month to a year after this decree before the divorce actually becomes legally final and the couple is no longer husband and wife. If a spouse dies within this period, the surviving "spouse" has all the rights of the surviving spouse, just as if divorce proceedings had never been initiated, and even if the deceased spouse was efficient enough to have changed his or her will, the surviving spouse is entitled to take her forced share of the estate. If the spouse did not get around to changing his will (and the will happened to provide for his "spouse"), the survivor would then have the chance of either accepting the bequest under the will or taking a forced share, whichever gave her more.

This potential problem is even more exaggerated when the spouses are legally separated but not divorced, or when they are simply "estranged." In either case they are still considered husband and wife, with all the attendant rights on the death of a spouse.

In all of the above cases (a nonfinal divorce, a legal separation, and even an estrangement), it is advisable for the spouse with the larger estate to have the other spouse enter into an agreement (even if a price has to be paid for it) providing that in the event of the death of a spouse, the other agrees to waive (not to exercise) any rights she may have to the other's estate. If the agreement is properly drafted and consideration (payment or some other valuable concession) is given, such agreements (discussed below in greater detail) can be legally binding and can avoid the problems mentioned above.

EFFECT OF DIVORCE ON A WILL

While in most states marriage automatically *revokes* a will made before the marriage (unless the will was made in anticipation of the marriage), the opposite rule often applies to divorce, at least prior to the enactment in many states of modern laws, such as the Uniform Probate Code, to address this problem. That is, formally, as a general rule, a divorce does *not* revoke an existing will. Because of ignorance of this rule, the families of many deceased ex-spouses found themselves sharing the estate with the surviving ex-spouse who was named as a beneficiary of the will, which the deceased forgot to change, or didn't bother to change because he thought the divorce somehow changed it. As a result of the clear inequity of such situations, almost all the states have enacted laws that provide that although a divorce does not revoke an existing will, it *does* revoke the provisions of such a will that favor the divorced spouse. The Uniform Probate Code also revokes all fiduciary appointments of the divorced spouse (and his family members) and terminates any powers of appointment granted by the divorced spouse.

For instance, say that Tristan has a will leaving three-fourths of his estate to his loving wife, Isolde, and the remaining one-fourth to his son, Wagner. The will also provides that if Isolde does not survive Tristan, the entire estate will pass to Wagner. After many years of a harmonious marriage, however, the music stops and the couple obtains a divorce. After the divorce, Tristan immerses himself in his work of setting the Dead Sea Scrolls to music and so forgets to change his will. Suddenly one day, while writing an aria for the lead camel, Tristan aspirates on his pen point and dies. When the will is later offered for probate, Isolde arrives to claim her share. She is informed, however, that in Alaska, where they resided, the law provides that a divorce revokes any provisions in favor of a former spouse (the divorce was final), and since Isolde was only a former spouse, the bequest to her in Tristan's will was revoked. In such a case, the will is treated or interpreted as if Isolde (the divorced spouse) *predeceased* Tristan (even though in fact she did not), and so the estate would pass to their son, Wagner.

Despite state laws revoking will provisions for a divorced spouse or, in a few states, revoking the will altogether on divorce, it is important to note that such measures have *no effect* on beneficiary designations that the deceased spouse may have made on life insurance policies, retirement plans, and the like. Many court battles have been fought, and *lost,* in an attempt to recover insurance or other proceeds paid to the ex-spouse as beneficiary because the deceased simply forgot to remove her name.

The laws of some states go one step further with this concept of revoking will provisions for a former spouse, and, in the event of divorce, *also* revoke the appointment of a former spouse as *personal representative* of the deceased spouse's estate. Obviously, it can be embarrassing if the divorced spouse is appointed executrix to administer the estate for the benefit of the deceased's new bride! To avoid creating such a difficult situation, it is a lot easier, less traumatic, and cheaper to simply make out a codicil after the divorce, stating your wishes for the disposition and administration of your estate.

Premarital (and Postmarital) Agreements—and Wills

It is interesting that, as a general rule, first marriages are not accompanied by a premarital agreement, whereas second (and further) marriages are almost never without one. Whatever the reason, if either party of a marriage, first or otherwise, is at all concerned with limiting the rights of a spouse on divorce, separation, or death, an agreement should certainly be considered. Here, we will concern ourselves with the use of such agreements to prevent lengthy estate contests and to avoid the disruption of the forced share otherwise available to a surviving spouse.

For many years, the law effectively prohibited a married couple from entering into legal contracts with each other on the theory that to allow one spouse to sue the other would undermine the family unit, which is viewed as the cornerstone of our society. Eventually, as lawsuits for divorce and related property disputes became more common, it was successfully argued that each member of the couple was a legal individual and should be able to contract with anyone, including the other spouse. It is, of course, now widely accepted that for most purposes a couple can enter into a legally binding agreement with each other, and, as a result, couples began to discover that such agreements could even include, to a point, their financial responsibility to each other under a variety of circumstances. It should be noted here that a contract to do something that is against a particular law or against public policy will not be enforceable in any event, so that a husband could not avoid by contract, for example, his legal responsibility to support his wife and children.

Marital agreements fixing a spouse's rights at death are becoming quite common, especially where there are children from previous marriages. Such agreements are available in every state, including the community property states. Since the law is different in each state, it is difficult to outline the precise form of such an agreement in every case, but briefly, the agreement would state the share, if any, of the respective estates that each agrees to give the other on death. In return for such a share, the surviving spouse agrees to waive all other rights he or she may have to take anything further, such as (and specifically including) his or her right to waive the will and take a forced share of the estate. Furthermore, the agreement should also contain some provision regarding any jointly held assets that the couple may acquire. First and foremost, it is important to set a default definition of joint property for property that does not have a formal title document. For example, the agreement might state that all after-acquired property is considered joint property unless designated in writing by both parties to the contrary. As to disposition, if it is desired that the jointly held assets should pass to the survivor on the death of one, the agreement should clearly say so. And if it is desired that the jointly held assets should go to the surviving spouse *in addition* to any other share stated in the agreement, it should state that as well. Note that such an agreement could also provide that *no* share of a deceased spouse's estate will be taken by either spouse, so that each retains his/her own property, the consideration being the reciprocal waivers of rights.

Perhaps the most important element to ensure the enforceability of marital agreements is *independent representation.* Do *not* allow the same attorney to represent both parties. It is absolutely essential that each party have independent counsel advising each of their rights, and many attorneys make it a practice to have the attorneys sign the agreements as well, stating that they have explained the agreement to the client and they are satisfied that the client understands the contents and the rights and liabilities involved.

Although most marital agreements are premarital (made *before* the marriage), it is quite possible in most states to enter into *postmarital* agreements. If, for example, a couple is married for twenty years and decides to fix their respective rights at death (it usually happens after a dispute, but not always), they can at that point enter into a postmarital agreement. Generally, all of the same principles apply here as apply to premarital agreements, subject, of course, to the laws of a given state; it can be every bit as binding on the surviving spouse, and, like the premarital agreement, it can avoid a will contest.

There are two additional requirements to both premarital and postmarital agreements essential to their enforceability. The first is a full and complete disclosure of the assets of the parties. Any material omission can be the basis for the uninformed party to reject the terms of the agreement. The second is that the agreement will be fair and reasonable at the time of its implementation, although states differ as to the application of this rule on divorce versus on the death of a spouse.

Where a postmarital agreement is involved, it is also important to show that there was no fraud employed to induce a spouse to enter it. For example, in a Massachusetts case where a married couple was having some problems, the wife told the husband that if he would sign a postmarital agreement and transfer certain property to her, she would remain married to him. Wanting to stay married to her, the husband did so. Shortly after the deal concluded, the wife left him and sued to get the property under the agreement. The court held that such agreements induced by fraud would not be enforced.

Children's Rights Under a Will

Most people are under the mistaken impression that they *must* leave their children something in their estates, since if they don't, an omitted child has the right to contest the will and take a share of the estate. Perhaps the most common offshoot of this misconception is the practice of leaving one dollar to a child you wish to disinherit.

In fact, in every state, with the very limited exception of Louisiana, a parent has the power to disinherit a child simply by leaving his estate to someone else (other than the child). Whether the child is left one dollar or nothing at all, she may contest the will, but not simply on the basis that the deceased was a parent. What gave rise to this practice of leaving one dollar to a disinherited child are certain laws based on the presumption that parents normally do not wish to disinherit their children. The laws that reflect this presumption provide that if a child is accidentally omitted from a parent's will, he is nevertheless entitled to a certain share of the estate (these are called "pretermitted" child statutes).

In general, these laws protecting omitted children are of two types—one is the Missouri and New Hampshire type, which provides that if a child is not mentioned in the will, he or she will automatically take a share of the estate, regardless of the reason for the omission; the second is the Massachusetts type, which provides that if a child is not provided for in the will, he or she will take a share of the estate, *unless* the omission was intentional on the part of the parent.

In order to show that the omission was intentional, lawyers would have their clients (who wanted to disinherit a child) leave the child one dollar, or perhaps have them include a statement declaring their intent, such as, "I intentionally make no provision for my son, Randolph." When advised of the need to make such a statement, a number of testators have felt compelled to go a step further, embellishing the intentional omission with more colorful comments, such as the New Yorker who left his son "the generous sum of one dollar, which is twice what he is worth."

This is not to say that such language or intentional omission prevents a child from contesting a will. As explained in detail in chapter 10, anyone who has standing and who has a reason can contest a will, and children who are disinherited are often likely contestants. The point is that there is *no* legal obligation on the part of a parent to leave something to a child, even though the child may be a minor whom the parent was legally obliged to support while he (the parent) was alive. This rule (where a minor child survives a parent), however, has changed in a few states, and there may well be a trend developing across the country not to allow a parent otherwise responsible for providing for a dependent child to avoid the responsibility on death.

Sometimes a child is omitted unintentionally because she was born or adopted *after* the parent made out his will. Because of the presumption in favor of children, most states provide that a child born or adopted after the parent made out the will is entitled to a share equal to the share she would receive if the parent died without a will. As noted above, however, some states will not allow the child to take a share if it appears that the omission of the after-born or adopted child was intentional. Unfortunately, the question of intent of the deceased parent in either case is, in most instances, strictly interpreted, so that an intentional omission of a child on the mistaken belief that the child was dead, for example, is still an intentional omission. This has led to some very sad results. There have been a number of cases, for instance, when a parent who has not heard from a child for ten or twenty years or more omits him from the will, thinking he is dead. In such cases, the omission was intentional and therefore enforceable, even though it was based on a misunderstanding on the parent's part. (Note that the language of the will in such cases is important. As explained in an earlier chapter, if the mistaken belief is actually stated in the will as the basis for the omission, then even though the omission was intentional, thereby precluding the child from taking a share under the omitted-child law, the child may be able to void that portion of the will on the grounds of mistake. An example would be, "Because my son John is dead, I omit him from this will.")

Assumed death and actual disappearance are not the only causes for omission based on a mistake that can leave a child without a share. There have also been a number of cases where a father omitted a child because he thought the child was not his own, as in the case of Owen Schlock of New York.

Owen and his wife, Sarah, were caretakers on a parcel of property in upstate New York. According to the records, Owen's "only fault" was that he drank too much. Several months after his marriage to Sarah, he heard some rumors around town that Sarah was not "true to him." About a year and a half after the marriage, their son, Homer, was born. It was not until eight years later, however, on a night Owen came home intoxicated, that he accused Sarah of having had "connection with someone other than himself," claiming that Homer was not his son. For the next thirty years Owen continued to make similar comments, but only while intoxicated and never in the presence of anyone but Sarah. Finally, he made out a will leaving nothing to his son, Homer, who was, in fact, his son.

Under these circumstances, since Owen was of sound mind (he was sober when he made out his will), and since he deliberately omitted his son from his will without mentioning his reason for doing so, Homer was effectively (though unjustifiably) disinherited, and there was nothing he could do.

As discussed above, there are a number of states, such as New Hampshire, Missouri, and Alabama, that do not require proof that the omission was intentional in order for the omitted child to take a share. The mere omission is sufficient. In those states, a child not provided for or mentioned in the will automatically takes a share of the estate, regardless of the reason for the omission.

Interestingly, when a child is improperly omitted from a parent's will, the rights of that child can pass down to the child's children if the child is already deceased at the parent's death. For instance, say that Mallard asks his lawyer to prepare a will leaving all of Mallard's estate to his three children, Huey, Dewey, and Frank. When she comes to Frank's name, however, the lawyer's typist misses a few keys and the will leaves the estate only to Huey and Dewey. The will is signed by Mallard without realizing that Frank has been inadvertently omitted. As it happened, shortly after the will was signed, Frank was killed in an auto accident, survived by his wife and two young children. And shortly after that, Mallard died of a heart attack at the sight of his lawyer's bill.

Because Frank was not intentionally omitted from Mallard's will, he should be entitled to a share, his children argued. But Huey and Dewey come forth and say, "Personally, we liked Frank, and had he survived, we probably would have shared the estate with him, but it's a shame he didn't. Frank's children were never entitled to a share." In fact, those states that have laws protecting omitted children provide that the rights of an omitted child can be exercised through that child's *lineal descendants* if the child is deceased, and case law supports the fact that the omitted child need not have survived the parent for this to be so.

In my example, therefore, Frank's two children would have the right to share one-third of their grandfather's estate because of the fact that their father, Frank, was an improperly omitted child.

Remember that *any* mention of the child in the will is adequate to show that she or he was not accidentally omitted, so that even if the child is merely referred to in some context other than a bequest, such as naming him personal representative, it is probably sufficient evidence of an intentional omission.

An even more difficult question arises where an after-born child is the result of the artificial insemination of the deceased's sperm after his death. Here it is difficult to argue that the child was omitted intentionally since the child was not even considered to be in existence at the time of the testator's death, let alone the time he made his will. This issue of whether such children qualify as "omitted" children has yet to be resolved by the courts, but, as noted in the discussion below, it has been considered in a few states in regard to whether such a child would qualify for Social Security benefits.

Surprisingly, an omitted child does not get his share by contesting the will, since, presumably, the will was properly executed. Rather, before distribution is made to the other beneficiaries, the child must ask the court to order that a distribution be made to him as an omitted child, under the appropriate law of the particular state.

A parent who wishes to disinherit a child must also be careful that the remainder of his estate is properly disposed of under his will; otherwise the intentional omission statement may be useless, and the undisposed-of property will be treated as "intestate" property (as if the parent died without a will)—and, of course, under the law the child will take a share of that. Therefore, be sure your will has a "residuary" bequest (it would be unusual if it didn't, but it *has* happened, especially with home-drawn wills), leaving "all the rest, residue and remainder" to so and so.

Adopted children. For purposes of inheritance, adopted children are treated the same as natural-born children. They will inherit from their adoptive parents and *not* from their natural parents. When they are adopted, they *lose* the right to inherit from their natural parents' estates. This does not prohibit, however, both sets of parents from providing for the child voluntarily.

Children born outside of marriage: Today, two-fifths of all children are born to unmarried women. Until very recently, the general rule was that a child born outside of marriage could only inherit from his or her mother and not from the father, unless the father acknowledged the child to be his (although the father could, of course, voluntarily provide for the child). A 1986 U.S. Supreme Court decision changed all that, holding that such laws were unconstitutional and that a state may not prohibit a child born outside of marriage from inheriting. The effect of this decision gives such a child the same inheritance rights as a child born to a married couple, including the right to a forced share if he is improperly omitted from the will.

Assisted reproduction. Modern science is creating complicated legal problems, many of which were totally unanticipated while developing the related technological advances. A number of these surprise issues surface in the area of inheritance law. For instance, say that Jack and Jill are married, but Jack is terminally ill at a relatively young age. Both of them are desirous of having more children, so Jack preserves and stores his sperm for this purpose. After Jack's death, Jill is impregnated with Jack's sperm as they planned, resulting in another of "their" children, but this one is born nearly four years after Jack's death. Does the child have rights to Jack's estate long after it is settled? And what if Jill dies before Jack, Jack later remarries, and dies sometime later. After Jack's death, his second wife learns of the stored sperm, is impregnated with Jack's sperm, and bears Jack's child. Does this child have any rights to Jack's estate even though Jack never consented to the arrangement?

One Massachusetts case, decided in 2002, dealt in part with the former issue (where the deceased consented), but the legal question that arose was whether the child born after the one parent's death would increase the surviving spouse's rights to Social Security benefits. The case involved a young couple married three and a half years with no children. It was discovered that the husband had leukemia and would likely be unable to father children once the disease progressed. The couple arranged to store the husband's semen and preserve it for possible future use by the wife. In October 1993 the husband died, and in October 1995 the wife gave birth to twin girls after being artificially inseminated with her husband's sperm. The wife then applied for mother's benefits and child's benefits under Social Security. Her claim was denied by Social Security on the basis that she did not establish that the twins were her deceased husband's "children." Subsequently, a U.S. administrative law judge held that the children did not qualify for benefits because they were not entitled to inherit from the father's estate under Massachusetts law. Then Massachusetts's highest court, the Supreme Judicial Court, reviewed the case. The court held that the children did qualify as children of the deceased husband and that the surviving spouse's benefits should be measured accordingly. The court went on to note, however, that such an opportunity should not be allowed to take place at just any length of time after the father's death and that a reasonable time period, perhaps two years, should be established as a limit beyond which such rights would be cut off. Otherwise, it would not be equitable or reasonable to require other heirs or legatees to wait indefinitely for their rights to the estate to be settled. (The court also held that paternity must be clearly established and that the deceased father must have affirmatively consented to posthumous conception and to the support of any resulting children.)

In another case on the same issue as to whether an after-born child who was not "in utero" at the time of the testator's death would qualify for child's Social Security benefits, a lower court decision against the child was appealed to the federal circuit court of appeals. That court (in the Ninth Circuit) held in 2004 that the child did qualify as a "child of the testator" and should receive benefits. It was also noted, however, that the issue continues to be unsettled and unpredictable.

Perhaps an even more potentially troublesome issue arises with "anonymous" donors, typically resulting where healthy men donate sperm and healthy women donate eggs, both being paid for the donation, to be purchased and used by infertile couples or single individuals who wish to produce children. Depending on the arrangements made with the donation center, it may be possible for the purchaser or the child to discover the identity of the donor. Does the child in such a case have any rights to the natural parent's estate? Typically, two situations apply. In many instances, a couple unable to otherwise bear children will utilize the donation resources. Since the resulting child is the biological child of only one spouse, the other spouse might legally adopt the child, and the rights of the child to the estate of the natural parent are then cut off. When this does not happen, however, it may be that the child does have rights to the natural parent's estate, but it is not always clear. In one case in the state of Washington, for instance, the court held that the previously anonymous male donor had no (lifetime) responsibility for the support of minor children produced by his sperm. To (help) avoid the question of rights and liabilities in such cases, it is typical for the anonymous donor to sign a legal waiver of financial and parental responsibilities on making the donation and for the recipient/purchaser of the sperm or egg to also sign a release, waiver, and confidentiality agreement on receipt. But in the eyes of the law, who can sign for the child? In such cases, it is not at all clear that a parent can waive the legal rights of the child.

All this adds up to a potentially risky situation for the donor, unless, as noted, the child is later legally adopted. As to the legitimate spouse who stores gametes for use after death, the spouse would be well advised to simultaneously establish some form of trust for the child or children who may result from the use of the gamete, since it could be that, depending on how long after death the child is born, the law might not provide the child with any rights. (Note that such a trust would present some very interesting drafting challenges and should only be undertaken by an attorney expert in the field of trust law.)

Special Family Allowances

Every state has laws that offer some protection for the welfare of a surviving spouse and, to a lesser extent, minor children of the deceased in cases where the deceased did not provide for them in his or her will or where the family requires financial assistance while the estate is being settled. For the most part, these provisions favor the surviving spouse, and amounts allowed for the care of minor children, surprising as it may seem, are usually quite limited. In Massachusetts, for instance, while a widow's allowance is only limited by need and by the proportion the allowance bears to the total estate, allowances for minor children may not exceed $100 per child. As noted previously, however, a minor child has the right to sue the estate of a Massachusetts parent for support, since the parent had the legal obligation to support the child while the parent was alive. Most states, however, do provide shelter, at least, for the minor child for a period after the parent's death.

Such "shelter" provisions, frequently called "homestead" rights, usually allow the surviving spouse and the deceased's minor children to continue to live in the home (even though it may have been left to someone else under the will), at least until the children reach the age of majority, and, in some cases, the surviving spouse may continue to reside there for the rest of her life, whether there were children or not.

WIDOW'S ALLOWANCES

Actually, *widowers* are now generally permitted to receive allowances from the estate too, but for hundreds of years such allowances were given only to widows because of the husband's legal obligation to support and provide for his wife. These widow's allowances stood in addition to any homestead allowance.

The purpose of the allowance, which is paid out of the deceased spouse's *probate* estate, is to provide for the care and support of the surviving spouse *during the period of administration* of the deceased spouse's estate. Knowing how long it can take to settle an estate, and considering the fact that distributions are not normally made to beneficiaries for many months at best, the probate courts are empowered under the laws of every state to order that payments be made from the estate to the surviving spouse from the estate for his or her maintenance and support.

The widow's allowance ordered by the court takes priority over all other debts of the estate and may be paid to the spouse even though the estate is insolvent, or being sued or contested. It may be given to the spouse whether or not she is named as a beneficiary under the will, and even where there was no will. Furthermore, the allowance is available to the spouse *in addition* to any forced share she may take or other benefits she receives from the estate. Since it takes first priority, the allowance could, if large enough in proportion to the rest of the estate, disrupt or even reduce other bequests. In fact, if the estate were small enough, it could be used *entirely* for the widow's allowance and there would be no "estate" to administer, despite the fact that the deceased spouse left a will that contained bequests to others.

The amount of the allowance is always up to the court, which takes into consideration the size of the estate and the circumstances of the widow, such as age, health, general needs, and manner of living. It is this last consideration that often gives rise to the greatest discrepancies between what the widow thinks she should get, what the estate thinks she should get, and what the court gives her.

In one case in Georgia, the widow, Marylou, applied to the court for a year's allowance from her husband's estate, which was valued at over

$300,000. In Georgia, the procedure was to appoint an appraiser to determine approximately how much money Marylou would need for the twelve-month period. The appraisers came up with a figure of $75,000. After the personal representative (a bank) of her husband's estate recovered from the shock, they appealed to the court on the basis that the amount was excessive. The court agreed and reduced the allowance to $50,000. The personal representatives, still unhappy with the amount, appealed to a higher court, arguing that while Marylou's husband was alive, he never spent more than $1,800 a year for support of the both of them! Since when did her manner of living warrant an expense of $50,000 for twelve months? The higher court agreed that the lower court was too generous and suggested that the amount of $3,500 would be more appropriate.

That was in 1950. Only a year later, another case on widow's allowance illustrated even more dramatically how the accustomed manner of living has a great deal to do with the allowance. In this case, Millicent Hearst (yes, that Hearst!) asked the court for a mere $10,000 a month to tide her over while the estate of her husband, William Randolph Hearst, was being settled. In view of Mrs. Hearst's accustomed style of living (and, of course, the size of Hearst's multimillion-dollar estate), the court granted her request.

Although the court has wide discretion in deciding the amount of the allowance and, in most cases, the length of time it will be paid, it has no discretion as to the persons who are entitled to be paid. For instance, even though a spouse may have been legally separated from her husband for years before his death, she may still be entitled to a widow's allowance on his death. And no matter how needy a widow may continue to be, if she remarries after her husband's death, any widow's allowance will immediately cease, as she is then no longer a widow.

The allowance is not automatic. It must be applied for by the surviving spouse within a reasonable time after the death of the other spouse, and, as noted above, if the personal representative of the estate or the beneficiaries feel it is excessive, they can appeal the order. Few spouses would voluntarily waive the allowance after the other's death, but if the couple executed a prenuptial agreement waiving or limiting the spouse's allowance, this would obviously have a bearing on the court's order.

Since most estates take quite some time to settle, it is a good idea to consider applying for the widow's allowance soon after the death of a spouse to provide quick, liquid funds for the support of the survivor. However, if the surviving spouse already has adequate funds (from joint bank accounts, etc.) and is the beneficiary of the estate as well, she may forego the allowance, use her own funds for support, and simply wait for the estate to be settled. On the other hand, if she is not the only beneficiary, or if there is a substantial number of creditors who stand to take too large a bite out of the estate, then the surviving spouse should definitely apply for the widow's allowance.

Keep This in Mind

Every common-law state contains certain "protective" provisions for a surviving spouse, so it is difficult to disinherit a spouse without some careful legal maneuvering. On the other hand, it is relatively easy to disinherit a child, if done intentionally. In both cases, certain types of trust can facilitate the disinheritance, but that typically requires the assistance of knowledgeable legal counsel. Where multiple marriages are concerned, this also calls for expert advice, as well as premarital and postmarital agreement documents.

8

Estate Management

Five hundred dollars shall be expended by my personal representatives for the purpose of buying booze and canapés for my friends. On second thought make it eight hundred dollars because I don't want my friends to go away sober or serious.

—from the will of Wayne Morris

Clearly the above is not a bequest but rather a direction to the personal representative of Morris's estate to spend a certain amount of money in connection with the postfuneral "ceremony." As such, is it a valid expense of the estate? If the expenditure were larger and therefore reduced the shares of the beneficiaries, would it still be honored? Is it paid before creditors of the estate are paid? Is it the personal representative's obligation to pay all such expenses out of estate funds? What if he uses his own funds? Can he later recover the money from the estate?

Who Pays the Debts and Expenses of the Estate—and When?

The administration of an estate operates on the same principle that applied when the testator was alive—a person must first attend to his own debts and expenses before he can give away what is left. With the exception of certain priority allowances given primarily to the surviving spouse (as discussed in chapter 7), the beneficiaries of an estate can only take what is left after the appropriate debts and expenses of the estate have been paid. This, of course, leads to the questions of which expenses must be paid first and what is appropriate. In early English law (on which much of our law of wills is based), the deceased's funeral expenses and the costs of proving the will were given first priority over all other debts and expenses, and this is still generally the case. Using the general assets of the estate (that is, assets that are not already specifically encumbered by a mortgage or lien), the priority of payment is as follows:

1. Funeral expenses
2. Administration expenses
3. Taxes (federal and state)
4. Expenses of last illness
5. All other debts

Out of respect to the deceased and because of the obvious need to dispose of the body with dignity, funeral expenses are generally paid before any other debts or expenses of the estate. As explained below, however, there are certain limitations. For instance, funeral expenses must be reasonable in proportion to the entire estate, if possible, though in an estate of only a few thousand dollars this may not possible, for the entire estate may be consumed by the funeral expenses. On the other hand, the cost of a huge and extravagant monument may appear quite reasonable in a $10 million estate.

If the estate is insolvent (i.e., where the debts exceed the value of the estate), the funeral costs are still given priority but are often limited in amount. Furthermore, in such cases, the court would understandably not be so lenient in what it allowed as a funeral expense, although reason and respect for the deceased would still prevail. For instance, in one Pennsylvania case where the estate was insolvent, an unusually high sum had to be paid for a special oversized casket because of the huge size and weight of the deceased. The cost was questioned by the creditors as unreasonable (it wasn't clear what they suggested as an alternative), but the judge found it to be proper and allowable, since there was no other, less expensive way to inter the deceased with dignity.

In situations such as the one above, the deceased's creditors have to act fast because the burial often takes place right after death and long before the will is probated or the personal representative is appointed. If the person is already buried (and the expense incurred) before the creditors have a chance to challenge the incurrence of the expenses, they can subsequently challenge the *payment* of those expenses, asking that their own claims be given equal priority. If the court feels that the burial expenses were excessive, it could limit the payment of such expenses and the gravedigger or funeral director might just have to take less than they bargained for. The typical estate, however, is *not* insolvent, and so in most cases the funeral and burial expenses are given their due priority, and, if reasonable, they are seldom questioned.

Funeral expenses have been held to include not only the direct costs of the funeral and burial but also the cost of burial plots, perpetual-care contracts, masses, and, more commonly, tombstones and monuments, keeping in mind the ever-present requirement of reasonableness in proportion to the estate. If in your will, for example, you direct that your personal representatives engage a sculptor to carve a twenty-foot-tall marble statue of you holding a golf club, it is unlikely to happen unless you have a multimillion-dollar estate and a place to put the statue. Furthermore, unless you tie the direction for such an elaborate memorial into a conditional bequest (as discussed in chapter 6), there is always the chance that your heirs will challenge the instructions. This is just what happened in the estate of Billy Rose, the famous showman and at one time the largest individual shareholder of AT&T.

Rose's will directed that a large and elaborate mausoleum be built for him (although Billy himself was an unusually small man). Unfortunately, his two sisters, who stood to inherit the $30 million estate, didn't agree and instigated a lengthy court fight to revise the will. Poor Billy had to lie in cold storage for two years before the case was finally resolved and he got his mausoleum.

Quite often, a surviving spouse will pay funeral expenses out of accessible funds in a joint bank account, even though there are other assets in the probate estate. If the estate is solvent and the surviving spouse is the sole beneficiary of the estate, this is not a problem. If the estate is insolvent, however, or if the spouse is not the only beneficiary, she should seek reimbursement from the estate for the funeral expenses she paid; otherwise, she would just be increasing, at her own expense, the amount available to creditors and other beneficiaries.

Finally, the question of whether allowable funeral expenses would include the cost of refreshments, or "booze and canapés" as directed by Wayne Morris at the outset of this chapter, would depend on whether the estate was solvent and on whether the expenses were reasonable in proportion to the estate. This is just the type of expense that would be disallowed in an insolvent estate but unquestioned (if reasonable) in a solvent one. I suppose if there is a question, you could always give your personal representative the option of having a "cash" bar.

After funeral expenses come expenses of administration. Commonly, these would include personal representative fees and attorney's fees in connection with proving the will, handling all matters for the personal representative in administering the estate, and defending an attack against the will or the estate. In addition, they would include all costs in discovering, collecting, and maintaining estate assets. As with all priority amounts, however, administrative expenses must be reasonable under the circumstances, and anyone having an interest in the estate, such as creditors or beneficiaries, can ask the court to review and possibly disallow them if they are unreasonable.

Next in order of priority come taxes or other amounts due to federal and state governments. Of these, the federal taxes take first priority, then the state government. The type of taxes that fall into this level of priority normally include estate and inheritance taxes and income taxes owed by the deceased (and assessed by the government) *up to the time of death.* Taxes that accrue *after* that date are generally not given the same priority. Note that many states and the federal government have laws that override this general rule and direct that payment of an estate tax generated by a particular asset owned by the deceased at death gets paid out of that asset. For example, the beneficiary of insurance proceeds may be liable for any estate tax caused by the inclusion of the proceeds in the taxable estate of the deceased.

After taxes come the expenses of the deceased's last illness, but not in all states. In many states, these expenses are simply lumped in with all other expenses after the three enumerated above. In those states that give priority to expenses of the last illness, such expenses would normally include costs such as physician's and hospital bills and medication relating to treatment of the illness that ended with the deceased's death.

After this category, the states vary considerably in giving preference to any other items of debt. Some, for example, recognize wages due to employees or rents due from the deceased as a tenant. However, as a general rule, the first three—*funeral expenses, administrative expenses,* and *taxes*—are given priority in all states.

The person responsible for the payment of all such charges is the personal representative of the estate. This responsibility is a very serious one, since if the personal representative fails to pay a debt that should (and could) have been paid or pays a debt that should not have been paid, he will be *personally* liable for those funds out of his own pocket unless he can show good cause for his error. As noted in earlier chapters, the personal representative normally will *not* pay any questionable debts until the creditor makes a claim against the estate for payment; every state provides a specified "open" period within which such claims must be made. If an unsecured creditor fails to make his claim within that period, he is likely to lose his right to recover unless he can show in court that justice and equity require the payment of a late claim and that he has not been culpably neglectful in failing to pursue his claim.

Many claims are not questionable, however, and the personal representative may, if he wishes, pay them at any time, assuming there are available funds to do so. If a personal representative in good faith uses his personal funds to pay a valid claim, he may later be reimbursed by the estate. In fact, if a third party advances funds to the personal representative for payment of a valid estate debt or if the third party pays the debt herself, she is similarly entitled to reimbursement from the estate, as illustrated above where a wife paid her deceased husband's funeral expenses out of her joint bank account. In either event, however, whether it is the personal representative or a third party, if the debt was overpaid or should not have been paid, there would only be partial or no reimbursement, accordingly. If the estate is insolvent, then a prudent personal representative will pay *no* debts at all until he has received approval of the probate court, since overpayment or improper payment will result in the personal representative being personally liable.

Even though an estate may be solvent and have plenty of assets to cover all costs, the next logical question is which of the estate assets are used to pay them. For instance, say that Uncle Mike left an estate consisting of $10,000 in cash and a home worth $80,000. His will leaves Ike a specific bequest of $10,000, and "all the rest" goes to Aunt Agnes (Uncle Mike's sister). As it turns out, there are debts and expenses of $13,000. Where does the money come from? Will Ike lose his $10,000 bequest?

The general rule is that unless the will provides otherwise, debts and expenses are first taken from the "residuary" estate, leaving the specific bequests, to the extent possible, intact. Therefore, in my example above, Ike would receive the $10,000 bequest because there is enough value in the residuary estate to cover the debts and expenses. Unfortunately for Aunt Agnes, however, there is only the home. In such a case, Agnes would either have to come up with the $13,000 on her own or sell (or mortgage) the home to pay the estate expenses. Relatively speaking, she would be much better off if she raised the money on her own, since a sale of the home under these circumstances would involve considerable additional estate expense, which *she* would indirectly have to bear.

If, on the other hand, there was enough cash or other liquid assets in the residuary estate, then the rule is that these assets are used first, and the real estate, if any, is *not* sold until the cash and other assets ("personal property") are used up. After the personal property in the residuary estate is used, then the real estate (in the residuary estate) may be sold and used to pay the expenses. When *all* of the residuary estate is used up, then and only then (*unless* the will states otherwise) are the specific bequests used to pay the debts, in the proportion they bear to each other. (This is called "abatement" and is discussed in detail in chapter 5.)

Investing Estate Assets

After paying all of the estate's debts and expenses, or perhaps while waiting until it is time to pay them, what do you do with all of the estate's money? Can you just deposit it in a simple bank account? If there are securities, must you hold them or should you sell them? In short, is the personal representative responsible for actively investing the estate's assets?

In past times, and in states that have not updated their probate laws, unless the will or the laws of the particular state specifically direct otherwise, the personal representative was under *no* duty to invest the estate funds. His primary responsibilities include discovering and collecting estate assets, paying all appropriate debts and expenses, and distributing the balance to the beneficiaries. This is not to say, however, that the personal representative could not pay attention to existing investments or that he could leave funds "idle." At the very least, any cash or liquid funds should be deposited into interest-bearing bank accounts. In this context, he is not necessarily bound to search for the highest income-producing investment; his first consideration must be protection of the principal, even if it means accepting a lower return.

If, on the other hand, the state has enacted the Uniform Probate Code, or the will instructs the personal representative to invest estate funds, then he must do so; and, when doing so, he must follow the "prudent investor rule," which basically suggests that he invest using the "modern portfolio theory" of an integrated portfolio of equities, bonds, cash, and other assets in a typical portfolio. (No cryptocurrency, at least while this type of asset remains new and volatile.) Occasionally, the personal representative "inherits" a questionable investment that the deceased was holding during his lifetime (like that cryptocurrency) and has instructed in his will that the personal representative must keep and cannot sell. The personal representative is faced with the choice of making an unauthorized sale or watching the investment gradually sink in value. In such a case, he may not be obliged to sell, but prudence should motivate him to ask the court and/or the beneficiaries for permission to do so. Obtaining the permission of either would normally take the PR "off the hook" for selling in violation of the terms of the will.

If the questionable investment consists of something the personal representative cannot sell, such as shares of stock in a small or privately held company, then he is under no obligation to take action other than to exercise the estate's right to vote as a stockholder of the company and to keep aware of the status of the stock and the company.

Since in modern times the personal representative has a duty to invest as a prudent investor would, what is the risk of personal loss for bad investments? What if there are two or more personal representatives and the investments are entrusted to one of them? This often happens when a family member and a professional person, such as an accountant, are named co–personal representatives. Usually, the nonprofessional will let the professional do the investing, paying little or no attention to what he does with the funds, unaware that he could be personally liable for the professional's bad judgment. This is almost exactly what happened in the Shoddenfart estate.

Willi Shoddenfart's will named his brother, Otto, and his accountant,

Morris, as co–personal representatives of his estate. After Otto and Morris were appointed by the court, Otto, not being very familiar with the technicalities of the job, left everything up to Morris. Although Willi's will made no mention of investing, there was quite a bit of cash in the estate—around $250,000—and Morris felt it would be in everyone's best interests to invest it "wisely."

During the next year or so while the estate was being settled, Morris did some investment "research," consulted with certain experts, and finally placed the estate funds in a number of securities that he thought would surely appreciate, as well as some very high-yielding bonds. Since Otto was co–personal representative, he was asked to co-sign the checks Morris made out to pay for the investments as well as checks to pay estate bills, but Otto never even inquired what the checks were for. In fact, he was quite pleased that Morris was taking care of all estate matters, feeling that even if he asked, he probably wouldn't have understood anyway.

As it turned out, a few of the stocks didn't do as well as Morris had hoped (they dropped about $57,000 in value by the end of the year), and two out of three of the high-yielding bonds defaulted on their interest payments. In the meantime, Morris didn't forget to take his personal representative's fee of $7,200, and Otto was thrilled to receive a check for $3,000 as his "fee."

Willi's spouse and son, the beneficiaries of his estate, complained to the court, asking that Morris and Otto be held responsible for the stock losses and lost interest and that they return their fees as well. Morris claimed that he acted in good faith and that he took the trouble to get expert advice, so he should not be liable. Otto argued that he had nothing to do with the whole matter, that he didn't know a bond from a doughnut, and that Morris never told him a thing about what he was doing, so how could he be responsible?

The court noted that Willi's will gave the personal representatives no authority to invest the funds, and therefore, any investments made by the personal representatives were made at their own risk. Furthermore, as co–personal representatives, they had the duty to act jointly. When Otto was asked to sign checks, he had at that time an opportunity *and an obligation* to inquire of Morris where the estate funds were going and why. He could not avoid that responsibility by ignoring it, and so he was held to be *equally* liable with Morris for the losses, and they were ordered to return the fees they received as well.

Today, with the widespread imposition of the prudent investor rule,

Morris's good-faith effort to invest wisely based on the advice of a competent wealth advisor might get him off the hook of personal liability, as long as he monitored the account statements on a monthly basis and regularly met with the wealth advisor to review the performance of the portfolio. Even so, it can often be advantageous for the personal representative to keep the beneficiaries informed of asset performance. More on that below.

Accounting to the Court and to the Beneficiaries

One of the primary duties of a personal representative or administrator may be to provide an "accounting"—a detailed and accurate report to the probate court of all estate assets and transactions relating to such assets. We say "may" because under the modern Uniform Probate Code there are several levels of probate: voluntary, informal, formal, and supervised. Not all levels require an accounting. That said, often an accounting is required and it is instructive to understand what it is.

As explained in chapter 1, the personal representative is first required to determine the extent of all probate assets belonging to the estate, and then, if required under state law, list the assets on the inventory that is required to be filed with the probate court. The inventory is *not* an accounting but generally serves as the starting point of the personal representative's account, since those are the assets he has to administer and deal with in the settlement of the estate. As also noted, the *inventory,* and now the personal representative's *account,* deals with *probate* assets. Therefore, jointly held assets, insurance proceeds payable to a beneficiary other than the personal representative, and assets held in a trust will *not* be included in either the personal representative's inventory or the personal representative's account unless the personal representative takes the position that despite the ostensible title or arrangement to avoid probate, they are *probate* assets, and he intends to take the necessary legal steps to bring them into the probate estate, as discussed in chapter 2.

After his appointment by the court, the personal representative is sometimes required to file an accounting at regular intervals, usually on an annual basis, although the probate court can order him to account at any time. If no account has been filed and the estate is ready to be settled, and depending upon the level of probate where levels exist, the personal representative will file his "first and final" account, although the account may encompass more than a single year as appropriate.

The first annual account will usually begin with the assets shown on the inventory; then it will show any additional assets that have come into the personal representative's possession. It will list all income and sources of that income, and it will show any losses realized, as well as all disbursements, including payment of estate debts, widow's allowances, expenses, and taxes. The balance of all this is what the personal representative has in his hands at the time of the account. This report will be filed for each year until the estate is settled, showing the complete status of the estate (in probate) at the end of each accounting period. If the account is a final account, it will also show distribution or proposed distribution of the balance of the estate to the beneficiaries, so that the balance shown on the account to the probate court is zero. When this happens and the court (and all other interested parties) approve of the account, the personal representative is discharged and the estate is closed. Note that under the Uniform Probate Code, if an estate is closed "informally," then the court does not discharge the personal representative from liability but instead closes the estate, and if no problem arises during the following year, the personal representative is then free from liability in most instances.

If after the estate is closed the personal representative discovers additional estate assets, he must file a supplemental account and go through the approval process once again as to the new assets.

Where there are co–personal representatives, only one account need be filed, but each personal representative must account to the court for all estate assets in his actual possession, and, as discussed above, each is fully responsible for administering the estate, even though only one does the work.

If someone other than the personal representative is in possession of estate property but won't give it up, that third party may be compelled to account to the court as to that property. Indeed, this very important legal mechanism is often used to recover estate property that has been taken by someone without authorization.

In one case, for instance, one of four daughters was taking care of her mother and decided, after her mother died, that she would help herself to the mother's jewelry. The mother's will named another daughter as personal representative and left her jewelry to the four girls equally. The personal representative filed a request in the probate court asking that her sister be ordered to give an "accounting" of the jewelry she had in her possession and to deliver it to the personal representative for administration in accordance with the mother's will. The other daughter steadfastly refused, and the court finally ordered her arrested for contempt of court with the threat of jail if she didn't comply. This persuaded her to turn over the jewelry.

Similar exposures to penalties such as personal liability and even jail time face the personal representative who fails to account when obliged to do so. It is not only the court that can compel an accounting from the personal representative, but *any* party who has an interest in the estate can ask the court to order him to account. Obviously, this includes all beneficiaries of the estate, but it also includes creditors of the estate. The creditors of a *beneficiary* (as opposed to creditors of the *estate*), however, may not compel an accounting unless they have legally attached the beneficiary's interest in the estate. (In this case, the attachment would occur when a court, in recognition of the creditor's potential claim against the beneficiary, ordered the beneficiary's share of the estate to be held in abeyance pending the outcome of the creditor's claim.)

When an accounting is required, typically a beneficiary, and anyone else having a legal interest in the estate, is entitled to notice of the personal representative's accounts; otherwise, the accounts cannot be approved by the court. Where a charity is a beneficiary, often state law requires the state attorney general receive a notice of the account. Notice usually consists of sending the beneficiaries and other interested parties a copy of the proposed account. This is required in order to give the beneficiaries and other parties an opportunity to review the personal representative's financial administration and see that their interest and assets are being properly handled. It also gives the beneficiaries the opportunity to *object* to the personal representative's account if there are any entries or transactions that the beneficiary wishes to question. The beneficiaries' objections to entries or transactions should be sent to the court in writing with a copy to the personal representative, and should be very specific as to the items that are in question and why. A general objection to the account without specifics will usually be dismissed by the court.

Despite all of these serious requirements to account to the court and the beneficiaries, the personal representative's account can be waived in most states if all interested parties assent to the waiver. Of course, this assumes that all creditors have been paid and that no new creditors will surface within the allowable period. Dispensing with the account, where allowable, can help to keep the estate "private," since the account, like all other documents filed in the probate court, becomes *public* information once it is filed.

Waiver of accounts, and in many cases even inventories, is not uncommon in estates of the rich and famous in order to keep estate matters private, even though the will or the estate had to be probated. In the case of President John F. Kennedy's estate, for instance, the probate records at the Suffolk County Probate Court in Boston show that he left a will and that a personal representative was appointed, but that's it. There is no inventory, no accounting, and no other estate information in the public file. Since no interested party ever complained about it, nothing else was done, and technically, to this day, the estate was never closed!

However, if the personal representative's account is never filed and the estate is not closed, the personal representative is never discharged from responsibility. This means that at some future date a beneficiary could decide to challenge the personal representative's acts and, if the beneficiary was successful, the personal representative would be personally liable, long after the estate was "settled." For this reason, most professional personal representatives (such as attorneys or banks) will always file their accounts, including a final account, and ask that the accounts be allowed (approved by the court). Once the final account is allowed, the personal representative is discharged from liability.

Remember, only parties in interest can compel an accounting and, except in a very few states, the court will seldom take it upon itself to compel one unless there is some apparent reason to do so, such as fraud or deceit or other improper conduct. If all the creditors are paid and all the beneficiaries are happy with the settlement, the estate could be settled quietly and privately, although there are risks of reopening for some reason at a later date.

When You Can Get Your Share

After all debts, expenses, and taxes are paid, and the final account has been approved or the probate process otherwise concluded, the beneficiaries can finally get their shares, although this does not usually happen as quickly as the beneficiaries would like. Because the personal representative, in most cases, must wait until the allowable period for creditors' claims has expired and until the tax authorities are satisfied, it may take a year or more, under the best of circumstances, before final distribution of the estate. Meanwhile, however, it is possible (and is often the case) for the personal representative to make *partial* distributions to the beneficiaries if such distributions clearly will not affect the ability to pay creditors and all other costs, including taxes.

Unfortunately, the personal representative has the right to withhold distributions if administration or circumstances of the estate call for it. For instance, distribution may be withheld pending resolution of a lawsuit against the estate, or where there is a contest over beneficiaries' rights under the will. Many states provide a certain period after which beneficiaries must be paid unless a court or the will permits otherwise. And even where a justifiable delay occurs, the beneficiaries would then be entitled to interest on their shares starting after the prescribed period by the laws of the state or under the terms of the deceased's will. For instance, in Massachusetts, unless the will provides otherwise, beneficiaries are entitled to begin receiving interest on their bequests if the bequests are not paid by one year after the date of death of the deceased. But if, for example, the deceased's will directs that the beneficiaries be paid six months after his death, interest on their bequests will begin at that time, not after one year. Similarly, if the deceased provided that payments would not be made until two years after her death, interest on unpaid bequests would *only* begin to run after the two-year period provided in the will. A provision in the will to pay bequests early, by the way, does not give the personal representative the right to pay them out before debts, expenses, and taxes are paid; it merely determines the time when interest begins.

How you get paid. Unless the will provides that you should receive a specific item of property, your share may be paid out to you in any manner that gives you your fair share of the estate. For instance, if the will leaves you one hundred shares of Amazon stock, then you will get one hundred shares of this stock and not cash. If the estate does not have one hundred shares of Amazon stock, and the bequest was not "adeemed," as explained in chapter 4, the personal representative must purchase the shares to fulfill the bequests.

With residuary shares, however, the beneficiaries often receive a combination of both cash and "in kind" distributions. A distribution "in kind" is one where you receive a share of the items that are left in the estate. For instance, say that after all debts, expenses, and taxes have been paid, there are three equal beneficiaries who are to divide $150,000, three hundred shares of stock, and a car. Unless otherwise agreed, each will get $50,000 in cash, one hundred shares of stock, and one-third the proceeds from the sale of the car (although, if they wished, they could own the car as tenants in common). Alternatively, if the car was worth about $12,000, two of the beneficiaries could receive one hundred shares of stock plus $54,000 in cash, and the other beneficiary would get one hundred shares of stock, $42,000 in cash, and the car. If the beneficiaries cannot agree on a split (such as where the item is not divisible and more than one wants it), then the personal representative can order the item sold and divide the proceeds, and if the item is auctioned off, then the beneficiaries can battle it out there. Where there is an "in kind" distribution, it is a best practice for the personal representative to obtain valid appraisals of the property to be distributed in kind (where such values are not readily attainable), and submit to the beneficiaries a "proposal for distribution," giving the beneficiaries time—often thirty days—to object to the valuations or method of division. Modern probate laws state that after such notice, the personal representative will be free of liability if a timely objection is not made.

If a beneficiary owes money to the estate (because he owed money to the deceased), his share of the estate may be reduced by the amount he owes and he will have little to say about it. This happens quite frequently, as where a child continually pressed the parent for "loans," which the parent advanced. If over a period of time the parent advanced a disproportionate amount to one child, she may decide to mention that fact in her will and provide that the child's share should be reduced by that amount. When this happens, the share *will* be reduced, regardless of whether the child ever signed a "legal" note, and regardless of whether any such note was enforceable. About the only defense a child would have in such a case would be proof that he paid back the funds *after* the will was signed.

When the time comes to divide the spoils, the personal representative must make the necessary transfers to the beneficiaries. Shares of stock or other securities, for instance, can either be endorsed over to the beneficiaries or, as happens more often, be re-registered by the personal representative in the beneficiaries' names (or as they direct) and have them delivered to the beneficiaries. Cash or other liquid funds are, of course, paid by check, and personal property (such as furniture, jewelry, etc.) is often transferred by mere delivery of the item to the beneficiary, although occasionally it will be accompanied by a letter of "deed" stating that it is being transferred. If it is a valuable item of personal property, such as a work of art or a stamp or coin collection, you should ask for and keep some written verification that it came to you through the estate, as well as the value of the items as reported by the estate on the estate tax return.

Real estate is handled differently for distribution purposes. In most states, persons who inherit real estate (called the "devisees" where there was a will, or "heirs" where there was no will) *automatically* take title to the real estate on the death of the person from whom they are inheriting, subject, of course, to debts, expenses, and taxes of the estate (some states, such as Massachusetts, impose an automatic estate tax lien on real estate that must be removed to clear title). That is, there is *no* need for the personal representative to deed the property over to them nor for the court to order a transfer. The property becomes theirs on the deceased's death. This is occasionally the source of some confusion among beneficiaries, since they wonder how the property could be theirs if it is still "in the name of" a deceased parent and the beneficiaries have no deed with *their* names on it. The change in title is made "legal" by referring to the probate proceedings and the will at the registry of deeds where the property is recorded. The registry thus verifies the change of ownership, and, therefore, there is usually no need for the personal representative to deed the real estate to the beneficiaries. If, however, the property is being *sold* from the estate to a third party, then the personal representative, after obtaining the court's permission to sell the property (in the event the will does not dispense with this requirement), will give a deed from the estate to the third-party buyer.

Even though the beneficiaries inherit the property as of the date of the deceased's death, it does not necessarily follow that they can sell it immediately. Because it may be subject to the payment of estate costs and taxes, a buyer would be reluctant to purchase it until he is satisfied that he can take the property free and clear of all such costs and related liens (as noted above). The buyer will usually ask for some form of assurance (usually a release from the tax authorities and/or court approval of the sale) before the sale is finalized.

Real estate that is left to more than one beneficiary will pass to those beneficiaries as tenants in common (with no survivorship rights) unless the will provides otherwise. Thus, a bequest of the home "to my sons, Clark and Clive, in equal shares" leaves Clark and Clive as tenants in common. This makes sense if this is the deceased's intention, because under this form of ownership, if Clark dies, his half of the real estate will pass to his heirs, and vice versa. Where the real estate is vacation property that has been in the family for generations, a more nuanced plan is often preferred, so the "outlaws" don't inherit the property to the detriment of the descendants of the deceased.

Quick Settlement Procedures for Certain Estates

Many states have special, abbreviated probate procedures if the estate does not exceed a certain amount, if no one objects to the use of the "small estate" settlement procedure, and, of course, if the will does not direct otherwise. The amounts vary, but we note here that under the Uniform Probate Code, "voluntary administration" is possible if the entire estate consists of "personal property" (not real estate) with a value of $25,000 or less (not including the value of a car).

The small-estate procedures only apply to *probate* property. Thus, if an estate consisted of a half-million dollars' worth of stocks and bonds the deceased held in *joint* names with his spouse (or in a living trust, which is preferable) and a $9,000 bank account in his own name, the estate could qualify for a *small*-estate administration, since the probate estate only consisted of $9,000, which is below the $10,000 limit for small estates in most states.

Remember, however, that the use of the small-estate procedure is always subject to denial if anyone contests the disposition of property or if a valid creditor is prejudiced by it or if the testator's will instructs otherwise.

Whether the estate is large or small, however, the important thing is that it is properly settled and that the beneficiaries get their money as quickly as possible—at least that's how the beneficiaries see it. Occasionally, the deceased anticipates their eagerness to get at the money and provides for a waiting period of his own. A somewhat extreme example of this was the estate of Mr. Zalewsky, who must have had quite a sense of humor. Mr. Zalewsky left his will in an envelope bearing the instructions: "To be opened after my death." It was so opened, and inside there was another envelope with the words: "To be opened six weeks after my death." After the prescribed six weeks, that envelope was opened, only to find a third envelope, which directed: "To be opened one year after my death." Out of respect (there is no legal obligation to follow such instructions—in fact, if the location of the will is known, there is an obligation to produce it to the court within a very short time after the death), the heirs waited a year, opened the envelope, and, you guessed it, found a fourth envelope! Between envelopes, indecision, and ignorance, they ended up waiting *five years* until Zalewsky's will was finally uncovered and read, and when it was, it proved to be just as eccentric as the envelope game. Zalewsky provided that half of his estate was to be liquidated and the funds deposited in a bank account, to stay there with interest accumulating for one hundred years, at which time it would be divided among his descendants. Now *that's* a long time to wait.

Keep This in Mind

Settling an estate can be a time-consuming, sometimes expensive process, or it can be quick and easy, depending, obviously, on the size and complexity of the estate. Further, even a relatively simple estate can be in the former category if there is a dispute over property or a contest, or faulty documents. If you're the one in charge of the settlement, the first thing to do is get a reputable opinion of what you're in for, and don't be hesitant to delegate (or decline!). If you do delegate, the estate will pay for it, and there will be less stress on you to accomplish tasks you know little or nothing about.

9

Personal Representatives

I want it that mine brother Adolph be my personal representative and I want it that the judge should please make Adolph put up plenty bond and watch him like hell. Adolph is a good business man but only a dumpkoff would trust him with a busted pfenig.

—from the will of Herman Oberweiss

Although Herman may not have been very articulate, he seemed to have a pretty good understanding of the role of the personal representative. And even though he didn't trust his brother, he knew that the court could "watch him like hell" and that if Adolph messed up or ran off with some of Herman's money, Herman's beneficiaries would still be protected since they could collect on Adolph's "bond." But if Herman was so worried, was his brother a good choice? Should you generally name a family member as personal representative? Does it make a difference if the personal representative you name is also a beneficiary? Or should you name your lawyer? Or a bank? What if your personal representative resides out of state? Or in another country? Or what if you simply don't have anyone you can name, should you still make out a will?

The Russian term for personal representative (executor) is *dushe prikazchik,* which means "spokesman for the soul." And this is just what the personal representative is: one who speaks for the deceased in the settlement of his estate and the carrying out of the instructions in his will. If you make out a will, therefore, it would be remiss not to name a personal representative. If there is simply no one you can name, it is possible, as you will see, to make out your will and leave the selection of personal representative to be done after your death by someone or some institution you trust. In any case, the choice of personal representative should be well thought out, as it is an important job, and the correct choice can make a tremendous difference in the smooth settlement of your estate.

Personal representative vs. trustee. The very first distinction you must understand is the difference between "personal representative" and "trustee." Most people think they are one and the same, but their functions are *very* different. Your *personal representative* simply settles your probate estate (reminder: assets in your own name) and has no authority to decide who gets what portion of your estate. His job is finished when the estate is settled, which is usually a year or so after your death. Your *trustee* manages and distributes the money and/or property you left in *trust*, which often takes place after your estate is settled, and your trustee may well have substantial discretion to pay or withhold benefits to or from your surviving spouse, children, or others, depending on your instructions. The trustee's job may last for many years after your death or after your children's deaths, or, in some cases, for years after the deaths of your grandchildren. Even when the personal representative and trustee are the same person or organization, the courts treat the positions as entirely separate.

Briefly, the personal representative's job is to collect and preserve all probate estate assets, pay all appropriate debts, expenses, and taxes, and distribute the remainder according to the terms of your will. (The personal representative is also responsible for burying the deceased testator in a manner suitable to his estate and his station in life unless the deceased gave this power to someone else, such as a healthcare agent under a healthcare proxy.) If you have no will, an *administrator* is appointed by the court to do all of this, except that instead of distributing to people you choose, the administrator would distribute your property according to state laws of intestacy. You cannot name your own administrator if you leave no will, but states often have an order of priority as to who is named administrator.

The procedure for appointment of a personal representative usually takes thirty to sixty days in most states. If there are pressing estate matters that must be taken care of immediately after death, those states allow for the quicker appointment of a "temporary" personal representative. The temporary personal representative may be appointed very quickly (usually only a few days after application, if no one objects) and serves until the permanent personal representative is appointed.

Of course, if you have no estate to administer (that is, no *probate* estate), then it may not be necessary for your personal representative to be appointed by the court, although, as discussed in detail in chapter 2, this does *not* mean you won't need a will. And, in some states, the will must still be filed with the probate court for "informational purposes only" or, under the Uniform Probate Code, the original will need not be filed in the court but instead must be held by a person who could open probate should the need arise.

If you do have a probate estate to administer, then on your death your will is submitted for probate and the court will appoint the personal representative you chose in your will, unless someone objects and claims the named personal representative is unfit to serve. No matter where you made out your will and no matter where your property is located, your will is submitted for probate in the county of your *domicile* at the time of your death, even though you may have died in another county or another state or another country. If you left property in your own name in another state, however, another set of probate proceedings will have to be taken out in that "foreign" state (called "ancillary administration"), but only after your will is first approved and your personal representative appointed in the state of your domicile. Your personal representative would then attend to the ancillary administration of the property in the foreign state. (This is usually a time-consuming and costly procedure and can be completely avoided with proper planning, as explained in chapter 11.)

The personal representative's bond. To secure the performance of his duties without damage or loss to the estate, the personal representative is required to file a "bond," which is simply the personal representative's personal promise to pay or make good any such damages or losses caused by him. This, of course, is only helpful if the personal representative is financially able to repay the loss, and it also assumes he is still around to do so! If you leave your millions and all probate assets to your children, and your personal representative takes title to your probate assets and runs off with your spouse and your money, the personal representative's personal bond won't do the children much good, since he and the money are gone. For this reason, most states require the personal representative to have "sureties" on the personal representative's bond. A surety is someone *else's* personal guarantee that if the personal representative causes losses to the estate and doesn't pay (or runs off with the money), then that person who provided the guarantee will pay. A surety can be personal (another individual) or corporate (an insurance company that insures against the executor's losses). Using individual sureties is less costly because you would normally use a friend or relative, and it is unlikely that he or she would charge you for this favor. Perhaps if friends and relatives realize the potential risk, however, they would charge you, if they agreed to do it at all. In most instances, they sign as sureties on your bond without fully understanding what it means. Clearly, a corporate surety is best for the estate, and although it does involve a cost to the estate, it is usually very reasonable in light of the added safety it offers.

Unlike Herman Oberweiss, however, many testators have so much confidence in their personal representatives that they include a provision in their wills that *dispenses* with the personal representative's bond, and many but not all states allow this. Most of the states that do not allow the dispensation of a bond will instead allow the dispensation of sureties, so that the personal representative must give his personal bond but need not secure guarantees on it. Whenever a bond is required, the personal representatives will not be appointed by the court until the bond is filed with the court. In general, most prudent professionals feel that a bond should always be required, whether you have a brother like Adolph or not.

Who Can or Should Be Your Personal Representative?

You are free to choose just about anyone you want to act as personal representative of your estate, within certain limits of course, and if your choice is within these limits, the court is obliged to follow your choice in most cases. Generally, you may not appoint a minor or incompetent person or, in many states, a convicted criminal. Otherwise, the appointment will not be rejected even though the person is extremely old, or suffers from a handicap, or has no business experience, or is a heavy drinker, or is a creditor of the estate, or is a witness to the will, or is a beneficiary, or is thought to be mentally or morally "impure." Having all this in mind, it is relatively safe to say that the law recognizes your right to select any competent person you choose and does not demand a high standard for the position. This is not to say that a court would approve an appointment that would lead to nothing but trouble, but, in general, it would give preference to your selection.

Don't forget that apart from court approval, one other approval is essential to your selection of personal representative—that of the personal representative himself. It's a good idea to discuss the matter with the person you choose to be sure he will accept the position. After all, it is not an easy job you are assigning him, there is personal liability that can result from mismanagement of the role, and he can, if he wishes, decline the appointment after your death. If this happens, then the successor personal representative named in your will (if, in fact, you named one) steps up to the plate—to decide again whether to accept or decline.

Since there is this right to decline, as well as the possibility of the personal representative you originally selected dying before you or becoming ill, or, in the case of a lawyer, a bank, or a trust company, going out of business, or for any other reason being unable to accept the position, you should always name at least one successor personal representative. Although there is no limit to the number, it is rare to see more than two successors named. If you initially name two or three co–personal representatives (that is, "I appoint my sons Andrew and Alexander as co–personal representatives of my estate"), you must consider whether you want one or the other to serve alone if either can't serve.

You can also make the appointment conditional upon some other occurrence, such as the attainment of a certain age, completion of college, remaining single, being a resident of your state, etc. Again, if it is against public policy, the restriction may not be enforced by the probate court.

Nonresidents, provided they otherwise qualify, are generally acceptable in most states, although appointing a nonresident may not be a good idea. First of all, there are practical problems a nonresident will face in dealing with property and creditors in another state, as well as in appearing in court, if necessary, and signing documents for the court, etc. Also, there may be added expenses, because when a nonresident is appointed, he must in some states appoint a resident "agent" in the local state for legal purposes. Furthermore, the estate will incur additional expenses in paying for the nonresident's travel to and from the local state to attend to the estate administration. If at all possible, therefore, try to keep your selection local. Even more complicated is the nomination of a personal representative who is not a U.S. citizen and resides outside the United States, thus triggering obvious logistical problems of communication, understanding, and the signing of documents. And, in the modern age of increased regulation of the financial sector, some financial institutions may not even be able to take direction from a non–U.S. citizen.

And if for some reason you are simply at a loss to come up with any logical choice, then you can leave the choice up to someone else. That is, your will can say, "The personal representative of my will shall be chosen by the senior partner of the law firm of Nailem, Dodgem and Chargealot, but shall not be a member of that firm," or, "The personal representative of my estate shall be nominated and appointed by the then-serving Rabbi of Temple Hillel in Boston, Massachusetts," etc. Very few testators use this substitute appointment approach, but if you decide to be one of the few, be sure the person or organization you choose to do the selecting is one that will make a sensible choice, and remember that it is preferable to choose a position rather than an individual (i.e., "the senior partner of the law firm of Clark & Cluck," rather than "John Clark, Esq.").

Whomever you choose or whatever method you use, it must be *clear* and *definite.* If your will is considered to have failed to name a personal representative, the court will appoint one for you. This is illustrated in the case of Marshall Blackburn, who appointed "one of my sisters" as PR of his will. When Blackburn made out the will, all three of his sisters were alive, but when he died only *one* survived him. Therefore, it should have been pretty clear, you would think, that the one sister surviving would be the one to be appointed personal representatives. Not so, the court said. The appointment of "one of my sisters" was ambiguous and therefore an insufficient appointment. The "one" could easily have been either of the two who died, and, if so, the surviving sister would have no right to be named personal representative. To hold otherwise, the court would be rewriting Blackburn's will, and courts are always reluctant to do that. Blackburn could have easily avoided the problem by saying "my oldest sister who survives me," which would have clearly selected a particular one, whether all three or only one survived.

Whether the original or the successor or one nominated by some other source, the personal representative is appointed only after notice is given to all interested parties that he was nominated by you and is about to be appointed by the court, as long as no one has a valid objection. Notice for the appointment of the personal representative usually accompanies and is integral to the notice for the probate of the will. Anyone objecting to the allowance of the will automatically objects to the appointment of the personal representative, since there can be no personal representative without a will. It is quite possible, however, to consent to the allowance of the will but object to the appointment of the personal representative simply by wording your objection accordingly, but remember, you can't object simply because you don't like the person; you must have some valid grounds for objection.

As noted earlier, the standards for appointment of a personal representative are not very high, so grounds for objection are somewhat limited. That is to say, the person named by the testator in his will is normally appointed by the court, despite lack of intelligence or experience and despite the fact that the named person stood in a hostile or potentially hostile position with the heirs and beneficiaries. For example, we have seen a number of cases where the testator named his ex-wife as personal representative to administer the estate for the benefit of his widow, and at least one case where a married man named his paramour as personal representative. In all such situations, although the family and beneficiaries may fume with anger over the appointment, there is usually very little they can do, absent incompetency or undue influence, since that particular relationship does *not* disqualify the personal representative from serving. In such cases, the court's response is, "We must appoint her; but if she subsequently fails to properly perform her duties as personal representative, you are free to ask us to remove her."

Good choices/bad choices. Whether you made a good choice or a bad choice in naming your personal representative—that is, whether your personal representative will accomplish a smooth, tax-wise, and efficient settlement of your probate estate or whether he will instead milk the estate dry, prolong settlement, make questionable tax decisions, and continually fight with the beneficiaries—can only be determined after the fact. Other than the protection offered by the personal representative's bond, there is no guarantee that your lawyer will do a perfect job, or that a bank won't botch up the investments, or that your brother-in-law won't run off with the money. There are, however, some guidelines that may help reduce the possibility of a bad choice.

The first issue to consider is whether you should choose a professional, such as an attorney or a bank, or a nonprofessional, such as your spouse, your brother-in-law, or your barber. To a great extent, this depends upon the size and nature of your estate. If the estate is of moderate size (i.e., no complicated tax issues involved) and very liquid (i.e., savings, investments, and a home), and if you do not anticipate any family disputes, then we would say it would be acceptable to have a family member, such as a spouse and/or an adult, responsible child, as personal representative of your estate. If you do anticipate family disputes in the settlement of your estate (even though it may only be over who gets the grandfather clock or mother's engagement ring, which is often the start of a larger dispute), then you should consider having an independent, disinterested personal representative, not necessarily a professional but at least someone outside the immediate family.

If, on the other hand, your estate is somewhat more extensive, such as one that includes income-producing real estate or out-of-state property or a closely held business, or anything else that will require expertise in handling, or if the estate is simply a large one, then you should definitely consider a professional personal representative. If you do have a professional, remember that you can also name a family member to act as *co–personal representative* with the professional. This way a member of the family can keep closely involved with the process of settlement as well as all the necessary decisions and elections that must be made, and this in turn will remove some or all of the mystery that often accompanies a professional's handling of the estate that can make a family suspicious.

If you do make a bad choice (of course, *you* will never know it—unless cryonics works, you go into the deep freeze, and come back to check out how your estate was handled), your beneficiaries do have the right to ask the *court* to remove the personal representative, as discussed in detail later in this chapter. As you will see, you might also consider giving them the right to remove the personal representative and appoint another. Although there is no certainty the *court* will honor your directions (we know of no case or law on the issue), it certainly can't hurt.

Powers of the Personal Representative

How many of you have heard the story about the newspaper advertisement that read, "Practically New Cadillac Sedan in Perfect Condition. Estate Must Sell—$50." Most readers dismissed the ad as a hoax, but one adventurous young man decided to check it out. Sure enough, he found a gorgeous, gleaming Cadillac, and the seller, who was the personal representative of the deceased owner's estate and also his widow, confirmed that the young man could have the car for only $50! It seemed, so the story goes, that in his will, the widow's late husband specified that his Cadillac was to be sold and the proceeds paid to a close "personal friend" of his who turned out to be his mistress. Is this a true story? Did the widow/personal representative have the power to do this?

One of the most common misconceptions about personal representatives is the extent of their powers in administering an estate. It is often thought that the personal representative has the ability to change or withhold bequests or to otherwise exercise control over how estate assets will be sold or distributed, disregarding the provisions of the will. *This is simply not so.* As noted several times before, the personal representative's job is simply to settle the estate and distribute the remaining assets *according to the terms of the will* and in the best interests of the beneficiaries, whoever they may be.

The story of the Cadillac, the widow, and the significant other, therefore, is *not* true. If it were true up to the point of the sale for $50, then the story would go on to say that the significant other asked the court to order the widow to pay, out of her own pocket, the difference between the $50 and the fair value of the Cadillac. And the court would do it.

In fact, the personal representative's powers are derived from the will. That is, your will can contain extensive powers for the personal representative or none at all. If no powers are specifically granted, it is nevertheless presumed that the personal representative has the basic powers necessary to carry out the terms of your will and the settlement of your estate, with the possible exception that if real estate must be sold, the personal representative must obtain formal permission from the court to do so (a "license to sell"). Although many simple form-book wills omit reference to the personal representative's powers, it is unwise to do so—if there is a subsequent question of his authority, he must appeal to the probate court to decide the question, which adds unnecessary delays and expense to the settlement of the estate.

For this reason, attorneys drafting wills will usually grant the personal representative all "statutory" powers given by the particular state (most states have standard powers that may be granted simply by reference to the particular law), or they may enumerate specific powers. It is not unusual to make these powers very broad so there will be no question as to the personal representative's authority to enter into any necessary or advisable transactions in the settlement of the estate. For instance, a personal representative may, and in some cases should, be granted the power to employ agents, attorneys, stockbrokers, etc.; to exchange, mortgage, or lease property; to lend or borrow money on behalf of the estate; to compromise claims (reach a settlement with the claimant) for or against the estate; to retain existing investments or make new investments; to take control of digital assets; and, if a business is involved, to continue the business.

Whether you want or need to grant any or all of these powers to your personal representative depends on the size and nature of your estate. The important thing to remember is that even though you may grant your personal representative broad powers, it does *not* mean that he can change your wishes as expressed in your will. For instance, the power to "mortgage, lease, or exchange property" does *not* mean that your personal representative can swap the Cape Cod summer home you left to your daughter for a winter home in Florida, nor does it mean he can place a big mortgage on it or lease it to someone else before he gives it to her. The only reason he would be authorized to do any of these things would be if it became necessary in the course of settling the estate for payment of debts, expenses, and taxes. And as discussed in chapter 8, specific bequests are generally the last items to be touched for payments of estate expenses.

Remember, it is the duty of the personal representative to act in the best interests of all parties of interest in the estate, and this clearly includes the beneficiaries, whether or not they all get along.

Fees of the Personal Representative

Under early English law, the personal representative of an estate was considered to be an honorary position (and it still is, to an extent), so his services were to be performed without compensation. In the United States that practice quickly changed. It is well established that personal representatives are entitled to "reasonable compensation" for the services they render to the estate and the beneficiaries, and this is the case even though the personal representative may also be a beneficiary of the estate. Taking a fee is certainly not mandatory, however, and, in fact, it is not uncommon for a family member to serve without compensation. But when the personal representative is also a principal beneficiary, there are situations in which taking a personal representative's fee can actually save the estate some money, particularly in larger estates where a tax is due, even though the personal representative's fee is taxable income to the personal representative. For instance, if the estate is large enough to be in a 40 percent estate tax bracket and the personal representative has little other income and is in a 28 percent income tax bracket, taking a $50,000 fee will only produce a $14,000 income tax to the PR, but it will save the estate $20,000, a net savings of $6,000.

To be properly payable, the personal representative's fee should be approved by the court, and it is then normally taken from the residual estate. If a beneficiary objects to the amount of the fee, she would usually do so at the time the personal representative files his account, or as soon as she learns of it if the account is not yet filed. And *don't* confuse the personal representative's fee with the attorney's fee. They are separate and distinct roles and generate separate and distinct fees. The special situation where the attorney also acts as personal representative is discussed below. In both cases, by the way, the fees must always be "reasonable."

What is reasonable depends on the particular circumstances of the case and is based on the amount of time, trouble, and responsibility involved in settling the estate and the manner in which the personal representative performs his duties. It is also based on the value and nature of the assets that come into the personal representative's possession and for which he is held accountable. The question also arises as to *when* the value is taken. Should it be at the date of death or at the date of estate settlement? Or some average value in between? If the estate is worth $100,000 at the date of death, and if oil is discovered on estate land, increasing its worth to $5 million at the time of settlement, what value should be used? Since the size and extent of the estate's assets have a direct bearing on the personal representative's responsibilities, newly discovered assets or an increase in value of existing assets will usually entitle the personal representative to a larger fee. However, if the increase in value has no bearing on his duties or responsibilities, such as a jump in the stock market that increases the value of the estate's investments, then the personal representative's fee would not normally be affected.

Using value as a strict basis of compensation can be arbitrary. For instance, consider the situation of the personal representative of a $200,000 estate consisting of rented real estate and involving battles with tenants, housing authorities, and disgruntled beneficiaries and compare it with the personal representative of a $2 million estate held entirely in bank accounts and publicly traded stocks, all payable to the personal representative (as the beneficiary of the estate): is it fair that the second personal representative should receive a fee four or five times that of the first, when the first may have put in much more time and trouble? In such a situation as that of the first personal representative, it is likely that the court will approve a fee higher than normal in view of the circumstances. In the second situation, however, it is unlikely that a beneficiary (if it were someone other than the personal representative) would be successful in getting a court to *reduce* the fee because the estate was so simple to settle.

The actual amount of the allowable fee varies from state to state. Many states simply adopt the "reasonable compensation" approach with no fixed amount, while others publish a commission schedule, establishing what are considered reasonable fees based on a percentage of the estate. New York, for instance, has a permissible personal representative's fee schedule that is 5 percent on the first $100,000 in the estate, 4 percent on the next $200,000, 3 percent on the next $700,000, 2.5 percent on the next $4 million, and 2 percent on any amount above $5 million. So a personal representative in New York would receive a $59,000 commission on a $2 million estate. Note that this commission may be severely reduced if the personal representative is the lawyer who drafted the will. In that situation, to receive the full commission, the lawyer must make written disclosures of the fee to the client prior to the signing of the will. And if there were *two* personal representatives on a probate estate of $300,000 (less certain adjustments), *each* would receive the full commission! If there are more than two personal representatives, they must split the two full commissions (unless the will provides otherwise). (Many states require co-PRs to share the fee, as discussed below.)

California's schedule may appear a little more "reasonable." Its rates are 4 percent on the first $100,000; 3 percent on the next $100,000; 2 percent on the next $800,000; 1 percent on the next $9 million; 1.5 percent on the next $15 million; and for all amounts above $25 million, a reasonable amount as determined by the court.

If we move the $2 million New York estate to California, the personal representative's fee would "only" be about $33,000. Texas, on the other hand, always likes to think big, and this includes its PR's fees. In this state, the fee can be as high as 5 percent of the value of the entire estate. If our $2 million New York estate were situated in Texas, the fee could be as much as $100,000 (almost as good as being a beneficiary under the will!). Note that these illustrations assume an "orderly" settlement of the estate without will contests, tax audits, or other disruptions.

For a few more comparisons of the fees on our $2 million probate estate:

- In Florida the fee would be $55,000 (and *double* that if there are two personal representatives!).
- In Iowa the fee would be $40,140.

In *all* states the standard fees may be increased, as noted above, if "extraordinary services" are rendered. Extraordinary services that can generate extra fees typically include the sale of real estate, defending a claim against the estate, a will contest or other beneficiary dispute or claim, or handling an estate tax audit.

In any event, it is *always* a good idea for the personal representative to *keep very careful records* of the time he spends on all estate matters, including details of conferences or trips made on behalf of the estate and conversations and conferences with the estate attorney. This information can be very valuable in the event that the personal representative's fees are questioned. It can also be valuable if the personal representative changes her mind about taking a fee, such as when she may have thought at first no fee would be charged, because perhaps the personal representative is a family member, but after the time spent on the matter and considering its emotional toll, she decides a fee is in order (as is a vacation!).

Occasionally, the question of PR fees is addressed in the will. That is, some testators attempt to fix the compensation of their personal representative by providing a specified amount in the will. If a testator does so and the named personal representative subsequently accepts the position, then in most states he is bound to do the job for the stated fee or resign (assuming the court allows him to do so). Some states, although not the majority, allow the personal representative in such a case to ignore or even remove the will provision limiting fees and take a "reasonable" fee instead. If the will provides for no personal representative's fee or a ridiculously low fee, it is likely that most states would nevertheless allow the personal representative to take a reasonable fee, as it would not be in the best interests of the beneficiaries to do otherwise.

Occasionally, a testator who is overly concerned about the personal representative's fees may discuss the matter with his proposed personal representative and reach an agreement for fees. If you are certain that this person will outlive you and you have a pretty good idea of when you will die and how large your estate will be at the time, this might be a good idea, since the personal representative would be bound by the agreement he signs with you, assuming he subsequently accepts the position. In general, however, such agreements are rare, since few people are in a position to foretell the future.

Where there are two or more co–personal representatives, the question of fees can be a problem. Should they divide a single fee? Or should each take a full fee? Unfortunately, the states are not consistent on this point. Some require them all to share a single fee, others allow a full fee to each, while still others simply look at all of the services performed and attempt to arrive at a reasonable fee for everyone concerned, which would appear to be the fairest approach. In view of this, if you plan to name three or four co–personal representatives, you should first check the law in your state (if you care about the fees).

Frequently, because the testator has so much confidence in his attorney, he will name the attorney as personal representative of his estate. This raises the obvious question of whether the attorney should be allowed a fee for acting as personal representative, as well as a fee for acting as attorney for the estate. There have been various arguments over the years, but today's view is that a personal representative who also performs services as the attorney for the estate is entitled to fees for all services rendered in both capacities, provided that such fees are disclosed to the client in an "engagement letter," which the client signs, and are reasonable under the circumstances. In any case, remember that any interested party has the right to object to both personal representative's fees and legal fees and that both the personal representative's fees and the legal fees must be approved by the court.

Removing a Personal Representative

Removal of a personal representative is always an adverse proceeding, where the personal representative and the parties seeking removal each have their own counsel. There is a court hearing, and a decision is made on the matter. This shouldn't be confused with the voluntary resignation by the personal representative when he simply does not want to or cannot continue his duties. (Even in that case, the personal representative's resignation is valid only when accepted by the court, and there must be a valid reason for it, although it is usually accepted, provided the resigning personal representative files his accounting up to the time of his resignation.) Forcible removal of the personal representative by angry beneficiaries is entirely another matter.

Once the personal representative is chosen by the testator (as stated in the will) and appointed by the court, the creditors and beneficiaries of the estate are usually stuck with him unless he dies or becomes incompetent, or unless they can prove serious misbehavior on his part. This is not to say that it is impossible to remove a personal representative, only that it is very difficult. In most cases, beneficiaries wish to remove the personal representative because he is moving too slowly, or he is rude and unfriendly toward them, or he acts like the estate "belongs" to him, or he repeatedly refuses to give the beneficiaries information, or he keeps the estate funds in a bank account instead of investing in something else. None of these reasons is grounds for removal.

The general rule is that a court will remove a personal representative only for "cause," that is, if it can be *shown* to the court that he is *incapable* of performing his duties, or that he is *unsuitable* for the position, or that he has breached his fiduciary duty, or that he mismanaged the probate estate, or that he has become *disqualified* since he was appointed.

Disqualification would occur, for example, where the personal representative was convicted of a crime (unrelated to the estate) and sent to jail. Becoming incapable of serving would include, as mentioned before, any physical or mental disability, whether permanent or temporary, that would prevent him from performing his duties. A breach of fiduciary duty would occur where, for example, the personal representative misappropriated funds from the estate or engaged in a transaction with the estate to his own benefit. The last criterion, "unsuitable," is the one that requires constant interpretation.

Although the term *unsuitable* can encompass a variety of conditions that would cause a court to question a person's ability to impartially serve as personal representative, two that seem to arise more than any others are *conflict of interest* and *misconduct* by the personal representative. Conflict of interest might occur, for instance, when the personal representative is required to sell closely held stock from the estate to a company in which he himself is a stockholder. As personal representative he would want to sell at a high price, whereas as stockholder he would want to buy at a low price. By itself, this type of situation is *not* a reason to remove the personal representative. If the deceased knew that the situation would arise when he named the person personal representative, then it is highly unlikely that the court would second-guess the deceased. If the situation arose subsequently, there is still not cause for removal, unless it can be *shown* that the personal representative is about to conclude a sale of the stock at a price unfavorable to the estate. At that point, the court might remove him as personal representative, and, of course, he would be personally liable for the loss.

Perhaps the most common reason for removal or attempted removal of the personal representative is misconduct, which for all practical purposes is often a breach of fiduciary duty. As noted above, what constitutes the necessary level of misconduct to warrant removal may be one thing in the eyes of the beneficiaries and quite another in the eyes of the court. Generally speaking, the misconduct has to be pretty serious, to the point where it is actually damaging or threatens to damage the estate. It can include everything from habitual drunkenness to stealing from the estate. In between, causes for removal would include failure to file an inventory or accounting (although filing late is not cause for removal), failure to obey a court order, failure to perform his duties as personal representative, and generally any waste or mismanagement of the estate. Some of these terms, such as *waste* and *mismanagement,* are as vague as the term *unsuitable,* and about the only way to explain it is by referring to the U.S. Supreme Court's response when asked to define pornography: "We can't define it," the Court said, "but we know it when we see it."

A clear example of misconduct that constitutes grounds for removal was in a case involving an estate that included four pieces of income-producing real estate. Some of the real estate needed repairs, and so the personal representative hired carpenters and painters to do the work. While they were at it, however, the personal representative thought he might as well have them do a little work on his own home, to the tune of about $11,000. The workmen obligingly billed the personal representative for work done on estate property, including the work on his home. The charge was only discovered when one of the beneficiaries checked the accounting and thought the bill for repairs was unusually high for the work done. An investigation quickly revealed what had happened and the personal representative was just as quickly removed, but only after he repaid the $11,000 plus interest to the estate.

Misconduct is not always so clear, however, and not always the type of misconduct that warrants removal. In another, slightly more colorful case, Arthur Friswald, a widower who left his entire estate to his three daughters, thought he was wise in choosing his accountant, John Hoopes, as his personal representative. In performing his duties as personal representative, Hoopes found it necessary to communicate regularly with the sisters, and in doing so, he became somewhat friendly with them. In fact, he became more than friendly with two of them and began seeing each privately. Neither realized he was having an affair with the other, until one night when one decided to confide in the other and told her of the affair with Hoopes.

Not surprisingly, the two sisters became furious, and in addition to certain other actions and epithets irrelevant to this book, they immediately petitioned the court to remove Hoopes as being "unsuitable" for the position. In his own defense, Hoopes pointed out that he faithfully and meticulously performed his duties as personal representative of the estate, and his relationship with the sisters in no way interfered with this. He further pointed out that he did not charge the estate for any of the private "conferences" he had had with the sisters. The court had to side with Hoopes. As contemptuous as his behavior may have been, the court said, it was unrelated to and did not affect the proper performance of his duties as personal representative of the estate. The fact that Hoopes performed additional "duties" was not cause for his removal.

As angry as they were over the court's denial of their petition, the Friswald sisters reached an increased state of rage when they found that their father's estate would have to pay the legal fees for Hoopes's "defense" and that they would have to pay their own legal fees.

In fact, as a general rule, the question of who pays the costs for the removal proceedings depends upon the outcome. If the incumbent personal representative successfully resists the attempted removal, his legal fees will be paid out of the estate on the basis that there was found to be no wrongdoing, and it is in the best interests of the estate to keep the personal representative on board. On the other hand, if he is found unsuitable and is removed, then the removed personal representative will not only pay his own legal fees but may be ordered to make restitution to the estate for any damages, which may include the return of fees previously paid to him.

Similarly, if the parties seeking to remove the personal representative are successful (the action may be brought *only* by a party interested in the estate), then their legal fees may be paid from the estate, on the basis that their action resulted in a benefit to the estate, in the form of removal of an unsuitable person who interfered with the proper settlement of the estate. If unsuccessful, like the Friswald sisters, they pay their own way.

To possibly avoid situations like this, a testator might consider including a carefully drafted provision in his will allowing the beneficiaries to remove the personal representative, if in *their* opinion he is unsuitable or becomes unsuitable for the position. Although there is no law on the validity and effectiveness of such a provision, and although one could argue that since the personal representative is appointed by the court, his removal is solely within the power and discretion of the court, there would nevertheless be no harm in including such a provision. The most that could happen in such a case is that the provision would be ineffective and ignored, and the best (short of it helping to facilitate a removal) is that the personal representative, upon seeing such a provision, may simply be more careful about doing his job properly for fear of testing the removal provision in court.

Keep This in Mind

Choose your personal representative (executor) carefully, largely on the basis of competence, not closeness to you. It can be a time-consuming and stressful job, and you are not doing the selected person a favor. If you really want a close relative or friend to direct the settlement of your estate, consider naming an experienced professional as a co–personal representative to serve with the layperson.

10

Will Contests, Lost Wills, and Beneficiaries' Rights

I leave my cousin Irving the sum of one dollar, and I wish absolutely that he not get a penny more under my will. He has been responsible for my death and God will punish him. If he fights this will in any way, I shall always haunt him and do everything possible to scare him.

—from the will of Quincy Bigger

At some point, the threat of a possible will contest crosses the mind of just about everyone who makes a will. It is commonly thought that anyone who is related to you can somehow challenge or upset the settlement of your estate just by hiring a lawyer to contest the will, and it won't matter how *well* the will was drawn, unless you left the rascal one dollar.

Can *any* will be contested by *anyone* who wants to make trouble for the deceased's estate? At what point can the will be contested, and who pays for it? Did Quincy Bigger have to leave his cousin one dollar to prevent a contest? If threatening to haunt the potential contestant, as Quincy said he would do, is not enough, is there anything else you can do?

Although the facts of a juicy will contest can have all the excitement of an Agatha Christie novel and therefore often make the headlines, only a very small percentage of wills are contested, and most of the contests are *unsuccessful.* Studies have shown that over 99 percent of all wills offered for probate are ultimately admitted to probate. Unfortunately, the potential threat from a practical standpoint is not whether the contest will be successful but whether an attempt at contest will be made. This is because many disgruntled, would-be beneficiaries will hire an attorney to contest the will and "tie up" the estate, primarily in the hopes of forcing a settlement rather than on the basis of legitimate grounds for a contest. Given the tremendous expense of litigation, questionable claims are all too often settled, although they lack merit. As we will see, however, the laws are gradually changing in this area, and contesting a will is no longer a matter of mere whim or angry reaction.

In any case, don't confuse a *contest* of the will with a *claim* against the estate. If the deceased owed you money for goods or services, or for a loan you made to him, or if he has property of yours that you intend to get back, the necessary procedure is to make a claim against the estate *after* the will is allowed by the probate court, which in most cases is a lot less expensive and time-consuming than contesting the will.

Who May Contest Your Will

Contrary to popular belief, not anyone can contest a will. The general rule is that only persons "interested" in the estate have standing and are allowed to contest the will. A person is "interested" in the estate if he stands to gain something if his will contest is successful. For instance, if you die without a will, your estate will pass to your spouse and children in various percentages depending on the controlling state law. Therefore, a child often has standing to contest a will, since if he is successful in overturning the will, he will gain a share of the estate. As pointed out in chapter 7, however, this does not mean that you *must* leave something to your children. It is not that they have a *right* to a share of the estate, but only that they have *standing* to contest your will if they have grounds for a contest. If a person would receive more under the terms of your will than he would receive if you had no will or under a prior will, then he may not contest it, since he would not gain anything even if he were successful. A person who seems to have no connection with the deceased may nevertheless contest a will that excludes him if he were mentioned in a previous will (and can prove it).

In general, all "heirs" who would inherit if you left no will, but *not* heirs of the surviving heirs, have standing to contest the will. For instance, say that your only living relatives are your mother and brother. The law provides that if you die without a will, your mother will inherit your entire estate. You make out a will leaving everything to your companion, Clarence, who is despised by your brother but accepted by your mother, since he has always been kind to her and never failed to remember her on Mother's Day. On your death, your brother desperately wants to contest your will, but your mother does not. In this case, only your mother has standing as an heir to contest the will, and there is nothing your brother can do unless he was mentioned in a previous will. If, on the other hand, your mother died before you, or even after you but within the allowable period for filing a will contest, then your brother would have standing, as he would be your direct heir (if your mother predeceased you) or he would be able to contest the will as the beneficiary of your mother's estate.

Remember that a spouse's taking his or her "forced share" as explained in chapter 7 does not constitute a contest of the will. The forced share is a statutory right regardless of the provisions of the will.

Because of the "interested party" requirement, you need not, as a general rule, worry about stepchildren or divorced spouses, although these are often the source of the greatest concern to testators. A divorced spouse has no standing to contest, even though he or she was mentioned in earlier wills as a spouse. A stepchild has no right to inherit, but if a stepchild was mentioned in an earlier will, he or she would have the right to contest, as would any other beneficiary who had been omitted in a subsequent will. In some cases, the court's strict adherence to the interested-party rule where stepchildren are concerned can appear unfair and unjust, as in the case of Sally Everbrook. Sally's mother was divorced from her father, and when Sally was six years old, her mother married Sally's stepfather, Douglas Huber. Shortly after the marriage, Sally became known as Sally Huber. She was enrolled in school under the name Sally Huber, was baptized under that name, with the baptismal records showing Douglas as her father, and all school and hospital records showed her as Sally Huber and Douglas Huber as her father. And although Douglas had never legally adopted Sally, he continually referred to her and treated her in all respects as if she were his natural daughter. In 1978, Sally's mother died, and about a year later, her "father," Douglas, died.

Douglas's will, which was made out just after his marriage to Sally's mother, left his estate to Sally's mother, if she survived, otherwise to his brothers and sisters.

Sally contested the will on the basis that considering all the facts and circumstances as well as the behavior and acknowledgments of Douglas, she should be considered his legal heir and be entitled to inherit at least a share of the estate. The court conceded that Douglas clearly treated Sally as his daughter, but this, unfortunately, did not change the fact that she wasn't his daughter. *Douglas,* for some reason, never legally adopted Sally and, therefore, she had no standing to contest the will or take a share of the estate.

In other will contest situations, there may be no family relationship at all, but merely a business connection between the deceased and the contestant. In one case, for instance, the testator made out a will leaving a substantial share of his estate to a business, the Mantis Corporation, to allow it to use the funds for business purposes, and left his stock in the corporation to other family members. Later, he made out another will, leaving nothing to the business and everything to his family. When the second will was offered for probate, a stockholder of the Mantis Corporation contested its allowance. The family asked the court to reject the contest on the basis that the stockholder had no standing to contest the will. Not so, the court said. Standing is not restricted to beneficiaries who are actually named in the previous will, but includes persons who may be affected by the carrying out of the terms of the will. As a stockholder of the Mantis Corporation, the contestant would have indirectly benefited by the previous will and, therefore, was definitely in a position to contest the subsequent will.

Creditors of the estate do not have the right to contest the will, nor do creditors of a beneficiary or heir in most cases. It is possible in many states, however, for a contestant to "assign" his rights to contest a will to someone else. In other words, an heir who has standing to contest could transfer his right to contest to another person either by sale, gift, or exchange, like any other property right.

When it comes to will contests, you can't eat your cake and have it too. If you have accepted benefits from the estate, you cannot then turn around and contest the will, unless you can show you were somehow deceived into accepting such benefits just to prevent you from contesting the will. This might happen, for instance, where the personal representative offers you money or other property as a part of your "share" of the estate and has you consent to the will without seeing it. If this happens and you later wish to contest the will, you should attempt to return whatever was given to you to preserve your right to contest.

Grounds for a Contest

You *cannot* contest a will simply because you don't like the provisions, or because you received less than you felt you should have received, or because the provisions were, in your opinion, unfair. You must have *legal* grounds, which, if supported by the evidence, would cause the will to be rejected by the probate court. Briefly, legal grounds include:

1. **Lack of testamentary capacity**—the testator was insane or incompetent at the time the will was signed.
2. **Improper execution**—there were not enough witnesses, or for some other reason the will was not properly signed.
3. **Undue influence**—someone took advantage of the testator's susceptibility and caused him to make out a will different from what he would have made on his own.
4. **Fraud or mistake**—the testator was induced to sign the will as a result of fraud, deceit, or mistake.
5. **Revocation**—the will was canceled or revoked by the testator.
6. **Bogus will**—the will offered for probate was not the will of the decedent. (This might include forgery, for instance.)

You needn't choose only one of these grounds to contest the will. If you have evidence that could lead to rejection of the will on more than one ground, you may contest accordingly. For instance, you may feel that there has been undue influence, but you may also have evidence that, when the will was signed, none of the required witnesses was present. The comments that follow on the several grounds are for your general understanding only and are not an exhaustive discussion of the issues; your attorney will be able to advise you in greater detail. Furthermore, in reading this section on grounds for will contests, remember that in most instances the detailed description of each of the grounds is contained in another chapter; for example, the issues relating to an improper execution and testamentary capacity to make a will are discussed in chapters 3 and 4.

1. LACK OF TESTAMENTARY CAPACITY

As the question of testamentary capacity applies to wills and will contests, it is often very difficult to disprove. The court presumes that the testator was sane and competent, which means that if you feel the testator was incompetent at the time the will was signed, you have to prove it. This could be quite difficult if the will was signed several years earlier, for instance, since it would mean that you would have to produce witnesses and other evidence relating to the specific time the testator signed his will. And remember that eccentricities are not necessarily indicative of incompetence or lack of understanding, and that persons who are suspected of being incompetent can have moments of lucidity, so that even credible evidence of weird behavior and occasional incompetence may not be enough to support a will contest based on lack of testamentary capacity. And if the will was signed in a lawyer's office, you have an even slimmer chance of proving lack of capacity, because most attorneys are extremely careful in monitoring the signing of the will, which normally includes a brief discussion with the testator to satisfy the witnesses that he knows and understands what he is signing.

2. IMPROPER EXECUTION

Assuming there is some substance to the claim, improper execution may not be quite as difficult to prove as lack of testamentary capacity, since it goes to the actual facts and circumstances surrounding the signing as opposed to an evaluation of the state of mind of the deceased from a distance. The requirements for proper execution of a will are discussed in detail in chapter 3, and, if it can be shown that *any* of the necessary requirements was missing, the will may be declared invalid and the contest successful. As noted above, however, if the will was signed in the lawyer's office, the chances of proving improper execution are slim. But many testators (to the delight of many lawyers who are paid to contest wills) write their own wills and also arrange for the signing and witnessing. Such cases are the ones most likely to sidestep an important legal requirement, as in the case of Claude Boxe.

Boxe was a well-to-do widower who lived alone in Buffalo, New York. He hated lawyers and so decided to write his own will. He had a brother, William, with whom he never spoke, and a sister, Virginia, who was a known prostitute. His will, therefore, left his entire estate to his only friend, Stanley Gillis, who lived nearby and was always ready to help Claude when he needed it. Aside from being poorly drafted and neglecting to name a personal representative, Claude's will made it clear that he wanted his brother and sister to receive nothing, and that any claims they made against the will or the estate were to be fought "at all costs, even if it means spending everything on those blasted lawyer's fees."

On the night the will was to be signed, Claude called in two of his neighbors to witness his will. When they arrived, he signed the will and asked them to witness it. Just as the first neighbor stepped forward to sign, the doorbell rang, and Claude left the room to answer it. It was his sister, Virginia, who had heard that Claude made out his will, and she wanted to try to make amends with him. Refusing to listen, Claude slammed the door in her face and returned to the room where the neighbors, who had by then finished witnessing his will, were waiting. Claude apologized for the interruption and then dismissed them with his thanks. Later that night, he wrote a letter to Virginia, telling her never to come to his house again and that he "fixed it" so that she and "that no good brother of hers" would not get a dime from his estate.

About a year later, Claude died and his friend Stanley Gillis offered his will for probate. Virginia and William contested the allowance of the will, however, on the basis that it was improperly executed. When the facts came out, it became clear that there was an improper execution since the witnesses did not sign in Claude's presence, as required by law. But it was Virginia's fault, Stanley argued. She knew they were signing at that time and came to the house for the very purpose of disrupting it. Furthermore, Claude's intentions to omit Virginia and William were clear, not only in the will but also in the letter he wrote Virginia. That didn't matter, the court said. The letter had no legal effect and there was no indication of fraud on Virginia's part. Even if she had planned it, Claude was free to sign his will again (or to acknowledge his signature) in the presence of the witnesses. He did not; the will was not properly executed and was, therefore, invalid. And despite Claude's instructions to fight it to the end, there was plenty of money left to be split between Virginia and William (and their lawyer, of course).

3. UNDUE INFLUENCE

When someone influences a testator to make out his will and leave his property in a manner that he would not have done were it not for the influence, then the will is the result of "undue influence" and invalid. Almost every would-be beneficiary who is left out of a will thinks he has a case of undue influence against another beneficiary who is suddenly named to receive most or all of the estate. This seems to happen very often, for instance, where children are omitted in favor of a new spouse or another child. Unfortunately, undue influence is extremely difficult to prove, as even where it is present, it is usually done subtly, over a period of time, and there is no specific act or incident that clearly reveals it. Therefore, it must almost always be shown by circumstantial evidence. (Here's an example of circumstantial evidence: You checked your mailbox and found some mail. Then you noticed prints in the snow of exactly the type of boot your mail carrier wears in the winter. Although you didn't actually *see* him deliver the mail, the *circumstances* strongly indicate that the mail carrier delivered it.)

To *prove* that your stepmother mentally coerced your father to make out a new will that excludes you is no easy task. It is not enough to show that she nagged him constantly, or that she just pretended to love him, or that she threatened to leave him unless he would make out a will in her favor, or that it is not fair that she should get everything and you, the child, get nothing. You must be able to show that your father (or whoever the testator may be) was *susceptible* to the undue influence of another, that the culpable person (in this case, your stepmother) was in a *position* and had the *opportunity* to exert undue influence, that she did, in fact, exert it, and, last but perhaps most important, that as a result of the undue influence, the testator (your father) *changed* or made out his will in a manner reflecting the undue influence.

As you can see, none of these requirements can be quantified or stated as a specific, identifiable rule of law, the violation of which would make your case winnable. It is not at all similar to proving that the will was not witnessed by two people. With undue influence, every case must be judged on its own particular circumstances, and the courts are required to *begin* their evaluation on the presumption that the will they see before them reflects the *uninfluenced* wishes of the testator. The burden of proving that the testator was unduly influenced rests with the contestant. This is not to say, however, that it is an impossible burden, but rather that because of the difficulty (and therefore, expense) in doing it, the estate must be fairly large before it becomes worthwhile.

Here is one case where it was worthwhile. Nathaniel Cooper was a brilliant businessman who, through a series of shrewd investments, made himself millions of dollars. He owned posh homes in Philadelphia, Manhattan, and Long Island and was attended to by a chauffeur and a battery of butlers and maids. He had one child, Robert, from his first marriage, and a second, Gerald, from his subsequent marriage to Roslyn Cooper. The relationship between Robert and Roslyn was strained.

In the late 1950s, Nathaniel had a serious stroke that left him physically handicapped; although he could get around, he was not the same man. He became hypochondriacal and would regularly carry with him a suitcase full of medications, which helped lead to his becoming anxious and depressed. Throughout this period, his wife, Roslyn, attended to him, and Nathaniel became quite dependent on her. The thought of losing her made him "utterly despondent." Despite this, he had times, particularly in the mornings, when he could transact his business and attend to his investments. He continued to read voraciously and, in general, was in control of his financial affairs.

Nathaniel thought highly of his son Robert and loved him very much. He paid for his education and subsequently loaned him $3,000, but only after the loan was "approved" by Roslyn. He once said, "Someday he [Robert] will be a very wealthy man." Although she approved the first loan to Robert, Roslyn dissuaded Nathaniel from making a subsequent $10,000 loan to him because of their strained relationship, causing Nathaniel to say to his son, "If you could only get on good terms with Roslyn, I could do a lot more for you, but she knows every step I'm up to and she will make my life hell."

Nathaniel made a number of wills during his lifetime, and in every one but the last, Robert was one of the principal beneficiaries. In fact, on July 16, he made out a will, naming Robert as one of the principal beneficiaries, as he had done in the past, but then on July 19, just three days later, he made out another leaving virtually all of his property to Roslyn. It seems that during the three-day period, Nathaniel and Roslyn had a heated telephone conversation, after which Nathaniel went to his attorney and directed him to prepare a new will, leaving almost everything to Roslyn. Nathaniel died about eighteen months later, and Roslyn submitted his "last" will for probate. Not surprisingly, Robert contested it. What's your guess? Was there provable undue influence?

At the probate court level, Robert won. Then Roslyn appealed and she won. Then Robert appealed to the state's highest court, and he finally won. The whole business took almost *ten years* to litigate! And one can only guess at the legal fees involved.

Another interesting and illustrative point is this: the effect of the court's final decision was to throw out Nathaniel's "last" will and revert to the one he executed just before that, under which Robert was a principal beneficiary. But so was Roslyn and so was her son, Gerald! Although Robert "won" and Roslyn was found "guilty" of undue influence (it's not a crime unless some other fraud takes place), this did not affect her share under the previous will.

The problem with illustrating the principles of undue influence through case studies is that no two people and, therefore, no two cases are the same. You may have a situation that appears to have an identical fact pattern to a particular case but could have a totally different outcome in the courts. That is, the same or nearly the same fact pattern may not constitute undue influence if it did not affect the way the testator made out his will. And remember that forcing the testator to *make out* a will is *not* undue influence. The test of undue influence is whether he made out his will exactly the way *he* wanted to, provided, of course, he had not been tricked into doing it.

It has been said that nothing is as intricate as a devious mind, and the challenge of influencing another to do one's bidding without realizing it is too tempting a challenge for the devious mind to pass by. If we start with the premise that we are not allowed to change a person's desire in making his own will, why not offer him facts that themselves will cause him to change his desire on his own? That way, the testator could not be said to have been unduly influenced, since he is doing exactly what *he* wanted to do. For instance, if a woman is convinced that her husband has been unfaithful to her, she may be inclined to change her will *voluntarily* and leave everything (in excess of the husband's statutory share, as discussed in chapter 7) to her children. Then all we need to do is convince her of that (untrue) fact. Would this be undue influence?

In one case based on a similar approach, the children of an ailing testator placed a bottle of poison (complete with a label sporting a skull and crossbones) next to their father's bed, together with a note saying, "Mrs. B., give this to Mr. B. One-fourth of this bottle will kill the old devil; don't put it in his eggs as you did before; put it in his coffee. I'll be over Sunday. G.F." This, together with a few other carefully placed comments and bits of evidence, caused the father, Mr. B., to believe that his wife was trying to poison him, whereupon he made out a new will and gave the bulk of his property to his children. Shortly thereafter he died (*not* from poisoning), and his wife, upon learning that she had been bypassed, contested the disposition of his property. The children made the mistake of telling certain other parties of their plot, and the bottle of poison and the note were found not far from their home. They were ordered to give the property back to their mother. This type of plot overlaps between undue influence and fraud, and to contest the will successfully it is essential that the statements and facts presented to the testator were false and the testator must have relied upon them in making the will. If they were true, then the contestant has no case.

The person perpetrating the undue influence need not be a beneficiary under the new will, although in most undue influence cases it is surely done for the money. It has happened, however, that the undue influence is applied merely to get revenge against a beneficiary or to benefit a person in whom the perpetrator is interested.

Occasionally, the "new" beneficiary will be so eager to get the testator to sign the will that the beneficiary himself will prepare it. Although by itself this approach is not illegal, such a will definitely will be subject to careful scrutiny by the court, and if there is a suggestion of undue influence, the beneficiary will probably have the burden of proving that undue influence did *not* take place. In general, it is *not* a good idea for the principal beneficiary of the will to prepare the will. If at all possible, an independent attorney should be consulted, and she should confer with the testator, privately if possible, and explain the terms of the will. And so long as the attorney is not a beneficiary, your will has a much better chance of surviving an attack. (The question of attorneys as beneficiaries is covered in chapter 14.)

4. FRAUD OR MISTAKE

As mentioned above, these categories, particularly fraud, can often be closely associated with undue influence, and in many will contests the contestant will allege *both* fraud and undue influence. Fraud will occur when the testator makes or signs a will as the result of having been willfully deceived as to the nature or the contents of his will or as to some facts that bear upon the disposition of his property. Mistake is the same, but *without* the willful deceit by a third person. The common element between the two is that the testator acted on false information. The sometimes unfortunate difference between the two is that a will is almost never invalidated because of mistake, whereas it is readily rejected where fraud can be shown.

Fraud can occur either by tricking the testator into signing a will when he doesn't realize it is a will or by giving the testator false information *with the intention of causing* him to make out his will based on the false information. An interesting example of the first variety occurred where one Randolph Brinkley decided that his elderly and ailing neighbor, Ms. Constance Hildreth, should finally repay him for all his "kindness." On a friendly visit to her home one day, Brinkley invited Ms. Hildreth to join an organization, of which he was a member in fine standing, devoted to the care and preservation of cats. Having three of her own, Ms. Hildreth was pleased to sign the "application form" that Brinkley had conveniently brought with him.

The form was actually Ms. Hildreth's will, neatly printed and leaving her entire estate to Brinkley. Realizing that the will had to be witnessed, Brinkley then visited two more of his neighbors and asked them if they would "sponsor" Ms. Hildreth as a member of this wonderful organization for cats, and they did.

Not long after, old Constance checked out of this life, and Brinkley brought the will in for probate. It quickly occurred to him, however, that he might have a problem when the witnesses were asked to testify that they saw Constance sign the "will." His only solution, he thought, was to get rid of the witnesses. So, on another of his neighborly visits, Brinkley brought them a gift of some delicious breakfast cake. Saving it for the next morning, the neighbors left it on their table. In the meantime, while the neighbors were out, the landlord and his wife stopped by, and within minutes of helping themselves to a bite of the lovely cake, they both died of convulsions. Constance's will was declared invalid and Brinkley was hanged for murder.

The other type of fraud, referred to as fraud in the inducement, is more common than the one in the Brinkley case discussed above. Normally, it results from the concealment of a material fact, which causes the testator to make out his will in a fashion that he would not have done were it not for the false information. An illustration of this not uncommon type of fraud is the Holmes case.

Samuel Holmes made out his will, leaving everything to his two nieces, Daisy and Florence. On Samuel's death, Daisy filed for probate of Samuel's will and listed herself and Florence as Samuel's only heirs (probate petitions normally require a statement showing all the known heirs of the deceased—relatives who would inherit if there were no will—whether or not they are mentioned in the will). The will was admitted to probate, but then another niece, Wilma Hober, surfaced to contest the will.

Wilma offered testimony from witnesses stating that Samuel thought his sister (Wilma's mother) was dead and that she had no children; otherwise, he would have made the will in her favor. There was also evidence to show that

Daisy knew that Samuel had another niece. In fact, Daisy had letters to Samuel from Wilma but destroyed them. And on Samuel's death, she took no steps to notify any heirs other than her sister. From all the evidence, the court concluded that Daisy fraudulently withheld information from Samuel that caused him to make out his will in her favor and differently than he would have otherwise. What is interesting, however, is that the court did not declare the will invalid, but merely the bequest to Daisy. The bequest to Florence was allowed to stand, as she had no part in the fraud, and Wilma got her fair share.

The problems that sometimes arise with the question of fraud are the cause and effect of the fraud. If the mistaken belief had nothing to do with the making of the will, the fraud may not overturn the will. For instance, say that Bartholomew seeks a CPA to head up the accounting department of his company. He hires Morris, who presented a phony résumé. In fact, Morris was not an accountant but had extensive experience as a bookmaker in New Jersey. He does an extraordinary job, however, and becomes so close to Bartholomew that Bartholomew, who has no close relatives, names Morris as beneficiary of his estate. Is Morris guilty of fraud? Well, he may be as to the securing of the position, and if he didn't get the position, then he never would have been mentioned in Bartholomew's will, but does this fraud negate the will? Probably not, since it was Morris's good and faithful performance, as well as his close relationship, that led to the will, *not* his fraud in gaining employment.

Change the facts just a little, however, and we may have more of a problem. Say that Abbie and Kendall meet and fall in love. Kendall proposes, Abbie accepts, and they are married. The only problem is that Kendall is already married, but he decides not to tell Abbie, as he feels it would definitely put a crimp in her day. After they are married, they make out wills leaving everything to each other, as most couples do. Abbie dies first, and Kendall proceeds to take her estate under the will. Can Abbie's parents contest? Was Kendall guilty of fraud?

Or how about this—Abbie is seventy-six and Kendall thirty. Abbie has a few million and Kendall a few dollars. Does this change the picture? Would it matter if they were married for twenty years?

There is no hard-and-fast rule, except that if it can be shown that Kendall lied about his marital status *primarily* to gain access to Abbie's estate, then it is likely the will would be overturned for fraud. On the other hand, if it can be shown that Abbie would have provided for him even if she had known of the deceit (which might have been the case after twenty years but not after one year), then the bequest might be allowed to stand.

Mistake in making a will, as noted above, is virtually the same as fraud but *without* fraud. In the absence of fraud, a will is unlikely to be invalidated on the basis of mistake, except in the rarest of cases. That is, no matter how unfair the results seem to be, the courts will not reject a will simply because the testator mistakenly believed, for example, that his son was dead or that his daughter didn't need the money, or that he didn't know that he left it all to his grandchildren, so long as the mistakes were innocent and no fraud was involved. An unfortunate illustration is the case discussed in chapter 7 where the testator disinherited his son because he mistakenly believed the son was born outside of marriage. Many other cases exist where the testator omitted one relative or another on the mistaken belief that the person was dead. In such cases, the will stands, and the mistakenly omitted beneficiaries have no recourse. The *only* time that there may be relief for mistake is where the mistake is apparent on the face of the will *and* it is equally apparent on the face of the will that the testator would have provided for the omitted beneficiary had he known the true facts. For instance, in the case of the supposedly out-of-wedlock child, the results would have been different if the father's will had said, "I leave my estate in equal shares to my lawful children, excluding my son, Irving, because I believe him to be the child of someone else."

Other types of mistakes, such as a misspelled or incorrect name, or mistake in the description of property, or leaving the same property to two beneficiaries, generally are resolved by offering evidence to the court as to what the testator meant or intended. They are seldom, if ever, reasons for voiding the will, and as a result, they do *not* involve a will contest but merely a request of the court to interpret the terms of the will.

For instance, say that Donna leaves "my apartment number 3 in building 819 to my son, Alexander," but she does not own that one; rather, she owns apartment number 9 in building 813. If it can be shown that Donna intended the bequest to be apartment 9, then the court will acknowledge the mistake and allow her son to take the corrected bequest. Similarly, if a bequest is made to "my daughter's son, Robert Jenkins" and the daughter's son is named Ronald Jenkins, the bequest will be honored.

In the above illustrations, the mistakes do not appear significant, and the intention of the testator can be made clear or confirmed with admissible evidence. More serious issues arise in instances where the mistake is that the testator thought he was signing his will but in fact signed something else. In the case of Constance Hildreth discussed above, the document she signed was not intended to be her will, so it could have no effect as a will—testamentary intent is essential. But what about a case where I sign a document as my will, but which in fact is somebody else's will? Clearly, even though I had testamentary intent and the document was a will, it would nevertheless seem to be the type of mistake that would cause it to be invalid. Or would it?

Consider the odd case of Harvey and Rose Snide of New York. Pursuant to their instructions, their lawyer prepared wills for each that simply gave the whole estate to the other, and if one did not survive, to their children. Each spouse was named executor of the other's estate. In other words, the wills were completely identical except for the names.

They met one evening at a friend's house, with the lawyer and witnesses, for the signing of the wills. Their attorney, Knot Toobrite (not his real name but an appropriate one for him), removed the wills from his briefcase and presented one to Harvey for signing and one to Rose, indicating to each that they were signing their will. The problem was that the lawyer gave each spouse the *other's* will, so that Harvey signed Rose's will and Rose signed Harvey's. (Apparently, even after the wrong wills were signed, Knot Toobrite didn't notice it!) Harvey died, and when his "will" was submitted for probate, the guardian ad litem for Harvey's minor child contested its allowance on the basis of mistake and lack of testamentary intent, since it wasn't Harvey's will! In an unusual holding seemingly inconsistent with prior New York law, the court decided that the facts of this case were unique and that the wills would be reformed to the effect that Rose's name would be substituted for Harvey's where it appeared and Harvey's for Rose's, to conform to Harvey's intentions.

As a practical matter, it is *highly* unusual for an attorney to allow this to happen. After the signing of any documents, let alone a will, any competent attorney would examine each signed page for signature, date, notarization, etc., and the document as a whole would be reviewed for integrity (all pages present and in order, etc.).

5. REVOCATION

Revocation, as grounds for a will contest, would occur when a party offers a will for probate but the contesting party contends that the will has been revoked. This could happen, for example, where a subsequent will had been made, revoking the will offered for probate, or where the will offered for probate has been revoked but the instrument was not destroyed. For instance, a case discussed in chapter 4 describes the testator who threw his will into a fire with the intention to revoke it and left the room. The beneficiary rushed to rescue the will, which was intact except for a slight charring. As pointed out earlier, the will was legally revoked by the testator, but if the beneficiary offers it for probate after his death, the testator is not around to dispute it. It is easy and convenient to offer such examples in a book to illustrate legal principles, but as a practical matter, unless the contestants of the will can offer some testimony or other evidence that the testator thought he destroyed the will, the contest may be lost.

"Partial" revocation, however, is what gives beneficiaries the most trouble and perhaps generates the most in legal fees. Drawing lines through someone's name or bequest in a will and then initialing it generally spells trouble. (In fact, you might just as well write the word *trouble* across the page and leave it at that.) In most states this is not a revocation but rather an invalid attempt at changing the terms of the will, which can only be done through a properly executed codicil. *So don't do it.*

6. BOGUS WILLS

A bogus or inauthentic will generally involves fraud and, like certain other grounds for contest, overlaps with it. The story of Constance Hildreth's cats and Randolph Brinkley, discussed above in the section on fraud, is an illustration of a will that was rejected as not being the will of the deceased. The same would apply, for instance, where the will was originally that of the deceased but someone made an unauthorized change to it, then offered it for probate. This method can be quite difficult to detect, since, in most cases, the will was properly signed by the testator and witnessed according to law. But, as is often the case, those stealing from the dead are usually amateur thieves and don't cover their tracks very well, as illustrated in the case of the estate of Nora Winkle. About five years before her death, Nora had her lawyer make out her will, which was properly signed, witnessed, and notarized in the lawyer's office. The will left Nora's entire estate in trust for her husband for his lifetime, and on his death the remainder was to go to Nora's stepdaughter.

On Nora's death, the will was offered for probate. At first glance everything looked in order. The will was properly signed by Nora, the witnesses had signed, everyone's signature was notarized, and Nora herself had even placed her initials on every page. But something had changed. Instead of the remainder passing to the stepdaughter, the first page of the will stated that on the husband's death, the remainder should pass to Nora's brothers and sisters. Naturally, the stepdaughter stepped in to contest the will.

It seems that after Nora made out her will, one of her brothers went to Nora's lawyer and instructed him to make out a new will because Nora had changed her mind and decided to leave the remainder to her brothers and sisters. The brother specifically asked that the lawyer have the will typed on the *same* typewriter as that used on Nora's first will. The lawyer did so (very unusual without speaking to the client first!) and waited to hear from Nora. Then one day while the lawyer was out, the new draft of Nora's will mysteriously disappeared from his office. In court, he later identified page one of the will in probate as the *second* will he had drafted and *not* the one signed earlier by Nora in his office. The brother (or someone) had placed Nora's initials on the *new* first page, substituted that page for the earlier one, and offered the "original" will for probate. Nice try, said the court, but no cigar. And no will either. The will offered for probate was not Nora's will and was therefore rejected.

How to Contest a Will

The exact procedure for contesting a will varies considerably from state to state, but certain basic steps and principles apply, nevertheless. With the important reminder that this is not a legal textbook and that the assistance of a competent attorney is *vital* to success, particularly in the case of will contests, the following are the basic principles.

States follow one of two methods of probate of a will—the first is *with* notice to the heirs, the surviving spouse, and the beneficiaries under the will, and the second is *without* notice. In those states that allow a will to be probated without notice, such as New Hampshire, the contest of the will is filed with the probate court *after* the will is probated. In these states, you usually have a much longer time within which to file your contest against the will. In New Hampshire, for example, it is generally six months after the probate court has accepted the will. But the longer you wait, the greater the chance that estate assets will be used or expended. Once you file your action to contest the will, however, the probate process is usually suspended until the case can be heard or until interim administrators can be appointed to administer the estate while the contest is proceeding. It may be a period of years after the will is probated, but it is usually tied to the period of administration of the estate. That is, you should file your contest before or within a very short time after the estate is settled and before the court issues a decree releasing the personal representative.

In those states that require notice *before* the will is allowed for probate, such as New York, Massachusetts, and Maryland, you must file your objections to the allowance of the will *before* the date set for the court's review of the will, which is often only a month or less after the petition is filed by the person who wants to probate the will. If you fail to file within that period, you may lose your right to contest the will. A few states that require notice allow you to contest on certain grounds before or after the will is allowed. It is *not* a good idea to wait, however, if you feel you have grounds to contest.

Whatever the state you file in, once your objections to the will are filed, the probate is effectively suspended, and this, if nothing else, gives you a little leverage to gain a settlement if a settlement is desired or possible. But as noted below, do *not* file groundless objections for the sole purpose of forcing a settlement, or you may find yourself with nothing but the requirement to pay legal fees—for *both* sides. If the estate requires management (and it almost always does) while the contest is pending, an administrator will be appointed by the court to continue the administration. Often coadministrators are appointed—one from each side (you should aim for this)—to keep matters honest. But if this is not agreeable to the parties or to the court, an independent administrator (usually an outside attorney) will be appointed by the court to serve until the contest is settled. Of course, the administrator gets a fee for this.

If you decide to contest the will, the very first thing you should do is consult with an attorney to determine whether you have grounds to contest and how soon you must file your objections. Remember, you should *not* delay in consulting an attorney and filing; otherwise you may lose your right to contest. And you want thoughtful legal advice, not a rushed opinion. You should bring with you to your attorney's office copies of any notices you have received in connection with the probate or proposed probate, copies of any correspondence to or from the deceased (or anyone else) relating to his intentions or his estate, copies of any previous wills or trusts that you may have, and, in general, any information that bears upon your contest and involvement with the deceased or his estate.

If your attorney decides you have grounds to object, she will prepare the necessary pleadings to file a formal objection to the allowance of the will (or to revoke the allowance); at some point this pleading must specifically state, in detail, your objections, the *grounds* for your objections, and the *facts* on which your objections are based. While at one time it was relatively easy to tie up an estate on questionable grounds, the current trend in the courts is to *punish* frivolous and groundless objections by requiring the troublemaker to pay the costs and fees for *both* sides, so don't be surprised if your attorney discourages you from proceeding despite what might look to you like a good case.

If you get to the point where it is decided that you have a case worth pursuing and objections are to be filed, the next thing to do is to get out your wallet and get ready for a long, expensive, and unpleasant ride.

Costs and Delays of a Will Contest

After you get over the anger and hurt of being left out of your favorite aunt's will, or your father's will because he left his estate to his new wife, you should think long and hard before you rush in to contest the will. As noted above, the first thing to do is establish whether you have grounds for a contest. If so, then you should think long and hard again because it can be a lengthy and expensive procedure with *no* guarantee of success. Even though you may have what appears to be a solid case, remember that you are bucking a strong presumption that the will is valid and that it accurately reflects the last wishes of the testator. The statistics show that only a very tiny percentage of will contests is successful.

If, despite this, you decide to proceed, you should realize that *you yourself* are responsible for the fees and other costs of the contest, while the other side—the personal representative and the noncontesting beneficiaries—is financially backed by the estate. Assuming that you would not challenge the will unless the estate was substantial in size, this means that they can afford to go the distance, while you may end up mortgaging your home to do so. Most competent attorneys expert in the field will not take a will contest case on a contingent fee (you don't win, you don't pay) basis. There are, of course, exceptions to this, but in most cases your attorney will want a retainer as well as your commitment to pay costs plus his ongoing fees (perhaps at a reduced hourly rate against a percentage of whatever you may win) to pursue the case actively. Costs would include stenographers' costs for depositions (there will probably be a lot of them), investigators' fees, and travel expenses if the depositions must be held in other states. It is not at all unusual for legal fees and expenses to run $10,000 to $75,000 in an "average" will contest and in an "average" estate, and probably much more if it goes to trial. (We have seen legal fees in protracted will contests climb into the hundreds of thousands of dollars!) Considering, again, that you may not be a winner, you must ask yourself if you can afford this kind of sport.

The good news is that, if you are successful, you will at least indirectly recover your fees and expenses from the estate, and the bad guys in most cases must now pay *their* costs out of their own pocket. It's sort of the winner-take-all concept, except that, in some cases, if the personal representative has acted in good faith, the courts have discretion to allow him legal fees, even though the will was ultimately rejected.

You must also consider the time involved. These fees are not expended over a month or two. They are more likely to represent a year or two, and much of your own time is often required. And then there is trial. Even after the preliminary pleadings and "discovery" period (depositions and other sources for information), there are potential delays in finally reaching the time for trial. And if you make it that far, then there is the possibility of appeal. And there may be more than one appeal. Just look at the Nathaniel Cooper case discussed earlier; it took *ten years* for that case to be finally resolved! Unless you have an "ironclad" case, therefore, you might be better off spending the money on a psychological counselor to help you get over the hurt and realize that the money will not make you happier (unless, of course, it is a *really* big estate, the receipt of which has been known to be a mood elevator).

How to Prevent a Contest

Money can be a great rationalizer, particularly where estates are concerned. People who originally would not dream of suing their brothers, sisters, parents, or cousins suddenly feel quite justified in vigorously seeking their "rightful" share of an estate by contesting a will that left them out or did not leave them "enough." It is no secret that will contests are public, painful, and expensive, no matter who wins or loses, but is there a way to prevent or at least discourage a contest?

Basically, there are four ways to prevent a will contest: (1) include an anticontest provision in your will and give the beneficiary something to lose; (2) during your lifetime, enter into a written agreement with the beneficiary where she agrees not to contest; (3) have the will admitted to probate while you are still living; and (4) put all of your property in a living trust.

ANTICONTEST ("IN TERROREM") PROVISION

Although we feel that a provision of this sort belongs in just about every will, for some reason it is very seldom used by the average law firm. While it is impossible to take away a person's right to his "day in court," it is quite possible to discourage him from exercising that right by giving him something to lose if he makes that choice. Because of the lack of an anticontest provision in most wills, the contestant in the majority of will contests has nothing to lose except the expenses of waging the contest. And while such expenses may not be minor, they may pay off in the form of a settlement with the personal representative or the heirs and beneficiaries. What's more, the contestant may still be entitled to any bequest left to him under the will.

For instance, say that Dad has four children, Eena, Mina, Minnie, and Moe. In his will he left Eena, Mina, and Minnie $150,000 each, but only $20,000 to Moe. Moe contests the will and settles with the estate out of court for $30,000. Depending on the terms of the settlement, Moe might not only get this $30,000 but *also* the $20,000 left to him under the will. In effect, Moe has nothing to lose except the cost of the contest. (To make matters worse, the estate will have to pay its own legal fees, which in some cases could have the effect of reducing the other children's bequests under the will.)

An effective way to discourage people like Moe would have been to include an anticontest provision (also called a *noncontest* provision, a *forfeiture* provision, and an *in terrorem* provision) in Dad's will. In simple terms, provisions of this type say that anyone who contests the will automatically forfeits any bequest made to him under the will; this provision is quite enforceable in most states.

Thus, if Dad's will in the example above provided that the $20,000 bequest to Moe was subject to the condition that he not contest the will, it is likely that Moe would have thought twice before contesting the will and waving his $20,000 good-bye, not to mention the out-of-pocket legal fees he would incur. A noncontest clause, however, will be useless to prevent an omitted beneficiary from contesting the estate unless he has something to lose, and this is the price you must pay to discourage the contest.

To make the clause work, the amount at risk must be a meaningful amount to the beneficiary, an amount that will make him think before he rushes to his lawyer's office and starts running up legal fees. The $1 bequests are certainly useless, as are those in the hundreds, we would say. And you can always get creative and offer payments over a period of years, say $5,000 (or more) per year for five years, depending on the size of your estate and how much you want to discourage a contest, but this may only prolong settlement of the estate.

Including a noncontest clause in your will does *not* mean that a contest is legally prohibited. It merely means a contestant will lose his bequest or share of your estate if he attempts to interfere with the probate of the will. If the contestant is willing to risk that loss and the contest is subsequently successful, the presence of the noncontest provision will be moot because the will itself would have been overturned.

For instance, say that you are the victim of undue influence, but you don't realize it. Your daughter has manipulated you into a position where you are totally dependent on her, and, thanks to her stories, you are becoming resentful of your other children. As a result, you make a will leaving 50 percent of your estate to your daughter and 25 percent to each son, providing they do not contest the will. But your daughter is not satisfied with this. Before you sign the will, she changes the figures so that she receives 80 percent and the sons 10 percent each, again with the noncontest clause. The changes are imperceptible and you do not notice them when you initial each page and sign the will. After your death, the sons find out what their sister has done, but now they must decide whether to risk loss of their 10 percent (each) of your estate. What would *you* want to happen in this case?

To prevent such inequities and fraud from escaping judicial review, many experts object to the enforceability of noncontest clauses on the basis that they can discourage an otherwise valid contest and allow a "defective" or fraudulent will to prevail, as in our example above. In fact, a number of states, such as Iowa, Missouri, New Jersey, and California, provide that a noncontest clause will *not* be enforced against a beneficiary who is found to have *probable cause* for his contest. In as many other states, however, including Georgia, Pennsylvania, Massachusetts, and New York, the courts have held that a noncontest clause can be effective, regardless of whether the beneficiary had probable cause to contest the will.

In other words, in the "probable cause" states, even though you had a noncontest provision, the beneficiary could contest the will and still receive his bequest even though he *loses* the contest, *provided* he had good cause for filing the contest. What constitutes probable or good cause will depend on the facts of each case. Obviously, a court can decide if there was probable cause only after a sufficient number of facts have been disclosed.

If you do decide to include a noncontest clause in your will, you must be sure to provide what will happen to the forfeited bequest if the beneficiary does contest. This is called a "gift over," and without it, the clause will be invalid. For instance, you might say (*not* in these exact words), "Any beneficiary who contests this will shall forfeit his bequest, and such forfeited bequest shall pass to the other named beneficiaries hereunder, in equal shares," or, "shall be treated as if the contesting beneficiary has predeceased me," or, "If my son George contests this will, his bequest shall pass instead to my son Charles."

The most frequent problem with this noncontest strategy of giving them something to lose is that if you really want to disinherit someone, you probably don't want to leave them anything like $10,000 or $50,000 (or more, depending on the size of your estate). This problem can be avoided almost altogether by leaving your property through a living trust rather than through your will, as discussed later in this chapter.

Types of noncontest provisions. If you are about to include one in your will or trust, remember to consider whether you wish the forfeiture to apply to the descendants of the contestant. For example, if you left $25,000 to your son John provided he does not contest the will, consider whether John's contest should cause any bequests to his children to be likewise forfeited.

Further, carefully consider what constitutes a "contest." Some attorneys use language that includes "any filing against the allowance of the will." But other proceedings could be filed that do not technically fall under that definition but nevertheless cause trouble and expense for the estate, which is just what you are trying to avoid. Therefore, a much broader definition should be used, including not just the allowance of the will but also the appointment of the personal representative and the administration of the estate generally. Furthermore, instead of filing a formal objection, the would-be contestant could engage an attorney to "investigate the possibility of contesting" but without doing so. That investigation would cost the estate money in the form of additional legal fees in dealing with the would-be contestant's attorney. Thus, the provision might provide that such expenses will be taken from the would-be contestant's bequest, if not forfeited for that reason.

AGREEMENT WITH THE BENEFICIARY

As infrequent as noncontest provisions may be, agreements with the beneficiary are even less common, with one exception—marital agreements. As discussed in chapter 7, premarital agreements or postmarital agreements or separation agreements usually contain a provision that neither spouse will contest the will of the other. Since fair consideration was given for this promise, it will be enforceable and can be used to prevent or stop a will contest in violation of its provisions.

Where beneficiaries other than a spouse are concerned, however, the occurrence is quite rare. If you are not on friendly terms with a beneficiary to begin with, it would seem highly unlikely, to say the least, that he would sign an agreement not to contest your will, even if you paid him. And as to beneficiaries with whom you have a good relationship, they will probably be taking a fair share of your estate anyway, so a noncontest provision in your will would do the trick and eliminate the embarrassment of asking them during your lifetime. Nevertheless, if somehow the unusual circumstances arise, it is possible to enter into an enforceable agreement with beneficiaries not to contest your will.

LIFETIME (PRE-MORTEM) PROBATE OF THE WILL

A New York trust company once reported one of the shortest wills on record—"All to Mother." While it may have succeeded in passing the deceased's estate to his mother, the problem was that he called both his mother and his wife "Mother." Thus, a court had to get involved. Wouldn't it have been great if the deceased could have explained what he meant? Those involved often wish they could just ask the deceased what was meant by one phrase or another, or why a key provision or name was somehow omitted. Instead, contestants are typically faced with long, drawn-out, and expensive battles accompanied by a desperate search for supporting evidence and a knowledgeable expert to prove their case. If only one could offer the will for probate while the testator was alive. Actually, there are eight states at the moment that make this possible. Alaska, Alabama, Delaware, Nevada, New Hampshire, North Carolina, North Dakota, and Ohio all have statutes that offer a procedure for the pre-mortem probate of a will. Although the specific procedure may vary somewhat from state to state, it typically involves a court petition to "prove the will." All interested parties (beneficiaries, heirs, intestate heirs) must receive notice and have the opportunity to respond. Once the will is ruled valid by the court, it may not be later challenged on the testator's death, unless, of course, the testator substantially modified it in the meantime, although some states, such as Arkansas and New Hampshire, allow the modified will to be considered validated. Generally, in other states, a minimal modification, such as a change in the named personal representative, would not reopen the opportunity to challenge, except perhaps for the suitability of the new representative.

The advantages of such a procedure are obvious. A party may be far less inclined to challenge a will while the testator is alive, for fear of the testator's obvious angry or surprised reaction, and far more inclined to do so after his death. A parent whose competency is challenged can defend her competency and is not likely to look kindly on the child who raised the issue. The disadvantages are that in some jurisdictions, such as North Dakota and Ohio, the contents of the will are made public, as with any will contest. Nevertheless, this procedure may be far more effective than an "in terrorem" clause, which causes a beneficiary to lose his share if a contest is made. Of course, an in terrorem clause may still be included in a will offered for pre-mortem approval, provided it is enforceable in the particular state.

But aside from being good cocktail conversation (among lawyers anyway), this lifetime probate process does not help testators in states without these laws, as the procedure is only available to wills made by a domiciliary of the respective state, and many might think they are out of luck if their state law does not contain provisions for pre-mortem probate. Nevertheless, there may be a viable alternative. Four of the above states allow a *trust* to be validated even though there may be no issues or disputes at the time, and the settlor of the trust need not be a domiciliary of the state. So long as the trust is governed by the law of the state, the pre-mortem validation will apply. The problem with the Alaska, New Hampshire, and Nevada procedure in this regard is that they require a formal petition to the court and a subsequent adversarial hearing on the matter, involving time, expense, and publicity. Delaware alone has sidestepped entirely the requirement of a court petition and hearing, and requires only written notice from the trustee to all interested parties. If a person wishes to contest the validity of the trust, whether revocable or irrevocable, the person must petition the court within 120 days after receiving such written notice from the trustee. Failure of the person to do so forever waives any right they have to contest the validity of the trust, but only those who receive notice are bound by the 120-day window.

For purposes of planning in states without these laws, the Delaware pre-mortem validity of trusts law may offer a unique opportunity even though a testator's state does not offer a pre-mortem probate.

USE OF A LIVING TRUST

As we have noted several times throughout this book, your will relates only to property that is in your *probate* estate. It follows, therefore, that the contest of a will affects only the property in your probate estate, and that property passing *outside* your probate estate may not be affected by the will contest. Contesting the will, therefore, becomes worthwhile to the contestants *only if there is a substantial amount of probate property.* Without that, a will contest can be meaningless. For instance, say that Attila, who is single, has an estate consisting of three tons of gold and six small countries, all in his own name. He makes out a will leaving everything to his twelve sons, and nothing to his daughter, Honey. Since all of Attila's property was in his own name, it will pass according to the terms of his will, but *only* after the will is allowed for probate. If Honey contests the will, therefore, all of the probate property will be tied up, and the sons will get nothing until the will contest is disposed of.

Placing the property in joint names with his sons might avoid this exposure to a certain extent, but, as pointed out in chapter 2, jointly owned property can be attacked as probate property and in many instances can be brought back into the probate estate. This is not, therefore, a reliable way to avoid a will contest. So what should Attila have done if he didn't want Honey to inherit?

Attila could have placed the gold and the real estate into a living trust during his lifetime. He could, as discussed in chapter 11, keep control over all the trust assets during his lifetime and provide (in the terms of the *trust*) that, on his death, whatever remained would pass directly to his sons. Although a trust is not impossible to attack, it is far more difficult to attack than a will. A will does not take effect as a legal instrument until the death of the testator and, even then, not until the probate court has allowed it. A trust, on the other hand, becomes effective and operative as a legal instrument as soon as the settlor (the person who creates the trust) places assets into it. Since he does this during his lifetime, and since the trust is operating with his full knowledge and, in most cases, control, it is difficult for a contestant of the trust to argue that the settlor lacked the capacity to do it, that he was unduly influenced, that it was improperly executed, or that someone fraudulently induced the settlor to set up the trust. In fact, it is extremely *rare* to hear of a case where a would-be beneficiary successfully attacked a living trust.

Another reason such attacks are far less frequent and far less successful than will contests is that the contestant has no "leverage." That is, through a will contest, the contest can tie up the assets of the estate for years, preventing everyone from getting the full benefit and use of the property. As a result, the estate has an incentive to settle with contestants just to get rid of them and begin enjoying property. When the assets are in a living trust, however, except in rare cases where trust assets are rapidly disappearing or the claim is over the entire trust, the contestant has no right to tie up the trust assets while he is attacking the trust, and so the existing trust beneficiaries can go on enjoying the benefits despite the contest. Because of all this, trust contestants usually find themselves wasting a good deal of time and money only to find that they have little or no chance of breaking the trust. (For the details on how to have your own trust, see chapters 11 and 12.)

Finally, if you want to double your protection against a contest, you should also consider including an anticontest provision in your *trust* as well as your will. All of the same rules and considerations relative to the inclusion of the anticontest provision in wills apply to its inclusion in trusts. And this includes the necessity of giving the contestant something to lose. That is, as with a will, if you want to discourage a beneficiary from contesting the trust, you should make a bequest to him, conditioned upon his agreement not to contest or attack the trust.

Despite all of this, it seems that if there is enough money involved and someone feels shortchanged, it's a good bet that somebody will contest something for some reason, whether it be under a will or a trust, even though that party may realize that the only guaranteed winners are the lawyers.

Probating a Lost Will

The mention of probating a lost will may cause you to ask two questions: If we are probating a will, even a lost one, what does this have to do with a will contest? And how can you probate a will if it is lost?

As to the first question, it is not unusual for a person to make more than one will. It is also not unusual for someone to offer for probate a will that may not be the last will of the deceased, on the basis that if the last will cannot be found, it must be lost. In cases where, despite a diligent search, the will appears to be lost, many states make the rebuttable presumption that, because the will was in the testator's possession and cannot now be found, he must have cancelled or destroyed it. In such cases, the preceding will, if there is one, may be offered for probate. But not everyone may agree that the lost will was destroyed by the testator, and so they would contest the allowance of the earlier will and, at the same time, offer to probate the lost will, in the manner to be reviewed shortly.

There is also the more devious situation in which the beneficiary of an earlier will who is omitted from the last will destroys the last will and offers the one before it for probate. If the other beneficiaries do not have a copy or any other evidence of the existence of the lost will, they could be out of luck. Furthermore, the same dastardly deed could be committed even if there was no prior will. This would happen, for example, where the wrongdoers stood to inherit more if the deceased died without a will, as happened in the case of LaVerne Ketcham.

LaVerne lived with her two sisters for many years. All three of them being single, they enjoyed a good relationship, and each made out a will leaving her estate to the other two. About two years before her death, however, LaVerne met young Adolfo, who swept her off her seventy-two-year-old feet. After a year of intense courting and romance, they became engaged to be married, and as a gesture of their faith and devotion to each other, LaVerne and Adolfo wrote out new wills leaving everything to each other, whether or not the marriage took place. Unfortunately, only a few months before the scheduled wedding, while LaVerne was boating with Adolfo, the boat capsized and LaVerne drowned.

Grief-stricken, Adolfo immediately asked Laverne's sisters for the will (which she left at home) so he could attend to Laverne's last wishes. The sisters carefully searched through Laverne's private papers, all of which were kept in their home, but said they could find no will. The sisters then petitioned for administration of Laverne's estate on the basis that she left *no* will, in which case the two sisters, as Laverne's only heirs, would inherit her entire estate. When Adolfo raised the question of the will LaVerne had recently signed, knowing that it was among Laverne's papers, the sisters replied that they knew of no other will and that, even if there was one, the fact that it could not be found raised the presumption that LaVerne herself destroyed it with the intention of revoking it. Adolfo continued to object, claiming there *was* a will, but that it must be lost, *not* revoked. He told the court about their pledge to each other, and even offered his own will as evidence to show proof that each provided for the other in a will. Therefore, he said, he should be entitled to Laverne's estate. Was this enough? If the court believed Adolfo's story, could it allow Laverne's estate to pass to him?

Generally, to probate a lost will, you must be able to prove, by satisfactory evidence, the contents of the will *and*, in some states, its proper execution. If a copy of the lost will is available, this would certainly be acceptable evidence of its contents, and if the copy was taken after the will was signed and witnessed, then this would be convincing to help show that it was in fact signed and witnessed. By itself, that may not be enough, however, just as it would not be enough if it were the original. In those states that require evidence of proper execution, one or all of the witnesses must testify as to the execution of the will by themselves and by the testator. In other words, in a "proper execution state," a lost will must be proved just like any other will, except that the original is not available. If there is no copy of the will, the will may nevertheless be proved and probated if evidence of its contents and execution can be determined. This may be difficult to prove, although it is not necessary to prove the exact words of the will, only the substance of the contents and intent. Nevertheless, it is still difficult, since witnesses do not usually read the will and unless there is some corroborating evidence such as testimony or the files of the attorney who drafted it, proof is unlikely to be available. Adolfo lost his case because he did not have a copy of LaVerne's will and had no idea who the witnesses were or who the lawyer was who made it out. Without this, the will could not be reconstructed.

Perhaps one of the most famous (although not terribly fascinating) attempts at probating a lost will was that in Howard Hughes's estate. After the much more interesting case of the "Mormon" will (discussed in chapter 1) was disposed of, it was then contended that Hughes had made out a valid will many years before, but it had been lost. The proponent of the lost will was the Howard Hughes Medical Institute, a charitable organization founded by Hughes during his lifetime. The opponents were Hughes's distant heirs, who stood to inherit what was left of the several billions after the estate debts and expenses were paid. In its 1977 petition to probate the lost will, the institute attempted to show that Hughes had signed a will in 1925, leaving his entire estate to the institute. Although the institute presented a rough draft of the will, it was unable to show that it was ever signed, and could not produce witnesses or any other corroborating evidence of its execution. As a result, the court rejected it and in 1980 decided, once and possibly for all, that Hughes left no will. (Now, if you can just prove you were related to him . . .)

Occasionally, a will can be considered lost even though its whereabouts are known but no longer accessible. In a very bizarre case illustrating the point, justice won out. Young André Laysse was shocked at the sudden death of his wife, but even more shocked when he found that she had left him only the legal minimum from her small fortune. As soon as his wife's will was offered for probate, Andre and his mother went forthwith to the probate court and asked to examine the original will, since they felt his wife was insane at the time she made it out. When the court clerk removed the will from the file, André's mother snatched the will from the clerk's hands and, as the clerk ran around his desk to recover it, she handed it to André, who, according to the *New York Times*'s account of the story, "quickly put it into his mouth, chewed it violently, and swallowed it without a pause, before the eyes of the astonished clerk."

Here was a truly lost will. Unfortunately for André, however, a carbon copy of the will was available, as well as the necessary testimony of the witnesses. Accordingly, the will was probated as written and, in addition to the small amount he was left under his wife's will, thanks to André's antics, he was also left with a case of indigestion.

Keep This in Mind

If you are in charge of settling an estate, just hope there won't be a will contest. Few legal battles are more time-consuming, expensive, and stressful. In fact, if not out of the question, consider resigning your position in favor of an experienced professional who knows the ropes.

If you are the one contesting a will, *be sure* you have

1. An expert opinion that confirms you have a strong case,
2. An understanding of the effect of the noncontest clause if there is one,
3. $25,000 to $250,000 (or much more, depending on the size of the estate and the determination of those you are fighting) to fund your contest, and
4. Lots of time.

11

Avoiding Probate and Wills Altogether

The key here, I think, is not to think of death as an end, but to think of it as a very effective way to cut down on your expenses.

—Woody Allen

Actually, death can *increase* the expenses for many estates, especially when there is a will contest, as we have seen. And even if there is no will contest, everyone knows that probating an estate can be more time-consuming and expensive than avoiding probate. Other than staying alive, then, is there any effective way to cut down on these expenses? Is it really worthwhile to avoid probate? What is the best way to do it? Should you just put everything in joint names?

Avoiding Probate Through Joint Ownership and Other Do-It-Yourself Methods

There are four ways to transfer property at death. Only one is through probate. The other three are the result of some arrangement or disposition made by the deceased during his lifetime but designed to cause a "transfer" at his death. They include: (1) contractual arrangements, such as life insurance, where the promise of the other party to the contract involves a payment or transfer to named beneficiaries on the deceased's death; (2) joint ownership, where on the death of one of the joint owners the jointly held property is supposed to pass to the other; and (3) living trusts. (Gifts and life estates involve lifetime transfers; nothing is actually transferred at death of the donee or life tenant.)

LIFE INSURANCE AND OTHER CONTRACTS

Contractual arrangements that can avoid probate include life insurance policies and company benefit plans, although these are often most seen as probate-avoidance schemes by the average person. When you pay insurance premiums, for instance, you are transferring funds to the life insurance company, and the company agrees to pay the death proceeds to your named beneficiary. Meanwhile, assuming you retain ownership of the policy, you can have access to the cash value of the policy during your lifetime, and on your death the proceeds are paid directly to your beneficiary without the need for the probate process. There is, in effect, a legal contract between you and the insurance company, so no court or other outside party needs to be involved to authorize payment of the proceeds to the person named—*unless,* that is, you make the mistake of naming your "estate" as the beneficiary. Briefly (and as also noted in chapter 2), there are four reasons you would name your estate as beneficiary of your life insurance policies: (1) to make the proceeds available to contestants of the will and creditors of your estate; (2) to increase the probate costs and attorney's fees; (3) to be sure that there will be a substantial delay before your beneficiaries receive the money; and (4) to be sure the proceeds will be subject to estate or inheritance taxes. In case you don't get our drift, if anyone advises you to make your insurance payable to your estate, get another advisor—fast!

Another illustration of a contractual arrangement that avoids probate would be certain company benefits that are paid after the employee's death, under an agreement or contract he had with his employer, such as a deferred compensation agreement. For example, a contract might provide that on an employee's death his spouse will receive $25,000 per year for five years. These amounts are paid directly to the spouse (or other beneficiary) and do not pass through probate, since there was a contractual agreement to pay them to a specific person or persons (or to a trust, as described later) after death of the employee. Note that retirement plan benefits are paid through a *trust* and not the contractual agreement we speak of here.

Finally, certain business agreements can provide that buyouts or interests in the business can be paid or transferred directly to a named person (or to a trust) on death. A partnership agreement, for instance, could provide that on the death of a partner, the partner's spouse will be paid fair value for the transfer of his share to the surviving partners, or that she can become a partner, thereby avoiding the probate of his share.

JOINT OWNERSHIP

Joint ownership of property is probably the most popular way of avoiding probate and transferring property at death, although this popularity may not be justified. The basic understanding of a joint tenancy between two owners is that on the death of one, the survivor automatically owns the whole of the jointly held property. It is thought of as a sort of inheritance.

From a legal standpoint, a valid joint tenancy is not a transfer at death at all, but rather the result of a *lifetime* transfer that "vests" or becomes the property of each succeeding survivor by operation of law. In other words, the property really already belonged to the survivor, subject only to the claim of the other joint tenant. The property, therefore, is *not* inherited. When a joint tenant dies, his interest and any claim he might have held in the joint property disappears, so the property, which belonged to the survivor subject to the claim of the other, is now the survivor's free and clear of any claim. This transfer of ownership is said to take place automatically by "operation of law" and needs no outside action or verification by probate courts, lawyers, deeds, or the like. It can be quite a smooth transition from one tenant to another. That is, of course, if there are no objections. Unfortunately, where money and emotions are concerned, things don't always work the way they are supposed to.

Joint tenancies enjoy as many challenges inside the courts as they enjoy popularity outside of them, because they are treated in such an arbitrary fashion by the creators of the joint tenancies. This, in turn, makes them quite vulnerable to attack.

Using joint tenancies to avoid probate can be extremely risky. It not only invites litigation when there is the slightest question of the deceased's intent but can also (depending on the size of the estate) produce extra taxes and even extra administrative (probate) fees—the very thing the joint ownership was intended to avoid! We have pointed out in chapter 2, for instance, that a disgruntled heir or an aggressive personal representative can take the position that the jointly held property should be *probate* property because it was not a "true" joint tenancy.

Another risk of joint tenancy is the simultaneous death of the joint owners. Basically, this has the effect of converting the joint tenancy into a tenancy in common. This would result in one-half the property passing through the probate estate of each joint tenant, and would bring about extra fees, delays, and taxes, unless the will or trust of one of the joint tenants contains a provision dealing with simultaneous death.

And even if the joint property succeeds in passing to the survivor on the death of a joint tenant, there is still the problem of the property being probated in the estate of the survivor, who is then the sole owner. To hope that the survivor will create some new joint tenancies in the future is merely to defer to a later date the risk of the same tax (discussed below), probate, and legal problems.

A possible and important exception might occur when the home—the principal residence—is held jointly by spouses. (In some states there is a special kind of joint ownership for spouses called "tenancy by the entirety," which affords a degree of creditor protection.) Seldom are there objections or interferences with the surviving spouse taking this property on the death of the other. Therefore, unless some other type of ownership is recommended by advisors, married couples owning their home jointly or as tenants by the entirety need not rush out to change the title, unless they want to place it in a trust, which can offer all the advantages of joint ownership with none of the disadvantages. Similarly, a bank account or money market account of "nominal" size in joint names of spouses is helpful for quick access to funds on death or disability of the other. By nominal size, I mean an amount sufficient to meet emergency needs in the context of your particular family's lifestyle.

For some families it may be $1,000, for others, $20,000. You must decide for yourself. (For a discussion of how joint property is taxed, see chapter 13.)

In short, it may happen that joint property will avoid probate, but the risks that it will not, and that even if it does it will produce other problems and concerns, far outweigh the possible benefits.

LIVING TRUST

A living trust, simply stated, is a revocable trust created during your lifetime that usually provides for the disposition of assets that are in the trust upon your death. In other words, you could provide that your living trust will pay out to you whatever you ask for during your lifetime and, on your death, whatever is left would be given to your spouse. Since there has been a lifetime transfer of the property to the trust, and since the trust provides what is to be done with the property on your death, there would be no need for the probate court to be involved in the transfer of those assets on death. (Trusts are discussed in much greater detail in the section that follows.)

The *trustee bank account* is a special breed of living trust and deserves a few comments and caveats here because of its excessive popularity and the unnecessary risks involved. In the typical case, A will place his funds in a bank account titled "A, trustee for B" or "A, in trust for B," each meaning the same thing, which is that A is to have complete control of the funds during his lifetime, and on A's death B takes what is left, without probate in A's estate. This is a flimsy, very risky, but sometimes workable trust arrangement, which, like the joint bank account, *may* avoid probate of the funds in the account in A's estate, provided no one objects. It is quite possible—and there is a good deal of litigation on the question—for A's executor to attack the validity of the "trust" and attempt to bring the funds into A's probate estate. Then there is also the possibility that B will predecease A and the funds will definitely be in A's probate estate. (Note that many people *mistakenly* think that if they place the beneficiary's Social Security number on the trustee bank account, he or she will be taxed on the interest. This is *not* so. Because the trustee has complete control of the funds and no completed gift has been made to the beneficiary, the *trustee* will be taxed on the income, regardless of whose tax identification number is on the account.) Furthermore, all of the funds in the trustee bank account will be subject to tax in A's estate.

Finally, assets in a retirement plan trust, such as a company pension or profit-sharing plan, an IRA or Keogh plan, or an IRA rollover account, will avoid probate provided they are payable to a named beneficiary and *not* payable to your estate. As noted, all of these arrangements are held through a trust, or something similar to a trust, even though you may not have realized it. For this reason, your named beneficiary will receive the funds or benefits without the need for probate.

Everything else you need to know about trusts is covered in chapters 12 and 13. For now, here is a summary of why the living trust option offers all of the advantages of joint ownership—including avoidance of probate—but with far less risk of interference:

Different Types of Co-Tenancies and Their Characteristics

QUESTION	JOINT PROPERTY	TENANCY BY THE ENTIRETY	TENANCY IN COMMON
Survivorship rights?	Yes	Yes	No
Right to sell your share?	Yes	No	Yes
Right to divide (partition) the asset?	Yes	No	Yes
Can creditors reach the share?	Yes	Maybe*	Yes
Included in the estate?	Yes	Yes	Yes
	(Varies 100%–50%)	(50%)	(Your % share)

*Depending on the state where the property is located. A number of states (e.g., New York, Massachusetts, Florida) prohibit creditors from reaching certain property held under a tenancy by the entirety.

Joint Property vs. Living Trust

QUESTION	JOINT PROPERTY	LIVING TRUST
Avoids Probate?	Probably	Yes
Can save estate taxes?	No	Yes
Helps avoid creditor attack?	No	Sometimes
Provides for the unexpected?	No	Yes
Affected by your disability?	Yes	No
Affected by simultaneous death?	Yes	No
Affected by divorce?	Yes	Yes
Easy to obstruct?	Yes	No
Can provide for a succession of interest, such as first spouse, then children, then grandchildren?	No	Yes

QUESTION	JOINT PROPERTY	LIVING TRUST
Can be protected from a beneficiary's creditors?	No	Yes
Can predict outcome?	No	Yes
Reduces overall costs and expenses?	No	Yes

AVOIDING PROBATE IN MORE THAN ONE ESTATE

As mentioned above, any assets that are *in* your living trust at the time of your death will completely avoid the probate process, *provided* that you have named beneficiaries in your trust to receive the assets. For instance, in a typical case, one spouse (the *settlor* or creator of the trust) will create a trust to provide for himself and his spouse while he is alive, and on his death the trust will distribute what is left to the surviving spouse. (In larger estates, this is modified somewhat to save estate taxes—see chapter 13.) In this case, when the settlor dies, the trust assets will be given to his spouse, free of probate, and the assets will then be the surviving spouse's to use and enjoy. But the problem is that at the surviving spouse's later death (or disability), all of the assets will then be fully probated. This can be avoided.

It is quite possible to design the trust in a way to avoid probate in *successive* estates. For instance, in the example above, say that the settlor's trust provided that on his death, all of the assets would *remain* in trust for his spouse's benefit, and the spouse could withdraw whatever was needed. Whatever was not used or withdrawn would remain in the trust, and on the spouse's death, what was left would pass to their children. This would cause the assets to avoid probate in both spouses' estates. It is possible to go even a step or two further and avoid probate in children's estates, etc., but there may be some complicated tax considerations to this and the details should be left to your tax lawyer.

Out-of-State Property—Double Your Probate, Double Your Legal Fees

Probate once is bad enough, but probate twice (or more!) can double the trouble, expense, delay, etc. And this is just what happens when you die a resident of one state while leaving property in another state. For instance, Jack has his home in Massachusetts, a second home in New Hampshire ski territory, and a third home in Florida. Each of the "out of state" properties is in Jack's name alone. On Jack's death, neither the New Hampshire nor the Florida property can pass to other members of his family according to his will until probate proceedings have been taken out in *each* of these states. The procedure is called "ancillary administration" (meaning probate in another state or jurisdiction), and this cannot be done until Jack's will has been probated in Massachusetts and a personal representative appointed. Even under the smoothest of circumstances, all of these procedures could take the better part of a year, not to mention the expense of hiring lawyers in all *three* states. And this is if nothing goes wrong. If Jack's will is contested in Massachusetts, the other properties are likely to just sit there until the dispute is resolved.

There are two simple ways to avoid *all* of this: one way is to place the out-of-state property in joint names. This way, on your death the property will avoid probate in the foreign state and the survivor will receive it straightaway. That's the good news. The bad news is that joint ownership can, as we have pointed out earlier in this chapter, lead to much more trouble than you ever bargained for. Just for openers, what if your joint owner dies before you? And if not, what happens on the death of the survivor? Answer: more probate, then more probate. By far, the better option is the second one, a simple living trust.

By using a living trust to hold the out-of-state property, you can avoid the exposure of double or triple probate, and you can easily provide for contingencies no matter who dies first, not to mention all the other advantages enumerated above. It may be that the particular state in which your property is located requires a special form of trust, but we can assure you, this is nothing compared to the time, trouble, and expense your estate will bear if you leave the "foreign" property in your own name.

Avoiding Probate with a Durable Power of Attorney

Most people associate *probate* with *death.* Few, other than those who have had to deal with it, realize that probate may be necessary during a person's *lifetime*—specifically, on the person's disability or incapacity. If a person becomes legally incompetent to manage his estate, then his financial matters cannot be dealt with unless he has a legal representative appointed to do so. Such a representative is appointed by the probate court in the form of a conservator to act on behalf of the "protected person." Note that if the person is so incapacitated that he is also unable to handle his personal affairs, such as obtaining housing, food, and medical care, the probate court will also appoint a "guardian" to handle these personal needs, and the same person may wear both conservator and guardian hats, or the court may appoint two different people. This bifurcation between the role of the guardian and the role of the conservator is relatively new, and is embodied in the Uniform Probate Code, which many states have enacted.

The procedure for appointment of a guardian or conservator is not unlike the procedure for appointment of a personal representative under a will, including notice to heirs and other interested parties, filing an inventory and annual accountings, and, of course, the opportunity of heirs and interested parties to object anywhere along the way. In other words, it is time-consuming, expensive, and very public, but, like probate at death, *it can be avoided.*

WHY A DURABLE POWER?

It is possible to appoint someone to act legally for you in the event of your disability or incapacity, and this is done through a "durable power of attorney."

The difference between a regular power of attorney and a *durable* power of attorney is crucial in this context. A regular power of attorney may give someone the authority to act legally for you, but that authority automatically *ceases* if you should become legally incompetent. If this happened, then it would become necessary to initiate probate proceedings to appoint a conservator for you despite the existence of the regular power of attorney.

A *durable* power of attorney, on the other hand, survives your disability or legal incompetence and provides that the person or persons you named under the power will be able to act legally for you *even though you are incompetent.* Therefore, at least for purposes of financial dealings, it will normally *not* be necessary to have a conservator appointed for you if you have a valid durable power of attorney. The durable power of attorney, which is recognized in all states, is a legal instrument, signed by you (it is a good idea to have it notarized and witnessed as well, since some states require this), that names a person (it could be more than one) as your "attorney-in-fact" to act on your behalf and do almost everything you could do if you were available.

SCOPE OF POWER

The durable power of attorney can authorize your attorney-in-fact to sign checks, enter contracts, buy or sell real estate, deposit or withdraw funds, enter safe-deposit boxes, create trusts, run your business, make healthcare decisions on your behalf (although this is more appropriately done through a "healthcare proxy," in itself a form of durable power of attorney), make gifts and other transfers of property that you might have made (*including transfers to your living trust*), and just about anything else that you could have done, all *without* the need of seeking probate court permission to do so.

Note that the power could also be restricted to certain acts or for a certain period of time. While this type of "temporary" power is not the one usually contemplated in an estate plan, it can be useful when, for instance, you are going to be away for a while and want to appoint someone to handle financial matters during that period. Or perhaps property is scheduled to be purchased or sold during your absence. You can appoint someone to negotiate and sign any documents, including a deed, to carry out the transaction in your absence. In any event, the power of attorney must be a *durable* one. Nowadays it is almost impossible to get any third party to deal with or honor a power of attorney that is not a durable one.

Obviously, giving someone all this power is a two-edged sword. While it ensures privacy and will save money and avoid publicity, the durable power of attorney at the same time can place tremendous powers into the hands of your attorney-in-fact. Actually, she could wipe you out with little trouble, and your only recourse would be to sue her (for breach of her duty to you), *if* you could find her. So be careful whom you select as your attorney-in-fact. Some advisors feel that a fair safeguard to this potential problem is to name *two* attorneys-in-fact, who must act together on your behalf. We agree that this will at least reduce the risk, but it also necessitates two signatures on every transaction if you want the precaution to work.

THE SPRINGING POWER

When they hear of the extent of the powers that are customarily given to the attorney-in-fact, some people get a little nervous about it and ask if there is another way, especially if the chosen attorney-in-fact is someone other than a spouse. For this reason, some attorneys (*not* including the authors) recommend the option of having a power of attorney that does not become effective *until* a doctor certifies that you are unable to care for yourself. This is called a "springing" power, and it will at least defer the risk of being wiped out until you are incompetent, and by then perhaps it won't matter to you. Personally, we think springing powers only invite legal questions regarding the start date, the timing, and continuance of the power.

For instance, a springing power must contain a number of additional, carefully drafted provisions (thereby adding potential problems in themselves) that define specifically what "springs" the power. Is it merely a doctor's letter, or must it be something more formal? Can it be any doctor? Your primary care doctor? A doctor who specializes in incapacity? Two doctors? What must the letter say? (If the language in the letter is unclear, you can bet it will be near useless to spring the power.) Must the letter or certificate be recently dated? What if the doctor's letter is, say, six months or a year old? Does the third party have a duty to ask for a new one? Or a duty to contact the doctor to verify that the letter is still valid? As one can quickly see, the springing power is, in our experience and strong opinion, fraught with potential problems and is generally a bad idea, since there is a much better way to accomplish the same thing.

Instead, we recommend that you have the instrument confer the power *when it is signed*, but advise your attorney (i.e., the lawyer who drafted your documents) to *hold* the instrument in her office vault until some later date or when the incompetence comes about. For instance, say that you sign a durable power of attorney, naming a spouse or a child as attorney-in-fact. Without the original instrument or a copy of the *signed* instrument, your spouse or child has no authority to act under the power. In the meantime, the original is left with your attorney with written instructions to deliver it to the attorney-in-fact upon the attorney's receipt of a letter from a physician stating that you are unable to handle your own affairs. Delivery of the instrument would then allow your attorney-in-fact to act under the power and take any necessary steps to complete your estate plan and carry out transactions, including transfers of assets to your trust. In comparison to the springing power, it would also avoid third-party questions as to whether you were, in fact, incompetent, since the durable power would not require that you be incompetent before it takes effect.

DURABLE POWERS AND JOINT OWNERSHIP

Many people are under the misconception that any assets they hold in joint names with a spouse or other person can easily be reached in case of an emergency or, for that matter, at any time. While this may be true for jointly held bank accounts, and while the *death* of either joint tenant will normally cause the survivor to have complete access to the asset, this is *not* true for jointly registered securities or jointly held real estate while both (or all) joint tenants are alive. In those (and certain other) cases, and in cases where property is held under a tenancy by the entirety, if one of the joint tenants becomes incompetent, the only party that can deal with the incompetent joint tenant's share is the incompetent joint tenant's court-appointed conservator or an attorney-in-fact under a durable power of attorney. Thus, even in the case of jointly held assets, a durable power of attorney can save time, legal fees, and court costs in dealing with assets.

SIGNING SEVERAL POWERS OF ATTORNEY

Where there are two or more family members (or others) that the principal would like to name, but he wants them to be able to act completely independently, there is the possibility of creating and signing separate powers for each. This will work if everyone is in concert and no dispute arises, but if the different parties named should disagree, then the situation could become somewhat chaotic and expensive. There is no simple way to deal with this possibility in the document, so choose your attorney(s)-in-fact carefully.

OUT-OF-STATE POWERS OF ATTORNEY

Most states will honor a durable power that was validly executed in the state of your domicile. This may work for bank accounts or tangible property in the "foreign" state, but it may not help where real estate is concerned. State laws regarding transfers of real estate are very precise, and a durable power of attorney that is valid in one state may not be sufficient to transfer real estate located in another state. Therefore, if you have real estate in more than one state, it would be a very good idea to make sure that your lawyer includes all the necessary varying requirements in a single durable power of attorney or to execute separate durable powers of attorney, each complying with the law of the foreign state with respect to durable powers *and* the laws regarding transfers of real estate. In both alternatives, it is a good idea to have a local lawyer in each jurisdiction "approve" of the durable power of attorney prior to its execution.

COMPENSATING THE ATTORNEY-IN-FACT

Usually the attorney-in-fact is a spouse or other close relative, so compensation is not an issue. Nevertheless, as a "fiduciary," the attorney-in-fact is entitled to reasonable compensation for the services rendered. What is reasonable depends on the circumstances and the nature of the services rendered and is always reviewable by a court if reported, or the durable power itself might include a third party to review compensation requests by the attorney-in-fact, but factors to be considered include the time involved, the responsibility, and the urgency of the matter. It is acceptable, although not necessary, to include a provision such as, "My attorney-in-fact shall be entitled to reasonable compensation for the services rendered in my behalf."

NAMING A SUCCESSOR ATTORNEY-IN-FACT

Your durable power should also provide for a *successor* attorney-in-fact if your named attorney-in-fact ceases to serve. And if appointment of a conservator or a guardian becomes necessary despite the durable power (other relatives could insist on it), then in most states you can also nominate who you would like to serve as a conservator or guardian in the power itself. The probate court will typically appoint the person so nominated, unless someone can establish by clear evidence that the nominated person would be an inappropriate choice.

IT'S NOT THAT DURABLE!

Despite its flexibility and advantages, however, you should remember that a durable power of attorney *ceases at your death.* It is not a substitute for a living trust, and although it will help avoid probate during your lifetime, it will *not* do so on your death.

WHERE TO KEEP YOUR POWER OF ATTORNEY

While many people who do not leave their original documents with their attorney are inclined to keep them in a safe-deposit box, it is generally *not* a good idea to keep your durable power of attorney there. As noted repeatedly, the durable power is the key to dealing with assets and avoiding probate on your incompetence or incapacity. If the document is safely locked away in a safe-deposit box and you become incapacitated, your named attorney-in-fact (or the successor) may not have access to the box, and therefore the document will be useless, at least until access can be obtained. In general, it is a good idea to have your attorney store the durable power of attorney document (most law firms have facilities for the safekeeping of original documents) along with the instructions described above under "Springing Powers" to deliver the document to your attorney-in-fact at the appropriate time. This will avoid the unnecessary hassle, delay, and expense of dealing with the bank (or the court) to get access to the safe-deposit box.

Why You'll Still Need a Will

Even if you think you have transferred *all* of your property to a living trust or have it arranged in some other way to avoid probate, you'll *still* need a will.

This is because there is no way of knowing exactly what you will own and how it will be held at the time of your death. For instance, you may have all of your property in a trust, but then your great-aunt dies and leaves you one-fourth of her estate. Now you have another "asset" in your name, and unless you are efficient enough to transfer this to your living trust (a trust *can* hold *the right* to receive inheritances before they are received but not before the other person dies), your probate estate will include this inheritance.

Then there is property or rights that may arise just *after* or *as a result of* your death. With these types of assets, it is impossible to avoid probate. For instance, say that, for some reason, a death benefit from your employer is payable to your estate. Or you lived in an assisted-living facility that refunds your deposit at your death, and you forgot to have the facility agree to have it paid to your living trust. If you have no will, these amounts (as would *any* property that passes through your probate estate where there is no will) will pass to your heirs under the laws of intestacy.

Another type of "after-death" asset that must pass through probate would be damages resulting from some accident that caused your death. If, for instance, you are struck by a car and you die after suffering for a time, your *estate* would have the right to sue the driver of the car for "conscious pain and suffering" as well as for "wrongful death." Some or all of the proceeds recovered from the lawsuits, depending on the laws of the particular state, would pass under the terms of your will. Without even a simple will, this process becomes unduly complicated and expensive for your heirs.

Finally, as noted in more detail in chapter 2, there are options you have that are only exercisable through your will, such as the naming of a guardian for your minor children and the naming of a personal representative of your choice to be responsible for settling your estate.

Therefore, even when it is virtually certain that there will be no probate, we still recommend that you have a will, exercising all of the available options in accordance with your wishes and having the bulk of your estate "pour over" into your living trust. This way, any loose ends that may arise are covered and coordinated with your estate plan. If it later turns out that, in fact, there is no probate estate and no need to use the will, then the will is simply not actually submitted for probate. Even if it is not actually probated, some states require that any person in possession of a deceased's original will must *file* the will with the appropriate probate court. Other states simply require the named personal representative under the will to retain the original in his possession for a reasonable time.

Keep This in Mind

Although the probate system has developed a bad name over the years, many see it as a necessary procedure that can serve certain essential functions. For one, it operates to validate and approve a person's will, and for another, it facilitates the passage of legal title from the name of the deceased to his or her legatees or heirs when no other title arrangements have been made. Unfortunately, with all the necessary safeguards and reporting, it is generally not a simple and quick process, and it is public. Thus, a movement began around the 1960s to take steps to avoid the probate process, and today most people are aware that there are ways to do so (most commonly joint ownership, beneficiary designations, and trusts). These alternatives help maintain privacy and get our property where we want it to go.

12

Everything You Need to Know About Trusts

Put not your trust in money but put your money in trust.

—from a Chinese fortune cookie

For many years now, trusts have been acquiring increasing allure and attention from large segments of the public. Few people clearly understand what trusts can do or just how they work, but nevertheless, everyone seems to be pretty sure that trusts can do just about anything and can work wonders. That's almost true.

A trust can certainly provide for you and for your family; it can allow easy access to property (such as real estate), bank accounts, and securities while you're alive as well as during your illness or upon your death; and it can certainly save taxes and cause your property to avoid probate.

But there are many different types of trust, and the different trusts contain different provisions. Some may do the job you want, whereas others will not. You must be careful that your trust accomplishes your specific wishes, has all the necessary ingredients, and will do the job you chose it for. To help you understand whether or not it will, you'll need to know something about the basics of trusts and how they work.

The Basics of Trusts—A Working Overview

The fundamental trust arrangement involves a transfer of property to someone on his promise that he will hold it for another according to the transferor's instructions. It is a unique and useful relationship that clearly reflects its very name—a trust. And like many legal principles and relationships, the modern-day trust has evolved over the years to embody the latest legal and tax developments in many different areas. Nevertheless, no matter how complicated the trust instrument may be, the basics remain the same, and if you understand these, you will understand how a trust can help you.

According to some trust experts, the concept of the trust traces back nearly two thousand years to the reign of Emperor Augustus Caesar. At that time, a Roman citizen and his wife, who was not of the Roman Empire, wanted to leave their property to their children, but under Roman law the children were not allowed to inherit because their mother was not a Roman. To circumvent this law, the Roman left his property through his will to a friend, also a Roman, on his friend's promise that he would use the property to provide for the Roman's children after the Roman's death.

As it happened, the friend did not keep his promise. He betrayed the trust that the Roman had placed in him and used the property for himself. Emperor Augustus, shocked at the betrayal, referred the matter to the Roman court for disposition. Prior to this, the use of such a bequest (in trust) had never been formally recognized by the court, but after the emperor's approval, the trust arrangement became so popular that a special court had to be established to answer inquiries and determine the treatment of such cases.

This was one of the earliest recorded forms of a trust (and not all legal historians agree that this was the origin of the trust), but it contains all the basic ingredients of today's trusts. The Roman (called the *donor* or the *grantor* or the *settlor* of the trust) transferred property (sometimes called the *corpus*) to his friend (called the *trustee*), who promised to follow instructions to hold and use the property for the benefit of the children (the *beneficiaries*).

From its simplest form to the most complex, every trust is based on the same principles and contains the same basic elements: a settlor, one or more trustees, some property, and one or more beneficiaries. A *living trust* is any trust that you create while you are alive. It is sometimes referred to as an "inter vivos" trust—meaning "among the living." A trust created upon the settlor's death is a *testamentary trust.*

The trust created by our Roman was a testamentary trust—that is, it was created at his death by instructions contained *in his will.* In order for the trust to take effect, then, the Roman's will had to be approved by a court through the probate process. If the Roman had created a living trust and had transferred his property to the trust *during his lifetime* with instructions for its disposition after his death, there would have been no need for the probate court to make the transfer. *The property already in the trust would have avoided the probate process.*

Interestingly, the evolution of our law of trusts comes not from the Roman law at all but rather from the English common law dating back to the sixteenth century. The discussions that follow, then, reflect in large part the "common law" of trusts, referred to as such because it was developed on a "case-by-case" basis in the English courts. Since then, of course, numerous jurisdictions have peppered the common-law principles with some statutory embellishments. Where important, we will do our best to point them out.

REVOCABLE VS. IRREVOCABLE TRUSTS

Under most living trusts, the creator or settlor will reserve the right to "alter, amend, or revoke" the trust. This simply means he can change the terms of the trust at any time; he can even cancel (revoke) the trust and take the trust property back. In short, the settlor can do whatever he pleases with the trust or with any property held in the trust. The retention of a right to change or revoke the trust—called a *revocable* trust—does *not* provide the donor with any immediate tax benefits but *does* allow the property in the trust to avoid the costs, delays, and publicity of probate if so provided, and it *can* save estate taxes in future estates. Trust language should be *clear* about rights to amend or revoke and exactly what is required to do so. For instance, amendment or revocation is usually required in writing and delivered to the trustee. A change in the trustee's duties or responsibility may require the trustee's consent, but we prefer instead to give the trustee, in such a case, the right to resign rather than a veto power over such amendments.

The opposite of a revocable trust is an *irrevocable trust.* If a trust does not specifically contain the right to amend or revoke, some states' laws provide that it is automatically irrevocable, meaning that it generally cannot be changed "by the donor," but the modern trend is just the opposite. States that have adopted the Uniform Trust Code generally provide that unless a trust specifically states otherwise, the trust is revocable, and this seems like a safer approach. Note, however, that certain powers to change (even revoke) the trust can be given to others, so that while the trust would still be irrevocable as to the donor, it could nevertheless be amended or revoked by another party who is granted the power to do so. Although current tax savings can be realized through the use of an irrevocable trust, you should consider one only after proper advice and counsel. This is because you will be required to give up benefits, if not control, of the property, and since the document is relatively permanent, recovery of the property transferred to such a trust is unlikely. (The tax implications of trusts are covered in detail in chapter 13.)

HOW A TRUST WORKS

Whether your trust is living or testamentary, whether it is revocable or irrevocable, whether it is a simple trustee bank account (as discussed earlier) or a complicated family trust, once the trust takes effect it will work the same way. When property is transferred to the trustee, the trustee immediately begins to manage, maintain, and, if appropriate, invest the trust property, whether it be cash, securities, real estate, or other property, according to the instructions given by the donor. For example, say that John gives $10,000 to Mary with instructions that she give him (John) all the interest it earns, and upon John's death, she should turn the balance over to his sister Adele. Mary's duties are quite clear. She will pay John all the interest up to the time of his death, then she will transfer the remaining funds over to Adele directly. Adele then owns the money outright, without probate; Mary's job as trustee is completed and the trust is terminated.

Of course, the instructions and/or the duties could be much more involved. John could have transferred real estate to Mary, or a large portfolio of securities, and Mary, as trustee, would be responsible for the proper management of the trust property. If real estate, this might include renting the property, and would include keeping it properly insured and in good repair, and so on. If she were holding securities, she would be responsible for keeping track of the progress of the various companies whose stock she was holding, or she might simply hire an investment advisor. In any event, once the property is transferred to the trust, the trustee's responsibility is to care for it while carrying out the donor's instructions and the duties of the trustee.

WHAT CAN A TRUST DO?

The trust instrument is one of the most flexible legal tools available today. Rather than enumerate all that it can do, the scope of its flexibility is better understood by stating what it cannot do: it cannot be created to do anything that is illegal or against public policy. Anything else is permissible. For example, a trust can:

- Run a business
- Provide for minors or elderly or disabled persons
- Pay medical or other bills
- Create and distribute scholarship funds
- Provide for retirement, education, marriage, and even divorce
- Help carry out the terms of a premarital or postmarital agreement
- Hold real estate, cash, securities, or any other type of property
- Provide protection for property against creditors of the donor and other beneficiaries
- Avoid probate and some administrative costs for property in the trust, not just on the first death but on one or more subsequent deaths
- Receive and administer funds for charitable purposes
- Save taxes

Our Roman citizen established a trust to care for his children. Simple enough, and also one of the most common reasons for a trust. The Roman must have been a wise person. Even in the year 5 AD he knew that a youth and his money are soon parted, and that rather than give his children the money outright, it might be better to allow them only the use of the property until they reached an age of greater maturity, when they might better appreciate the value of money and the responsibility that goes with it.

Your reasons for creating a trust may be some, all, or none of the above. Or you may just want to avoid probate. Whatever the reasons, your trust can be specially tailored to accomplish your objectives, leaving little to chance. In light of this, it is foolhardy to rely upon the whimsical joint ownership form to dispose of your property when a simple trust can accomplish the same thing and more, with less risk.

WHO SHOULD BE YOUR TRUSTEE?

If you *fund* your revocable trust (place some or all of your assets into it) while you are alive—and you are foolish not to—then you should usually be your own trustee. Many people—even some attorneys—raise eyebrows at this, since, for some reason, it is regarded by some as a little unconventional. We have had many clients and readers tell us that they have consulted an attorney on the matter and that he or she said it couldn't be done. Regardless of what you are told, even by such poorly informed lawyers, it *can* be done and it is *highly advisable,* assuming you want to keep direct control and access to your funds and other assets. Note that this is rarely the case with an irrevocable trust, and that it is done far more in the United States than elsewhere. In the United Kingdom, for example, it is rarely done.

Under trust law, it is quite permissible for you to be donor, trustee, *and* beneficiary of your trust all at the same time, so long as your trust provides for some other beneficiary (or beneficiaries) after your death—this is called "a gift over." The gift over requirement is a simple one but nevertheless extremely important, for without it, your trust where you are the trustee and beneficiary could end before it begins. This is because the legal concept of the trust is the division of ownership into legal ownership, which rests in the trustee, and beneficial ownership, which rests with the beneficiary or beneficiaries. If A is the sole trustee of a trust that provides for A as sole beneficiary, the law treats the legal ownership of A as trustee as merging with the beneficial ownership of A as beneficiary, and this collapses the trust. If A were to simply add B as beneficiary on A's death, there would be a "gift over" and no "merger of title." The trust would continue with a new trustee appointed to replace A and to manage the property now for B. Naming yourself as initial trustee allows you to maintain full control over your property as long as you wish and are able to do so. In the event of your death or disability, your trust would provide for a "successor" trustee, who would take over that position for you and administer the trust property for your own and your family's benefit.

The successor trustee, who takes over if you are ill or deceased, or if you just don't want to act as trustee, is guided (and restricted) by the terms of your trust and applicable state law. He cannot use the funds for his own benefit (unless the trust allows it) or go against your instructions. If he does, he will be personally responsible for his breach of "fiduciary" duty, the duty of a trustee always to act in the best interests of the beneficiaries and in accordance with the terms of the trust.

Although naming yourself as a trustee is an easy choice, selecting a successor trustee is often not so easy. For larger estates, the successor trustee in many trusts, depending on the provisions, must often be an independent one (unconnected to you or any of the beneficiaries) for tax purposes. This would be the case, for instance, where you wanted the trustee to have maximum discretion to distribute trust income and/or principal to your spouse and children after your death. In this case, having a spouse or child as the trustee could cause a loss of tax benefits, although your spouse or child could serve as a co-trustee with the independent trustee, so long as the trust provides that she may not make unrestricted distributions to herself.

On the other hand, if you don't mind providing for a modest restriction on the trustee's discretion, you *can* name your spouse (and/or children) as successor trustee of the trust under which she is a beneficiary. Yes, you read that correctly. All that is necessary is to include what is called an "ascertainable standard" to guide the trustee in exercising discretion. The actual language would be something like, "The trustee may pay to my spouse such amounts of the income and principal of this trust as the trustee in her sole discretion determines is appropriate for my spouse's health, education, maintenance, and support." The words *health, education, maintenance,* and *support* are the magic tax words that comprise the ascertainable standard and serve to keep the trust assets (i.e., those in the "bypass" or "family" trust) out of the surviving spouse's estate, *even though* she is the trustee and the beneficiary and has wide, but not absolute, discretion on how to distribute the trust property.

Unfortunately, many attorneys like to get fancy and creative with the ascertainable standard and use words, for reasons we are at a loss to understand, that the IRS and the tax regulations have not approved. If the IRS tells us *exactly* how to do it, why mess with it? The simple addition of the word *comfort,* for example, to the four approved magic words has proved *fatal* in a great number of cases, causing the entire bypass trust to be taxed in the surviving spouse's estate. Note that this is not like a $50 fine. The wrong word can cost hundreds of thousands in unnecessary tax dollars.

In many smaller estates (say, $1 million or less—we know that $1 million is not exactly "small," but in terms of modern-day estates and estate taxes, it is considered "small"), the settlor is often named as the initial trustee of the trust that provides for his and his spouse's benefit during his lifetime. On the settlor's death, his spouse becomes the successor trustee and the trust continues for the spouse's lifetime. On the spouse's death, a child becomes the successor trustee, and at that point the child (as trustee) merely divides the remaining trust property (after payment of expenses and taxes) among the children. (More details on the options and tax implications of trustee selection are discussed later in this chapter.)

Our Roman citizen named his friend as trustee, and it turned out to be a poor choice. His friend had no experience in such matters and proved to be untrustworthy. In those days, perhaps, there were few people who could have had much experience, but a more honorable person may have at least carried out the donor's wishes.

Being a trustee may be easy if you are the donor as well as the beneficiary. You can do with the property as you please and you have only yourself to answer to. If you become a trustee where *someone else* is the beneficiary, however, you're in a whole new ball game. Everything you do is subject to review and question by the beneficiaries. Investments, distributions, the timing of both, selling, buying, leasing, preparing and filing tax returns and trust accounts, all must be done with your fiduciary duty in mind; otherwise, you could find yourself covering your mistakes with your own money! People who really understand the serious responsibility and duties involved usually do not wish to act as trustee for someone else unless they have considerable experience—and the time to do it—and are getting paid for it. As a result, when it comes to choosing a successor trustee, more and more people are relying on those organizations that have the experience and the time to give the trust the necessary attention. They are called "corporate" trustees.

A corporate trustee is a bank or trust company chartered by the state to accept funds from members of the public under a trust agreement. Although there may be something to be said against corporate trustees, there are many more important points in their favor. Most corporate trustees have been in the trust business for years and know how to manage a trust. They have a reputation to uphold and so do not want bad press if they can avoid it. They have financial backing and stability, so the chances of their running off with your money are slim, if not nonexistent. Their fees are regulated by law or by the probate court and are required to be disclosed to you before you name them as trustee.

On the other hand, corporate trustees have been accused of being cold and unresponsive to the members of the family, and they have been known to be somewhat stiff and inflexible when it comes to interpretation of the trust provisions. All of these "other-handed" objections, however, can be dealt with by adding two provisions to your trust: First, have your spouse or another family member act as co-trustee with the corporate trustee. This will add the warmth and sensitivity that some feel is lacking in a corporate trustee. Second, give your spouse (or other responsible family member or members) the right to remove—for any reason—the corporate trustee and appoint a successor (corporate or independent) trustee. If your trustee is performing poorly, this will facilitate a transfer to one that has a better record. Be wary of a trust that only permits the family to remove a trustee "for cause," as this simply permits the trustee to litigate the reason for the removal, typically at the expense of the trust itself. We believe an unlimited removal power in most instances is best.

In some cases, the power to remove and appoint a new trustee can have tax implications as noted in this and the next chapter. Furthermore, the power to remove can be abused, and in the wrong hands it can jeopardize the proper administration of the trust; but you'll just have to trust someone. One option for a settlor who worries her children will simply churn through successive trustees until they find one to do their bidding (i.e., simply give them all the money!) is to limit the power to remove to once every two or more years, thus giving a trustee the time to settle in and the children time to learn to work with the trustee.

For "smaller" trusts, say $500,000 or less, corporate trustees are not economical, and in most cases they would not want such a small trust. In these situations, a trusted family member or professional (such as an attorney or accountant) may be your only choice, so choose carefully, and don't forget to consider including the power to remove the trustee in the terms of the trust.

Remember, this is a brief overview. There are many other legal and, more particularly, tax considerations in the selection of a trustee. These issues are discussed in more detail in chapter 13.

THE TERMS OF YOUR TRUST

If you are going to have a trust, be sure it has terms that the trustee can follow and that properly reflect your wishes. The lazy man's trust, the trustee bank account, for example, or the inadequate preprinted form, or the trust from do-it-yourself books or legal websites are a little better than a joint account, but in many cases these options offer more risks. The trustee bank account, as discussed earlier, is a trust that, in effect, has no terms other than the trustee's absolute right to make deposits and withdrawals as he sees fit and the right of the beneficiary (subject to easy interference) to receive the funds on the trustee's death.

In order for the terms of a trust to be carried out, there have to be some terms. Where there is none or where the terms are incomplete or contradictory or confusing, there will be trouble.

The terms may be simple or they may be complicated, but they must be clear. They should cover lifetime distributions of income, principal, or both; the conditions or guidelines for distributions to beneficiaries; and the possibility that a beneficiary may die before the settlor or before receiving his or her trust distributions in full. There should be provisions for successor trustees and for adequate trustee powers, as well as protection of the funds from claims of creditors (called a "spendthrift" provision), to name only a few. Attorneys experienced in drafting trusts are well versed in the numerous provisions that can and should be included, but the following is an explanation of the more important ones.

SPRAY PROVISIONS

A very common and valuable provision seen in most family trusts, and invariably in "dynasty" trusts as discussed later, is the "spray" or "sprinkle" provision. Where there is more than one beneficiary, this provision allows the trustee to distribute (spray) the income and/or principal among the beneficiaries in varying proportions as the trustee feels appropriate, having in mind their individual needs and circumstances from time to time. In other words, the trustee need not make equal distributions among the beneficiaries, but instead can vary the distributions according to their particular needs, which undoubtedly is exactly what the parents would do were they alive. Sometimes a trust will be a spray trust until the youngest child reaches a certain age, say twenty-five, and then it divides into separate shares for each child. Ah, the flexibility of trusts!

STAGED DISTRIBUTIONS TO BENEFICIARIES

One of the considerable advantages of a trust over a will is the ability of the trustee to hold the beneficiary's share over an extended period of time, and during that time to provide for the changing needs of the beneficiary through trust distributions. But the question then arises: "At what point do we give Johnny his money?" If parents die before their children reach a "responsible" age (no one knows exactly what age that is), it is a routine matter to allow for the trust to continue as explained a moment ago, but for how long? Unless a beneficiary is incapacitated to the point of being unable to manage money and will never be capable of receiving a lump sum, or unless there is a dynasty trust that by its terms is designed to last for several generations, we need to think about the best way to make a distribution of Johnny's share to Johnny.

In the typical family trust, after the death of the surviving spouse the trust will provide benefits for the children until they reach a certain age, at which time the trustee pays out the shares and terminates the trust. The "certain age" differs with most families, but even in the case of relatively "small" estates, since we are talking about the distribution of a couple hundred thousand or more per child, certain sensible safeguards must prevail. For instance, most would agree that it is a little foolhardy to hand over $250,000 in cash to a twenty-one-year-old, or maybe even a twenty-five-year-old. And what about larger estates where the children are to receive upwards of $500,000 or $1 million each?

In such cases, estate planners will almost always recommend spreading the distribution over a period of years. This will give the beneficiary the opportunity to learn (hopefully) how to handle the money, or, if he spends it or manages it poorly, the experience is likely to cause him to be that much more careful with the next distribution.

In the typical case, distributions are slated for one-third at, say, age twenty-five or thirty, another third (i.e., half the balance) at thirty or thirty-five, and the balance at thirty-five or forty. Remember that while the child is waiting for these distributions, he remains a beneficiary of his share and can receive periodic distributions of income and principal according to his needs until the final distribution of his share is made. For instance, if a child gets married, or needs help in buying a home or starting a business, the trustee could make lump-sum distributions to the child, even though he has not yet reached the age specified in the trust. Many trusts contain language making it clear that the trustee can make such special distributions. Furthermore, if a child dies before his share is distributed, the trust may provide that the child may decide what happens to the remainder, and to the extent the child does not exercise his power (called a *power of appointment*—discussed later on), the remainder of the share will pass to or be held for the child's children, to be distributed to them at a certain age, or to the child's siblings, etc. This way, the remainder of the child's share avoids probate in the child's estate, although the power of appointment, depending on the type of power it is, may cause the child's share to be subject to the estate tax.

TRUSTEE ACCOUNTING

Most states require a trustee to notify a beneficiary that a trust exists for her benefit. And, at some point but typically on an annual basis, every trustee of every trust *must* account to the beneficiaries for his administration of the trust. Generally, a trustee's account is a detailed financial report of what the trustee received on behalf of the trust, what he did with the assets over the course of the accounting period (receipts, payments, expenses, etc.), and what assets are left at the end of the accounting period. Traditionally (and legally), the normal accounting period is annual, although most corporate (bank) trustees are set up to account to their beneficiaries on a quarterly basis.

Although there is a legal duty for the trustee to account to the beneficiaries whether the trust states it or not, it is nevertheless important to have a provision calling for an account so that the details can be spelled out as to when and to whom the accounts are to be given.

Where the settlor is also the trustee of the trust, it is not necessary that he account to himself. The accounting requirement is normally to protect beneficiaries who are not also trustees. In that event, with rare exception, it is not permissible in most states for the trust to dispense with an accounting, and any trust provision that attempts to do so would be ignored by the courts as being against public policy.

But is it wise for a minor child to know she is a beneficiary of a trust and to know the amount within the trust? What would be the incentive to complete an education, to become a productive member of society, when the child knows there is a couple of million waiting to be distributed to her at age twenty-five? Recognizing this concern, a number of states have passed laws allowing the creator of the trust to dispense with such notice and periodic reports until the beneficiary reaches a certain age, such as twenty-one or twenty-five (the latest age permitted). In the meanwhile, the beneficiary would have no knowledge of the trust or the amount in it. Thus, this arrangement is often referred to as a "secret" trust, a "quiet" trust, or a "silent" trust.

Many of these states allow the settlor to direct that no information regarding the trust be given to the beneficiary until she has reached age twenty-one (for New Hampshire trusts) or age twenty-five (for South Dakota trusts). Depending on the settlor's wishes, a New Hampshire silent trust could be established by a Massachusetts settlor, for example, and when the beneficiary reached age twenty-one, the trust could be moved to Massachusetts. In Delaware, there is no limit to the length of the "silent period," and the trust instrument can tie the silent period to an age of a beneficiary, the death of a settlor, a particular date, or the occurrence of a specific event. During the silent period, a "designated representative" serves as a presumed fiduciary to bind the beneficiary in a nonjudicial or judicial proceeding, to approve trustee accounts, or to institute a proceeding on the beneficiary's behalf.

It is important to keep in mind that the silent trust is still a trust, and except for the nondisclosure feature, the trustee still has the same duties of loyalty, impartiality, and diligence, and the beneficiary still has the same rights of recourse for a trustee's breach of fiduciary duty, except that barring emergency action that right of the beneficiary could be carried out by a surrogate. In that case, the enforcement of such rights by the beneficiary would be postponed until the end of the silent period. It must also be remembered that the trustee is still charged with administering the trust for the benefit of the beneficiary. This would include not only investing the trust fund but also making discretionary distribution to or for the beneficiary's benefit. The only difference here is that if and when the beneficiary receives a distribution, the beneficiary may not ask, "Is there more where that came from?" (Well, she can ask but she won't get an answer.) If there are distributions from the trust, there would likely be tax reporting by the beneficiary, and the trustee would provide any necessary reporting information, but none of this would reveal any meaningful information about the trust.

Due to the restrictive nature of a beneficiary's rights in the silent trust, we believe it would be wise for drafters to provide for the appointment of a "trust protector" with powers that would add flexibility to the arrangement. Such powers might include, for example, the power to amend the trust, change trust situs, or accelerate distribution. Further, the protector or another party (such as the Delaware-designated representative) may be given the right to review and approve the trustee's accounts while the beneficiary is kept in the dark.

Once the beneficiary reaches the prescribed age, or some other triggering event occurs, she would have the right to review all of the trustee's actions and accounts over the years, including the silent period. Thus, some advisors recommend appointing a third party in the trust instrument—like the protector—who can review and approve the trustee's accounts on an ongoing annual basis to provide some closure for the trustee.

The silent trust is not for everyone, and it must fit the particular needs of a certain client. Some might, in fact, consider it harmful, preferring instead for the next generation to be actively engaged in learning the responsibilities of wealth from an early age rather than be shielded from the reality of their future. While opinions can differ, we can all agree that when discovering the goals of our clients, silence is never golden.

Accountings must be given in writing to the beneficiaries (or to a third party in a silent trust) in a form that is reasonable for them to understand. If a beneficiary questions any part of the account or the behavior of the trustee, he has the right to request an explanation from the trustee. Trustees who refuse or mismanage the trust are always subject to review and possible penalties by the probate court. If a trustee is found by a court to have acted improperly, the court will "surcharge" the trustee, meaning that the trustee will be ordered to pay the costs or expenses or damages *out of his own pocket.*

NONCONTEST TRUST PROVISIONS

In chapter 10 we explained how to contest a will and how to prevent a will contest. Briefly, a will contest is prevented by giving the troublesome beneficiary (or his children) a bequest that is *conditioned* upon his not contesting the will. In almost all states, this will work, although some states make an exception if the contesting beneficiary had reasonable cause to wage the contest. Trusts are no different in this respect, except that the provisions in the trust and the will can be coordinated so that the bequest, whether it be in the trust *or* the will, can be conditioned upon the beneficiary not contesting either document or interfering with its operation in some other way.

To illustrate, say that Uncle Sam wants to leave $1 million of his estate to his nephew Bill, but fears that his other two nephews will make trouble. Uncle Sam could leave his other nephews, say, $25,000 each under a bequest in his will and establish a separate living trust solely for the benefit of his nephew Bill. The will could contain a noncontest provision stating that if a nephew either contested the will *or* brought any action to set aside, interfere with, or attack the living trust, he would lose his bequest. Note that, in this case, if the noncontest provision was in the trust and not in the will, it would be ineffective unless the $25,000 bequest was then placed in the trust. That is, the provision must be included in the document that gives the bequest, and the noncontest condition could then extend to cover the other document.

USING PREPRINTED FORMS—OR, THE BEST WAY TO INCREASE LEGAL FEES AND EXPENSES

Everyone likes to save money, and saving money on legal fees is even better. As a result, there is a huge and extremely profitable market in preprinted legal forms of every type, from adoption papers to zoning applications, but by far the most popular have been the forms for living trusts. Being members of the public as well as lawyers, we can understand the feeling that if some lawyers use preprinted or "master" forms, why shouldn't you forget the lawyer and use them as well? But in our opinion, you ought to approach preprinted forms in the same way you would a cheap suit of clothes bought from a mail-order supply house. The price may be right, but you'd be a fool to think it will fit or be fit to wear. So it is with these forms.

On many popular websites and in many self-help books there are several hundred pages of a variety of trust forms, with step-by-step "instructions" on their use. The instructions, however, often fail to take into consideration all gift tax or other tax results (in fact, some instructions could result in additional taxes). In addition, they fail to consider the possible conflicts from one preprinted form to another when compared with your overall estate plan; they fail to consider adequately death or disability of your beneficiaries; they completely overlook coordination from one form to another; and, most dangerously, they encourage you to go merrily along arbitrarily filling in the blanks, without knowing the slightest thing about what you are doing. And for what? For a savings of legal fees, since the last thing you should do—such sites and books tell us—is consult a *lawyer.* The fact that thousands, or hundreds of thousands, or maybe millions of your dollars are involved doesn't seem to mean much to the forms salesforce, but it's an awful risk for your family. The unguided use of such forms *might*, if you're lucky, result in avoidance of probate with some of your property, but it will more likely result in *added legal fees* for court interpretation of conflicting documents, *added taxes,* and *added costs* in the estates of the beneficiaries. You might as well have spent your money on a cheap mail-order suit.

When you think of the tens of thousands of dollars in savings that can definitely—not maybe, as with uncoordinated forms—be saved through the use of a professionally drafted and funded trust, properly coordinated with the rest of your estate plan, it is silly and reckless to try to do it yourself with the help of forms you know nothing about that are mass-produced for the unknowing, uninformed public. The only ones who benefit from these forms are the company who sells them to you and the estate-planning lawyers who help the family navigate the horrors of a failed do-it-yourself plan.

Coordinating Your Plan—Putting Your Trust to Work

Some of you reading this may feel complacent because you already have a trust. If this is so, congratulations—maybe! Set aside your complacency for the moment to see if your trust has been "funded." (Most living trusts typically are *not!*) A trust is funded when property is transferred to it. Your trust will operate or have effect *only* as to that property that has been actually transferred to the trust.

Perhaps the most common estate-planning mistake is having a trust, then failing to fund it. By funding we do not mean a transfer of $10 or $100, or by naming the trust as beneficiary of your life insurance policy. We mean funding it with just about all or at least the major part of your property, as well as naming the trust as beneficiary of your life insurance policies (unless you have a separate life insurance trust, discussed later in this chapter) and, in some cases, provided your tax advisor approves, your retirement plans. Depending on the state in which you live, you may need a different trust to hold your real estate, but this can easily be drafted to coordinate with the terms of any other trust (or trusts) you have.

The big mistake is going to the trouble of having a trust but continuing to hold most of your property in joint names, or in your own name alone. Your jointly held property will, unless someone objects, pass to the surviving joint tenant and *not* to your trust. As to this property, then, your trust becomes worthless. Property in your name will, of course, have to pass through probate. And then it may pass to your trust, but only if that is what your will provides and if no one successfully contests it. In either case, you have lost a very important feature that the living trust offers: avoidance of probate in your estate and possibly future estates. Furthermore, failing to coordinate your assets with your trust could foul up your *entire* estate plan.

For instance, we recently had a case in which a father had gone to a great deal of trouble to create a trust for his daughter who had an intellectual disability. With an attorney's help, he had set up an elaborate, well-drafted trust that provided for the daughter's care for the rest of her life, since she was unable to care for herself. On the father's death, his widow came to us to determine the next step so that the trust could begin to provide for the child. An examination of the father's assets disclosed that everything he owned was in joint names with his wife. Nothing passed to the daughter's trust!

In the more common situation, one spouse will have a marital and a family trust to accomplish his estate and tax planning, but most of his property, being jointly held, will pass outside the trust, rendering the trust useless and frustrating the estate plan unless the family acts fast following the death.

Funding your trust, then, to the maximum practical extent possible will allow you to get the benefits intended by the trust, during life as well as after death. One of the important lifetime benefits is realized if you become disabled. If jointly held securities or real estate is involved, at least one-half the value of the joint property would be "frozen," and in any event a sale would not be allowed until the probate court appointed a conservator for you (or it could be carried out through a durable power of attorney). If, instead, you had placed this property in a living trust, *no* court action would be required. The property would be immediately accessible by the trustee to provide for your care and treatment. This can be extremely important in the case of a widow or widower or other single person.

Once you have some familiarity with the trust concept, call your attorney and ask him how familiar he is with *funded, inter vivos* (living) trusts and whether he can develop an estate plan for you that is designed to *avoid probate.* Be frank and direct in your questions. If your attorney gets overly defensive or tells you that you cannot be your own trustee, he is probably not familiar enough with the area, and you should look around for another attorney.

Most bar associations have lawyer referral services, and they should be able to give you the names of two or three local attorneys who have indicated they have a familiarity with tax and estate planning. But, as discussed in chapter 14, don't assume that the lawyers referred to you are experts either. You may have better luck with a national organization of trusts and estates lawyers called the American College of Trust and Estate Counsel (ACTEC). ACTEC maintains a searchable database of its members (called "fellows") on its website at www.actec.org.

Don't be afraid to call these (or other) attorneys to request an initial conference—preferably a free one. Many attorneys are willing to give you fifteen minutes or a half hour (you shouldn't expect more than that) without charge to determine whether they can help you and to see if the "chemistry" is right.

Once you have selected and met with an attorney, make sure your other advisors are kept in the loop as the estate plan develops. Should you have a wealth manager, accountant, or insurance advisor, it is a great idea to give those advisors permission to talk to your attorney, so as the plan develops your "team" is all working together in your best interest. Such collaboration and openness results in the best plan.

Part of your plan will undoubtedly involve funding or transferring property to your trust (if it doesn't, you probably don't have the right plan). This is the legal move that actually starts your trust. As previously discussed, once the trust is funded, it then takes effect. Funding, or placing property in the trust, is a lifetime disposition of the property, and from that point on the property will be administered and distributed according to the terms of your trust because it is *in* the trust, even though you may be the trustee. Following are basic instructions on how to fund your trust.

BANK ACCOUNTS

Once your attorney has prepared your living trust and you have made the decision to fund it, you should take a copy of the signed trust to your bank and have the bank either change the title on your existing accounts or simply open up a new account in the name of your trust, showing yourself as trustee. The bank will usually want to keep a copy of your trust on file; this is acceptable since its privacy is still respected.

If you are asked for a tax (or entity) identification number (sometimes called a "TIN" or an "EIN"), and either you or your spouse is a trustee of the trust, you should give the bank your Social Security number, since all interest on the account will be taxed to you. If, out of ignorance, the bank insists on a TIN (which is actually against the tax regulations!), this is still not a problem, as discussed in chapter 13. If a third party is trustee, you'll have to apply for a TIN, but all income is still taxed to you. Application for a TIN is done online with the IRS.

Once you have opened a new account in the name of your trust, nothing else will change. You may make deposits, withdrawals, and loans, open new accounts, pay bills, and anything else you would do on your own. The difference is that now the funds in the account are "managed and disposed of" according to the detailed terms of your trust rather than according to chance.

Where all bank accounts are changed to the trust, one must be mindful of any direct "deposits" or direct "bill pay" linked to the bank account(s). Those automatic transactions must be changed so that they are deposited into or withdrawn from the new account titled in the name of trust.

Note that some spouses prefer to keep one joint bank account to use for the payment of day-to-day expenses, and so they do not have to change the "linked" accounts. This is fine as long as it is a "money in, money out" account that rarely has a balance over a nominal amount, such as $25,000. In the unlikely event both spouses pass away at the same time, this type of account can be closed through a relatively simple probate process called "voluntary administration" in most states. To avoid probate altogether, spouses could ask if the bank permits a "pay on death" (or "POD") designation to the joint account, and if so the spouses can name the trust as the POD beneficiary to receive the account when they are both deceased.

STOCKS AND BONDS

Transferring securities to your trust can be a little more involved than transferring a bank account to the trust, but do not be discouraged. Whatever it takes, it's worth it, and there is a shortcut.

If the securities are *registered* in your name or in joint names, you must first determine whether or not you want to transfer them to your trust. Remember that for income tax purposes the dividends or interest on these securities will be taxed to each joint owner equally, and if this arrangement is saving you some income taxes, this might be a consideration. Furthermore, depending on the size of your estate, there may be estate tax implications to changing all of your securities from joint names to a trust, so, especially with larger estates, you should check with your tax attorney first.

A transfer of registered securities to your living trust is effected by signing or by having each joint tenant sign the back of the stock certificate (or a "stock power," which is a separate paper, available from your stockbroker) and by submitting these to the transfer agent whose name will appear on the certificate. Before sending these, you must have the signatures "guaranteed" by a stock-brokerage house or by a commercial bank, so the transfer agent can rely on their authenticity. (Certificates should always be sent by registered or certified mail, or any way that can be tracked and receipt confirmed.) The transfer agent will also want a copy of the trust. Fortunately, there is a shortcut.

We have found that a *much* easier way of transferring securities is through your stockbroker (often now called a "wealth manager" or "financial advisor"). If the securities are in street name (held by your broker) or are registered, you may simply open a *new* brokerage account in the name of your trust and have your broker place the securities into this new account. If you intend later to take delivery of the securities, you will ask the stockbroker to re-register them in the name of the trust. Some houses charge a nominal "accommodation fee" to make the transfer for you, and whatever it is, pay it! Transfer agents are extremely difficult and unnecessarily picky when it comes to trusts, and the aggravation you are avoiding makes the accommodation fee well worth spending.

After the transfer, you, as trustee of your trust, may deal with the securities just as if you personally owned them. There will be no restrictions, except that if you want to trade on margin or deal with options, the brokerage house (for its own protection) will usually request special language in your trust. If you intend to make these transactions, instruct your attorney when the trust is being drafted. If you forgot or did not know, you may amend the trust to add the necessary language (the brokerage house will be glad to tell you the specific language they would like).

As with the bank account, you may "wheel and deal" with your stocks without interference, and if you are disabled, your successor trustee may take over, but his wheeling and dealing is subject to more scrutiny by you and your beneficiaries. You (and the successor trustee) must always remember that the successor trustee may be personally responsible if the terms of your trust are breached. In this way, you and your beneficiaries are protected.

REAL ESTATE

Real estate is unique in many respects. For one, every transaction relating to the property is formally recorded at an official registry. The names of the old owners, the new owners, and the mortgagees, the discharge of mortgages, any attachments, and so on are all on record. And in many but not all states, when the real estate is transferred to a trust, the trust itself is recorded as well. Once the trust is recorded, it may be that any changes or amendments to your trust may also be required to be recorded, and in some cases this could be inconvenient. For this reason, most attorneys have a simple form of trust especially designed to hold real estate.

Before you transfer any of your real estate to your trust, have a local attorney advise you as to any potential tax issues involved, as well as local laws regarding the holding of real estate in a trust, to be sure you are not creating any new problems. For instance, many states do not recognize a declaration of "homestead" that is made on a principal residence held in a trust. Typically, a homestead declaration that is properly made and recorded can protect the residence from attachment and sale by creditors of the homeowner. Although a few states (like Delaware, New Jersey, and Pennsylvania) offer no homestead protection, the protection can be quite substantial in others. In Massachusetts, for instance, it is $500,000 (twice that if the homeowners are over age sixty-two), and in Texas, Kansas, Iowa, Oklahoma, and Florida it is unlimited. Note, however, that the Bankruptcy Abuse Prevention and Consumer Protection Act of 2005 imposes its own overriding limitations on homestead protection. Furthermore, if the property is mortgaged, be sure the transfer does not violate the terms of your mortgage. A bank holding a low-interest mortgage may like nothing better than to call the balance due on the mortgage because of some technical breach of the mortgage contract, even though the new owners are essentially the same as the old. Normally, the mortgage would not be called just because a declaration of homestead is recorded, especially since the homestead would *not* prohibit the bank from collecting on the mortgage note. Federal law prohibits a bank or other lender from calling a mortgage if the transfer of the property is to a living trust under which the borrower or spouse is the beneficiary. In any case, you should consult with your attorney.

Also, it is a good idea to check with your insurance agent. A home in a revocable living trust is just as insurable as a home owned individually, but the terms of the agreement may need tweaking, such as having the trust added as an additional "payee."

BUSINESS INTERESTS

The trust to hold your business interests, whether they be in the form of a partnership, limited liability company, corporation, or sole proprietorship, may be the very same living trust that holds your bank accounts and securities, or it may be a special, separate trust recommended by your attorney. Here, particular attention should be given to selection of the person or organization (the successor trustee) who will have control of the business after you. It should be someone capable of handling that responsibility. If the person or organization you wish to name as successor trustee is different from the person you wish to run your business, this can easily be arranged either by a separate trust or by a special provision in your primary trust. Remember that under a trust you can provide that control of the business will be in one person's name, whereas benefits (payments of one type or another) may go to your family. If the business is jointly held, all of these choices are taken away from you. If the business is held in your own name, all of these choices are delayed by the probate process, and the business is subjected to the other exposures of probate as well.

MOST OTHER PROPERTY

Virtually every type of property may be held in a trust. Anything that is not mentioned above that you wish to put into your trust can be done so, merely by taking the necessary steps to transfer it legally to the trust. If there is a question or the manner of transfer eludes you, just ask yourself, "How was the item transferred to me in the first place?" It may have been by a bill of sale, deed, etc. In most cases, you can use the same approach, although it would not be a sale, since no payment is being made for the transfer to the trust. Then there may be assets that you didn't acquire in an obvious way but you nevertheless own them, such as an inheritance or the royalties to a book you wrote, or a song you composed, or something you invented. Since you are the owner, you would transfer ownership by a "deed," simply stating that you transfer all your "right, title, and interest" to the trust, but keeping in mind that there are federal laws that control intellectual property, and an expert in this field should always be consulted. As such, this is another area where an attorney can help you over the rough spots.

Items of tangible personal property usually have no formal title documentation, with the possible exception of automobiles and certain boats, which have "certificates of title." If you wish to hold tangible items of property in your trust, such as antiques, jewelry, furniture, etc., this can be done through a simple written statement describing the items in detail and indicating that you are holding them in your trust. You may also declare who is to receive the items on your death. Such a statement might say:

> I hereby declare that I have transferred the following items of tangible personal property to the Bove Family Trust, dated August 19, 1988, and that I am holding the same, as Trustee, under the terms and conditions of that trust:
> [list and description of items]

Upon my death, such items are to be divided equally between my two children. If either predeceases me, all to the survivor. If they both survive me and they cannot agree upon a division of the items within three months after my death, my trustee is directed to sell the remaining items and divide the proceeds equally between my two children.

/S/ Alexander A. Bove, Jr.

[Witness and/or notary is generally not necessary, but either or both won't hurt.]

Incidentally, life insurance policies are not usually transferred to a revocable trust, although they may be. Instead, it is customary to name the trust as *beneficiary* of the policies. By itself, this does not constitute a change of *ownership* of the policies. If actual ownership of the policies is to be transferred to a trust, it is usually an *irrevocable* trust, designed to save estate taxes on your death. (In this type of trust, you would *not* be the trustee, nor would you have any control over or rights to the trust assets. See more on this later in this chapter.)

If your plan calls for only one trust and all your property has been transferred to it, you should make a checklist of what is in your trust and keep the list up to date. New property should be acquired in the name of your trust rather than individually, if this is your plan, and you ought to review the whole arrangement with your attorney once each year.

Surprisingly, having a trust does not require any more record keeping than not having one. In other words, if you already have securities and bank accounts in your own name, you would, of course, keep your own records of these. If they are transferred to your trust, you'll keep the very same records, except that the title of those accounts will be in the name of the trust instead of your own name individually. Furthermore, unlike a will, a copy of the signed trust is adequate when you deal with brokers and banks, so the original can be safely left with your attorney or in your safe-deposit box.

Another advantage of a trust over a will is its "geographic" flexibility. When a family moves to a new state, they are often advised to make out a new will. If the same family happens to have a living trust, however, it would not normally be necessary to make out a new trust because the existing trust will be perfectly valid in the new state. And if this family does make out a new will, the new will can easily refer to the existing trust that was made out in the previous state. (Note that if you acquire real estate in the new state, special rules may apply to trusts holding real estate there.)

DIGITAL ASSETS

Do you store family pictures in the "cloud"? Do you have social media accounts for Instagram, Facebook, Twitter, or LinkedIn that you would want closed (or notice of your demise posted)? Most of our lives are tied to online activities, and most of these activities are done individually. In a well-drafted estate plan, your attorney-in-fact under your durable power of attorney and the trustee (or a special "digital trustee") would have been granted the power to access your digital assets, but what happens after you are dead and what kind of access will actually be granted is governed by the terms of use specific to each site. For example, Gmail in certain circumstances will permit access to a decedent's email account by the personal representative; and Facebook has a procedure where a decedent's account can be frozen in time and continued to be accessed by "friends" existing at death. If you would like to explore further how your digital assets will be treated, you should begin by revisiting the terms of use statement for each site you use and care about.

CRYPTOCURRENCY

Cryptocurrency is a complex subject. Suffice it here to say it is a digital (virtual) currency that can be used in the marketplace in a secure fashion. Cryptocurrency can be held in a crypto wallet, with the owner of the wallet having a private key made up of numbers and letters that grant access to the wallet. The key can easily be given to a trustee—write down the numbers and letters on a piece of paper and hand it over. A problem with cryptocurrency, however, is that often the private key is stored on a computer and easily lost when the owner dies, without adequate documentation. That is a virtual disaster.

DON'T LET THE IDEA OF A TRUST SCARE YOU

To many, the thought of a trust seems attractive, but then when they find that they must rearrange title to their assets, they get a little worried. Changing bank accounts, securities, business interests, and real estate can cause you to have second thoughts about the trust and question whether you're "doing the right thing." If this happens, remember that your trust is *revocable*—you can change it or cancel it, in whole or in part, anytime you wish at your absolute whim. Furthermore, *you* can be the trustee, so there is no loss of control.

Once you have separate trust accounts, you will find it much easier to deal with banks and transfer agents through your trust. Furthermore, you will become a little more accustomed to dealing with the trust yourself. In this respect, you will be buying and selling securities, opening accounts, etc., in the name of "John Hernandez, Trustee of the John Hernandez Trust, dated 12/3/04" instead of just "John Hernandez," or "John and Isabella Hernandez as joint tenants." From these basics all trusts are built, and they can be molded into some pretty intricate and complicated structures, designed to meet a myriad of objectives of the settlor. What follows is a brief explanation of the numerous types of trust created and used by attorneys for estate planning, generational planning, business planning, charitable planning, etc., keeping in mind that a competent and expert attorney can combine many of these trusts. Note also that a number of objectives can be satisfied by a single trust (although you should keep in mind that putting everything into a single trust is not necessarily a desirable goal). For instance, a marital deduction trust can readily be combined with a charitable trust or an asset protection trust, and a life insurance trust frequently doubles as a generation-skipping trust or a dynasty trust. Of course, these are all covered in detail in this chapter.

Trusts for the "Family"

THE BASIC ESTATE-PLANNING TRUST—PROVIDING FOR SURVIVING SPOUSE

For a married couple, with or without children, the typical estate plan will include, in addition to wills, durable powers of attorney, healthcare proxies, and one or more living trusts. In some states, such as community property states, one joint living trust can accomplish all the spouses' goals. In other states, especially those that impose an estate tax, two living trusts, one established by each spouse, is the norm. We'll discuss the estate tax in detail in chapter 13. For now we will look at how spouses typically provide for each other in trusts and, where children are involved, for them and possibly future generations.

Perhaps the first question to consider is whether spouses want to provide for each other at all. Most do, but not all. Where the marriage is not the first for each spouse, there may be other considerations. As discussed earlier, you may not disinherit a spouse in most states absent a binding marital agreement to the contrary. So what are the options? Here are but a few options of how one spouse may provide for the other through a trust. For all options, assume the first spouse has died, the living revocable trust is now irrevocable, and the deceased spouse wants the surviving spouse to be the sole beneficiary of the resulting trust:

- Hold the entire trust for the benefit of the surviving spouse. Allow the trustee to make distributions of income and principal to the surviving spouse for any reason. Permit the surviving spouse to serve as the trustee to control investment and distribution decisions. Grant the surviving spouse the power to decide what happens to the trust property at the surviving spouse's death, and permit the surviving spouse to transfer it to anyone in the world. (This transfer power is called a "general power of appointment.") Wow. Seems like complete ownership, doesn't it? The tax authorities would agree, and this trust would be taxed in the surviving spouse's estate at death. If there is anything left in the trust, that is.
- To change the estate tax result, should you wish to do so, and still have the surviving spouse serve as trustee with almost unlimited access to the trust property, the trust can provide that the surviving spouse receives all the trust income but can also limit distributions of principal (corpus) for the "health, education, maintenance, and support" of the surviving spouse. The surviving spouse's power to decide what happens to the trust property at the surviving spouse's death is curtailed a bit—the surviving spouse can decide to transfer the trust property to anyone in the world, including charities, but not to herself, her estate, her creditors, or the creditors of her estate. (This is called a "nongeneral power of appointment.") This trust might still be emptied by the surviving spouse, but what was left at her death would not be subject to the estate tax and would pass to the next generation of beneficiaries under the terms of the trust.
- To still achieve the estate tax avoidance and try to leave a little something for the beneficiaries who follow the surviving spouse (children, charities, friends, and the like), the power to make principal distributions can reside in an independent professional trustee, someone other than the spouse. So if the surviving spouse remarries, she can't just take the money and run, and then leave it to her new spouse.

The deceased spouse's assets are there for her should she need it, as determined by the independent professional trustee, but she must need it, not just want it. Some might find this too restrictive, in which case the surviving spouse can be given the power to remove and appoint the independent professional trustee.

TRUSTS FOR RETIREMENT BENEFITS

Often, one of the larger assets in an estate plan is the retirement plan account. If a spouse has such an account that represents a substantial part of his estate, it becomes important that the benefits are paid out in a way that not only takes advantage of any income tax relief but also qualifies for the estate tax marital deduction. Designating the surviving spouse as outright beneficiary will do the trick, but that is not always recommended by estate planners. Sometimes, where there is a surviving spouse, the settlor's spouse is named as the first (primary) beneficiary, and a trust is named as the second (contingent) beneficiary. The trust might be for the benefit of the spouse (a marital trust) or it might benefit others, such as the children. When this happens, the trust should contain some special provisions to ensure that the distributions to the trust qualify for the best income tax treatment. What is the "best" treatment varies as the law varies, with the most recent changes in the law occurring in December 2019. Briefly, the new law (called the SECURE Act) generally, and with some exceptions for minors and beneficiaries with disabilities, requires a nonspouse beneficiary to liquidate a retirement asset within a ten-year period. The retirement asset can grow income tax free until it is liquidated, at which point the after-tax proceeds can enjoy the protection of the trust structure.

MINOR'S AND CHILDREN'S TRUSTS

There are two types of trust most commonly used to provide for minors and children: "Minor's trusts" and so-called "Crummey trusts." In both cases the trusts are generally used to effectuate gifts to benefit minors and/or young adults without giving them direct access to or control over the gifted funds.

Minor's trusts. The "minor's trust" is also referred to as a "2503(c)" trust, which is a term suggesting a trust that conforms to the requirements of section 2503(c) of the Internal Revenue Code. This section states that if a trust meets certain requirements (noted below), then gifts to the trust will be treated as gifts to the child and will qualify for the annual gift tax exclusion,[2] even though the child may not receive the funds for a period of time. (As explained in greater detail in chapter 13, gifts that qualify for the annual exclusion are not subject to gift taxes and do not use up any of an individual's lifetime gift tax credit.)

To qualify for this treatment, a separate irrevocable trust instrument must be prepared, and the trust must provide that:

- The minor (child) must be the only beneficiary of the trust, except that if the child dies before all assets are paid out and he has not directed otherwise in a will, the trust assets may be paid to or held for others (typically siblings);
- Any income that has accumulated, together with all of the remaining principal, must be distributed to the child or made available to him at age twenty-one; and
- On the death of the child before age twenty-one, he must have a right to dispose of the trust assets through his estate (although, as noted above, alternative beneficiaries may be named if the child fails to exercise this right).

As a general rule, it is *not* a good idea for a parent to be a trustee of this trust; otherwise, there is the possibility that the trust assets will be included in the parent's estate if the parent dies before the trust ends. Once established, the trust cannot be changed during its term, although the trustee can have great flexibility in distributing or retaining income and principal for the minor. The term *minor's trust* and the required termination at the child's age of twenty-one may appear inconsistent, since in virtually all states the age of majority is now eighteen. The age of twenty-one stems from earlier times when that was the age of majority, and no need to change it was ever recognized where this type of trust is concerned.

In fact, even twenty-one is not generally regarded as a sensible age to hand over large sums of money to a child. Therefore, many minor's trusts contain a provision stating that upon reaching age twenty-one, the child will

---

[2] As discussed in chapter 13, the tax code allows for gift-tax-free annual gifts to an unlimited number of donees. Since 1982, the "annual exclusion" for tax-free gifts has been $10,000 per donee per calendar year. Beginning with 1999 gifts, however, the law directed that the $10,000 amount would be adjusted by the cost-of-living standard, but only by multiples to the nearest $1,000. In 2020 the amount is $15,000. For the current annual exclusion amount in subsequent years, you can check the IRS's website or the authors' website at bovelanga.com.

be notified that he has a right to withdraw the entire balance of the trust. If the child does not exercise that right by notifying the trustee within thirty or sixty days of such notice (the "window"), then the funds will remain in the trust, *outside* the child's control, for an additional number of years (usually five to ten years). Assuming the child can be persuaded not to withdraw the funds during the window, the trust will then continue for the stated period. During this extended period the child will be taxed on all the trust income and capital gains, whether distributed to him or not, so the trust should contain a provision requiring the trustee to pay or distribute to the child an amount equal to the attributable taxes or to pay the tax directly. Until the trust ends, the trustee will manage the trust assets for the benefit of the child, giving him what he reasonably needs but not necessarily what he requests. At the end of the period, all remaining assets are turned over to the child, who, at that time, will hopefully be wiser and more mature.

If a large amount has accumulated in the trust and a further safeguard is denied to discourage the child from unwise use of the funds, the trust could provide that if the child fails to withdraw the funds during the window, then at the end of the extended period, they may be withdrawn by the child, but only with the consent of another party. Of course, that party must be chosen carefully, and provisions should be made for a successor if the party is unavailable or for removal of the consent requirement at some point.

The tax implications of minor's trusts up to age twenty-one are fairly straightforward. Any income for the year that is held in the trust and not distributed to the child during the year is taxed to the trust. Income that is distributed to the child is taxed to the child (but be mindful of the "kiddie tax" if the child is under a certain age; see chapter 13 for more on that). There will be no additional tax when the trust terminates and the assets (and accumulated income) are distributed to the child. If the child dies before the trust ends, the assets are included in the child's estate for estate tax purposes, although in most cases no tax will result.

The other trust for children. Although children (and grandchildren) can, of course, be named as beneficiaries of any type of trust other than a marital deduction trust, the "other" trust most commonly used for children (although its use is certainly not restricted to children) is called, in estate-planning vernacular, the "Crummey trust."

The principal advantages of the Crummey trust over the minor's trust is that the Crummey trust can and often does have more than one beneficiary, and the Crummey trust does not have to end (nor must the funds be made available) when a beneficiary reaches age twenty-one, or any age for that matter. And like the minor's trust, gifts to the Crummey trust can qualify for annual tax-free gifts. This qualification can be particularly important when you have a potentially taxable estate and several beneficiaries whom you want to benefit and to whom you do not want to give the money (or other property to be gifted) outright. For instance, in 2020 a married couple with four children (and generous hearts) could transfer up to $120,000 per year (each spouse giving $15,000 to each child) of tax-free gifts to one Crummey trust for the benefit of their children.

In order to qualify for the annual tax-free gift, the gift must be subject to the "present enjoyment" of the donee (recipient). In other words, if the donee has to wait to receive the funds (as in the case of most trusts), a gift to the trust will not qualify as a tax-free gift and the donor will then have to apply a part of his "lifetime exemption" to the gift (more on this in chapter 13). The tax law provides a specific exception to this rule where a minor's trust is concerned (section 2.503(c) trusts as described above), but gifts to most other trusts will not qualify *unless* they are Crummey trusts or the equivalent.

A Crummey trust (named after a 1968 federal case on the gift tax question involving a taxpayer unfortunately named D. Clifford Crummey) is one that has a provision allowing each beneficiary the right or power (called a "Crummey power") to withdraw his or her share of the annual gifts to the trust, up to the annual tax-free gift limit. For instance, if Chester contributed $24,000 to a Crummey trust for the equal benefit of his three children, each child would have the right to withdraw $8,000.

As you may have quickly observed, it may not be a good idea to allow this withdrawal power to continue indefinitely or carry forward cumulatively from year to year. If we did this, what would be the sense of having the trust? The fact is that the typical arrangement is largely modeled after the original power that Crummey himself used.

The irrevocable trust established in 1962 by D.C. Crummey and his wife provided that each beneficiary would have the right to withdraw the lesser of the annual tax-free gift limit or his equal share of the annual gifts to the trust, *provided* he did so by December 31 of the year in which the gifts to the trust were made. If the beneficiary did not exercise his right to withdraw, he could not thereafter withdraw his share of that year's gifts, and such gifts would become a permanent part of the trust. Crummey, then, could *time* his gifts, making them, for instance, sometime in December, so his children only had a limited time in which to exercise their withdrawal rights. The IRS objected to this arrangement, Crummey brought the case to court, and that is how the Crummey case came to be. The court held that the right of withdrawal *did* give the beneficiaries the necessary present enjoyment (or at least the *right* to present enjoyment, even though some of the beneficiaries were so young that they could not, without a guardian, exercise their rights), and therefore Crummey's gifts to the trust qualified as tax-free gifts.

As a result of various disputes with the IRS, further requirements subsequently evolved from the Crummey case, giving practitioners a clear picture of how to draft Crummey powers to qualify for the tax-free gift without drawing inquiry from the IRS:

- The beneficiaries *must be given notice* of their right to withdraw, indicating the amount they may withdraw and the manner in which to do it;
- The beneficiaries must be given a reasonable amount of time after receipt of the notice to act upon it (called a "window," and the window is usually thirty days); and
- The fact that a beneficiary may be an infant or very young child is not an issue. (Typically, the notice of withdrawal right is sent to a parent on behalf of the child.)

As taxpayers use Crummey powers more and more aggressively to remove assets from their taxable estates, the IRS is liking them less and less and attacking aggressive cases more and more. In one case, at the time when the annual tax-free amount was $10,000 per donee, a taxpayer's Crummey trust gave sixteen beneficiaries the annual right to withdraw (allowing annual tax-free gifts of $160,000 to the trust), and provided that if they didn't withdraw, only four of the sixteen would be able to receive distributions for their lives. The IRS took the trust to court. As it happened, the IRS lost, but the IRS has publicly stated that it intends to actively pursue such aggressive uses of the Crummey power. Furthermore, there has been at least one proposal in Congress to pass legislation limiting the number of annual tax-free gifts a person may make.

It is not fatal if the trust does not have Crummey powers; in fact, many do not. Without Crummey powers, however, any gifts to the trust will have to be applied to the donor's lifetime exemption and, as explained in chapter 13, once that is used up, every gift (other than annual tax-free gifts) will then be subject to a gift tax.

The typical Crummey trust for children will be for a number of children and will terminate when a child reaches, say, age thirty or thirty-five or forty. In the meantime, the trust assets are managed by the trustee for the group of beneficiaries, and funds are distributed as needed to each of them. Crummey trusts for the benefit of grandchildren must follow some special rules and are discussed later under the section on generation-skipping trusts.

The *tax rules* relating to Crummey trusts are somewhat complicated, but briefly, the beneficiaries are taxed on trust income based on their respective proportions of cumulative tax-free gifts left in the trust. This is because a failure to withdraw is treated, for tax purposes, as if the donee *did* make their withdrawal and then *recontributed* the same amount to the trust under which he is a beneficiary. Similarly, a portion of the assets of the Crummey trust will be in the estate of a beneficiary who dies. All of the results can be modified by varying the provisions of the trust, and suffice it to say that such trusts should only be prepared by experts.

TRUSTS FOR UNMARRIED PARTNERS

When two people develop a long-term relationship that has virtually all the attributes of a "marriage" but without the legal contract of marriage, each of them should consider an estate plan that provides the other with benefits on a partner's death, without interference from the relatives of the deceased partner, and, if possible, with the benefit of any tax breaks that are available.

One basic tax break that is *not* available to unmarried partners is the marital deduction, since it is only available to individuals who are legally married (including common-law marriages in the few states that recognize such marriages). Nevertheless, unmarried couples are able to make annual tax-free gifts to each other and to establish trusts for each other. In fact, unmarried couples can enjoy one tax-advantaged strategy that is not available to spouses or to children. This is called a grantor retained interest trust (a "GRIT"). Until 1989 GRITs were used by individuals to transfer assets to a trust and retain the income for a period of years, after which the trust assets would belong to (usually) their children at a highly reduced gift tax value, thereby reducing the donor's estate. In 1990, however, the law changed to disallow GRITs for family members.

Since unmarried partners are not related to each other, the tax code does not prohibit one from creating a GRIT for the other. Briefly, a GRIT might work like this. During the term of the typical GRIT, the donor (creator) is only entitled to the income from the assets in the trust. Although the assets may be sold and the proceeds reinvested, the donor is never entitled to more than the income actually produced by the assets. For purposes of computing the value of the gift made by the donor to the residuary beneficiary, the tax regulations assume that a certain return was earned on the assets. In fact, the gift and estate tax advantages are increased if the assets grow more and earn less than the tax tables assume. If the donor dies during the term of the GRIT, all advantages are lost, and the full value of the trust is included in the donor's estate. This is not such a catastrophe as it may appear, however, as it merely leaves the donor in the same position as she was in without the GRIT; the only loss would be the costs of implementing the GRIT.

For instance, Elizabeth, who has substantial assets, wishes to provide for her partner, Jan. Elizabeth and Jan have chosen not to marry. Elizabeth establishes a fifteen-year GRIT and transfers $500,000 worth of securities to the GRIT. Under the terms of the GRIT, Elizabeth receives all the income from the securities for a fifteen-year period, and, thereafter, the securities (or whatever they have become) belong to Jan (or they could continue to be held in trust for Jan's benefit).

Because the GRIT is irrevocable and Elizabeth has no right to recover the principal (as opposed to the *income* generated by the principal), Elizabeth is deemed to have made a gift to Jan, the person who will receive the principal at the end of the fifteen-year period. But since Jan has to wait fifteen years to receive the funds, the gift is certainly not one for "present enjoyment." Since it is not, the gift must be discounted to reflect the present value of what Jan will receive in fifteen years. In fact, depending on Elizabeth's age and the income rate assumed by the federal rate tables at the time of the gift, the gift could be, say, only about 28 percent of the $500,000 amount actually placed in the trust, or $141,500. That is, to make a gift of $500,000 to Jan fifteen years from now, Elizabeth may only have to apply $141,500 of her lifetime exemption.

Although the GRIT for unmarried couples is not quite as advantageous as the marital deduction, it can in some instances come close. Note, however, that the advantage offered by the GRIT may be affected by the age of the donor (the creator of the GRIT). If Elizabeth, in our example above, was age eighty, a fifteen-year GRIT would not be a good idea, since she may not outlive the term, and no savings will be realized. And a five-year GRIT would offer considerably less tax advantage. This is because the closer we are (i.e., the less time) between the gift and the enjoyment of the gift, the lower the discount for gift tax purposes and, correspondingly, the less the savings.

Another potential drawback of the GRIT is that although the appreciation on the gifted assets escapes estate tax, the donee (the beneficiary who receives the assets when the GRIT ends—Jan) may face a capital gain on a subsequent sale of the assets. This is because the donee/beneficiary's cost basis is the same as that of the donor. This is most easily explained by illustration. Elizabeth (age sixty) places $500,000 of stocks in a fifteen-year GRIT, and at the end of the GRIT the stocks will be given to Jan. Elizabeth paid $200,000 for the stocks many years ago. If Elizabeth dies twenty years later when the stocks are worth, say, $1 million, only $141,500 will be included in Elizabeth's estate. The difference of $858,500 will be estate tax free to Jan. However, Jan's *cost basis* in the stocks will be the same as Elizabeth's ($200,000), so that a sale by Jan at the market price of $1 million will produce an $800,000 capital gain. Whether this makes economic sense depends upon a comparison of the capital gains rate (generally 20 percent) and the estate tax rate (40 percent in 2020) and, of course, whether or not either or both Elizabeth and Jan will be subject to the estate tax at all.

Note also that the GRIT need not actually produce any specified amount of income. Furthermore, it may be funded with *any* type of property, not just securities. That is, the donor could fund it with rental real estate or a patent or a copyright interest, or even a residence, which generally produces no income at all, if a single-family dwelling. This is one instance where it pays to be "unrelated" as the tax laws make it prohibitive to do a GRIT for a close family member. (Where a family member is involved, a GRIT funded with a residence must meet certain strict requirements, as discussed below.)

In fact, with the exceptions of the marital deduction trust, the qualified domestic trust (or QDOT), and the children's trust, *every* type of trust discussed in this chapter can be used by and for unmarried partners. The selections and individual trust provisions would be those suited to the objectives of the individuals involved.

Unmarried partners also make use of the Crummey trust (described in detail above). Although the amounts placed in the trust (generally equal to the annual tax-free gift per beneficiary per year) are lower than in the GRIT, the gifts can accumulate over the years, and there is no waiting period that must pass before the trust assets are out of the donor's estate. Furthermore, as described later in this chapter, "leverage" can be attained by using the trust funds to purchase life insurance on the donor. If properly structured, the trust can receive huge amounts of life insurance proceeds totally tax free for the benefit of the unmarried partner.

TRUSTS FOR INDIVIDUALS WITH DISABLITIES

When the family includes an individual who has disabilities, a special trust or special trust provisions should be considered to protect the financial interests of that person. Of course, the term *disability* can have a wide range of meanings. Generally speaking, I am referring here to individuals who would not be able to care for themselves or whose interests would be better served by retaining control and management of the person's inheritance or other assets in a trust, and in some cases, individuals who are formally diagnosed to be "totally and permanently disabled."

In some cases, certain types of trust are essential in order to preserve benefits the disabled person may be receiving. For example, in the case of a person who is eligible for Supplemental Security Income (SSI) benefits, the receipt of an inheritance or personal injury award would immediately disqualify that person from benefits, but if these funds are instead placed in a special trust for the individual's benefit, he would not be disqualified.

Even if a person is not receiving government benefits but is under a guardianship or conservatorship because of his disability, the outright receipt of an inheritance or gift will cause unnecessary complications and fees. Again, by placing the person's inheritance or other funds in a trust with appropriate provisions, the donor and the donee can avoid fees, publicity, and often even the need for court supervision. What types of trust and provisions are appropriate?

While it is virtually impossible to suggest the exact provisions that should be placed in every trust for a person with disabilities, there are certain guidelines that, if followed by a competent practitioner, will help protect the funds and the beneficiary.

In the typical case of a family with a child with disabilities, a parent (or other relative) may want to provide for the child on the parent's death. If the child is receiving or may in the future receive government benefits, an outright bequest to the child will, as noted above, disqualify the child from eligibility for benefits, which could be a very expensive loss. Although there are alternatives, such as leaving the child's share to other children on the basis that they will use those funds for the child with disabilities, such alternatives are risky and generally regarded as bad planning. Instead, the parent can consider placing the child's share in a "supplemental needs trust" or in a fully discretionary "special needs trust."

As indicated below, at some point both the supplemental needs trust and the special needs trust will be irrevocable, generally meaning in such cases that they may not be amended without a court order, which can be expensive, time-consuming, and not necessarily successful. Thus, either of these trusts could be left in a situation where a change in the law or in the circumstances of the beneficiary or his family renders one or more provisions of the trust inappropriate, disadvantageous, or in some fashion undesirable, but with no way to change it. One example is where the government recently revoked clothing as a basic need, but countless supplemental needs trusts are still out there stating that the trustee is prohibited from providing "food, clothing, or shelter" to a beneficiary. Later on in this chapter we will discuss how the use of a trust protector can solve this problem by amending the trust to accommodate the change in the law.

A supplemental needs trust is an irrevocable trust for the benefit of the person with disabilities (although in some cases it includes other beneficiaries in addition to the disabled person), and the operative provision states that the trustee may only make distributions to or for the person with disabilities to provide for the needs of that person *over and above* the person's basic needs for food, clothing, and shelter. The reason for this is the government regulation providing that if a person on certain disability benefits (SSI) has unrestricted access to assets in a trust to the extent that such assets may be used for the person's basic needs and support (i.e., food and shelter), then those assets will be considered available to the person. Since the SSI program is a welfare program and eligibility is based on a lack of assets available to the individual to provide for his basic needs, then the individual could lose his eligibility if the trust assets are considered so available. In order to eliminate the possibility of this happening, the trustee of the supplemental needs trust is actually prohibited, by the special provision, from making distributions for the beneficiary's basic needs of food and shelter.

Care must also be taken to ensure that the trust cannot be considered to be revocable by the beneficiary. Furthermore, many supplemental needs trusts have "self-destruct" provisions causing termination of the trust if the continued existence of the trust would cause the beneficiary to lose his benefits. While the self-destruct provision (discussed below) is seen as useful (by some), the trust should *not* provide that on such a termination the assets will be distributed to the beneficiary.

The problem with the typical supplemental needs trust is that it is fairly rigid and shortsighted in its operation and restrictions. For instance, the typical supplemental needs trust will directly or indirectly prohibit the trustee from making distributions to the beneficiary that are or may be used for "food or shelter" because such distributions could disqualify the beneficiary for SSI purposes or affect his benefits. In these cases, if the circumstances (or the government programs) change, we are stuck with the trust as it is (although the trust, if carefully drafted, could include certain special provisions such as a limited power to amend or a limited power of appointment held by a third party—both discussed elsewhere in this chapter). What the drafters of the supplemental needs trust clearly overlook (to the detriment of the beneficiary) is that unforeseen changes in the beneficiary's circumstances or even in the SSI program itself could warrant a more flexibly drafted trust. Furthermore, also apparently overlooked is the fact that a "prohibited" distribution from the trust for, let's say, rent does not actually disqualify the beneficiary from public benefits, but rather it has the effect of merely reducing a monthly benefit, at the most, by one-third the benefit under the "one-third reduction" rule.

With this in mind, many experts in this field use instead a fully discretionary trust that does not restrict the trustee to distributions for the beneficiary's supplemental needs. As explained earlier in this chapter, a trustee's powers and duties can range widely, dictated by the written terms of the trust. And distributions made from the trust to the beneficiaries can be mandatory (giving the trustee no choice) or discretionary. In addition, the trustee's discretion can be guided by additional provisions of the trust.

For instance, in the supplemental needs trust, the trustee has discretion to make distributions or not to make them, but *only* for the beneficiary's supplemental needs. In a fully discretionary special needs trust, the trustee has no such restrictions and may make distributions for any purpose whatsoever, at the trustee's discretion (usually accompanied by either or both of the words *sole* or *absolute*). In addition, the fully discretionary trust usually contains (and *should* contain) a statement requesting the trustee, in exercising its discretion, to take into consideration whether the proposed distribution would have a negative effect on the beneficiary's eligibility for government benefits. Although technically this does not limit the trustee, it is a reminder of the settlor's intentions and assists the trustee in making a decision. It does *not* by itself affect the beneficiary's eligibility for benefits, so long as the beneficiary himself did not establish the trust. Thus, for example, it would be permissible for the trustee to make a distribution of, say, $1,000 for the beneficiary's rent, which would have the effect of causing the beneficiary's SSI payments, usually about $600, to be reduced for that month by $200 or so. Doesn't that make a lot more sense and offer a lot more flexibility than providing that the trustee simply cannot make such distributions?

A fully discretionary trust should contain as little language as possible relating to the extent of the trustee's discretion, as too many words in that context could be fatal to the protection otherwise offered by the trust. For instance, *fully* discretionary means there are no restrictions or guidelines governing the exercise of discretion. If a trust says, "The trustee may make such distributions to or for the beneficiary as the trustee in its absolute discretion deems appropriate for the beneficiary's *support, maintenance, and welfare,*" it is *not* a fully discretionary trust. In fact, under the law of many (if not most) states, the beneficiary (and therefore the government, if the beneficiary is on a benefit program like SSI) can legally force the trustee to make distributions for the beneficiary's "support," etc. Accordingly, a well-drafted fully discretionary trust, if using the language above, would end that sentence at the word "appropriate."

The choice of whether parents (or other family members) should establish a supplemental needs trust or a fully discretionary trust for a child with disabilities depends in large part on family circumstances and almost as often on the family's legal advisor. A supplemental needs trust is frequently the choice only because the advisor is unclear on how the fully discretionary trust works. Many feel that the advantage of the supplemental needs trust is that its very language (of providing only for items *other than* food or shelter) more or less guarantees that the existence of the trust will not affect the beneficiary's eligibility for the SSI program. In fact, federal regulations do not require that such provisions be included to ensure eligibility. The regulations *only* look to actual distributions made from the trust and the *use* or potential use of those distributions. In other words, if a trustee of a fully discretionary trust was aware of the SSI regulations (and he would have to be if there was a trust beneficiary on SSI), and was therefore careful not to make distributions that would affect the beneficiary's eligibility, there would be no difference between the two trusts—except one important one: the special needs trust restricts the trustee in distributions and could leave the family in a bad situation if circumstances and/or the regulations change. On the other hand, the discretionary trust leaves the trustee with full choice as to whether or not to make distributions and as to the amounts of any distributions that are made, meaning, in effect, that the trustee can automatically adjust distributions to accommodate the changes.

Both the supplemental needs trust and the fully discretionary trust for an individual with disabilities can be established through the parent's will (a testamentary trust) or during the parent's lifetime (an inter vivos or "living" trust). Most knowledgeable practitioners agree that a living trust is the better choice. If a living trust is used, a parent may be the trustee, although if the parent has a potentially taxable estate and wants the proceeds of the special needs trust or discretionary trust to be out of his taxable estate, he may be better off having someone else serve as trustee, particularly if the trust is to hold life insurance on the parent's life (life insurance trusts are discussed later).

In many cases the trust will provide benefits for other children as well as the child with disabilities, and this arrangement can actually give the trust much more flexibility. This question, however, must be carefully considered in each particular case, especially where the trust is established with the beneficiary's own funds (a self-settled trust). In any event, provisions must be made to dispose of any remaining trust assets on the death of the person with disabilities. If it is possible that the person could have children, the parent may want to make provisions for them. Otherwise, the remainder will typically pass to the siblings of the child.

Self-settled trusts for individuals with disabilities. When a person establishes and funds a trust for himself, it is referred to as a "self-settled trust." (Note that a trust is still considered to be self-settled even though it may be established by a person's guardian or conservator, or at the order of a court, so long as it is funded with assets belonging to the beneficiary.) In some cases, however, a beneficiary with disabilities can establish a trust for his own benefit (with his own funds) and still qualify for government benefits. Briefly, if the person is on SSI and does not become institutionalized, he can establish a supplemental needs trust or a fully discretionary trust for his own benefit, being careful that no provision in the trust can be interpreted as giving the beneficiary the right to revoke the trust, and being equally careful not to include language that requires or requests the trustee to withhold distributions if they would affect the beneficiary's eligibility for benefits (this is called an "exculpatory" provision). This latter suggestion is because of case decisions and public policy rules relating to self-settled trusts.

Discussed in more detail below is the "Under-65 Trust." This is another type of self-settled trust for a person with disabilities that in some regards falls under the fully discretionary category but is regarded differently by practitioners because it is a "statutory" trust. That is, it is a trust for a person that is specifically described under the federal law relating to the Medicaid program. Briefly, it must be established for a person under the age of sixty-five (although it can continue past that age), and on the beneficiary's death it must provide for repayment to the state for Medicaid benefits paid to the beneficiary. Any balance remaining in the trust may be paid to others, such as family members. During the beneficiary's lifetime, the trustee may have full discretion over payments to the beneficiary.

Self-destruct clause. Since the establishment and continuation of the special needs trust or discretionary trust (but *particularly* the special needs trust) is conditioned on the beneficiary's continued eligibility for benefits, the trust's purpose may be frustrated if its very existence causes the beneficiary to become ineligible. Accordingly, many such trusts contain a self-destruct provision that says something like, "If the existence of this trust causes Johnny to lose his benefits under the Social Security Income or other program, then this trust shall thereupon terminate, and the trustee shall distribute the remaining trust principal and undistributed income to Johnny's then surviving siblings in equal shares." A similar provision, called a "forfeiture" provision, could be used, especially if there are other beneficiaries, where the share of the beneficiary with disabilities would automatically be forfeited (terminated) if the existence of the trust causes a loss of benefits.

Self-destruct clauses are quite legal (although they could present a problem if the trust is self-settled), and are commonly used in special needs trusts.

Trusts for personal injury settlements. These trusts typically fall into the category of "trusts for the person with disabilities," since the very nature of the personal injury settlement is to compensate a victim for injuries (a temporary or permanent disability) caused by another. Of course, not every personal injury settlement gives rise to the need for a trust. Smaller settlements and those where the victim has fully recovered by the time the settlement is received present a different situation. In those cases, while a trust may be advisable for general estate-planning purposes, it need not be a special trust designed around the circumstances of the settlement.

Where the individual has not fully recovered, however, or may never fully recover, and in cases where the individual is receiving SSI or Medicaid benefits to provide for his care, the use of a trust may be essential to preserve those benefits as well as to preserve the settlement funds to provide for future care and enhancement of the individual's quality of life.

Although trusts can be created for personal injury settlements after a lump sum has been received, in cases where all or part of the settlement is structured, it is *extremely important* that a trust expert be consulted *before* the final settlement is negotiated. In most circumstances where a large recovery is involved, the settlement is often "structured"—that is, paid in specified periodic amounts over an extended period of time. Again, it is important that the trust expert be consulted in structuring the settlement, not only to preserve eligibility for any benefit programs but also to avoid the tax traps often present in such cases (the tax traps are discussed in chapter 13). Note the reference here to a "trust expert." No matter how outstanding the personal injury attorney, it is unlikely that he or she would have the expertise necessary to design, draft, and fund the trust to best suit the particular circumstances.

Where a trust is established to receive the proceeds of a personal injury settlement, it will generally be considered a self-settled trust, as discussed above. As pointed out, however, properly drafted self-settled trusts may nevertheless allow the beneficiary to continue to qualify for SSI or Medicaid.

Typically, the self-settled trust for personal injury settlements will be a supplemental needs trust or a discretionary trust, or one of the qualifying Medicaid trusts. There are also cases, however, where such a trust is not self-settled. It is not unusual, for instance, for a personal injury award to be apportioned between the victim and his spouse, or between the victim and his parents. In these cases, the spouse or more particularly the parent may want to use her share of the settlement proceeds to fund a trust for the benefit of the child. This type of trust would *not* be a self-settled trust and offers considerably more flexibility in providing for the injured party, but at the same time it introduces some very complicated tax issues for the parent who establishes the trust. Accordingly, it should only be done by a trust expert.

Medicaid trusts. Medicaid is a needs-based (i.e., welfare) benefit program administered separately by each state, but funded in part by the federal government and in part by each state. A person qualifying for Medicaid is only allowed to have a minimal amount of assets, other than a home. Although each state may have certain differences in its particular Medicaid regulations, each must follow certain basic federal guidelines in order to be eligible for the federal subsidy. One of those guidelines is the waiting period imposed on a person who transfers assets and later applies for Medicaid benefits.

The basic rule (in every state) is that if a person makes a gift of assets and the gift is not connected with a trust, and if the person applies for Medicaid within sixty months of the date of the gift (the "look-back" period), then the amount of the gifted assets will be taken into consideration in determining whether the person will be entitled to Medicaid benefits subject to the notable exceptions for certain trusts as described below. However, if assets are transferred to a trust, and if the trust to which the assets are transferred allows any benefits to be distributed to the person who established the trust, then the look-back period may not apply to all of the transferred assets, because federal law provides that the assets of a trust, to the extent they may be paid to the person establishing the trust, will be considered accessible to him for Medicaid eligibility purposes.

For instance, say that Chester creates and funds an irrevocable trust that provides that the trustee can pay to Chester any part or all of the trust income or principal as the trustee in its discretion deems appropriate. In this case, *all* of the trust assets are considered available to Chester, whether or not they are paid to him, and it will not matter whether he applies for Medicaid ten months or ten years after the trust is established. Keep in mind that even if the trust directs the trustee *not* to make any payment that would jeopardize or terminate Chester's eligibility for Medicaid, *all* of the trust assets would nevertheless be considered available to Chester. Such a provision (called an "exculpatory clause") is useless to protect the assets of a self-settled trust.

In this type of trust where *no* discretion is given to the trustee, it does not matter who acts as trustee. It can be the settlor and/or the settlor's spouse, for example, or one or more children.

(This is but a cursory overview of only a few of the Medicaid rules, which are extensive, very complex, and frequently subject to exceptions. Readers who wish to do Medicaid planning should consult an expert in that field.)

Using these rules as a basis for planning, if we restrict the benefits we can receive from the trust and if we wait sixty months before applying for Medicaid (where relatively large transfers are made), then the restricted amount or portion can be protected. Here is how it can work in practice: Margo establishes an irrevocable trust to which she transfers $400,000 worth of investments. The terms of the trust allow the trustee to pay to Margo any dividends and interest from the investments, but *under no circumstances* is Margo to receive any of the trust principal. About fifty months after the trust is established, Margo enters a nursing home. The *income* from her $400,000 trust is applied toward Margo's nursing home costs for the following ten months and Margo's family pays the balance of the costs. Just *after* the sixty-month period following the transfer to the trust, Margo applies for Medicaid benefits. Assuming she has no other assets (and assuming Margo does not reside in one of the so-called income-cap states, which deny Medicaid benefits to anyone receiving more than a certain amount of income[3] even though the person may have no assets), Margo will then qualify for Medicaid. Although she will have to apply the trust income toward her care, the state will pay the balance of her care costs and the $400,000 of investments (plus whatever growth is realized) will be protected for her family.

It is common and advisable for the income-only Medicaid trust to contain estate-planning provisions allowing for the trust to continue for the benefit of Margo's family after her death. It is also generally advisable, especially in view of the rapidly changing law in this area, to provide for a "safety valve" in this type of trust. This frequently takes the form of a provision that allows a trustee (*other than* the settlor or her spouse) or some other party outside the trust to direct principal distributions out of the trust to the settlor's children or grandchildren, thus allowing the principal to be protected in the event of a later change in the law.

Special exceptions to the Medicaid trust rules. Under a 1993 change in federal law, three types of trust were recognized as exceptions to the rules that would otherwise "count" the assets in a self-settled Medicaid trust and therefore disqualify the beneficiaries of such trusts. These three trusts are commonly called the "under-65 trust," the "pooled trust," and the "Miller trust."

Miller Trust. The Miller trust, named after a court decision on a Medicaid issue, is a trust that is suitable to be used only in "income-cap" states. As noted above, the hard-to-understand rule in these states is that a person, even though certified to be in need of care and having zero assets, will not be able to qualify for Medicaid if her income exceeds the state-prescribed amount. For instance, say that Sally lives in Florida, an income-cap state. She has advanced Alzheimer's and needs institutionalization. She has no assets but receives a company

---

[3] The income-cap states are: Alabama, Alaska, Arizona, Arkansas, Colorado, Delaware, Florida, Georgia, Idaho, Indiana, Iowa, Kentucky, Louisiana, Mississippi, Nevada, New Jersey, New Mexico, Oklahoma, Oregon, South Carolina, South Dakota, Tennessee, Texas, and Wyoming.

pension of $1,510 per month. If the income cap in Florida is $1,500 per month, then Sally's income exceeds the cap, and she *cannot* qualify for Medicaid!

The Miller trust law, however, provides that Sally's guardian can petition the Florida court to establish a Miller trust for Sally. The court would order that Sally's monthly pension be paid into the trust, and the trust would provide that the trustee may then pay to Sally (or to the nursing home) a monthly amount equal to $10 less than the income cap, thus allowing Sally to qualify for Medicaid. The law also requires, however, that any funds remaining in the trust on Sally's death (which wouldn't be much) be paid to the state to help reimburse it for the benefits paid to Sally without interest. Any type of income, including Social Security income, may be paid into a Miller trust, but *only income* may be used to fund this type of trust.

Pooled Trust. The pooled trust is a trust designed to hold the assets of more than one disabled individual (in separate accounts) and must be established by a nonprofit organization for this purpose. The same nonprofit organization must be the trustee of the trust. The individual's account within the pooled trust may be funded by the individual himself, by his guardian, parent, or grandparent, or by a court. Although the individual's funds are assigned to a separate account, they may be invested in a "pool" with the funds of other disabled individuals. While the funds are in the pooled trust, the trustee may distribute such funds attributable to the individual's separate account and/or the income from those funds to the disabled individual on a discretionary basis. Since this is one of the "excepted" or "safe harbor" Medicaid trusts, the funds in the trust are not considered accessible to the individual, and therefore do not affect his eligibility for Medicaid. Like the Miller trust, there must be a payback provision on death, but the pooled trust payback is slightly different. On the individual's death, the remaining funds in his separate trust account must either be applied to pay down the amount owed to the state for Medicaid benefits paid to or for the individual (without interest) or simply added to the accounts of other individuals (who typically are totally unrelated to the individual). (Note that some states appear to be interpreting this provision rather harshly, attempting to limit the amount that may be retained by the pooled trust for other beneficiaries.) If there are adequate funds to reimburse the state in full and the state is, in fact, reimbursed, then any funds in excess of such reimbursement may be paid to those beneficiaries *outside* the trust as the individual designates in the trust (including his family).

Under-65 Trust. The under-65 trust is by far the most useful and common of the three, since it allows for a greater possibility of preserving some of the individual's funds for his desired beneficiaries while still allowing the person to qualify for Medicaid. But like the other two trust exceptions, strict rules must be followed. The under-65 trust may be established by the individual's parent, grandparent, or legal guardian, or by a court. Unlike the pooled trust, it may *not* be established by the individual with disabilities himself. Furthermore, the trust must be established before the individual reaches age sixty-five, although, once established, it may continue beyond that age. The trust must be for the "sole benefit" of the individual. That is, *no one* but the individual may benefit from the trust until the state is reimbursed in full (without interest) on the individual's death. Thereafter, family members or other beneficiaries may receive benefits if any trust assets remain.

There are two distinct advantages to the under-65 trust. One is that transfers to this trust are not treated as disqualifying transfers for Medicaid purposes, so an individual under age sixty-five could have his assets transferred to this type of trust and immediately qualify for Medicaid. A second advantage is that the trust does not require an independent trustee (as does the pooled trust), so a family member may have control over the trust investments, which in turn could be arranged to ultimately benefit the individual and his family. In addition, the under-65 trust (as well as the pooled trust) allows the individual to take advantage of the "spread" between the amount the state pays for nursing home care (which must later be paid by the trust) and the private pay costs of care, which are generally 20 to 50 percent higher. Therefore, even if full reimbursement were made to the state, it would inevitably be less than if the individual paid on his own.

Asset Protection Trusts

It seems that we all want protection from creditors, whether we need it or not. Trusts are one form of legal vehicle that can be used to protect assets, and there are a number of variations of these, both domestic and foreign. But there are also laws intended to discourage asset transfers, including transfers to trusts a person makes for creditor protection purposes. In fact, a great and very complicated body of law has developed around the issue of whether an individual is or should be permitted to transfer his assets for the purpose of placing them beyond the reach of a creditor or potential creditor. Many such transfers may be attacked by the creditor as "fraudulent."

A fraudulent transfer (or "conveyance") is not fraudulent in the criminal sense of the law, but rather it refers to a transfer that is unfair to creditors and in violation of the concept of good-faith dealings with the rest of society. (The trend in the law is to now call such transfers "voidable" transfers, as courts can order them rescinded.) This is not at all to say that planning for creditor protection is automatically fraudulent or voidable. When properly done, it is quite legal and can positively protect assets. On the other hand, there should be (and there *are*) rules to prevent someone from, say, incurring a large debt and then intentionally transferring his assets away, thereby leaving him unable to pay the debt. These rules are called the fraudulent transfer (or fraudulent conveyance) rules, and whether they have been violated is usually decided by a court (after the creditor wins a suit for his money or claim) based on the facts and circumstances of each individual case. Understandably, there are many thousands of cases on the subject.

Furthermore, efforts made by creditors to rescind or reach transfers based on the fraudulent transfer rules are "actions within actions." That is, a creditor must take a *separate legal proceeding* during which the court conducts a separate hearing to determine whether a transfer was fraudulent. Such proceedings themselves can be drawn out and expensive.

In addition, there are time periods (called the "statute of limitations" or "period of limitations") within which a creditor must act; otherwise, his right to attack the transfer is lost. Typically (although some states differ), the limitations period for attacking a fraudulent transfer in the United States is four years after the transfer. (Note that special rules and longer periods may apply in bankruptcy proceedings, but this situation is outside the scope of this discussion.)

As a general rule, if you make a transfer that falls into any of the following categories, it is likely that the transfer will be considered fraudulent:

a. Transfer made with the actual intent to hinder, delay, or defraud a creditor. Your "intent" is often difficult to prove, so the law contains a number of telltale actions that may be considered by the court, such as concealment of the transfer, transfer to close relatives or "insiders," transfer for less than full value, transfers that leave you "insolvent" (i.e., more debts than assets), transfers made right after you discover that you are being sued or about to be sued, or transfers made when you know that you have done something that has damaged someone and they are likely to sue you.

This last criterion often surprises people since the common misunderstanding seems to be, "If I haven't yet been served with the legal papers, I can still make some transfers." *This is not the case.*

b. Incurrence of a debt beyond your ability to pay. This, of course, presumes that you made a transfer for less than fair value before the incurrence of the debt, and that had you kept the transferred asset you would have otherwise been able to pay the debt.

For example, say that you want to borrow $75,000 for an investment you think will make you rich, but you don't want to use your own money, so you arrange for a loan. Just prior to taking out the loan, you transfer $100,000 to your spouse, leaving you with assets of about $150,000 and debts of about $140,000. You then borrow the $75,000 from the bank, which is glad to loan you the money because of your long and good financial standing with them. Unfortunately, the investment goes sour and now you can't pay the bank. Under those facts, the bank can recover what you owe from the $100,000 you transferred to your spouse, on the basis that it was a fraudulent transfer.

c. Transfers that actually leave you insolvent. This type of transfer may include those mentioned under "b" above, and both may be attacked by your present or *future* creditors—they include transfers made *while* you are insolvent as well as those that *make* you insolvent.

For instance, in the example in "b" above, say that you gave your spouse $150,000. This would have left you with more debts than expenses even before the bank loan, so the transfer would have rendered you insolvent. Under both rules, the bank would be able to go after the transferred funds.

d. Transfers for less than fair value when you are engaging or are about to engage in business (the "undercapitalization" rule). Say that you intend to start a business that normally requires $50,000 in capital to operate. You have $50,000 (and that is all you have), but you don't want to risk it. You transfer $40,000 to your spouse and proceed with the business, putting in only $10,000. You run up $40,000 in business debts *or* you are faced with a $40,000 claim from a customer and decide to close the business. Under the thin capitalization rule, your creditors or the customer could attack the gift to your spouse.

e. Transfer to an insider (relative, employee) to pay a preexisting debt, where the insider had reasonable cause to believe you were insolvent. You have run up quite a lot of debt, which includes $125,000 due to your brother-in-law for funds he advanced to you. You have about $380,000 in debt and $160,000 in assets, and you are thinking of filing bankruptcy or at least just throwing yourself on the "mercy" of your creditors. However, you first pay your brother-in-law, who is aware of your problems and has growing concern over the $125,000 you owe him. (You are probably motivated to do this, believing that later on he may be willing to reloan you the funds, and besides, if you don't pay him, your sister will never speak to you again.) Unfortunately, you are not allowed to favor him as a creditor and, under these facts, your other creditors will be able to attack the funds paid to your brother-in-law.

As a result of the application of these rules over many years, we are left with the following potential outcomes where a *fraudulent transfer* is deemed by a court to have been made:

- Your creditors can reach assets or benefits that you can reach.
- Your creditors can receive what you have a right to receive.
- Your creditors can *reverse* an "unfair" (fraudulent) transfer.
- Your creditors can have your assets placed in the hands of a court-appointed receiver.
- Your creditor can attach, freeze, and/or force a sale of your assets.

And in certain cases,

- Your creditors can force you into bankruptcy. This can increase the statute of limitations period in the event a trust or "similar device" is involved, leaving transfers more vulnerable.

(This is an extremely brief overview of the fraudulent transfer rules. Anyone concerned over the issue should consult an expert in the field.)

Of course, the other side of this coin is that if none of the above rules applies to you, or if the transfers were made some time ago, *outside* the period of limitations, then the assets will likely be protected and unreachable by your creditors. But that, of course, is only part of the answer. The examples above, for instance, illustrate giving the assets away to spouses, in-laws, etc.—who really wants to do that? What we really want is an arrangement where *we* can continue to enjoy our assets, at least to some extent, while still keeping them beyond the reach of our creditors. Is there a way to do this? Actually, there are a number of ways, and most involve the use of legal vehicles such as the corporation, the limited partnership, the limited liability company, the trust, or various and creative combinations of any or all of the above. In this case, however, since we are discussing trusts, we will focus on the *asset protection trust.*

WHAT IS AN ASSET PROTECTION TRUST?

Generally, an asset protection trust is one where the settlor (the creator of the trust) can continue to enjoy benefits from assets she has transferred to the trust while placing those assets beyond the reach of her creditors. (This type of trust is called a "self-settled" trust—more on this later.) In addition, the asset protection trust must at the same time be designed to take advantage of appropriate estate-planning and tax benefits. Whether the assets in such a trust can be reached by creditors depends on two essential factors:

1. Did the transfer of assets to the trust constitute a fraudulent transfer?
2. What rights does a creditor have against the trust assets under the law of the jurisdiction governing the trust?

As noted in the discussion above, if a transfer is deemed to be fraudulent, it won't matter what the law is regarding the trust, since the fraudulently transferred asset(s) can be reached as if the trust did not exist.

If the transfer is not fraudulent *or* if the period of limitations within which a creditor must attack the conveyance has expired, then we must look to the law of the jurisdiction of the trust (the governing law) to determine the creditor's rights.

WHAT LAW GOVERNS YOUR TRUST?

Somewhere in every well-drafted trust, usually toward the end, you will see a statement like this: "This trust is established in [*the selected state or other jurisdiction*] and all matters relating to the trust shall be construed, administered, and governed by the laws of that jurisdiction."

Is this all that is necessary to have the trust governed by the laws of a favorable jurisdiction? Does it matter that the person creating the trust does not live there? Would this mean that every time a question arises someone has to go to a court in the particular jurisdiction?

When we form a corporation or a partnership or a limited liability company, we have the freedom of choosing any state in the United States, or any country in the world for that matter, simply by filing the necessary organizational documents in that state or country. It does not matter that we may never actually carry on a business or any other activity in that jurisdiction, only that we organized the entity there according to its laws. (How many times have we heard or seen the reference "a Delaware Corporation," when it is apparent the company has no connection with Delaware other than having been legally incorporated there?) Once we do that, all legal matters relating to the administration of the entity and the rights of its shareholders, partners, or members will be determined by the laws of the selected jurisdiction, even though the business and the shareholders are elsewhere.

Trusts are different. While the jurisdiction of a trust may also be freely selected by the settlor, in order for his selection to be binding on the trust and the beneficiaries, the trust must have a *connection* (the law calls it a "nexus") with the chosen jurisdiction. For instance, say that Barry, a resident of Oklahoma, creates a trust for the benefit of his children, who reside in California, and funds it with real estate he owns, located in New York. He then names his brother, who lives in New Jersey, as the trustee. Barry decides that Delaware law would be best for his trust, so he includes a statement in the trust that it shall be governed by the laws of Delaware. Is this valid? If not, what law would apply? The law of Oklahoma? New York? California? New Jersey?

First, since there is no connection whatever to the state of Delaware, the provision in Barry's trust attempting to make it a Delaware trust would be invalid. Next, in determining what law would apply, the court in this case would probably apply the law of New York, because when a trust's principal assets are real estate, it is the law of the location of the real estate (the "law of the land") that will determine the jurisdiction (called the "situs") of the trust. If the trust had property in several states, the court would then have to consider all of the circumstances and, as a general rule, would apply the law of the jurisdiction that on balance has "the greatest interest" in the trust. In this case it could be California, because that is where all the beneficiaries are, but a definitive answer cannot be given.

This is why a settlor wishing to have his trust governed in a jurisdiction other than his own must *provide* a connection. Perhaps the easiest way to do this is to select a trustee in the desired jurisdiction. The situs of the trustee is an adequate connection and one of the first used to establish the situs of the trust. Thus, had Barry simply selected a trustee in the state of Delaware, even (in some cases) to act as co-trustee with his brother, this would in most cases have been sufficient to bind the trust and establish the governing law.

This would be the case even though at some future date the Delaware trustee resigned, although if he resigned immediately after appointment there would likely be a different result. But note that where asset protection is the goal, it is best to have more than just the trustee as the connection to the jurisdiction you wish to govern the trust. Factors to consider include the residence of the settlor (does the settlor live in the desired jurisdiction?), the residence of the beneficiaries, and the location of some of the trust assets within the jurisdiction.

In most cases, a settlor will choose the state of his domicile as the governing law of his trust, as that is typically where the assets (or most of them) and the beneficiaries (or most of them) are located. In fact, unless the settlor is choosing a jurisdiction specifically for that jurisdiction's protection of the trust assets, or specifically because of the location of the settlor's own assets (such as real estate), or because most of the trust beneficiaries are located there, then the normal choice would be the settlor's domicile jurisdiction. But if, on the other hand, the objective is asset protection, then the settlor has the option of choosing among several other jurisdictions, both domestic and international as we will see.

It is also interesting to note that the situs of a trust can be *changed* if the terms of the trust allow it. This can have far-reaching and complicated effects and should only be considered with expert advice.

THE SPENDTHRIFT TRUST RULES

The general rule of creditor protection in the United States where a "self-settled" trust is concerned is that your creditors can reach whatever benefits may be paid to you out of the trust, regardless of a trust provision to the contrary. This is called the "spendthrift trust" rule. A self-settled trust is one where the settlor names herself as a permissible beneficiary. A spendthrift provision in a trust is one where the trust expressly prohibits any creditor of a beneficiary from reaching or attaching the beneficiary share or interest in a trust. Combining them would result in a settlor being able to establish a trust for her own benefit while preventing creditors from reaching the trust assets. As noted below, however, in most states, this arrangement is considered against public policy and not allowed.

Here is how the rule works. Denise creates and transfers assets to an irrevocable trust with an independent trustee, which provides that the trustee may pay to Denise and/or her children any part or all of the trust income and/or principal as the trustee deems appropriate in its sole discretion. In other words, Denise cannot order the trustee to make any payments from the trust; it is totally up to the trustee. In addition, the trust contains a spendthrift provision. This is a self-settled spendthrift trust, and in all states except (as of this writing) Alaska, Colorado, Connecticut, Delaware, Hawaii, Indiana, Michigan, Mississippi, New Hampshire, Nevada, Ohio, Rhode Island, South Dakota, Tennessee, Utah, Virginia, West Virginia, Wyoming, and possibly Oklahoma and Missouri (as discussed later), Denise's creditors can reach *all* of the assets in the trust. The fact that Denise's children are also beneficiaries has no bearing on that result. If the trust were revocable by Denise, the issue would be even clearer, since, as a general rule, her right to revoke the trust and take back all the assets could be reached by her creditors (except in Wyoming).[4] Oklahoma allows revocable trusts, but the settlor may not be a beneficiary, so they are not "self-settled." Note that if Denise were *not* a beneficiary and the transfer was not fraudulent, her creditors could *not* reach the trust assets—although neither could she. It is this aspect of the spendthrift trust rule that actually makes it attractive to most families. That is, when a person creates a discretionary trust for the benefit of one or more *others* (such as spouses and children), creditors of those beneficiaries may not reach the trust assets. Many parents or other ancestors protect their beneficiaries' inheritances with this form of arrangement, often called a "third-party spendthrift trust."

To illustrate, Steve, a widower with a substantial estate, made out a will leaving everything to his two sons equally. He knew that one child was a little "loose" with money and the other had a shaky marriage, but he didn't know there was anything he could do. After Steve's death, his concerns proved out: one child spent most of his money and lost the rest gambling, while the other was forced to give most of his share to his wife as a divorce settlement.

If, instead, Steve had established spendthrift trusts for the benefit of his two children (he could include their children as well), providing the usual safeguards prohibiting a beneficiary's creditors from reaching trust assets, then Steve's money would have been protected and remained intact to continue to provide benefits for his two sons for their lives and even for their children, despite the debts or the divorce.

In the ordinary course of the typical estate-planning practice, the situation often arises not just when planning for someone like Steve but also when planning for Steve's children. When individuals are getting estate-planning

---

[4] Wyoming law allows the settlor to retain control over the trust.

or even financial advice, it is standard procedure for a good estate planner to ask about potential or expected gifts of inheritances. If the circumstances warrant, the advisor will recommend that the parent or other relative of the individual who has named them as a beneficiary consider instead establishing a spendthrift trust for that person. This would give the person benefits and reasonable access to the inheritance but would keep the inheritance beyond the reach of the beneficiary's creditors, and, if properly drafted, the trust could escape taxes in his estate as well.

To illustrate, say that during a conference with her estate planner, Sally reports that a malpractice claim has recently been made against her and she is concerned that her insurance won't cover it. She also states that her eighty-four-year-old aunt, Sadie, recently made out a will naming Sally as the sole beneficiary. Aunt Sadie's estate is about $3.9 million, and Sally's estate is $1.6 million, which she intends to leave in trust for her children. If things are left as is and Aunt Sadie dies, Sally will receive the $3.9 million, which will then be immediately available to her creditors. In addition, Sally's estate will jump to $5.5 million, and in some states this amount would generate an estate tax on Sally's death.

If Sally's estate planner is worth her salt, she'll advise Sally to speak to Aunt Sadie about changing her will. She'll suggest (through Sally) that instead of an outright bequest to Sally, Sadie should establish a spendthrift trust for Sally's benefit, with liberal distribution arrangements for Sally. On Sally's death, what is left in the trust could go to Sally's children, *protected from Sally's creditors* and *completely free of estate taxes* in Sally's estate.

As mentioned above, there are exceptions to the rules—positive and negative. The negative exceptions to the spendthrift trust rules include the majority of states where a beneficiary's share of a spendthrift trust will be available to pay a creditor for "necessaries" furnished in good faith to the beneficiary and, in many cases, the beneficiary's child support obligations. In addition, in three states—Mississippi, Georgia, and Louisiana—spendthrift trust assets may be available to certain "tort" creditors of a beneficiary. (A tort is a wrong committed against another, such as assault and battery, stealing, or causing personal injuries by reckless driving or other negligent behavior.) These three states have carved out special exceptions to the spendthrift trust rules in certain of those cases, so if you are establishing a trust in one of those states, either consider establishing it elsewhere or consult an expert to be sure you understand the limitations that apply.

DOMESTIC ASSET PROTECTION TRUSTS

These are self-settled spendthrift trusts that are created, funded, and administered in certain states and offer or purport to offer protection of trust assets from the creditors of the settlor even though the settlor is a beneficiary. Because they are "domestic," they would, of course, be subject to the jurisdiction of U.S. courts and laws, including the spendthrift trust laws, if they apply. In the states mentioned above, and, to an extent, in Colorado (let's call them, and others that will undoubtedly follow, the domestic asset protection trust [DAPT] states), the spendthrift trust rule as it applies to self-settled trusts has been abolished by statute if the trust complies with state law. Briefly, compliance with the law generally requires that:

- The trust must be irrevocable by the settlor (except in Oklahoma and Wyoming);
- The settlor must not be in default of child support payments;
- Distributions from the trust to the settlor must be fully discretionary (in Oklahoma the settlor may not be a beneficiary);
- Some of the trust assets must be deposited and administered in the protective state (in Oklahoma, all of the trust assets);
- At least one of the trustees must be a resident of the protective state, or must be a bank or trust company with a principal place of business there; and
- Transfers to the trust must not have been fraudulent transfers.

Delaware has special exceptions to creditor protection even where all of the above requirements are met (e.g., alimony payments and certain personal injury claims), but aside from these special cases, the DAPT states apparently offer protection of assets without giving up use and enjoyment of those assets, in the ordinary course of events. Or do they? A number of experts in the field have raised the question of whether these trusts will stand up to a constitutional law challenge, that is, whether a creditor who obtains a legal judgment in, say, New York, against the settlor/beneficiary of an Alaskan trust can require the state of Alaska to honor the New York judgment under the "full faith and credit" rule of the U.S. Constitution. Proponents of the Alaska-type trust argue that such a judgment need not be given full faith and credit because it was not a judgment against the *trust,* as the foreign court had no jurisdiction over the trust. Countering further, the opposing critical experts argue that even if the full faith and credit argument does not work, the federal bankruptcy rules would override the state law and allow a trustee in bankruptcy (of the settlor/beneficiary) to reach the trust assets. (It should also be noted that for bankruptcy purposes, the trustee in bankruptcy has up to ten years to challenge a transfer to a DAPT as a fraudulent transfer.) In the former, the jury is still out. In the latter case, there have been a few bankruptcy cases where the trustee in bankruptcy has successfully challenged a transfer to a DAPT as being fraudulent, but remember, the majority of settlor/creditor cases take place outside of bankruptcy.

Despite the fact that there may not be prominently reported cases on the strength or weakness of the DAPT, this should not be taken to mean they do not work. In fact, it may be that the opposite is true. Remember, one key to asset protection planning is to make it difficult and expensive for the creditor to reach the assets. It is not inexpensive or expedient for a creditor to first obtain judgment in one state and then pick up and sue on the judgment in another state with no guarantee of success. In most cases, the creditor might agree to settle.

Another important issue where selection of a DAPT is concerned is the statute of limitations that applies in bringing a lawsuit in the DAPT state. They vary considerably, ranging from five years for preexisting creditors in Virginia, to two years in Nevada and South Dakota, to eighteen months in Ohio. Whether these shorter statutes would apply, for example, to a New York settlor/debtor's transfer to a DAPT in Ohio has not yet been decided by a court. In this regard, it should be noted that there is considerable commentary supporting the position that the law of the settlor's domicile will establish the open period for attacking the transfer as fraudulent, as opposed to the law of the trust. Nevertheless, it remains an uphill, expensive, and time-consuming battle for the creditor.

ASSET PROTECTION TRUSTS IN NON–ASSET PROTECTION STATES

There are also alternative options to create a self-settled asset protection trust in a state that does not allow such trusts. These trusts must be irrevocable as to the settlor and must contain certain limitations on distributions, but in the right circumstances they may offer an alternative to a DAPT.

Protection through powers of appointment. Generally, self-settled asset protection trusts established in non-DAPT states are a "step down" from the best of all worlds offered by Delaware-type DAPT trusts or offshore trusts. These alternatives involve an arrangement where someone other than the settlor is given the power to remove assets from the trust and place them elsewhere, such as in another trust. This power is called a "power of appointment." Power of appointment is the legal term meaning the power to redirect ownership of assets that are subject to the power. A power is a "general" power if the person who has the power (the powerholder) can redirect the ownership of the assets to *himself.* The power is a "limited" or "special" or "nongeneral" power if the powerholder cannot exercise the power to himself or for his own benefit, but only for others, called the "objects" of the power or the permissible "appointees." If the language creating the power permits it, the power can be exercised to place the assets in *another trust* (for the benefit of the individual objects of the power) rather than for the individuals directly.

To illustrate, Stewart creates a trust providing that the trustee can pay all the income to Stewart, but no principal. (Assume that Stewart's transfer is not fraudulent.) At the same time, the trust allows Stewart's wife, Carolyn, the power to direct the trustee to pay trust principal to or for the benefit of any or all of Stewart's children. In this case, Carolyn has a nongeneral power of appointment in favor of Stewart's children (the objects of the power), and, at any time and for any reason, without restriction, Carolyn can exercise it by directing the trustee to pay such part or all of the trust principal (assets) to the children as she chooses, or to a new trust for their benefit. Note that the exercise of such a power is *not* a new transfer. It is regarded as merely a completion of the initial transfer (by Stewart) that became subject to the power.

The beauty of this arrangement is that the exercise of the power to move the assets is *not* a fraudulent transfer by Stewart, since his transfer was made earlier when he funded the trust. And it is not considered a transfer by Carolyn since the trust assets did not belong to her. Furthermore, there is considerable law supporting the fact that a court could not order Carolyn to exercise or not to exercise her power under these circumstances. Accordingly, if the trust income being received by Stewart became in jeopardy of attack by Stewart's creditors, Carolyn could exercise her power and remove the principal of the trust, which in turn would remove the income.

The obvious problem with this picture is that Stewart now has neither income nor principal. Is there a way that we could leave "open" the possibility that at some future date Stewart could regain use of the income or the principal?

Remember that Carolyn's power over the trust principal included the children, and the terms of any exercise are at Carolyn's sole discretion. Thus, when trouble struck, Carolyn could exercise her power in a *revocable* manner (this is permissible, allowing her the opportunity of re-exercising it again later) into a trust for the benefit of her children. Then later, when the coast is clear, Carolyn could revoke the first exercise and make a second exercise of the power into a new trust for the benefit of Stewart.

Protection through the power to amend. Akin to the power of appointment is the power to *amend* a trust. Most people (including attorneys) instinctively regard this as a power held by the *settlor*. In fact, it is quite possible to give someone *other than the settlor* the power to amend the settlor's trust. (This is also discussed in the part on the trust protector below.) Under the law, a power to amend is considered a power of appointment, so that if this power is utilized, it must be drafted very carefully to result in the correct power being granted, presumably a nongeneral power.

The power to amend a trust would work in much the same way as a power of appointment, but with the added advantage that the trust assets need not be removed from the trust; the trust would merely be amended by the powerholder to achieve the desired effect. For instance, the desired effect may simply be to remove the settlor as a beneficiary. A benefit of using the power to amend is that unlike a power of appointment, an exercise of the power need not be accompanied by a statement that the exercise is revocable.

THE TRUST PROTECTOR

Though this may sound like the title of a new TV series, it is in fact a commonly used trust provision by attorneys specializing in asset protection planning and by many in estate planning as well. The role of protector is viewed by some as having originated in overseas trusts and family foundations. It typically involved a trusted family friend who would be given veto power over trust distributions that were to be made to beneficiaries, but in many cases the protector might have even broader powers, including the power to amend the trust and to add or remove beneficiaries. The protector would *not* be a trustee, but he may be given the power to remove and replace trustees. As can be seen, it is or can be a very powerful position "outside" the trust.

As explained several times, many of the trusts used in estate planning are or will become irrevocable at some point. Unless expressly provided otherwise in the trust (and many fail to provide this), such trusts are not easy to change if in the future changes occur in the circumstances of the beneficiaries or in the law that make a change desirable or necessary. In many such cases, a formal court "reformation" is required. This involves notice to every interested party, legal representation, and presentations before the court—a process that can be expensive and time-consuming. This is just one of those cases where a trust protector can save the day. The protector can be authorized to make the necessary changes quickly and without court approval.

Of course, selection of the protector must be carefully considered. It is generally a bad idea to name the settlor or a beneficiary as protector. Typically, it should be a responsible party with some knowledge of trusts and of the family makeup, though the latter is not a strict requirement. You should select a protector with the same care applied in selecting a trustee, depending on how broad the powers are that you give to the protector. This is in part because the protector's powers are superior to those of the trustee. Because the protector's powers are so important and integral to the proper administration of the trust, the purpose of the trust, and the interests of the beneficiaries, the protector is considered a "fiduciary," which means he has a duty to always act in the best interest of the trust and the beneficiaries. If he fails to do so and losses or damages result, he could be held liable. If your estate planner includes provisions for a trust protector in your trust, you should be sure that his role as fiduciary is stated in the trust. Some advisors believe otherwise and make it a point to state that the protector is not a fiduciary and will have no liability for his acts or failure to act. If you think it is a good idea for your beneficiaries to have no recourse for a protector's gross negligence or reckless misconduct, you'd better think again. Note that not all trusts will need a protector. The problem is that, except for very short-term trusts, you can't tell whether one will be needed at any point in the future for some unforeseen reason. In that event, we recommend you consider including a provision for a "springing" protector. This is where there is no permanent protector but the trust allows a protector to be appointed at any time, for a specified term or permanently, and with the powers to be determined when he is appointed. The appointment could be made by the trustee, or the beneficiaries, or a third party, or even a committee. When needed, the protector could be appointed for the desired period, he could carry out the desired transaction, and his term could then end. Simple as that.

There are numerous additional provisions that should accompany the appointment of a protector, such as compensation, power to resign, appointment of a successor, etc., but a competent estate-planning attorney will know what to include.

All that said, the use of a trust protector can be more effective for asset protection trusts than a power of appointment, due to the extensive powers that can be given to the protector. The extent of the powers can allow a broader planning perspective than a simple power of appointment, so that it is not a matter of just appointing the property/assets out of the trust. It is more like a power to amend, as discussed above, but with all the "accessories" to enhance flexibility.

If a protector is used in an offshore trust structured to provide asset protection for a U.S. settlor, it is important to provide that the protector may *not* be a U.S. person or entity, as they would ordinarily be subject to the jurisdiction of U.S. courts. More and more protectors are being used in domestic trusts as trust attorneys become more familiar with their use, although up until the past few years it was virtually unheard of in U.S. trusts. Now there are a number of states (e.g., Delaware, Ohio, New Hampshire, Utah, South Dakota) that have laws specifically providing for the appointment of a protector. As a general rule, the protector should not be a beneficiary of the trust.

Note that there are a myriad of legal and tax intricacies and potentially complicated consequences of maneuvers involving powers of appointment, powers to amend, and the use of trust protectors. These suggestions are only hypothetical to illustrate the potential uses of these provisions for domestic creditor protection purposes. Where domestic asset protection measures are not sufficient, the more serious planners will turn to the offshore trust—the "Great Wall" of asset protection.

Offshore Asset Protection Trusts

Ironically, there may be evidence that the concept of asset protection using foreign jurisdictions actually began in the United States. During World War II, many German (and other countries') citizens attempting to escape Nazi dominance and control moved their assets to the United States. As part of their move to confiscate assets, the German courts ruled that those assets had "illegally" moved "offshore" and should be returned to Germany and the Third Reich, and German judgments were issued accordingly. German representatives then attempted to collect on these judgments against funds held in the United States. The U.S. courts, however, held that in the absence of "comity" (where international jurisdictions may recognize certain of each other's judgments out of fairness and respect), these "foreign" judgments were neither recognized nor enforceable in this country, and there was certainly no treaty between the two countries providing for reciprocal recognition of judgments—hence those assets were unreachable by the individuals' German "creditors," even though the creditors had a legal judgment against them. This is the fundamental concept of how the offshore asset protection trust works, only reversing the direction of the assets and the location of the creditors.

In the typical foreign asset protection trust, a U.S. person will establish and fund a living trust in an offshore jurisdiction that has no reciprocal judgment recognition agreement with the United States and usually no tax treaty (although, as noted later, the offshore asset protection trust is rarely established to avoid taxes—almost all offshore asset protection trusts are tax "neutral," meaning that they offer no advantage or disadvantage, but are fully reportable to the IRS on mandatory informational returns relating to foreign trusts and foreign assets, as discussed further in this chapter). The assets that are to be protected will actually be transferred to this trust and held offshore. There is little benefit to leaving assets onshore as it simply leaves them vulnerable to the order of a U.S. court.

Once the assets are settled offshore in the trust, creditors must jump considerable hurdles at considerable expense to get at them. And by "creditors," we do not mean only your typical bad debt or personal injury claimant. Many offshore trusts have been established to avoid claims of forced heirship (see chapter 7) by spouses and children, and even to protect funds in the event of a divorce. In one case, a very wealthy businessman named Hess placed millions in a Gibraltar trust. His latest wife later sued for divorce, and she also sued in Gibraltar, claiming the transfer to the trust was fraudulent and should therefore be available to her as a creditor, only to have the legal door slammed in her face. The assets in Hess's Gibraltar trust were unreachable by her.

Due to the average person's concern about moving money a few thousand (or more) miles away and placing it in the hands of some bank or trust company they've never heard of, some onshore advisors recommend an arrangement whereby the funds and investments remain onshore in the individual's control until "the suit hits the fan." This result is typically accomplished by establishing a family limited partnership and transferring the targeted assets to that partnership. The individual (and her spouse, if appropriate) will act as the general partner (but holding only a 1 or 2 percent partnership share), and therefore they control all investments and distributions. The limited partner, holding a 98 or 99 percent share, is an offshore trust. Everything stays this way until trouble strikes, at which time all investments are liquidated (note that there may be a capital gains tax: to pay on liquidation) and the partnership is dissolved, with ultimate distribution of assets to the "partners." The liquidation of assets is necessary to facilitate an "immediate transfer" (e.g., by wire or cashier's check) to the offshore trustee. On dissolution, a partnership pays its partnership debts (here there would likely be none) and then pays out the funds to the partners according to their shares. One of the partners is the offshore trust, and since the offshore trust is a 98 or 99 percent partner, virtually all of the partnership funds would be immediately moved offshore, out of harm's way. Note that the term "immediately" is applicable as long as the foreign trust has already opened a foreign account and is ready to accept funds. If not, it can take several weeks, if not months, to open a foreign account.

As just noted, however, the assets must be moved outside the United States, and there must be an offshore trustee who is not subject to the jurisdiction of U.S. courts. And while the onshore partnership arrangement may offer a degree of comfort, since the assets remain nearby and under the control of the U.S. managing partners, it also involves the likelihood of paying a gains tax when the assets are liquidated, which is *not* the case if the assets have been placed in the offshore trust at the outset. Furthermore, while assets are held in the United States, or even where they may be offshore but held in U.S. companies, there is always the risk that a creditor can convince a court to reach or perhaps freeze those assets, preventing movement or protection offshore, as they are technically within the U.S. court's reach. For this reason, the really serious asset protection plan may involve offshore trusts holding the trust's cash and investments offshore. And in the really, really serious plan, the offshore trust only holds offshore investments, not stock in U.S. companies.

Although the typical offshore trust is irrevocable, this is not a deterrent to its establishment, since its provisions are extremely flexible. Such a trust is typically designed to provide exclusively for the individual and, if desired, for her family as well. Also, there are often provisions for amendment by the trustee or by a protector if deemed to be in the best interests of the beneficiaries, and for the appointment of a protector if one was not already appointed. As explained above, a protector is not a trustee but simply an individual or entity outside the trust who can have the power to veto distributions, add or remove beneficiaries, and hold other powers designed to insure flexibility. Since the settlor herself does not have these powers, a court could not order her to exercise them. Offshore trusts will also usually include a "flee" clause, which allows a party, such as the protector, to order the trustee to move the assets of the trust to another offshore jurisdiction if the assets are in jeopardy in its present jurisdiction.

In its actual operation, the offshore trust works just like any other trust. The trustee invests the assets and makes distributions to the beneficiaries as provided by the terms of the trust. Thus, so long as advisable, the settlor could receive income and principal payments as needed. If trouble strikes, distributions to the settlor would cease, and they could be made to his spouse (if a beneficiary) or even for other purposes, such as payment of the settlor's mortgage or other bills. Once the claim was settled, distributions to the settlor could be resumed. There would also be provisions for continued management of assets and distributions after the settlor's death. In fact, the trust will contain all the usual estate tax marital deduction and bypass trust provisions, and even generation-skipping trust provisions as discussed earlier, just as if it were an onshore trust. Furthermore, the individual's will would be coordinated with the trust, as is customarily done.

WHICH OFFSHORE JURISDICTION?

While this is definitely not the answer, virtually any offshore jurisdiction will be better than a U.S. jurisdiction. This is because getting a U.S. judgment enforced offshore is complex, time-consuming, and hugely expensive. But, as we said, that is not the answer to the question. The real answer depends on two important factors: First, does the jurisdiction recognize U.S. (or to them "foreign") judgments? And what is the period of limitations within which a creditor may sue the trust or attack the transfer to the trust? There are a few jurisdictions regarded as the "best" for asset protection purposes, but then, depending on your particular circumstances, there are some that are perfectly suitable, even though they do not offer what others do. The case of Mr. Hess with his Gibraltar trust is an example. Gibraltar has a long, open period of limitations, but if the transfer to the trust did not render the settlor insolvent, the protection is immediate (no open period).

Those at the top of the list are the Cook Islands, Liechtenstein, and the Bahamas. In all of these jurisdictions, foreign judgments are not enforceable, and the open period of limitations is two years or less (one year in the Cook Islands and Liechtenstein, with a difficult-to-overcome exception). Furthermore, where the debt or claim occurs any time after the trust is established, the protection is immediate. Such a creditor has no enforceable claim on the trust. And one more hurdle: even where the creditor sues within the allowable short time period, the only basis for the suit must be that the transfer to the trust was fraudulent as to *that* creditor, and the creditor must prove that it was, beyond a reasonable doubt!

OFFSHORE TRUST TAX ISSUES

Although the offshore trust will typically contain provisions designed to minimize estate taxes, as noted above, it is designed to be "tax neutral" for *income* tax purposes. This means there are neither income tax advantages nor disadvantages in establishing it (with the possible exception of the gain on liquidation if it is funded with assets liquidated from a U.S. partnership—but note that any gain is because of the need to liquidate the U.S. partnership and *not* because of the existence of the offshore trust). The tax neutrality is primarily due to the fact that the trust is intentionally designed to be a "grantor" trust for U.S. income tax purposes. As discussed in more detail in chapter 13, a grantor trust is one where, because of certain provisions contained in the trust, all trust income, losses, deductions, gains, etc., are *passed through* to the settlor. That is, the trust pays no income taxes; all taxes on trust income or gains are paid by the settlor, whether she receives them or not. On the settlor's death, the assets in the trust are treated like any other asset in her estate. Nevertheless, it is extremely important to note that although the establishment of a foreign asset protection trust does *not* normally bring about any extra taxes, it *does* bring about the requirement to file additional tax information forms each year. Failure to file the necessary annual foreign trust tax information forms with the IRS can result in a penalty of 35 percent of the amount transferred to the trust. (Taxes and the required tax forms are discussed in the next chapter.)

CREDITOR'S ATTACK ON A FOREIGN TRUST

Because the trust and the trust assets are located in a jurisdiction that does not recognize U.S. court judgments, a creditor would actually have to initiate *new* legal proceedings in the offshore jurisdiction. This means that he would have to hire an attorney in the foreign jurisdiction and pay legal fees up front—attorneys in asset protection jurisdictions do not work on a contingent fee basis. In addition, the creditor in most instances would have to produce evidence and witnesses to prove his case, as he would (or already has, at great expense) in the United States. Furthermore, some of these jurisdictions require that the creditor post a bond, usually a *cash* bond, before he is allowed to bring suit, to cover court costs and fees in the event he is not successful. Lastly (for now), the suit must be brought in the foreign jurisdiction within the short period of limitations, which, more often than not, will have expired by the time the creditor has a U.S. judgment and has conducted discovery to disclose the existence of the offshore trust.

In short, it is a formidable and expensive proceeding, chosen by only the most determined creditors and usually only in chasing large judgments, and with minimal chance of success. Unofficial but very reliable reports show that better than 95 percent of such attacks are either unsuccessful or settle for five to ten cents on the dollar. This is not to indicate, however, that all offshore trusts are creditor-proof, *nor* that you should or can create one in the face of a lawsuit.

In this sense, there is, perhaps, both good news and bad news with respect to offshore asset protection trusts. The good news is that the above observations illustrating the tremendous difficulty and expense that face a creditor seeking to attack such a trust are absolutely true and proven so. The bad news is that one way their virtual imperviousness to a creditor's attack has been proven is through a blatant abuse of their protective features by con men and other individuals of dubious character. The cases resulting from these abuses have, of course, been the ones that have made the headlines and the ones that in some respects have given a "bad image" to such trusts. This is quite unfair to those perfectly legitimate individuals who establish such trusts with nothing to run from and nothing to hide. Nevertheless, as badly motivated as they were, here are a couple of examples of actual cases dealing with offshore trusts.

In one case, a New York business owner who we'll call "Porky" needed additional funds to carry on his business. His company borrowed $1 million from a major New York bank, and Porky personally guaranteed the loan. Shortly thereafter, through a combination of a downturn in business and his own substantial withdrawals from the company, Porky and the company defaulted on the loan. When the bank came to collect on his personal guarantee, Porky filed for bankruptcy. After lying to the bankruptcy trustee as well as to the court, Porky finally admitted that he had transferred substantial funds (perhaps $1 million or more) to an offshore trust he had established in the Channel Islands (not the best jurisdiction). This was done while he knew of the company's circumstances and while his personal guarantee was in effect (in short, he had clearly made a series of fraudulent transfers). The net result, after proceedings in a New York bankruptcy court, was that the court refused to acknowledge the validity of the offshore trust and so considered the funds "available" to Porky, but the result of all this was not that any money was legally recovered from the offshore trust; rather, it was merely that Porky's debt was not discharged by the bankruptcy proceedings. What did the bank, his major creditor, do? According to reliable sources, they simply settled for twenty to thirty cents on the dollar, obviously deciding that to pursue Porky's money in the offshore trust was simply not worth it.

In another notorious and abusive case, a couple we'll call Bonnie and Clyde owned a chain of bookstores. Like Porky, Bonnie and Clyde needed money to carry on their business and so took out and personally guaranteed a $20 million (!) loan from a major bank. Undoubtedly, the bank extended the loan not only on account of the business but also on account of the fact that, unlike Porky, Bonnie and Clyde had substantial personal assets outside the company. As the story must go, the business went sour and the bank called the note. Bonnie and Clyde stalled and the bank brought legal action. Unbelievably, in the midst of and after legal proceedings against them, which resulted in an order for payment, Bonnie and Clyde established a trust in the Cook Islands and funded it with about $18 million of their assets. This time, the bank took forceful action against Bonnie and Clyde *and* their trust, even to the extent of suing in the Cook Islands as well as in the United States. All this took time (and lots of money), of course, and in the meantime, Bonnie and Clyde filed for bankruptcy. After numerous and expensive legal skirmishes that gained little ground, and with no certainty of success, the trustee in bankruptcy, in response to an offer on behalf of Bonnie and Clyde to settle the dispute for less than half the $20-odd-million debt, recommended to the court that the offer be accepted, which it was. Unlike in the movie, Bonnie and Clyde got away with the (balance of the) money.

In both of the above cases, the debtors clearly made fraudulent transfers, and it seems unfair that their legitimate creditors could not collect what was due them. As noted earlier, this may be the dark side of such planning, but it does demonstrate the strength of the concept in general. What is not so apparent or prominently reported are the thousands of legitimate professionals and businesspeople who in good faith and with no present claims against them establish offshore asset protection trusts and can then "sleep at night," knowing that a substantial part of their wealth is protected for themselves and their family. There is nothing unusual or unfair about this.

While in Porky's case the bank decided it would not be worth it to go to the foreign jurisdiction to attempt to prove the transfer fraudulent, in the case of Bonnie and Clyde, where many millions were involved, it clearly would have been worth it—*if* the bank could win. Once the bank got there, hired lawyers, and began the battle, however, the picture dimmed more than a bit. They definitely had a good case, at least on its face, but how do you prove a fraudulent transfer? Generally by showing evidence of the intent of the debtor/transferor. In this instance, the best way to show intent was the communications and correspondence between Bonnie and Clyde and the law firm that helped them create the offshore trust, and that's exactly what the bank's lawyers targeted. But this was clearly privileged attorney-client information—or was it? In fact, there is a "fraud" exception to the attorney-client privilege, and the court ultimately held that it applied here—but not to every document. All documents would therefore have to be examined, said the court, with opportunities for exceptions, objections by the parties' attorneys, and so on. With the prospect of months if not years of litigation on this matter alone, with no certainty or even a likelihood of success, it is not surprising that the trustee in bankruptcy recommended settlement.

It is also important to explain that the question of insolvency in this context often requires the person (the settlor) to take into consideration not only her actual debts but also those debts and claims that may be *pending* or *expected* (e.g., where you know you have caused damages giving rise to a claim, but the claim has not yet been formally filed). In this regard, most competent attorneys who practice in this area will have their clients make a complete disclosure and sign an "affidavit of solvency" before agreeing to prepare and implement an asset protection plan. Some attorneys even do a credit and background check and outstanding case review before proceeding with the plan. In addition, virtually all responsible offshore trustees will require a written statement by the attorney and another by the client, disclosing assets and liabilities as well as known or anticipated claims, and showing that the individual will not be rendered insolvent by the transfer to the offshore trust.

TRUSTS FOR NON-U.S. PERSONS

It has been said that one of the best-kept secrets in the trust world (and we do mean world) is that the United States is not only a tax haven but also an excellent asset protection jurisdiction for non-U.S. settlors of U.S. trusts. The applicable rules in this area are understandably quite far-reaching and complex, but we felt it may be helpful to offer a brief overview with the caveat that, as with so many topics covered in this book, expert advice is vital to proceeding with a plan.

For openers, if a foreign settlor (sometimes called a nonresident alien [NRA] or a nonresident noncitizen [NRNC]) establishes a trust here in the United States, and the trust is a "grantor trust" as to the NRNC, then interest and capital gains that the NRNC realizes on the investments in the U.S. trust will be income tax free to the NRNC. Furthermore, if the trust is settled in one of the many states that allow self-settled asset protection trusts, creditors of the NRNC may not reach the assets in the U.S. trust after the applicable period of limitations. (Note that the U.S. trust investments should be held in a foreign, non-U.S. corporation to avoid estate taxes in the estate of the NRNC. The foreign corporation shares would be held in the U.S. trust.)

Spousal Lifetime Access Trust (SLAT)

This type of trust might be regarded as a "have your cake and eat it too" trust, but HYCAEIT doesn't make for a very catchy acronym. Basically, it involves one spouse creating an irrevocable trust for the benefit of the other spouse and making a substantial gift to that trust (the SLAT). The nongifting spouse could be the sole beneficiary of the SLAT, or other beneficiaries, such as children, could also be included. The nongifting spouse could also act as trustee and have control over distributions, which in that case would be limited to distributions for the health, education, maintenance, and support of the beneficiaries (called an "ascertainable standard") including herself. The gift to the trust would be a potentially taxable gift, but, as discussed later, the allowable tax-free exclusion for gifts can run into the millions of dollars, so a gift tax on the gift is unlikely. The assets in the SLAT will not be includable in the gifting spouse's estate or in the nongifting spouse's estate. Further, those assets will be protected from the creditors of both spouses and the children until distributed—perhaps that's the frosting on the cake.

As a follow-up note, we do not recommend each spouse creating a SLAT for the other, unless the trusts are materially different (in beneficiaries and distributions, for example), otherwise the substantial benefits could be lost.

Decanting Trusts

Occasionally, the provisions of an irrevocable trust can become undesirable or inapplicable due to changed circumstances of the beneficiaries or changes in the law, but if the trust is irrevocable, what can be done? Although it has always been possible to petition a court to change ("reform") an irrevocable trust where unforeseen circumstances interfere with the original intention of the settlor (creator), recent years have seen a major trend in what is now known as trust "decanting." Analogous to the decanting of wine, this exercise is widely being used to move trust assets from one trust, where provisions have become outdated or inappropriate, to a new trust for the same beneficiaries and similar provisions but deleting the unwanted provisions. In fact, most trusts contain language that allows the trustee to make distributions "for the benefit of" the beneficiaries, which would seem to allow the trustee to "decant" to a trust for their benefit, but questions remain as to just how much leeway the trustee would have in such a case. The question became adequately widespread that as of this writing thirty-five states have enacted laws outlining their respective rules and requirements for decanting a trust. As would be expected, they are not all the same, but the basic theory is that when applicable, the law would allow a decanting into a new trust without the need for expensive, time-consuming court action. In any event, the many different issues in decanting can quickly be seen, such as: Can the new trust eliminate beneficiaries from the "old" trust? Can the new trust add beneficiaries who were not in the old trust? Do the present beneficiaries have the right to block a decanting or even to be given notice? What are the tax consequences of a decanting? And so on. Obviously, it is important to know of the existence of this option, but it is equally important to recognize the need for expert guidance and advice.

Special Purpose Trusts

As has become apparent, we hope, throughout the chapter, the trust is probably the most flexible document in the estate planner's book. As further indication of just how flexible, this section discusses three special purpose trusts (the actual number is limited only by the estate planner's imagination) designed and drafted to accommodate special situations or objectives, as well as a fourth, perhaps ultimate, special purpose trust, itself simply called a "purpose" trust. Keep in mind that the first three special purpose trusts, as with all trusts, will have one or more trustees, with a mechanism for trustee replacement; one or more beneficiaries, with provisions covering all possible changes, such as death, disability, etc.; a "corpus," or assets transferred to the trustee; and provisions covering the management and disposition of those assets in all circumstances, up to the termination of the trust. The fourth type, the purpose trust, need not have any beneficiaries.

THE NOMINEE TRUST

This is a "special purpose" trust that covers an almost infinite number of special purposes. That is, the nominee trust is often created solely to suit a particular situation requiring the use of a simple but private trust, although it does have two common functions—to avoid probate with privacy and to facilitate transfers of the trust property. The nominee trust is a unique type of trust that, in fact, is not always a trust. Also occasionally referred to as an Illinois land trust, a "blind" trust, and an agency trust, the nominee trust is often regarded as a relationship where the trustee merely acts as the *agent* of the beneficiaries. As an "agency" trust, the arrangement has, in some courts, been held to be a hybrid between a trust and an agency. An agency relationship occurs when you authorize someone to do something for you, giving specific instructions, and when the job is done the agency ends. This is not usually the case with the nominee trust, even though some nominee trusts are purposely drafted so that the trustee can *only* act as the agent of the beneficiaries, as specifically instructed by them. I raise this agency issue only because no discussion of nominee trusts would be accurate without it. Despite this, however, they are generally treated and structured as true *trusts*, and from here on we'll talk of the nominee trust as a *trust*.

The need for the nominee trust originated in those states that require a trust to be recorded in the state's registry of deeds if the trust is to hold real estate in that state. Because the typical estate-planning trust contains so much personal information that grantors would not want as public record, a trust was created that had virtually no personal information but would satisfy the state's conveyancing and title concerns. Effectively, the only provisions needed for recording such trusts would include adequate trustee powers to deal with the property, an orderly succession and notice of trustees, a provision protecting third parties who deal with the trustees, and little else. What's missing? The beneficiaries.

The truly unique feature of the nominee trust is that the identity and shares of the beneficiaries are set forth in a document *separate* from the rest of the trust, allowing the rest of the trust to be recorded (or a copy of the trust to be given to banks, stockbrokers, etc.) without disclosing the identity or shares of the beneficiaries or any other personal information. This separate document, legally a part of the trust, is typically called a "schedule of beneficial interests" (SBI), and it is a perfectly legal arrangement that does not affect the validity of the trust. Instead, it allows a copy of the trust (but *without* the SBI) to be readily recorded or given to parties dealing with the trustee who want to see a copy for their "protection" or, as in the case of banks or stockbrokers, who want to have a copy of the trust for their records.

Typically, the grantor (owner) of the assets will be the trustee of the nominee trust, succeeded by his spouse and/or children, or other close individuals. In small estates, the grantor and his spouse can be the beneficiaries, possibly followed by the children (all as stated on the SBI), and the primary function of the nominee trust—to avoid probate—will be carried out simply and quickly. In larger estates, however, the SBI would probably show the grantor's more elaborate estate-planning trust as the beneficiary of the nominee trust, thus completing the picture and allowing all assets to be easily placed in trust without disclosing any personal information. Since the nominee trust is normally a revocable grantor trust, it is ignored for tax purposes and does not complicate the overall plan.

As noted above, the nominee trust also greatly facilitates ownership and gifts of real estate, simply by changing the SBI instead of having to execute and record a deed for a fractional share of the property every time a gift is made. In cases where real estate is transferred piecemeal to a number of donees over a period of time, it avoids not only recording fees but also the need for twenty or thirty or more deeds. If this approach is used for such gifts, however, be absolutely *certain* that the grantor does not have the unilateral power, or even the power by majority interest, to amend the nominee trust or control the distributions to beneficiaries; otherwise, the IRS will claim that the full value of the property should be included in the grantor's estate, regardless of who is named on the SBI. It is also important to have the property appraised with each gift.

Further, it is an excellent way to hold real estate that is located in a state other than that of your domicile. This is briefly described in chapter 11, under "Out-of-State Real Property." In such situations, unless the real property is held under a survivorship interest or in a trust, it will be necessary to have double probate on your death (once in your own state and again in the state where the real property is located). A nominee trust can easily be used to hold the out-of-state property and avoid probate in both estates.

Don't be surprised if your attorney is not familiar with nominee trusts. Although they are valid and may be used in every state that recognizes trusts, they are not necessarily used in every state, particularly in those states, such as New Hampshire and California, that do not require a trust holding real estate to be recorded (only a "trustee's certificate" is required). Furthermore, in those states that truly have simplified probate, they are also less necessary. In any event, they are available as another way to avoid probate and ensure privacy, even in those states.

THE VOTING TRUST

The special purpose served with a voting trust is to transfer the right to vote shares of stock without losing control of the stock itself or any other rights associated with it, such as appreciation, dividends, or other distributions. The voting trust is most often used with closely held companies where it is deemed advisable to allow one or more specific individuals to vote the stock. It is the trustee of the voting trust who is entitled to vote the stock held in the trust, and thus the individuals who are to have the vote will be appointed as the trustees of the voting trust. A voting trust can be revocable or irrevocable; typically, they are irrevocable for a period of years, or for the life of the key person, or until the company is sold, or any other arrangement that suits the objectives and is within the law. Although many states have a special limitation period on voting trusts, typically ten years (e.g., New York), some allow the trust to last as long as any other noncharitable trust (i.e., about one hundred years, as discussed in the previous section).

A voting trust normally pays no taxes and files no tax returns, as it holds only the right to vote, and, if it receives any dividends, it does so merely as an agent of the shareholders. Funds or other trust assets are not managed as they would be with another type of trust. In practice, it is not uncommon for a closely held company to pay dividends directly to the shareholders even though the stock is held by a voting trust.

Shareholders wishing to establish a voting trust will actually transfer their shares to the trustees of the trust. The corporation is notified of the transfer, receives a copy of the trust, and actually issues a new stock certificate in the name of the trustees of the voting trust for the total number of shares transferred to the trust. The trustees in turn will issue to each shareholder a "voting trust certificate" for the number of shares they transferred to the trust.

When the voting trust terminates, both the trustee's and the shareholders' certificates are turned in, and the shares of stock are transferred back to the shareholders.

Voting trusts are often used when a parent transfers voting stock to a child or where a parent (or other relative) wants to leave shares of stock to one or more children through her estate on the condition that the shares subsequently be transferred to a voting trust with preselected trustees, to ensure the continuation of proper management and control of the company. As noted above, however, some states limit the term of such trusts to ten years, with one ten-year extension. If a more permanent arrangement is required, the stock could be transferred to a standard trust (i.e., not a voting trust) that can last for up to one hundred years in most states, or the company could simply issue two classes of stock—voting and nonvoting.

Remember, the existence of the voting trust has nothing to do with the disposition of the shares on your death. Accordingly, they should be dealt with separately, as any other asset. In this regard, there is no reason why the voting trust certificate could not be held by your living trust, so the shares will avoid probate and be distributed according to your estate plan.

STOCK OR BUSINESS PURCHASE TRUST

The special purpose of a stock or business purchase trust is to arrange for the purchase of a business interest or shares of a corporation on the death (and sometimes the disability) of a business owner or shareholder (the "owner"). It is primarily used where the owners are actively participating in a business or professional practice. In many such cases, it is wise to arrange for an automatic buyout on death or disability through a trust for a number of reasons:

- To produce an immediate source of cash to provide for the owner and for his family without having to wait for an estate representative to be appointed or a dispute to be settled;
- To produce funds to help pay any estate tax that may be due;
- To arrange for an orderly sale at a fair value rather than a forced sale at a bargain price;
- To allow a buyout at a previously agreed-upon price without interference from the deceased or disabled owner's beneficiaries; or
- To avoid having the surviving owner be forced to work with a new partner whom he or she may not want or who may not act in the best interest of the business.

In the typical business purchase trust the owners will transfer their interests in a form of escrow to the trustee of the trust. The escrow arrangement is one where the trustee has absolutely no obligations until such time as an owner were to die or become disabled (to the point where he could not perform his functions in the business). In the event of a disability, the agreement usually requires the owner to be disabled for a period of twelve months before the buyout would take place. In the usual case, the buyout is funded by life and disability *buyout* (not disability income) policies on the owners, and the policies are made payable to the trustee. This way, when the event happens, the trustee receives the funds, buys out the particular interest, and transfers the funds to the owner's beneficiary (if the owner is deceased) or to the owner or his representative (if the owner is disabled). Since the trustee already has the necessary transfer documents and the binding agreement to sell, he does not have to wait until the deceased's estate is probated or to get approval from the deceased's beneficiaries. This is not to say that it would be impossible to take legal proceedings to question the buyout, since legal proceedings can be initiated in just about any situation. However, there would be a binding agreement signed by the deceased or disabled person, and the burden of proof that it was somehow not binding or should be overturned would be on the challenger, at his or her expense. Note that in certain cases, the funding of a trust buyout with life insurance can result in tax complications. Be sure that your advisor is expert in this area.

If the agreement is not funded with life or disability insurance, then the payments must be made by the business or by the purchasing owner. In this event, care must be taken to work out a realistic arrangement for payment that does not bankrupt the business.

The price or formula for the buyout should be included in the trust agreement. It is usually best to have a formula that is simply applied to the facts and financial status existing at the time of the buyout. As a fail-safe provision, many agreements simply call for an independent appraisal to set the price.

As with all trusts, this one also requires the assistance of an attorney with considerable experience in drafting and implementing this particular type of trust, as well as the complicated tax implications of the different methods of funding the buyout.

PURPOSE TRUST

Briefly, a purpose trust is a trust established for a *purpose* rather than for specified or named beneficiaries. This concept is totally contradictory to one of the most basic principles of trust law, which is that a trust *must* have beneficiaries; otherwise there would be no one to enforce the trust and, therefore, no trust. In at least one respect, however, this concept is not new. After all, a charitable trust is typically established for a purpose and typically has no identifiable beneficiaries, but it has never raised the eyebrows of a trust lawyer or a judge. For instance, a trust established to maintain a public park or to fund medical research is nothing unusual, and if properly drafted is seldom questioned since such trusts are regarded as charitable and may be enforced by the attorney general for the benefit of the public. The "new" concept referred to here is the noncharitable purpose trust. An example of a noncharitable purpose trust would include one where a settlor established a trust to maintain his collection of antique automobiles, or perhaps one for the purpose of constructing a home for the maintenance and care of his pets and all their offspring. Such trusts would, under trust law, still be regarded as purpose trusts even though there may be individuals who happen to benefit from the trust carrying out its purpose, or beneficiaries who may take the trust's remainder when the purpose of the trust is satisfied or the trust terminates for some other reason.

For instance, in the illustration above, a valid purpose trust could be established for the maintenance of the settlor's collection of automobiles and, if the settlor's child or children were using the automobiles, they would indirectly benefit from the trust, although under the trust law that applies to purpose trusts they would not be considered beneficiaries and would have no standing to enforce the trust. Similarly, the trust could provide that if and when the automobiles were unusable or disposed of, or simply after a set period of time, the trust would terminate and the settlor's children would receive any assets (e.g., the automobiles) remaining in the trust. The fact that the children are designated remaindermen after the purpose is carried out does not change the character of the trust or by itself give it validity as a trust. Note, however, that in those states that do not recognize purpose trusts, a trust with these provisions would be totally disregarded as void, and one of two things would happen. Either the bequest would pass directly to the children without regard to the instructions to maintain the automobiles or the entire bequest would fail and pass by intestacy (absence of a will) through the settlor's estate. Cases have held both ways.

The offshore jurisdictions that have recognized purpose trusts have done so through formal legislation. They include, among others, the Isle of Man, Jersey, British Virgin Islands, Bermuda, Cayman Islands, Cook Islands, Liechtenstein, and Nevis. There are also a number of states that have effectively enacted purpose trust law by their adoption of the Uniform Trust Code, but in a far more limited way than the offshore jurisdictions. The thrust in the United States to adopt purpose trust legislation appears to be largely related to and motivated by the public's desire to be able to establish valid trusts for their pets, although other "honorary" trusts (such as trusts to maintain gravesites or masses) are usually allowed on the same basis

Generally, the states that allow purpose trusts limit the term of such a trust to twenty-one years. Interestingly, the wording of the law does not invalidate the trust after the twenty-one-year period; it merely declares the trust to be unenforceable. Presumably, then, a court could, upon petition, declare the trust invalid, inasmuch as its terms are unenforceable. When that happens, unless otherwise provided in the trust, the corpus would revert to the settlor or her estate. It would be unusual, if not a lack of foresight, if a drafter did not provide for disposition of the trust property after the purpose was carried out or in the event it could not be carried out.

A few states allow some form of purpose trust through case law (e.g.,

Pennsylvania), but whether through case law or a uniform act or code, the application and use of purpose trusts in the United States is extremely narrow and the term unnecessarily limited. For instance, if an individual wished to provide for the long-term maintenance of a private building without mingling that asset with other assets in a "person" trust (one that provided for individual beneficiaries, where dispositive disputes could arise and restraint on sale of the property could be overridden), why should he be limited to twenty-one years?

Accordingly, if a person in the United States wished to establish a purpose trust for a longer term than permitted in the applicable state, it would be a simple matter to settle one in one of the states that have adopted a specific statute allowing purpose trusts (see below) or in any of the several offshore jurisdictions recognizing such purpose trusts and then administer it in the state desired.

In addition to what we call the "bare-bones" purpose trust provisions contained in section 409 of the Uniform Trust Code, two states (as of this writing) have adopted their own "stand-alone" purpose trust—South Dakota and Oregon. In both states, the purpose trust can be perpetual, and while South Dakota allows the establishment of a purpose trust for any lawful purpose, the Oregon statute requires such a trust to have a business purpose and be funded with shares or ownership in virtually any type of business entity. New Hampshire does not have a purpose trust statute per se, but its private foundation law is such that virtually the exact equivalent of a purpose trust could be established under that statute. It seems that the New Hampshire legislature wasn't sure what it wanted, so it passed a law that straddled the two concepts.

Whether the purpose trust is created offshore or onshore, it must meet certain requirements, as with other trusts, or it will fail, despite the potentially broad scope of such a trust. The first requirement is that the trust be subject to enforcement. Most of the offshore statutes as well as the Uniform Trust Code require the trust to name an enforcer to enforce the terms of the trust (sort of a private attorney general) and provide for court appointment of one if the trust fails to do so.

Next, the purpose or object of the trust must be certain, reasonable, and possible. The case of the late famous author George Bernard Shaw is a good illustration of a purpose trust that seems to fail on all three counts. In his will, Shaw directed that the residue of his substantial estate be held in several trusts for, among other unusual purposes, the study of the advantages of developing a phonetic alphabet and the determination of the number of living persons who speak and write English based on the twenty-six-letter alphabet "at any and every moment in the world." The lengthy and complicated forty-seven-clause will, written in part at age ninety-four by Shaw himself, who is described by the court as having been "a kind of itching powder to the British public," generated the obvious question of whether the trusts were valid and enforceable. In its holding that they were not, on the basis that they were not for a charitable purpose (since the United Kingdom did not and still does not recognize noncharitable purpose trusts), the opinion also indicated that at least some of the purposes were virtually impossible to carry out.

Even if the purpose is possible to carry out, the court will not enforce it if it is wasteful, useless, or otherwise against public policy. An interesting illustration of this principle is the case of Anne Maria Burdett, whose will devised her home and contents to trustees, directing that on the day of her funeral the trustees arrange to have the doors and windows of her home bricked and boarded up "and nailed with good long nails," and basically kept "in state" for twenty years after her death; thereafter it would pass to named beneficiaries (remaindermen). Her will was contested by the remaindermen, but in the meanwhile the house was, in fact, bricked and boarded up as directed. Not surprisingly, extensive litigation ensued; ten years later the remaindermen's appeal was successful, and the court ordered the trust property unboarded, unbricked, unnailed, and sold, and the trust was to be terminated on the basis that it was wasteful, useless, and did not constitute a disposition of the property.

Of course there are numerous other terms to consider, such as selection of trustee and enforcer, successors to both, registration requirements, etc., as well as the purpose and duration of the trust. As to which jurisdiction to select, there are again numerous factors to consider, both domestic and offshore, including the purpose and term of the trust, the most logical place for administration, the laws of the jurisdictions under consideration (i.e., the flexibility of the applicable statute), and, perhaps, your travel preferences.

While the illustrative cases discussed earlier may be interesting if not entertaining narratives of would-be purpose trusts, what are the practical uses of such trusts that gave rise to their growing recognition and developing legislation? The answer is that modern-day purpose trusts can be used for personal or philanthropic purposes that do not otherwise qualify as charitable, for instance, to hold and provide for control of a family business (indefinitely, in jurisdictions not bound by the rule against perpetuities); for maintenance and preservation of family or business property without interference by beneficiaries; to provide complete privacy and creditor protection where, for instance, the purpose of the purpose trust is to maintain a noncharitable foundation for the benefit of the settlor and members of the settlor's family; and quite commonly, to hold ownership of companies that lease assets to other companies for off-balance-sheet transactions.

Keep This in Mind

It is safe to say that there may be no legal document that can do more than a trust. The most important thing to keep in mind, however, is that no one trust can do everything. Trusts are often created for special purposes, such as education, long-term care, or asset protection, and each of these trusts must contain special provisions that don't necessarily belong in the others. The most common public misconception, for example, is that "if my assets are in any type of trust, my creditor can't reach them." Wrong. There are various types of trust, and what each can do for you can vastly differ. Some provide asset protection, some do not. Just remember, one size does not fit all.

13

Probate, Trusts, and Taxes

There is only one difference between the tax collector and the taxidermist—the taxidermist leaves the hide.

—Mortimer Caplin, former director of the IRS

Anyone who has been through a tax audit might well feel that way. And anyone who has suffered through the deadly, double-barreled combination of a will contest *and* a tax audit usually comes to the painful realization that man is the only animal that can be skinned more than once.

What never ceases to amaze us, however, is that despite their loathing to pay taxes and equal loathing to pay legal fees, most people bring *both* a contest and an audit upon themselves and their families by failing to take a few necessary and fairly easy steps to avoid them. In chapter 12, for instance, we point out a way to avoid probate in not just one estate but two or more, inexpensively, and without the risks attendant to joint ownership, the expensive alternative that is used by most families. And in this chapter, we go further in pointing out how to save thousands in estate taxes by using one or more trusts—if you are one of the few lucky enough to have the wealth to trigger a federal estate tax, or you live in a state with its own estate tax. Will you take advantage of these ideas, or will yours be just another family that gets skinned more than once?

Probate vs. Taxes

One of the most common and persistent misconceptions is that avoiding probate means avoiding taxes. *This is simply not so.* It is quite possible (and becoming more common) to have an estate that totally avoids probate but that is fully subject to estate taxes. The legal principles and rules on which probate and taxes are based are completely different, and each serves a completely different function.

Remember, probate is the legal process in each state by which property that was in the deceased person's name alone (not jointly, and with no beneficiary designation) can pass to his heirs or beneficiaries after debts, taxes, and expenses of the estate are paid. By itself, the probate process does not generate any revenue to either the state or the federal government in the form of taxes.

Taxes, on the other hand—*estate* taxes, that is—are based on ownership, control, and enjoyment of property, *regardless* of whether or not the particular item of property was or was not probated. Jointly held property is a perfect example of this, as discussed in more detail below. For instance, say that after Mom's death, Dad places his home and all the rest of his estate in joint names with Daughter. On Dad's death, his entire estate will pass to Daughter as surviving joint owner without probate, but, at the same time, Dad's *entire estate* will be subject to estate taxes. Understanding this difference between the *legal* consequences of ownership (where it goes and who gets it) and the *tax* consequences (what is subject to tax) is essential to developing the best plan for your family.

A Word About Our Tax System

Justice Oliver Wendell Holmes said, "Taxes are what we pay for a civilized society." Well, we must be awfully civilized, since there is not much we do without paying a tax, sometimes a huge tax. The money we earn is taxed, and the money we earn on the money we earn is taxed; if we give money away we can be taxed; and what we have left when we die is subject to tax. We are not, however, any different from most other "civilized" countries, and you may be surprised to learn that when compared with other major countries, our taxes are actually *lower* than most.

Like most "civilized" tax systems, ours imposes taxes in three major areas: on income earned by the taxpayer; on gifts made by a taxpayer to another person; and on transfers made on account of a taxpayer's death. The last two are referred to as wealth transfer taxes and generally complement each other. But wait, there's more! There is a third transfer tax, the "generation-skipping transfer tax" (GST tax), and it, too, complements the other two transfer taxes. For instance, if there was an estate tax but no gift tax, a person could give away all of her assets during life and pay no tax on the transfer of that wealth to another generation, but our tax system requires a reconciliation of these gifts with your estate when you die. And what of the clever person who passes her wealth to her grandchildren and thus tries to circumvent the estate tax in her child's estate? That is where the GST tax comes in and applies an additional tax when transfers "skip" a generation. All of our tax laws are very carefully drafted to allow for a minimum of "loopholes" (note that a minimum is better than none), and this includes careful attention and consideration to the numerous situations where trusts are involved. As explained in more detail below, there are some cases where trusts are ignored for tax purposes and pay no tax, and other cases where the trust is taxed on its own. What follows is a brief explanation of how all this works, first with respect to what is included in your estate, then as to income taxes, then gift taxes and estate taxes, and finally generation-skipping transfer taxes.

What Is Included in Your Estate?

The next most common concern is the concept of what is included in your estate when computing the tax. Note that when we say something is "included" in your estate, we do not mean that the item is somehow taken back or handed over to your estate's personal representative. What we mean is that the *value* of the item for estate tax purposes (usually the fair value at the date of death) is added to and shown on the estate tax return for purposes of computing the estate tax. If the inclusion of these items produces a tax that the personal representative or trustee cannot pay, there is a legal mechanism by which the IRS can collect against the items themselves in proportion to the tax generated by each.

As to the general rule of includability, you can assume for starters that the value of any property over which you have *control,* or property that you have given away but retained the right to *use and enjoy,* or property that you simply *own* will be included in your estate for estate tax purposes. To expand on this just a bit, let's look at some specific items and forms of ownership and see how they are taxed in an estate.

1. Jointly owned property. If you were a joint owner of any assets with someone other than your spouse (or if it is your spouse and he is not a U.S. citizen), then the *full* value of the jointly held assets will be included in your taxable estate, *unless* (and to the extent) the other joint owner can *prove* to the IRS's satisfaction that he or she contributed to the property. Contributions by the surviving joint owner that can be traced back to gifts from the deceased are *not* considered contributions.

If you and your spouse were the only two joint owners and your spouse is a U.S. citizen, then only one-half of the joint property will be included in your estate. While it's true that this one-half will not be subject to federal estate tax because of the marital deduction, remember that the full value of that property will then be included in the estate of the surviving spouse on her later death, often costing extra in estate taxes.

2. Life insurance. If you were the *owner* of a policy on your life, or if you had any "incidents of ownership" (the right to change the beneficiary, cash in the policy, borrow against it, or cancel it), either individually or as trustee of a trust, or if the policy proceeds were payable to your estate or personal representative or required to pay debts, expenses, or taxes, then the *full proceeds* of the policy will be includable in your taxable estate—*even though* the proceeds avoid probate. Most people confuse ownership of a policy with designation of beneficiary. *The beneficiary is not necessarily the owner,* and, except as just noted, has little to do with the policy's includability in the estate, as explained in chapter 13.

3. Property in trust. As a general rule, your gross estate will include the *full* value of any assets in a trust created by you that is revocable by you, controllable by you (such as where you could change beneficiaries), or where you retained the right to receive income or principal for your life, or for a period that did not end before your death. In fact, the includability rules for trusts in the estate of the person who created the trusts can be divided into two categories: trusts in which the creator has retained some interest or benefit (retained interest trusts), and trusts in which the creator has retained some control (retained control trusts).

Similarly, when we apply the retained interest concept to asset protection trusts, special needs trusts (for Medicaid or other benefit programs), and personal injury settlement trusts established to receive a personal injury settlement, the result is that the full value of the trust assets is generally included in the deceased creator/beneficiary's estate.

In the typical case, all of the foregoing trusts but one will have either funds or property to use as a resource from which to pay any estate tax that may be due if there are no other funds available to pay the tax, and the trustee of the trust will be obliged to do so. The one trust where this may not be the case, resulting in a potentially serious problem, is the personal injury settlement trust funded with structured settlement payments (structured settlement trusts).

3a. Structured settlement trusts tax trap. Personal injury settlements are often "structured," meaning that the injured party (the "plaintiff") will accept periodic payments extended over a number of years instead of a lump sum. The choice is often motivated by the fact that such payments are usually income tax free. In most cases, as a matter of good estate planning (if not made otherwise necessary for Medicaid planning), such structured settlements are caused to be put into a trust.

Although structured settlements enjoy a special income tax break, however, there is no corresponding estate tax relief. Our federal estate tax laws are very clear in their treatment of unpaid settlement proceeds to which the plaintiff is entitled: they are *fully taxable* to the extent of their present value on the death of the plaintiff. This is the trap.

To illustrate, say that Henry, a minor, is awarded a settlement payable over his life but for no less than forty years. The settlement has a present value of $8 million. In year five, Henry dies and at that time the settlement has a remaining present value of $6.8 million.

Assuming no other assets in Henry's estate, and assuming that the contract did not provide for accelerated payment or commutation on Henry's death (something to ask for), the unpaid balance of the structured settlement is *fully includable* in Henry's estate and, depending on the year of death and the total value of Henry's estate, could generate a federal estate tax of about $1.6 million.

Since the insurance company is under no obligation to advance payments (unless negotiated in the contract as suggested above), how will these estate taxes be paid? Will the IRS agree to take a portion of each payment received by the beneficiaries? Further, if the estate tax liability is not paid by nine months after the date of death, interest begins to run on the unpaid amount.

Fortunately, the tax code allows for an extension of time of up to ten years to pay the tax. But even if the full ten years' extension is allowed, interest on the unpaid balance of the tax must also be paid, at a rate undoubtedly higher than the rate paid under the settlement. In most cases, therefore, the tax and interest could consume the settlement payments for years, and the named beneficiaries may get little or nothing until the estate taxes (and interest) are paid in full. In smaller estates, or in estates where there is a surviving spouse and the trust is designed to take advantage of the marital deduction, the problem can be lessened or even eliminated.

Although each case is different and special circumstances may allow a solution to the problem to be found (such as the purchase of life insurance on the plaintiff), there is no easy remedy, and in some cases, as with Henry, there is no remedy at all, *unless* the plaintiff or his attorney can get the settlement company to agree that if the plaintiff dies within the term, they will accelerate an amount of the payments sufficient to pay the estate tax on the settlement.

3b. Retained interest trusts. The tax code and numerous cases on the issue have been very clear about the following rule: if you transfer assets to a trust, and under the terms of the trust you are entitled to receive the income for your life or for a period that does not end before your death, then *all* of the trust assets will be includable in your estate at death. This will be so even though the trust is irrevocable and you have no right whatever to the principal or any rights to control the trust.

When we apply this concept to the retained interest trusts discussed in chapter 12, it should be clear that if the creator of any of those trusts should die before the end of the term, the full value of the trust assets will be included in the creator's estate (with the possible exception of the GRAT, where something less may be included in certain circumstances).

3c. Retained control trusts. This issue is much more involved, but the basic string leading to includability is where the creator keeps too much control over a trust. What is too much control is easy to describe in extreme cases, such as where the creator reserves the right to add or remove beneficiaries or change shares, or to change the terms of the trust, or where the creator names himself as trustee with unlimited discretion. In these cases, the *entire* trust assets are includable in the creator's estate even though the creator retained no benefits from the trust. The question is much more difficult in more subtle cases, such as where the creator reserves the seemingly harmless right to remove and replace trustees of a discretionary trust. Although that right, by itself, would only be a problem if the creator could appoint himself as trustee, as a general rule, retaining control of a nature that would, even indirectly, give the creator the ability to control trust distributions is dangerous. One way to deal with this is to give such control to one or more individuals who are close to the creator and whose judgment would likely be consistent with the creator's judgment in similar circumstances. Most tax attorneys prefer this route rather than to walk close to the line and risk estate inclusion by attempting to give the creator control that is just short of what would cause estate includability. But frequently, creator and third-party control can be combined to arrive at a satisfactory result.

For instance, as a general rule it is always wise to have a mechanism in a trust to change trustees. As suggested above, however, giving the creator the power to remove and replace trustees without limitation is considered somewhat aggressive. Instead, a third party who understands the creator's wishes in creating the trust may have the power to remove the trustee, and the creator may have the power to fill any vacancy in the trusteeship or vice versa. Note that this arrangement would *not* extend to the making of any changes to the trust's dispositive provisions (i.e., who gets what and when), and would not extend to the creator being able to name himself as trustee.

In short, a considerable degree of control of power to change the trust or even the beneficiaries can be given to others, but in general it cannot be retained by the creator without risking includability of the entire trust assets in the creator's estate.

4. Retirement plan proceeds. Fully includable in your estate (*and* in many—but not all—cases they will also be subject to *income* tax when withdrawn by the beneficiaries).

5. Gifts within three years of your death. *Not* includable, except in two cases. One is where ownership of a life insurance policy on your life was transferred by you within three years of your death, in which case the *entire* policy proceeds will be included in your estate for estate tax purposes. If you manage to live for more than three years after the transfer, the policy proceeds will escape tax, assuming there is no other reason they may be included. (Note that this rule has nothing to do with the adding back of lifetime taxable gifts, as there is no three-year limit on that.)

The second case where a three-year rule applies is where you have made a transfer of property, retained an interest in the property transferred (such as a life estate or an income or other interest in a trust), and given away or released that interest within three years of your death. On your death within the three-year period, the full value of the subject property will be added back to your estate.

6. Property held under a tenancy in common. Generally, only your proportionate share of the property is included in your estate.

7. Property in which you hold a life estate. A life estate is the right to occupy or use or receive the income from property during a person's (the life tenant's) lifetime. It automatically expires on the life tenant's death, and no further action is required for the owners (the remaindermen) to own the property. If you transferred the underlying property and retained a life estate, then the full value of the property will be included in your estate, *even though* you made a completed gift of the remainder (the full value of the property minus the calculated value of your life estate) on the original transfer. If *someone else* transferred the property and *gave you* a life estate in it, then *none* of the value of the property would be included in your estate, since you never had ownership of the property. (See also the comment in number 5 above.)

8. Assets held in your own name. Fully includable in your estate and fully subject to probate as well.

Taxable Value

The value at which all of the above assets will be subject to tax in your estate is the fair market value on the date of your death. There is also an election available to value the assets six months after the date of death, and, in some cases, this can prove advantageous (such as a big drop in the stock market within that time period). In addition, there are special use valuation elections for real estate used in a farm or other business, and a special tax break given to closely held businesses. These elections and tax reductions, however, only apply if certain specific conditions are met. Perhaps the biggest estate tax break is that given to surviving spouses in the form of the unlimited marital deduction (discussed in more detail in chapter 13), rendering estate transfers to the surviving spouse completely free of estate taxes.

Trusts and Income Taxes

Let's start with a *common misconception.* It is commonly thought that every trust must pay its own tax on income earned by the assets held in the trust. For some reason, this conclusion is thought to be even more definite if that trust is irrevocable. This is a dangerous, misleading, and often *costly* misunderstanding of the tax laws. Whether a trust will be treated as a separate taxpayer *depends on the terms of the trust*, and for our purposes, this can be boiled down to one simple rule.

If the trust is a "grantor trust" (explained below), it will be *ignored* for income tax purposes and will pay *no* income tax. All of the trust income (and losses and deductions) will pass through to the person who is treated as the "grantor" of the trust, whether it is paid out or held in the trust. If the trust is *not* a grantor trust, then, as described later, the trust will be taxed on income that is not paid out to its beneficiaries. The question then becomes, what makes a trust a "grantor trust"?

Grantor trusts. Because trusts can be so flexible and may be tailor-made to fit almost any situation, and because careful custom tailoring can often save income taxes, Congress decided many years ago to set down a number of rules that will determine whether a trust will be treated as a grantor trust. (These rules are contained in sections 671–79 of the Internal Revenue Code.) If by application of any one or more of these rules a trust is treated as a grantor trust, then all trust income, losses, deductions, and any other tax result, characteristic, or penalty will be attributed to the party treated as the *grantor.* It is important to note that it is also possible for a trust to be *partly* a grantor trust and *partly* a separate taxable entity, depending on the circumstances of funding and on the terms of the trust. Furthermore, depending on the same two issues, a trust can have more than one grantor. And sometimes the beneficiary of a trust can also be the "grantor" for income tax purposes. Don't blame us for the complexity. For the purposes of our discussions in this chapter, when we discuss the person who is the grantor, we will assume it is the creator of the trust.

The grantor is the taxpayer (who is usually, although not necessarily, an individual; it could also be an entity, such as a corporation or a partnership), who directly or indirectly transferred the money, property, or other assets to the trust, or who is treated as the "owner" of the trust due to the application of the grantor trust rules in the tax code.

More often than not, a grantor trust is intentionally made that way, but occasionally a slipup occurs and a trust that is intended to be a separate taxable entity (such as a minor's trust, as discussed in chapter 12) ends up as a grantor trust and is taxed to the person who funded it. The most typical example of a grantor trust is a *revocable* trust, designed primarily to avoid probate, or a revocable estate-planning trust. The creator's right to revoke such a trust causes the trust to be treated as a grantor trust.

Briefly, if a trust contains *any* of the following provisions, it will be treated as a grantor trust, *regardless of whether it is revocable or irrevocable,* and *regardless of whether the income* is *paid out to the grantor:*

A provision—

- allowing the creator or her spouse to revoke or change the terms of the trust;
- allowing the trustee to payout or accumulate the trust income for the creator or her spouse;
- allowing the creator or her spouse to withdraw trust funds;
- allowing the creator or anyone else to direct the trustee to pay trust funds to someone other than a beneficiary;
- allowing the trust assets to be returned to the creator or her spouse within a certain period;
- allowing the creator or her spouse to buy from or sell to the trust or to borrow money under less than fair market value terms; or
- allowing the trustee or anyone else to add beneficiaries to the trust.

In addition, a trust will be a grantor trust if a *U.S. citizen or resident* transfers assets to a foreign (offshore) trust that has a U.S. beneficiary (in which case the U.S. transferor is treated as the grantor *regardless* of the terms of the trust).

Note that the foregoing is an abbreviated review of the grantor trust rules. Although the discussion reflects the basic situations where the creator will be taxed on trust income, the rules can be extended to other situations, and they can be extremely complicated and tricky in their application. Nevertheless, this overview will give you a good idea of when you, as a creator and funder of a trust, may or may not be taxed on trust income, even though it is not distributed to you, and it will serve as a reminder to ask your lawyer about the income tax issues of a trust during the estate-planning process if he doesn't discuss it.

One might wonder why anyone would want to be taxed on the income of a trust when they are not able to benefit from the trust as a beneficiary? Comically, such a trust, which is intentionally drafted to shift the income tax burden to the creator of the trust, is often referred to as a "defective trust." Who in the world would want a defective trust, and what do we mean by "defective" anyway? In a number of tax-planning schemes, the creator of a trust may enter into a sale or other transaction with the trust, and if the trust is a "defective grantor trust," the transaction will generate no income tax consequences!

For instance, say that Fred creates an irrevocable trust for his children, and over the years the trust accumulates $400,000 of liquid assets. Fred is not a beneficiary and has no control over the trust. Fred happens to have a piece of real estate worth $350,000 that he would like his children to have. Fred's cost basis in the real estate is $50,000. Fred can sell the real estate to his children's trust for $350,000 cash, but of course, he will then have a $300,000 taxable gain since he and the trust are separate taxpayers for income tax purposes.

If, instead, Fred's trust were an irrevocable, "defective" trust (sometimes called an "intentionally defective grantor trust"), it would be classified as a "grantor" trust for income tax purposes, and Fred and the trust would be considered the same taxpayer. Since a taxpayer cannot sell property to himself, the sale of real estate from Fred to his defective trust, although still *legally* a sale, is ignored for tax purposes and therefore produces *no capital gain*.

The trade-off (with taxes, there has to be one) is that the trust will not get a new cost basis in the real estate. Its basis will be $50,000, the same as Fred's basis. But the family may not care, especially if the intent is to keep the real estate over the long term. There is still another benefit, however. All of the post-sale appreciation on the real estate will escape taxes in Fred's estate, because Fred and the trust are separate taxpayers for *estate tax* purposes.

With only a slight modification, the sale-to-a-defective-trust idea can be even more attractive for family planning. In the above example, say that the children's trust only had $50,000 instead of $400,000, and Fred's real estate is rental property, producing a good income. Instead of a cash sale, the defective trust can buy the real estate for a promissory note, bearing interest and providing for *only* interest payments, with the principal to be paid at a future date. Remember, the sales price must be a fair one, usually backed by an independent appraisal. The promissory note, however, need only bear interest at the minimum rate prescribed by the tax code. And since the income tax laws ignore the tax effect of the sale, the interest payments to Fred are not taxable to him. But don't get too excited about this, as the net rental payments *are* taxable to Fred, just as if he never made the transfer, since the trust is treated as a grantor trust. Fred is taxed on all the net income of the defective trust, even though the only payments he is entitled to receive are the *interest* payments on the note.

The advantage, again, is that on Fred's death, only the value of the *promissory note* is included in his estate; after the sale, all of the appreciation on the real estate escapes tax. Remember, though, that this is a brief illustration; the actual drafting and sale arrangements are complicated and should be undertaken only by expert tax attorneys.

It is important to note that there are certain instances where a trust can be a grantor trust as to the trust *income* but not as to the trust *principal.* The primary difference in this case is that if the trust is not treated as a grantor trust as to principal, then capital gains (which are generally treated as attributable to the trust principal) realized by the trust would not be taxed to the grantor but to the trust. Any competent tax attorney drafting a trust will know whether this arrangement is desirable and how to achieve it.

Nongrantor Trusts. For income tax purposes, a nongrantor trust is any trust that is not treated as a grantor trust. Interestingly, a trust could be drafted so that in some years it is a grantor trust and in others it is not. Lawyers refer to this as "toggling" from one income tax result to the other. For purposes of the following discussion we will assume the trust starts as and remains a nongrantor trust.

Simple and complex nongrantor trusts. Nongrantor trusts are separate taxable entities and are characterized (for income tax purposes) as "complex" or "simple." A simple trust is one that is required by its terms to distribute all of its income each year and may not make any charitable distributions presently or in the future. Any trust that is not a simple trust is a complex trust, but typically a complex trust is one that allows for discretionary distributions of income, principal, or both.

The basic rule of trust taxation for nongrantor trusts is that the trust is taxed on the amount of income it receives (actually or constructively) and does not distribute to its beneficiaries for the tax year. Distributions of trust income made from the trust to its beneficiaries in a given tax year are *deductible* by the trust to the extent of its taxable income for the year, and taxed as *income* to the beneficiaries, again to the extent of the trust's taxable income for the year. To illustrate in a simple manner, say that the Doright Trust (a complex trust) receives bank interest income of $5,000 on trust funds and distributes $3,500 to its beneficiary, Will Doright. The Doright Trust will report $5,000 interest income received, show a $3,500 deduction for distribution to beneficiary Will, and pay a tax on the $1,500 of income it did not distribute ($5,000 income less the $3,500 distributions). Will Doright will report the $3,500 trust distribution on his income tax return for the year.

If the Doright Trust distributed *more* than its income for the year, say $6,000, then $5,000 would be taxable income to Will Doright, and $1,000 would be a tax-free distribution of principal. This is a very simple illustration, and the application of these rules can get quite complicated. An example would be where the trust has different types of income for the year, such as dividends, interest, capital gains, and tax-exempt income, and where there are several beneficiaries, each one receiving different amounts of each. (As a general rule, capital gains are taxed to the trust.) It might also be noted that the tax law allows a trustee of a nongrantor trust to distribute income received by the trust in a given year up to sixty-five days after the end of that year (imaginatively called "the sixty-five-day rule"), and for income tax purposes the distribution may be treated as if it was made within the previous calendar year for both the trust and the beneficiary. There are also circumstances where a (domestic) trust may accumulate and pay a tax on income for years and then pay out the accumulated income to the beneficiaries without a tax. And then there are special rules when multiple trusts have been established for the same beneficiary. These situations are beyond the scope of this discussion, but your tax advisor should be able to guide you through such situations.

Trust Tax Reporting Requirements and Tax Rates

Nongrantor trusts. Trusts other than grantor trusts (and other than charitable trusts) must file an income tax return on IRS form 1041 for each year that the trust has *any* taxable income, or gross income (which may or may not be taxable) of more than $600 for the year. Such trusts must use a calendar year.

In addition to the 1041 form, the trustee must file copies of the K-1 forms the trustee sent to each trust beneficiary. If any beneficiary of the trust is a nonresident alien, then the trustee must file a 1041 form even if it has no income. The trust income tax return is due on April 15 following the calendar year of the trust, and, like individuals, trusts are entitled to an automatic three-month extension for filing the return by filing IRS form 8736.

Trusts must pay estimated taxes under rules similar to those for individuals. A trust need not pay estimated taxes on amounts distributed to beneficiaries, since these amounts are not taxable to the trust. Generally, the trustee would estimate the amount of income he expects to have left *after* distributions and deductible expenses, and pay an estimated tax on that amount. Since estimated taxes are paid quarterly, the trustee can calculate the amount on an ongoing basis. If the trustee pays too much in estimated tax, he can treat the excess as having been paid by the beneficiary. This way, the beneficiary would not have to pay as much additional estimated tax on the distribution. However, the amount the trustee credits to the beneficiary as an estimated tax payment is itself treated as an additional distribution from the trust.

Grantor trusts. Because the income of a grantor trust is taxed to someone other than the trust itself, does the grantor trust have to file an income tax return? Not surprisingly, the answer is somewhat complicated, and you'd want to make sure you, your lawyer, and your accountant are all on the same page. Very generally, in many instances the trustee of the grantor trust will obtain a separate trust tax identification number for the grantor trust and file a trust fiduciary income tax return (form 1041), but *no income taxes* will be paid by the trust. The numerical answers on the front page of form 1041 will be all "zeros" and the basic taxpayer information will contain only the creator's (grantor's) name, address, and Social Security number, indicating on form 1041 that the trust is a grantor trust by checking the appropriate box. The trustee will attach a statement to the 1041 showing the income received by the trust and stating that all income (and deductions and credits) will be reported on the creator's individual income tax return (form 1040). This is often called a "grantor tax information letter." A copy goes to the creator to include with her own income tax return.

In some instances, it is possible to avoid obtaining a tax identification number for the grantor trust and filing the trust's form 1041, but these alternative methods involve filing forms with all of the trust's asset holders to ensure that all trust income is reported under the creator's Social Security number and that the proper form 1099s are issued to the creator. Many find it easier to simply use the separate trust tax identification number method because once the creator dies and grantor trust status ends, a tax identification number will be needed for the trust at that time in any event.

Foreign trusts. Foreign trusts established by U.S. citizens and residents (typically for asset protection purposes) are now required to file a myriad of forms and statements with the IRS each year. Without discussing each form and statement in detail, this will give you an idea of the extent of the reporting involved: you *must* file IRS form 56, form Fincen 114 (this one filed electronically), form 1041, forms 3520 and 3520-A, a "background information" statement for the foreign trust, a balance sheet and income statement for the foreign trust, a foreign trust "owner statement," and a foreign grantor trust beneficiary statement. Obviously, a knowledgeable tax attorney or tax accountant familiar with those requirements must be employed. Note, however, that if there is a good reason for you to establish a foreign trust (e.g., for asset protection purposes), the filing requirements should not discourage the plan and are generally tax neutral (will *not* result in additional tax). Advisors who regularly do this type of work usually do it for a reasonable fee.

Nongrantor trust income tax rates. At one time (prior to 1994), the income tax rates of trusts were similar to those of an unmarried individual and offered an opportunity to save taxes by "shifting" income to a trust. For instance, a taxpayer in the 50 percent income tax bracket could create a trust for his children and place some of his investments in the trust, which would pay a tax as low as 11 percent on the same income. In some cases, he could later get the investments back from the trust. That was then.

In fact, it was this very arrangement that ultimately led Congress to enact the "kiddie tax," described below, and some of the grantor trust rules, described above, to prevent the shifting of income without giving up something in return. Nevertheless, the difference in tax rates continued to offer potential for tax savings until 1994, when Congress dramatically revised the tax rate tables for trusts, substantially curtailing any meaningful tax savings solely through the difference in rates. Thus, while there is still the possibility of shifting income to the lowest 10 percent bracket of a trust, it will only be of value for the first $2,600 of trust income retained by the trust because, as the trust income exceeds that amount, the rate quickly jumps to 37 percent, which is the highest rate for individuals and married couples. The following table should illustrate the dramatic difference in rates:

TAXPAYER	2020 TAXABLE INCOME	TAX RATE
Individual	$518,400	37 percent
Married couple	$622,050	37 percent
Trust	$12,951	37 percent

In view of the above, whenever possible, good tax planning will attempt to keep trust taxable income in the lower brackets and distribute the rest to beneficiaries who are also in lower brackets, so that the overall rate on the total trust income (both retained and distributed) is kept as low as possible. As noted with the next section, however, the trustee must also be mindful of the *age* of the beneficiary.

The Kiddie Tax. In its never-ending effort to attack tax savings plans developed by taxpayers and their advisors, Congress in 1986 adapted the kiddie tax, which has been amended from time to time, most recently in 2018, when Congress decided to apply the harsh trust tax rules to certain young individuals, and then again at the end of 2019 when Congress repealed the punitive 2018 rules. Today, the kiddie tax rules apply to children eighteen and under, but also to children between the ages of nineteen and twenty-four who are full-time students and whose earned income is less than one-half of the student's support. In either case, the child must have one living parent for the kiddie tax to apply. If the child is subject to the kiddie tax, you then look to see if the child's interest, dividends, and other unearned income (such as a trust distribution) is less than roughly $2,600 (in 2020). If so, the child's tax rate applies. Excess above this amount is taxed at the parent's tax rate.

Accordingly, trustees of minor's trusts and other trusts where the beneficiaries may be under age nineteen (or older than nineteen and a full-time student) at year end must always keep in mind the tax consequences of the distributions. Ideally, the trust distributions should be kept under the annual allowance. Alternatively, the trustee can invest in low-yielding securities or capital gain–oriented investments, or even tax-deferred (EE) government savings bonds. Zero coupon taxable bonds are no help since a portion of the interest must be reported each year. Once the child is free of the kiddie tax, however, all income received by or taxable to the child will be taxed at her own individual tax rate.

What a Trust Beneficiary Needs to Know

Income distributions. From the discussion above, it should be clear that trust beneficiaries are only taxed on income and in some cases capital gains that are distributed to them by the trust, *except* for trusts of which the beneficiary is treated as the *grantor*, and *except* for trusts under which the beneficiary has the *right* to receive all the income. In the latter two cases, the beneficiary is taxed on all the income whether or not it is distributed to him.

From the beneficiaries' perspective, however, the issue of beneficiaries' taxes is made quite simple because in cases other than grantor trusts, the trustee will give each beneficiary of the trust an IRS form "K-1" each year. A copy of the K-1 form must be filed with the trust's income tax return, and it tells the IRS and the beneficiary exactly how much income or loss and/or capital gains or loss that each beneficiary should report on his or her personal income tax return.

Termination distributions. When the trust ends, or when a final distribution is made of a particular beneficiary's share, there is generally no income tax on this distribution except to the extent that it might include the beneficiary's share of the current year's income and capital gains. The portion of the distribution that consists of principal is generally not subject to income taxes. In fact, there could even be a *loss* carried through to the beneficiary, since the termination and final tax year of a trust is the occasion that allows capital losses to be passed through to beneficiaries. However, if the beneficiary receives assets other than cash on a termination distribution, she may have a gain when she later sells these assets, depending on the "cost basis" of the assets. Cost basis means the "tax" cost of the asset for determining a capital gain or loss on sale. In general, on the distribution of an asset from a trust that is not an income distribution, the beneficiary's basis will be the same as the basis held by the trust. The trustee would give the beneficiary this information.

So, for example, if the trust has a cost basis of $2,500 in one hundred shares of XYZ stock worth $10,000 and distributes the hundred shares to Ben as his share of the trust, Ben will have a cost basis of $2,500 in the shares. If he later sells them for $10,000, he will have a $7,500 capital gain. On the other hand, if the trustee is required by the trust to give Ben a $10,000 bequest, and, in satisfaction of this, the trustee gives Ben the one hundred shares of XYZ stock worth $10,000, then the trust will have a capital gain of

$7,500, since it is satisfying a $10,000 obligation with an asset that cost only $2,500. Ben, in this case, would then have a basis of $10,000 in the stock, and if he sold it at that price he would have no gain or loss.

The Federal Gift Tax

Overview of the gift tax rules. Federal (and a few states') laws impose a *gift tax* on the transfer of property by gift from one individual to another for less than its fair value. Note that with the exception of gifts to charities and gifts between spouses, the gift tax rules apply whether the donee is a child, a grandchild, a friend, or anyone in between. There are exemptions and exclusions from the gift tax that change from time to time and that allow for gifts that are not taxed (commonly referred to as "tax-free" gifts). For instance, for 2020 a person (the "donor") could give up to $15,000 annually to each of any number of "donees" (the persons receiving the gifts) without paying a gift tax. The donee can be a relative or a nonrelative, literally anyone. This is called the "annual exclusion" gift. (You may be aware that for many years, the annual tax-free gift was $10,000 per donee. In 2002, due to an inflationary adjustment required under the tax law relating to annual gifts, that amount was increased to $11,000, then gradually to $15,000 for 2020.) The annual exclusion exists because as a tax policy the government does not want to keep track of small gifts—birthday gifts, holiday gifts, and the like.

In addition, a person can make a gift of *any amount* for qualified medical care (which includes medical insurance premiums and dental bills) and for qualified tuition payments on account of a donee without the need to file a gift tax return. However, to qualify for this gift tax exclusion, gifts for medical care and tuition *must* be paid *directly* to the educational institution or provider of medical care. If they are paid to the individual, they will be treated as part of and limited to the annual exclusion.

Since each donor is allowed an annual tax-free gift for each donee, then spouses, as *two* donors, can give up to twice the allowable amount to any number of donees they wish during each calendar year. Accordingly, in 2020, if Mom and Dad have four children and five grandchildren, they could give away $270,000 each year ($15,000 × 2 × 9), free of gift taxes—if they had the money.

And because of a special rule that allows one spouse to permit the other to use his annual tax-free allowance, the gift *need not come equally from both spouses.* For instance, if Mom has all the money and wants to make a $30,000 gift to Son, she can do so by having Dad consent to her use of his $15,000 allowance (note that in this case none of the gift actually comes from Dad). Dad does this by signing Mom's gift tax return (IRS form 709, due April 15 of the year following the gift, as explained elsewhere in the book), indicating his consent to the use of his annual exclusion allowance. If the couple is not married, they cannot split gifts like this. In that case, they would have to make their own separate gifts from their own funds. Note, too, that special rules apply if one spouse dies during the year of the gift.

The annual exclusion must be a "present interest" in order to be tax free. This concept can be complicated and elusive, but it basically means that the donee must be able to enjoy the gift when it is given to him rather than wait for years to get it. For instance, if Dad says to Son, "I have given your uncle $15,000 to hold for you until you get married," then unless Son is to be (and gets) married within the calendar year, the gift is not one of a present interest, and it will not qualify for the annual exclusion.

A popular use of the annual exclusion is to use it to save for a child or grandchild's educational costs by funding a "529 plan." This is also known as a "qualified tuition plan" after a provision in the Internal Revenue Code allowing for the income and growth on contributions to such a plan to be tax free if used for the beneficiary's qualifying educational expenses, which include college and postcollege tuition, fees, books, as well as room and board. Contributions are considered annual exclusion gifts for gift tax purposes and normally qualify for the $15,000 (for 2020) annual gift-tax-free exclusion. An interesting element of the 529 plan is that the annual exclusion can be taken up to five years in advance ($75,000 in 2020), but requires the filing of a gift tax return to do so. Traditionally limited to college and postcollege qualifying expenses, in 2018, 529 plans were expanded to include K–12 elementary and secondary school tuition for public, private, and religious schools. Note that the 529 plan distributions for K–12 tuition is limited to $10,000 a year. Also, starting in 2020, qualified education expenses include up to $10,000 to repay student loans and to pay for apprentice programs.

Gift tax exemption equivalent. Gifts that are within the annual exclusion may be repeated year after year without limitation. Gifts that exceed the exclusion or that do not qualify for the exclusion will be subject to the gift tax. Before a gift tax is actually paid, however, every individual is allowed a *credit* toward the gift tax, expressed in terms of an "applicable exclusion amount." Once a gift exceeds the tax-free exclusion amount, it generates a tax against which the donor's applicable exclusion *must* be applied; the donor does not have a choice. When the total gifts for the year exceed the allowable annual tax-free exclusions (if any apply), the amount must be reported on a gift tax return, IRS form 709, which must be filed each year by the same due date as the donor's income tax return (including extensions). Once the cumulative total of *taxable* gifts generates a tax that exceeds the donor's exclusions, then every taxable gift thereafter will generate an out-of-pocket gift tax, unless the lifetime exemption amount is increased by Congress. In 2020, the gift tax rate was 40 percent.

The allowable "tax-free" amount one may give away is commonly expressed in terms of the amount of dollars in gifts (or estate value) that may be transferred rather than in terms of the actual gift tax exemption itself. As of the publication of this book, the tax-free amount is set at $10 million per person, indexed for inflation starting in 2011. For instance, using the IRS gift tables and taking into account the inflation adjustment, in 2020, a gift tax credit converts to a lifetime gift exclusion of $11.58 million. In addition, the allowance and the tax rate are under a schedule of annual changes that run through 2025. On January 1, 2026, the tax-free amount per person drops back to a previous level of $5 million per person, also indexed for inflation starting in 2011.

To illustrate the relation between the annual exclusion and the tax-free allowance (the applicable exclusion amount):

- In 2020, Mom (a widow) makes a $60,000 gift to Daughter and a $40,000 gift to Son, never having made gifts before. Mom would file a gift tax return by April 15, 2020 (assuming she is timely filing her income tax return), showing the two gifts, but *each* would be reduced by the annual exclusion of $15,000, so the gift tax return would show taxable gifts of $45,000 to Daughter ($60,000 - $15,000) and $25,000 to Son ($40,000-$15,000). There would be no out-of-pocket gift tax to pay on the taxable gifts because together they total far less than Mom's tax-free allowance of $11.58 million. Mom's tax-free allowance is reduced by the $70,000 of taxable gifts ($45,000 + $25,000). Mom now has $11.51 million of tax-free allowance left.
- Mom can continue gifting without paying a gift tax until her tax-free allowance is exhausted.

As you can see, most taxpayers do not have to worry about paying a federal gift tax, although you do have to worry about complying with the rules and filing the gift tax return when required. As stated earlier, the lifetime exemption is scheduled to be reduced back to $5 million, and Congress could always reduce it further, so keeping track is important.

And what do you need to keep track of? In order for the gift tax to apply or even for a tax-free gift to be made, the gift must be *complete;* that is, the donor, in the words of the gift tax regulations, "must have parted with dominion and control" of the gifted property. An outright transfer to a donee with no strings attached is the clearest example, since the donee becomes the absolute owner of the property. Where gifts to trusts are involved, however, many tricky questions can arise. Certainly there is no question that a transfer to the donor's *revocable* trust is not a completed gift because the donor can simply revoke or amend the trust and take the gift back. Gifts to irrevocable trusts are not quite as conclusive, as explained in more detail below.

The gift may be one of money, jewelry, stocks, bonds, real estate, a life insurance policy, a royalty, even a copyright interest in a book. It can be anything that is capable of ownership and transfer. The amount of the gift for gift tax purposes is the *fair value* of the gifted property *on the date of the gift.* It does not matter that the donor paid much less than it is now worth. The only significance of the donor's purchase price is that it will generally determine the donee's cost basis if the gifted property is later sold. For instance, say that you paid $1,000 for a painting (your "cost basis") that is now worth $10,000, and you make a gift of it to your daughter, who sells it for $10,000. You have made a $10,000 gift *and* your daughter has a $9,000 capital gain. Note that you cannot get around this by "selling" her the painting for one dollar. Don't waste your time. A "sale" for one dollar is only a true sale if that's all the property is worth.

Gifts between spouses enjoy special treatment. There is no limit to the amount each spouse can give to the other without a gift tax (assuming the recipient spouse is a U.S. citizen). So if Bob gives his husband, Doug, a $5 million diamond for their anniversary, there is no gift tax and no use of Bob's applicable exclusion amount. Gifts to a spouse through the use of a *trust,* however, may not offer the same result unless the trust meets certain requirements. If the spouse has a full principal and income withdrawal power, it will be gift tax free, or if the trust qualifies as a QTIP trust, as explained later in this chapter, it will be gift tax free. Any other conditions, however, are likely to make the gift taxable.

Note that the above discussion on gift taxes is intentionally brief and very little more than an overview of the basics. It is offered only to give you a general understanding of such taxes to help you follow the concepts and tax savings ideas discussed in this book.

Gifts on creating a trust. As explained above, the gift tax rules apply when one person makes a gift to another. If a person makes a gift to a trust, who is the donee? Is it the trustee? Probably not, since we know that the trustee does not receive trust assets for his own benefit. Then it must be the beneficiaries. But if that is the case, what about the fact that the beneficiaries may not get to use or receive the gift for years, depending on the terms of the trust, or that some beneficiaries may never receive it at all? It is this fact that prevents a gift to a trust from qualifying for the annual exclusion *unless* the trust contains certain specific provisions.

The trust provisions required to obtain the necessary annual gift tax exclusion are somewhat simple in concept, but the tax and legal ramifications can be extensive and most are beyond the scope of this discussion. Briefly, for a trust beneficiary to be considered a donee with a present interest in the gift, she merely needs to be given the right to withdraw the gift from the trust. This right or power of withdrawal by the beneficiary has been ruled (first by the courts and then by the IRS) to be the same as making the gift directly to the beneficiary, thereby qualifying the gift to the trust for the annual exclusion. This is the case even though the beneficiary does not actually withdraw the gift. The right to withdraw is commonly called and widely known by practitioners as a "Crummey power," discussed earlier.

Trusts that contain Crummey powers are often referred to as "Crummey trusts," meaning that gifts to the trust will or should qualify for the annual exclusion because of the existence of the withdrawal powers. It is a safe bet that there is not a single tax attorney, tax accountant, or financial planner in the country who is not familiar with Crummey and his legacy. Little did Mr. Crummey know that his name would go down in tax history and generate a household phrase to be used by tax advisors for decades to come (although some of us might have preferred it if his name was "Nifty," or "Smart," or even "Super," as opposed to "Crummey").

The Crummey power is usually part of an irrevocable trust (remember, if the trust is revocable by the donor, no gift takes place) and typically provides that once the donor makes a gift to the trust, the trustee will notify the beneficiary of the gift and of the amount the beneficiary may withdraw. The beneficiary will have, say, thirty days after receiving the notice to advise the trustee if she wants to exercise her withdrawal right. If she does not notify the trustee that she wishes to withdraw the funds (some trusts require that she decline in writing), then the power to withdraw expires, and the funds that she could have withdrawn will remain in the trust and be managed according to its terms.

It is not unusual for there to be several beneficiaries of a Crummey trust, and the amount of the donor's gifts may be increased accordingly. For instance, if Peggy establishes a Crummey trust for her four children and the annual exclusion at the time is $15,000 per donee, Peggy and her spouse could contribute up to $120,000 each year to the trust, gift tax free ($15,000 per donor × 4 children [donees] × 2 donors). Crummey powers are very often used in irrevocable life insurance trusts to allow the donor/insured to pay the premiums on insurance policies on her life through gifts to the trust without gift or estate tax consequences.

When you think about it, this right of withdrawal or Crummey power is a pretty neat thing. If the beneficiaries holding the power never exercise it, quite a lot of money could pile up in the trust, gift tax free. And if we are pretty sure the power won't be exercised, we could name as many beneficiaries as possible to have the power, and then provide that once their power lapsed, other beneficiaries (the ones we really want) could receive distributions.

To illustrate, say that Leo has four married children who have a total of six grandchildren between them, five of whom are also married. Leo creates a Crummey trust providing that all of his children and grandchildren and all of their spouses will have Crummey withdrawal powers for thirty days after any contributions to the trust. After the thirty-day period, any amounts not withdrawn will remain in the trust for the benefit of Leo's four children, rather than for all of the "donees." Leo contributes $285,000 to the trust (four children, four spouses, six grandchildren, five spouses = 19 × $15,000 = $285,000). Leo claims nineteen annual exclusions. Will this fly? Could Leo add the parents of his sons- and daughters-in-law?

The IRS has repeatedly attacked this type of exaggerated situation and has vigorously taken the position that unless the beneficiary with the withdrawal power holds a real interest in the trust other than the bare Crummey power, the IRS will *disallow* the exclusion. In this case, only the four children were "real" beneficiaries. If the grandchildren stood to become beneficiaries after the children, the arrangement would probably be accepted, but as for the spouses, it would likely be a lost cause, since they have nothing more than the withdrawal power. It is also worthy of note that both the IRS and Congress are pushing for limitations on the number of annual exclusions a person can use each year. Expect to see more on this in the future.

Not every trust will have Crummey powers. There are situations where the donor will not want the beneficiaries to have withdrawal powers, or where, for tax purposes, it is advisable not to have them. A typical case would be a dynasty generation-skipping transfer (GST) tax trust designed to provide asset protection for its beneficiaries, discussed later in this chapter. If such a GST trust is to be established for a number of beneficiaries (say, children, grandchildren, and great-grandchildren), it is usually far more practical and desirable for long-term tax planning to *forego* the use of the annual exclusion and simply apply the donor's (and spouse's, if appropriate) gift tax credit to the transfers to the GST trust.

Gifts on terminating the trust. This is an easy one. If the trust is irrevocable and a completed gift was made on its creation, then there will be no further gift when the trust is terminated and the trust assets are distributed to the beneficiaries. As with anything that is as complex and far-reaching as the field of trusts, however, there could be exceptions, but the foregoing is the general rule. On the other hand, if the trust was revocable to begin with, then no completed gift was made at that time, and if the assets are distributed on termination to someone other than the original donor, there will be a gift of the fair market value of the trust assets on termination, from the donor to the recipient/donee of the assets.

The Federal Estate Tax

Individual state estate taxes. Before we discuss the federal estate tax regime, it is important to remember that individual states each have their own authority to impose a tax on the transfer of wealth. Prior to 2000, the majority of states did just that, but over time this has dwindled down to just thirteen in 2020. Generally, state estate tax laws fall into one of four categories.

First, there are states that do not have an estate tax at all. In 2020, the states with no estate tax are Arizona, Delaware, Georgia, Kansas, North Carolina, Ohio, Oklahoma, Texas, and Virginia.

Second, there are states that have an estate tax, but their local estate tax is tied to what is called the "federal estate tax credit." As the federal credit has been repealed by Congress, those states, in effect, have no estate tax, although one could come back if the federal credit is restored. In 2020, those states include Alabama, Alaska, Arkansas, California, Colorado, Florida, Idaho, Indiana, Iowa, Kentucky, Louisiana, Michigan, Mississippi, Missouri, Montana, Nevada, New Hampshire, New Mexico, North Dakota, Pennsylvania, South Carolina, South Dakota, Tennessee, Utah, West Virginia, Wisconsin, and Wyoming.

Third, there are states that have an estate tax. These states vary greatly in how the local estate tax is administered and who is subject to the tax. In 2020, the states with separate estate taxes are Connecticut, the District of Columbia, Hawaii, Illinois, Maine, Maryland, Massachusetts, Minnesota, New York, Oregon, Rhode Island, Vermont, and Washington.

Finally, a few states have an "inheritance tax," which focuses on the recipients of the inherited property and imposes the tax on them (rather than on the decedent's estate). In some instances the inheritance tax is in addition to a state estate tax. These states are Iowa, Kentucky, Maryland, Nebraska (applied on a county level), New Jersey, and Pennsylvania.

The federal estate tax. Provisions of the Internal Revenue Code go to great length to include in your estate the value of any and all property with which you are even remotely connected, and even some property with which you feel you have severed all connections. This is not to say that nothing escapes taxes, but rather it's meant to orient you to the theory of the tax laws so as to increase your general understanding and reduce the surprises that result from misunderstanding.

One of the more common misconceptions, for instance, is that every person's estate will pay an estate tax. In fact, it is just the opposite. Most estates pay *no* federal estate tax. This is primarily for two reasons, the first is because the portion of the estate that passes to the deceased's surviving spouse is tax free (this is called the marital deduction), and many people are married! And the second reason is that even where there is no surviving spouse, the substantial tax-free allowance renders most estates nontaxable. For instance, the federal tax-free amount for estates is currently $10 million, indexed for inflation. In 2020, that calculates out to $11.58 million per person. But, as stated above, Congress being as it is, this tax-free amount is subject to change, and indeed the current $10 million estate-tax-free amount is scheduled to "sunset" back to its previous level of $5 million at the end of 2025, absent congressional action.

Estates over the tax-free amount will pay a 40 percent tax (2020 tax rate), but only after allowable deductions. Remember that allowable deductions from the taxable estate, including the unlimited marital deduction for property passing to a spouse, will generally apply *before* the tax-free allowances are applied, so in some cases, the allowance may never get to be used, which is often a big loss for the family. Now, the surviving spouse is able to use the unused exemption of the deceased spouse via a concept that is known as "portability."

In simple terms, the surviving spouse can file an estate tax return for the deceased spouse and elect to "port" the unused exemption to himself. This concept is best explained by example: Ziggy dies in 2020 with an estate of $3 million, having never made a taxable gift in his lifetime, so that his entire $11.58 million estate tax exemption is available. He leaves the $3 million to his children, because his wife, Zelda, a real estate tycoon, has her own personal wealth valued at $15 million. Ziggy's available exemption shelters the $3 million in his estate from the federal estate tax. Zelda files a form 706 estate tax return for Ziggy's estate and elects to "port" Ziggy's remaining $8.58 million exemption to herself ($11.58 million available – $3 million used). She now has $20.16 million of exemption to use in her estate: her own $11.58 million and Ziggy's unused $8.58 million. If Zelda dies the next day, her entire $15 million estate escapes the estate tax, as she has more than enough combined exemption to cover her estate.

As with any tax rule (which may be evident by now as you read this book), there are special requirements that must be met for portability to work, such as, using the example above, Ziggy must be Zelda's last deceased spouse for her to be able to use his exemption. If Zelda had remarried, and the second spouse had died before her, Ziggy's ported exemption would die with Zelda's second spouse. Also, portability brings many planning opportunities, as the ported exemption can be used by the surviving spouse during her lifetime to make large gifts without using her own exemption. She would not have to wait until her death to benefit. So, portability is a very pro-taxpayer provision of the federal estate tax. (Importantly, many states that have their own estate tax do not permit portability.)

Another significant aspect of our estate tax system (an aspect that often is not clearly understood) is that all lifetime taxable gifts are *added back* to the donor's estate at his death. This does *not* mean that the donees of the gifts have to give them back; rather it means that the cumulative dollar amount of the donor's lifetime taxable gifts is shown on the donor's estate tax return to arrive at a "gross estate" figure that reflects *all* the includable property attributable to the donor on his death, which requires the addition of all of his lifetime taxable gifts. The term *taxable gifts* is the key because tax-free or exempt gifts are not added back. This is the primary reason that people with larger estates try to make as many annual exclusion tax-free gifts as they can before death, as these are not added back. So, if larger gifts are added back, why make them at all? Because all *appreciation* on the value of the gift after it is made escapes estate tax.

To illustrate, say that Jane, a widow, has an estate of $9 million that includes a parcel of choice real estate worth about $3 million. She decides to make a gift of the real estate to a trust for the benefit of her three children. She does so in 2020 and on April 15, 2021, she files a gift tax return (which should include a formal appraisal of the property with the return) showing the gift into trust of $3 million. Since this is below her allowable 2020 exemption of $11.58 million, Jane will pay no gift tax.

Ten years after the gift, Jane dies, with the remainder of her estate intact at $6 million ($9 million less the $3 million gift). At the time of Jane's death, however, the parcel of real estate she gave to the trust for her children had appreciated to a value of $7 million. Jane's estate tax return will show the $6 million she retained *plus* the $3 million lifetime taxable gift to her trust for her children, for a gross estate of $9 million. The $4 million *appreciation* on the parcel of real estate gifted to the children completely *escapes tax* in Jane's estate and is tax free to the children. Note that if Jane had kept the property until her death, her estate would have totaled $13 million. Would an estate tax have been due? If the tax-free exemption had remained at $11.58 million, the answer is likely yes, but it is hard to predict with fluctuating tax-free amounts. In any case, we can all agree an estate of $9 million is likely to pay a lower tax than an estate of $13 million.

The other side of the tax coin is that with the gift, the children would take Jane's cost basis in the property for the purpose of calculating the children's capital gain or loss (see discussion of this under gift taxes) and any depreciation deductions. But even if Jane's basis was near *zero* (unlikely but possible with depreciation), the children's tax rate on the long-term capital gain could be about *half* the estate tax rate (currently 40 percent). And if the gift was of property intended to stay in the family and not sold, the cost basis issue is of lesser importance.

The Generation-Skipping Transfer Tax

As if our tax laws are not complicated enough, we now have to contend with a special tax *separate* from the gift tax, the income tax, and the estate tax called the generation-skipping transfer (GST) tax. We will offer what we feel is a simple explanation (as simple as we can make it) of the GST tax for purposes of helping readers understand the potential, serious GST tax traps, and the basic reasons for some of the GST tax planning strategies discussed later in the chapter. But please heed this warning: the GST tax is one of the most complicated areas of the tax code, and you should *never* attempt GST tax planning without expert advice.

The GST tax is a tax imposed on transfers that are to benefit individuals who are two or more generations younger than the person making the transfer. Such individuals are called "skip-persons." Where family members are concerned (including nieces and nephews), the identification of skip-persons is pretty straightforward—it would include grandchildren (and more remote descendants) of the transferor, and grandnieces and grandnephews (and their descendants) of the transferor, regardless of the number of years in age difference between the transferor and the skip-person. Where nonfamily members are concerned, however, the rule calls for a thirty-seven-and-a-half-year age spread between the transferor and the younger beneficiary, who would then be a skip-person.

To illustrate, say that Herbert, age seventy-six, makes a gift to his grandnephew, Harvey, age forty. Even though their age difference is not thirty-seven and a half years, there would be a GST tax because the "family" rule will apply. On the other hand, if Herbert made the gift to his live-in companion, Anna, age forty, there would be *no* GST tax, since Anna is not thirty-seven and a half or more years younger than Herbert. What if Anna was thirty, and Herbert wanted to make a very large gift to Anna? He could marry her and pay no GST tax because spouses are always considered to be in the same generation regardless of their age difference.

As to trusts, a trust is a "skip-person" if all present beneficiaries are skip-persons or if the trust is one that only accumulates income and does not make any distributions at all until a specified time, and at such time distributions can only be made to a skip-person. (Is your head spinning?)

The GST tax is one that should be avoided at almost all costs, since it is applied *in addition* to any other gift or estate tax that is due, and there is only one rate, equal to the *highest* estate tax rate. However, everyone is entitled to a lifetime GST tax exemption. In 2020, like the estate and gift tax lifetime exemptions, the GST exemption is $10 million, indexed for inflation, for a 2020 number of $11.58 million. Thus, say that Rockyfella leaves $1 million of his gazillion-dollar estate to his grandchildren. Assuming his lifetime estate tax and GST tax exemptions have been used up and that the highest estate tax rate at the time is 40 percent, there will be a GST tax of $400,000 on the transfer and *another* $400,000 of estate tax—a total of $800,000 in combined taxes on the $1 million. (And believe it or not, when the GST tax is applied to certain lifetime transfers [gifts], the tax can be *more* than the amount given away!)

The GST tax applies to both lifetime and death-time transfers to skip-persons, although there is some slight relief in the tax code:

- The first item of relief is that lifetime gifts to most skip-persons (skip trusts have special rules) that qualify for the annual gift tax exclusion also qualify for the GST tax annual exclusion and are thus exempt from the GST tax. For example, in 2020 Grandpa can give $15,000 annually (as adjusted) to as many of his grandchildren as he wishes with no exposure to the GST tax.
- Second, the GST tax also does not apply to section 2503(e) gifts for qualified medical and qualified education expenses, discussed earlier.
- Third, the GST tax does not apply to gifts to 529 plans that stay within the annual exclusion rules.

In addition, as noted above, everyone is entitled to a GST tax exemption, the amount of which can vary, but which is $11.58 million in 2020. This exemption may be used during life or at death or a combination thereof, but can only be used until it is used up. And what is not used may *not* be "ported" and thereafter used by a surviving spouse; rather, an unused GST exemption remains unused. One interesting aspect of the GST exemption is that it can be automatically allocated by the government to an estate-planning transfer even if you don't want it to be! So it is tricky, and sometimes you must file a gift tax return to "opt out" of the automatic allocation rules because you wish to use your GST exemption elsewhere. As you can see, it is extremely important that a knowledgeable advisor is consulted when making transfers to gift trusts that include remote descendants as beneficiaries (or friends with a great age difference).

Tax-Oriented Trusts

A number of trusts have been designed for the primary purpose of taking advantage of certain tax laws, and they fall into two general categories: those that benefit only the family, and those that benefit the family and one or more qualified charities. These trusts are all subject to detailed requirements in formation and operation in order to realize the tax benefits.

The marital trust. Most spouses want to provide for each other at the first death; therefore, a person's living trust will typically state that upon the death of the creator, the trust becomes irrevocable, and is held for the benefit of the surviving spouse. When the marital trust is drafted correctly, it is unquestionably one of the most important trusts in the estate plan of a married couple with a potentially taxable estate. Why? If a trust is established for the surviving spouse and the requirements for qualifying for the estate tax marital deduction are accidentally missed, a veritable tax disaster (and probably a lawsuit for malpractice) will result. When the trust does qualify, *all* of the deceased spouse's assets that pass to the marital deduction trust will be free of estate tax in the deceased spouse's estate, without limitation.

It is called a marital deduction trust because our federal estate tax laws allow an unlimited deduction against the taxable amount of an estate for those amounts that "pass" to a surviving spouse. In other words, if John dies, leaving his entire $50 million estate to his surviving spouse (either outright or in a marital deduction trust), there will be *no* federal estate taxes. Technically, the calculation is:

Gross estate: $50 million

Less deductions against estate tax: (*$50 million*) marital deductions

Taxable estate: $0

Other deductions such as legal or accounting fees, debts, etc., are not used as the marital deduction in this case reduces the taxable estate to zero, before the other deductions are applied.

If the deceased spouse leaves the assets outright to the surviving spouse, there is no question about the bequest qualifying for the marital deduction. If the bequest is left to a *trust,* however, the trust must meet certain requirements; otherwise, the deduction could be lost.

For a trust to qualify for the marital deduction, the surviving spouse must be the *only* beneficiary of the trust during her lifetime, and she must either be given the unrestricted power to dispose of the trust assets on her death (a so-called "power of appointment marital trust"), or all of the trust income must be distributed to her at least yearly during her lifetime, in which case the spouse who *creates* the trust can direct disposition of the trust assets on the other spouse's death. This second type of marital trust is called a "QTIP trust" (for qualified terminable interest property trust). The QTIP trust is frequently used in the case of second marriages where one or both spouses have children from a previous marriage and the settlor spouse wants to provide for the new spouse but also wants to be certain that the children from the first marriage will receive the trust assets on the surviving spouse's death. For a QTIP trust to qualify for the marital deduction, an election must be made on the deceased spouse's estate tax return.

For instance, John and Mary both have children from a previous marriage, and each has an estate in excess of the tax-free amount. Each wants to provide for the other, but they also want to be sure that their respective estates will ultimately pass to their own children. They would each establish, on death, QTIP trusts (since they don't know in advance who will die first). Each trust would provide that all of the trust income would be distributed at least annually (although typically, trust income is distributed quarterly or even monthly) to the surviving spouse. The trust could also provide that the trustee could make discretionary distributions of principal to that spouse. (Note that *no one else* may receive principal or income of the marital deduction trust during the life of the surviving spouse.) On the death of the surviving spouse, the remaining trust assets would pass to the children of the settlor spouse. (*Remember,* as with all such trusts, this trust must be funded with the settlor spouse's assets in order for the plan to work. Jointly held assets or those accounts [such as a retirement plan] where an individual beneficiary is named will not pass to the trust, and the plan will be frustrated.)

The marital deduction trust is primarily tax driven. In some, if not most cases, a spouse is motivated to fund the marital deduction trust with a *smaller* amount than he or she otherwise would have in order to produce a lower overall estate tax in both estates. Because it is tax driven, in the current estate tax climate, with its large federal exemption, the pure marital deduction trust is not relevant in many estate plans of people who live in a state without its own estate tax. But the basic concept is still used in second marriages to provide for the surviving spouse, so that the marital trust will provide for the survivor but the trust assets will ultimately pass to the children of the first marriage.

Since we can't predict that the federal tax-free exemption will be when you die, we provide here an example of how a marital deduction trust would work if the tax-free amount was $5 million and no portability existed (as is true in most states with an estate tax). For instance, in the case of John and Mary above, say that John has assets of $6 million and Mary has assets of $4 million, and say that at the time of John's death the tax-free amount is $5 million. If John leaves his entire estate of $6 million outright to Mary, there will be no estate tax on his death. However, Mary's estate will now total $10 million (John's $6 million plus her own $4 million), and (assuming the same $5 million exemption at her death and a 40 percent tax rate) at her death Mary will have a "taxable" estate of about $10 million, producing a tax of about $2 million! If instead John leaves $1 million to a QTIP trust for Mary (no estate tax because of the marital deduction) and the $5 million balance in a family trust for Mary (he could also include his children as beneficiaries—no estate tax because it is sheltered by John's $5 million tax-free amount), there will, as above, be no tax on his death, but the greater advantage will come on Mary's death. Assuming the values and exemption remain the same, Mary's estate will total $5 million ($1 million from John's QTIP trust and $4 million of her own), and there will be no estate tax on John's death or on Mary's death, since Mary's estate is now sheltered by her $5 million tax-free amount, for a savings of $2 million and possibly *more* if their assets appreciate. In the case of previous marriages, the marital trust, as suggested above, is often a QTIP trust with an independent trustee, providing that on the spouse's death the remainder will pass to the first spouse's children. The other portion of the estate (typically, the "family" or "bypass" trust, as described below) may provide for the spouse, or the children, or both (or even the grandchildren in many cases). In any event, the spouse creating the trust has the option of deciding where the funds will go on the surviving spouse's death.

There may be cases—in fact, it is often the case—where neither spouse has been married before, where the settlor spouse wants the surviving spouse to have easy access to principal during her lifetime. There are a number of ways to accomplish this. One would be to give the trustee the power to make distributions of principal to the spouse. The trustee's discretion could be governed by a "standard," such as "comfort," "accustomed manner of living," or the usual "health, maintenance, education, and support." (Note that "standards" should not be used arbitrarily and without expert advice, since there can be serious tax implications to using the wrong standards in a trust.) This option could be enhanced by naming the spouse/beneficiary as the trustee. This is quite permissible from a legal and tax standpoint, but whether it is wise in a particular case will depend on the particular family circumstances.

Another way to provide access to principal of the marital trust would be to give the spouse/beneficiary the power to simply direct the trustee to make a principal distribution to her. This is called a "general power of appointment," and the power could be limited to a certain annual amount (e.g., $5,000 or 5 percent of the total amount in the trust, whichever is greater), or it could be unlimited (the entire balance). It would almost never be unlimited in a family trust or bypass trust, or any other trust that we did not want taxed in the spouse's estate.

As you can see, while a good deal of flexibility can be built into the marital deduction trust, there are some features that are inflexible if the marital deduction is desired. In addition to those explained above, the spouse's interest or benefits under the marital trust must be unconditional. That is, you *cannot* provide that benefits will cease if she remarries, or moves out of state, or fails to take care of the children or your elderly parent. Any such provision will cause the deduction to be *lost,* although you can condition benefits on the spouse's survival for a period not to exceed six months.[5]

Trusts for a noncitizen spouse. As described above, the marital deduction can provide a deferral of estate taxes on an unlimited amount of money. Congress allowed this based on the fact that on the death of the surviving spouse the government would collect its estate tax on virtually all the deferred amount. Several years ago, however, it occurred to Congress that if a spouse had a strong connection to another country, she might be tempted to move back to that country after the death of her U.S. spouse, taking the money with her. In that event, the U.S. government would never get its tax.

So, around 1988, Congress enacted a law that materially changed the marital deduction where the deceased is survived by a spouse who is not a

---

[5] Be sure to read also the part further below discussing retirement benefits and the marital deduction.

citizen of the United States. In fact, the law *disallows* the marital deduction for amounts passing to the noncitizen spouse unless the assets passing to (or for the benefit of) the noncitizen spouse are placed in a "qualified domestic trust" (dubbed a QDOT). If the assets are not placed in a QDOT by the time the federal estate tax return is filed for the deceased spouse's estate (even if filed late), then the entire amount will be subject to immediate tax.

To facilitate qualification for the deferral where the deceased spouse failed to create a QDOT for the noncitizen spouse, the law allows the noncitizen spouse to create her own QDOT after the death of the spouse. For instance, John dies and leaves his wife, Mary, who is *not* a U.S. citizen, an outright bequest of an amount that exceeds the tax-free amount. If Mary does nothing, all of these assets above the tax-free amount will be subject to estate tax. If instead she creates a QDOT within the time allowed and contributes the excess amount to the QDOT, no taxes will be due on that excess amount until she dies or, as described below, until the principal is distributed.

Mary can also eliminate the entire problem by *becoming* a U.S. citizen prior to the filing of the federal estate tax return (including extensions) in John's estate. In this case, the bequest would then qualify for the regular marital deduction, and no QDOT would have to be created.

If a QDOT trust is required, the QDOT election must be made by the personal representative of John's estate. The trust must be a trust for Mary's (the noncitizen spouse's) benefit, and it must provide that any distributions of *principal* (as opposed to income) will be subject to the trustee withholding the estate tax due on the distribution. (That is, the estate tax that would have resulted if the distributed principal from the QDOT was included and taxed in John's estate.) One of the QDOT trustees *must* be a U.S. citizen or a U.S. corporation. If the QDOT assets exceed $2 million, then one of the trustees must be a U.S. bank. If an individual trustee is used, then the individual U.S. trustee must post a bond or letter of credit to the IRS in the amount of 65 percent of the value of the trust assets to secure payment of the tax. If the trust assets are under $2 million, then no bond need be posted and a U.S. bank need not be a trustee, provided that no more than 35 percent of the trust assets consists of real estate located outside the United States. Also, if more than 35 percent of trust assets consists of non-U.S. real estate, then a bond *will* be required. If these requirements are not met, not only will the marital deduction be lost, but, if the assets are in a trust, the trustee of the trust will be *personally liable* for the tax. In short, the U.S. government wants to be sure it will get its money.

As noted, every distribution of principal from a QDOT to the surviving spouse during her lifetime or at her death will be subject to payment of estate tax (unless the distribution is due to hardship), and this tax is computed as if those amounts were included and taxed in the estate of the first spouse.

Accordingly, with a couple where one spouse is not a U.S. citizen, some careful attention to planning can yield valuable results.

Bypass trust. Like the marital trust, the so-called bypass trust is also tax-driven, since, if properly structured and administered, assets in such a trust can bypass (and therefore *escape taxation* in) the estate(s) of the surviving spouse and the beneficiaries. The bypass trust, also commonly called a "family" trust, a "credit shelter" trust, and an "exemption equivalent" trust, is designed to be funded, optimally, with the maximum allowable tax-free amount on the death of the creator (the settlor) of the trust. With this approach, there would be no estate tax on that amount on the settlor's death and no estate tax in the future upon termination of the trust. *Potentially taxable estates that do not take advantage of the bypass trust in one form or another are literally throwing money away.*

The bypassing of taxes in the estate of a trust beneficiary is based on the concept that the beneficiary did not create the trust, has no extensive control over it, or has limited control over it and cannot arbitrarily withdraw the principal. Under these circumstances, the assets in the trust will escape taxation in the estate of a beneficiary on the beneficiary's death (and as an added benefit, will not be reachable by the beneficiary's creditors).

Here's how it can work: Ralph creates a revocable trust for his own benefit during his lifetime. On his death, his trust provides that his wife, Alice, may receive as much income and principal as the trustee decides to pay out for her benefit during her lifetime (*not* a marital deduction trust). As it happens, the trustee is a "friendly" trustee and is liberal in making distributions to Alice. (There could also be situations where the trustee is instructed not to be liberal with distributions.) Even though Alice can benefit from the trust, on her death none of the assets in that trust will be taxed in her estate. The same result will occur if one or more children were beneficiaries of this bypass trust. That is, they could receive benefits for life, but the trust assets would not be taxed in their estate. However, if the assets pass to *their* children at death (Ralph's grandchildren), *then* this would be a generation-skipping trust as well as a bypass trust, and as explained above, there is a limit to the amount Ralph can place in a generation-skipping trust. There are additional benefits to a bypass trust, including protection of the trust assets from the creditors of a beneficiary and avoidance of probate of the trust assets in the beneficiary's estate. In short, there are numerous and significant advantages to using a bypass trust to provide for beneficiaries as opposed to just leaving them an outright distribution.

Charitable remainder trust (CRT). This is an irrevocable trust to which a person (the settlor) can transfer assets and retain either a fixed dollar amount of annual income (called a charitable remainder *annuity* trust), or a fixed percentage of the trust assets valued each year (called a charitable remainder *unitrust*). The tax code provides for minimums in either case for the trust to qualify. In the case of the annuity trust, the payment must be at least 5 percent of the initial value of the trust assets, and no assets may be added after that. With the unitrust, the payments must be no less than 5 percent of the value of the trust assets from year to year. Assets may be added to a unitrust trust at any time, but not to an annuity trust. It is also necessary that the projected remainder (based on the retained interest and the applicable IRS tables) be no less than 10 percent of the original contribution to the trust. Otherwise, the settlor could enjoy the tax deferral advantages of the trust and draw back most of the funds.

The income from either trust can be paid to the settlor for a fixed term of years up to twenty years, or for the person's lifetime. At the end of the period (if a term is chosen) or on the settlor's death, the balance remaining in the trust (the "remainder") must pass to a qualified charity. In either case there can be secondary (or more) beneficiaries after the settlor, but a secondary beneficiary other than the settlor's spouse produces adverse tax consequences and also can materially reduce the amount of the charitable gift.

Because the trust is irrevocable and the payments fixed or determinable, and because the remainder must go to a qualified charity, the settlor is entitled to an income tax *deduction* (up to allowable limits) *up front,* at the time the trust is funded. The amount of the deduction is calculated according to IRS tables (a complicated exercise that is usually and happily computed by the charity named in the trust), and it reflects the present value of the remainder that is to pass to the charity at the projected end of the trust. Although getting an income tax deduction today for a gift that will continue to be used by you (in the form of income) and may not be paid to the charity for many years ought to be enough of a bonus, there is an even greater bonus that accompanies this type of trust. The tax code provides that the trust itself is not taxable. The only tax that is paid is that which becomes due as a result of distributions from the trust to the individual beneficiary (typically the settlor or his spouse). This means that if a settlor transferred assets to a CRT and the CRT sold those assets at a huge capital gain, there would be *no tax* to pay on that gain unless at some point the gain was distributed to the settlor. This can result in an indefinite deferral of a virtually unlimited amount of tax.

Here's how it could work: Katherine, a single person age sixty, has 3,000 shares of stock in TechCo, her principal asset, which she acquired many years ago at a cost of about $40,000. At $165 per share, the stock is now worth $495,000. The problem is that TechCo pays a dividend of less than 1 percent, or about $4,000 per year on the 3,000 shares. Although Katherine could sell the stock and invest in a higher-paying investment, she is reluctant to do so because of a capital gain of $440,000 (which could result in a federal tax of about $124,000 [plus a state gains tax]).

Katherine is a perfect candidate for a CRT. She could create a charitable remainder unitrust paying her, say, 8 percent annually for her lifetime. On her death, the remainder would pass to her favorite charity. As soon as the trust is executed, Katherine can transfer the TechCo stock to the trust. The trustee of the trust can *immediately* sell the stock and, assuming it retains the same value, reinvest the full proceeds of $495,000. No tax will be paid on the gain by the CRT.

The particular investment return that the trustee realizes is important for long-term purposes, since Katherine will be receiving 8 percent of the value of the trust, valued *each year*, so if the value increases, Katherine's income will increase as well (and, of course, the converse would be true). In any event, for the first year, the trust will pay Katherine almost $40,000, and, assuming the value of assets remain constant, she will receive that amount each year for the rest of her life. Compared with the $4,000 she was receiving on the same amount, this is quite an improvement, at no cost to her (except for the document and setup).

The tax that Katherine will pay on the $40,000 income will depend on the trustee's investments and the source of the income derived by the trust. If the trustee received $40,000 of dividends and paid that out to Katherine, her income is deemed to be dividend income and taxed accordingly. Note that the trustee *must* pay Katherine 8 percent of the value of the trust assets, regardless of whether they actually earn 8 percent. If Katherine is paid out more than the trust earns, she is considered to be receiving back part of the principal (which would first be the capital gain).

For instance, if the annual payment is to be $40,000, but the trust assets only earned $28,000 for the year, then the balance of $12,000 is deemed to come from the principal, and this is when the capital gain on the stock would be drawn out. Thus, Katherine would have $28,000 of dividend income and $12,000 of capital gain to report. Often this is actually an advantage, since capital gain is generally taxed lower than ordinary income. Another important tax benefit is that Katherine would be entitled to an income tax deduction of about $125,000 in the year she funds the trust, for the present value of her gift to charity.

Note that there are many different options in structuring the income, one is explained below.

Charitable remainder trust retirement fund. And if Katherine's picture isn't attractive enough, it can get even better. A certain type of CRT can be designed to accumulate tax-deferred appreciation until such time as you decide to retire and take an income for life (or for a term of years). Where a unitrust is involved, the tax code allows the trust to provide that if the trust has no income for the year or less than the required percentage payment, then only the actual amount earned need be paid out. For instance, if the required payment was 6 percent of the assets but they only earned 2 percent, then only the 2 percent would be paid. This is called a net income CRUT (the "U" is for unitrust).

The code also allows such a trust to keep a running tab of the shortfall and to *make up* the shortfall in future years when the trust income increases. This is called a "net income with makeup" CRUT, or NIMCRUT. Even though the NIMCRUT can be structured to generate large distributions to the beneficiary/settlor in later years, the settlor's income tax deduction when the trust is created is calculated in the same manner as if the trust were a straight CRUT. Here is how a NIMCRUT might work.

Conrad has a large parcel of undeveloped land that he purchased long ago for a song. It is now worth about $500,000 and rising steadily because of the area. His plan has been to hold the land until he needs the money and then invest what's left after taxes to produce income for himself and his wife. Conrad creates a 6 percent NIMCRUT, which is to pay him 6 percent of the trust's value as income each year for his life, then the same amount for his wife's life, and then the remainder to three charities selected by them. If in any year the trust earns less than 6 percent, the shortfall may be made up in future years in which the trust earns more than 6 percent, to the extent of the excess income (over 6 percent) for that year.

The land is contributed to the trust and, based on Conrad's and his wife's ages and the 6 percent return, the $500,000 value of the land contributed to the trust results in a current income tax deduction to Conrad of about $120,000. The land produces no income, so no distributions are made, and the makeup account begins to build up. Furthermore, as the land appreciates in value each year, the 6 percent buildup also increases from $30,000 the first year to $72,000 in year ten when the land is worth $1.2 million. In that year the trustee of Conrad's trust sells the land for $1.2 million (net proceeds), and neither the trust nor Conrad will pay any tax on the gain in the year of sale (and may never pay a tax on it). The trustee invests the sale proceeds for a return of 8 percent, or $96,000 for the year.

Since the required payout is 6 percent, the trustee must first pay out $72,000 for the year (6 percent of $1.2 million). The income balance of $24,000 ($96,000 less $72,000) may then be applied toward the balance in the makeup account, which now stands at about $500,000. If the trust continues to earn 8 percent and the value of the principal remains constant, Conrad (and then his wife) will receive the full $96,000 each year until the makeup account is paid down, or about twenty years. If the return or the value of the principal changes, the payments will go up or down accordingly.

Each payment received by Conrad is first treated and taxed as ordinary income to the extent that the trust has any ordinary income that has not been distributed. If that is exhausted, then the payments begin to reflect capital gains that have not previously been distributed. In the typical NIMCRUT of this sort, the payments are made up largely of dividend or interest with only a small part, if any, being capital gain.

As noted, on Conrad's death, his wife will then be entitled to the 6 percent annual payout (or $72,000) if the value of the trust assets remains at $1.2 million. In addition, as stated earlier, she is entitled to recover any unpaid makeup amounts that accrued during Conrad's lifetime. The value of the unpaid makeup amounts and the wife's 6 percent income interest for her life is included in Conrad's estate for tax purposes, but there will be no tax on it because it qualifies for the estate tax marital deduction as a QTIP trust (see the discussion earlier in this chapter).

Charitable lead trust (CLT). A charitable *lead* trust (CLT) is, in a certain sense, the opposite of a charitable remainder trust (CRT). Whereas a CRT pays income to an individual for a period of time and then pays the remainder to one or more charities, the lead trust pays *income* to one or more charities for a period of time, then pays the *remainder* to one or more individuals. Like the CRT, the CLT must be irrevocable and can be a "unitrust" (a "CLUT") with fixed percentage of income for its term or an "annuity" trust (a "CLAT") with fixed annual payment for its term. Whether a CLUT or a CLAT, the lead trust, unlike the CRT, which can have a makeup provision if there is inadequate income in some years, *must* make its prescribed payments every year. And unlike the CRT, the CLT is not tax exempt and cannot defer tax on a gain. In fact, the income tax advantages of the CLT are usually negligible and sometimes negative. It is more often used for its estate tax advantages, which are gained by virtue of the *discount* the settlor receives on the remainder that passes to his beneficiaries. The discount is applied to the gift because the donee will not receive the gift for several years. Here is how it works.

If a person makes a gift of $100 today, the gift is clearly $100. If, instead, the person says, "I'm setting aside $100, which will be paid to you in ten years," then *today* the gift is not worth $100 to the donee. Taking it a step further, if the person says, "I'm setting aside $100; 7 percent of this will be paid each year to my church, and at the end of ten years, you'll get what's left," now we have still a different picture. If the account earns more than 7 percent, we'll have more than $100 left. But if it earns less, or substantially less, we may have nothing left. So, what is the value of the gift today?

The IRS has tables and procedures that enable us to arrive at a present value of the future gift based on the prescribed payout compared with the estimated rate of return established by the IRS over the period. In using these tables for planning purposes against what we believe will be the realistic rate of return, we can get a considerable tax advantage with the charitable lead trust.

To illustrate: Jack placed $200,000 into a charitable lead annuity trust providing that his alma mater will receive 8 percent, or $16,000, per year income from the trust for fifteen years. At the end of the fifteen-year period, the balance remaining in the trust will pass to Jack's two children. At the time Jack creates the trust, the IRS tables assume just over a 6 percent return (regardless of what is actually earned). Based on this return, the term of the trust, and the prescribed payment, the IRS will treat this as a gift of about $44,000 to Jack's children. If, in fact, the invested funds produced a return of 12 percent, the remainder value passing to the children at the end of the fifteen-year term will be nearly $500,000! In other words, in this example, Jack's children would receive $500,000 totally tax free and free of taxes in Jack's estate, and Jack would report a gift of only $44,000. Note that Jack would pay the income tax on the annual income of the CLT, reduced by the 8 percent passing to charity (unless he elected to deduct the present value of the charitable payments in full at the outset, in which case he would pay a tax on all of the CLT income for the term. This could be viewed as a negative tax result).

In effect, that Jack's paying a tax on the income accumulated for his children is an added benefit to his children, since they will receive the accumulated income on which Jack has already paid the income tax. Even though the children may receive substantially more than the calculated amount of the gift according to IRS tables, the table amount is the controlling factor. This is the principal advantage of the CLT.

The charitable lead *unitrust* can also be used as a generation-skipping device (to avoid estate taxes in a child's estate), but the lead *annuity* trust should not be used for this purpose. If the estate is large enough and the projected actual annual return sufficient, the CLUT can be very effectively used on a person's death to pass on a huge amount of funds, gift and estate tax free, to grandchildren. For instance, say that Jackie had a $30 million estate and no spouse. On her death she leaves $20 million in a CLUT with a rate of return for the charity and a term of years calculated at the time of her death so as to produce a remainder at or near zero, with the remainder at the end of the twenty-year period passing to her grandchildren (or great-grandchildren). This means that the $20 million would *not* be taxed in Jackie's estate, since there is *no* projected remainder to pass to her beneficiaries. If, however, the return on the $20 million was more than the applicable IRS rate on her death, the grandchildren could receive *millions* in tax-free dollars. In fact, this is almost exactly what Jacqueline Kennedy Onassis did in her estate (although for unknown reasons, it was not funded).

Tax-Oriented Family Trusts

These trusts are all motivated almost exclusively by tax laws that the trusts use to the family's advantage by saving gift taxes, estate taxes, income taxes, or any combination of these. Although tax planners are constantly coming up with new ideas, new trusts, or new versions of old trusts, the basic group of trusts in this category and discussed in this section include retained interest trusts, personal residence trusts, life insurance trusts, and spousal limited access trusts. GST trusts fall into this category too, but they were discussed above.

Grantor retained interest trusts (GRIT). This category generally includes trusts where the settlor (grantor) retains an interest in the trust for himself—typically, some amount of income or the right to use the trust property. In this section, it will be more appropriate to call the settlor the *grantor*, since this type of trust is commonly referred to as a "grantor retained interest trust" or GRIT. As discussed above, in a GRIT, the grantor usually transfers income-producing assets and receives the *interest* from those assets for a term of years selected by the grantor. At the end of the selected term, the remaining assets pass to the named beneficiary (the remainderman). The advantage is similar to that described in the charitable lead trust discussed above—a discount on the value of the gift of the remainder. If the grantor outlives the term of the GRIT, the trust assets will be excluded from his estate, regardless of their value. The bad news (for some) is that no savings and adverse tax consequences will result if the beneficiaries of the GRIT are members of the grantor's close family. The good news is that this does not include nieces or nephews, nor does it include unmarried partners.

Grantor retained annuity trust (GRAT). The sister to the GRIT, but with a much wider application, is the GRAT. This differs from the GRIT in that the grantor must receive *a fixed annual payment* for the term of the GRAT, and differs further in that the beneficiaries may be the settlor's close family. Like the GRIT, the term of the GRAT may be selected by the grantor; there is no minimum or maximum. The trick is, as it is with all of the retained income trusts, to select a term that the grantor will outlive, since if he dies before the end of the term, most, if not all, of the hoped-for tax savings will be lost, as explained below.

The most effective use of the GRAT will occur when the property transferred to the GRAT generates a higher income than the income assumed under the tax code (the so-called section 7520 rate), similar to the concept described above for the charitable lead trust. In this case, however, it is the *grantor* who will be receiving the income.

For instance, say that in September 2020 Sammy, age sixty-six, transfers shares of his closely held company to a twelve-year GRAT. The shares are appraised at $600,000 (after taking an appropriate discount for the minority interest and the fact that the shares are not readily saleable), and the GRAT must pay him $48,000 per year for the twelve-year period. The company is classified as an "S corporation," which means that its profits are passed through to its shareholders. At the end of the twelve-year term, the shares (or what remains) will pass to Sammy's three adult children. Based on the applicable IRS rate, after taking into account the payments that must be made to Sammy over the term of the trust (and assuming that the IRS agrees with the appraised value of the shares), Sammy is considered to be making a gift significantly less than the $600,000 that went into the GRAT—the gift will be about $100,000 when he creates and funds the trust. This is the case regardless of the actual income and regardless of what is actually left at the end of the term.

As it happens, the shares that Sammy has transferred to the trust are actually generating income of $126,000 per year, which is more than the required payments. In this case, the excess income remains in the trust, but because the trust is a "grantor" trust, the entire amount of the trust's taxable income, not just the amount he receives, is nevertheless taxed to Sammy. In this event, Sammy has the option, when he creates the trust, of giving the trustee the discretion to distribute to Sammy, in *addition* to the specified annuity payments, an amount equal to his tax liability on the undistributed income that remains in the trust. For instance, if after the required payments Sammy's tax on the undistributed amount was $16,000, then the trustee could distribute an additional $16,000 to Sammy to pay the tax; the remaining undistributed amount would remain in the trust to be invested with the trust assets until the end of the term, when it would all be distributed to the children, tax free.

Note that all required payments to Sammy, the grantor, *must* be made each year. If for some reason there was not enough cash to make the payment, then shares of stock, at their appraised value at the time, could be distributed in satisfaction of the payment. The GRAT may not issue a promissory note in lieu of making the annual payment.

If, by the end of the twelve-year term, the stock has appreciated in value to $2 million and there are additional accumulated cash and investments of $500,000, Sammy's children will receive the entire amount of $2.5 million totally tax free, even though Sammy's original gift was only about $100,000. The other side of this coin is that the children's *cost basis* in the shares will be the same as Sammy's original cost basis. Thus, a later sale of the shares is likely to produce a capital gain. On balance, however, the tax savings to the family will be huge, so long as Sammy outlives the term. If Sammy dies before the end of the twelve-year term, some of the tax savings will be lost, as a portion of the GRAT's assets will be included in Sammy's estate, generally the amount that would have been required to pay the remaining payments that stopped at Sammy's death. It should be noted that the grantor's grandchildren should *not* be the remainder beneficiaries of a GRAT at the end of the term. This is because the rules relating to the generation-skipping transfer tax as they relate to this type of trust would require the grantor to apply his GST exemption at the *termination* of the trust, when the value presumably would be at its highest.

During the twelve-year term of the GRAT, Sammy, if he wishes, can be the trustee with no adverse tax consequences. After the term, however, he should not remain as trustee, unless his only function is to terminate the trust and distribute the assets to his children. In some cases, especially where the children are minors or there is some other reason to keep the assets in trust, the trust will continue after the term, and in such event the grantor should *not* be the trustee. To do so could cause the trust assets to be included in the grantor's estate on his death after the term, when otherwise it would not be. A disastrous result.

One more thought regarding GRATs. It is possible to "zero out" a GRAT, meaning the payout to the grantor is calculated to equal the amount going into the GRAT, so that no taxable gift is made at all upon formation and funding of the GRAT. For a very simple example, Roxanne funds a two-year GRAT with $2 million, and the GRAT is designed to give Roxanne back the $2 million over the two years, plus whatever the IRS's 7520 interest rate requires to be distributed to Roxanne. If the 7520 rate was 2.2 percent, and the GRAT grew by 6 percent over the two-year term, about $2,066,000 would be distributed back to the grantor, and about $119,000 would be left in the GRAT to be distributed to the grantor's children (for example) without any reduction in the grantor's lifetime exemption amount. A good deal. To make it more attractive, the grantor could turn around and take the $2,066,000 and create and fund another two-year GRAT, and hope again for a growth in excess of the then-applicable 7520 rate. This is called a "rolling GRAT" strategy.

Grantor retained unitrust (GRUT). A third type of retained interest trust, mentioned only briefly here for the record, since it is generally of little use for estate planning, is the grantor retained unitrust (GRUT). We can recall from the discussion of the charitable remainder unitrust above that a unitrust is one where the grantor (in this case) retains the right to receive a fixed percentage of the trust assets each year. For instance, Gigi places $100,000 in a six-year GRUT, retaining the right to receive a 6 percent unitrust interest per year. The first year she would receive $6,000. Each year thereafter for the term Gigi would receive 6 percent of whatever the value was for that year. The main planning purpose of a retained interest trust is to "freeze" the value of the asset at the time the trust is created and to have increases in income and appreciation of the asset accrue for the beneficiaries. Since the GRUT would increase the income paid to the grantor as the asset appreciates, it is generally agreed that the GRAT is the far better estate-planning vehicle.

Qualified personal residence trust (QPRT). Like the other three retained interest trusts, the personal residence trust must be irrevocable, the term of the trust may be selected by the grantor, and the trick is to select a term that will end before the grantor's death. If you are able to select such a term and meet the requirements discussed below, it could result in substantial estate tax savings on your principal residence.

The benefit of the qualified personal residence trust (QPRT) is the ability to transfer a personal residence to chosen beneficiaries at a discount, often a very substantial discount, from its actual value. In the typical case, Mom and Dad own their home jointly. If they wish to establish one QPRT, it is generally advisable for one spouse to transfer his or her share of the home to the other, and that spouse will, a short while later, transfer the entire home to a QPRT. It is possible for the spouses to make a joint transfer to the same QPRT, but the drafting issues that must be properly addressed so as not to run afoul of the tax laws are too complicated to warrant it. If they must do it together, it is easier if each transfers his/her half to a separate QPRT. For obvious reasons, then, one QPRT by one spouse is the usual choice. And the choice of spouse is important as well. If possible, it should be the one who's younger or healthier (or both), so as to increase the chances that the spouse creating the QPRT will outlive the term.

As mentioned above, the choice of term is purely subjective, but one place to begin is the life expectancy tables used by the IRS. The reason these are significant is that the discount you will get at the outset will be larger as you get closer to your life expectancy and beyond. This, in turn, is because most QPRTs are (and should be) drafted to cause a termination of the trust and a "reversion" of the property to the grantor's estate if he dies before the end of the term. As the term gets closer to or exceeds the grantor's life expectancy, the likelihood of his outliving the term decreases, hence the less chance the beneficiaries have of ever getting the property, hence the smaller the gift. For instance, if a healthy eighty-year-old establishes a ten-year QPRT (more than his life expectancy) and if his residence has a market value of $300,000 at the time of the transfer to the QPRT, his gift, for gift tax purposes, will be only about $88,000.

The QPRT may only be funded with one *personal residence* (and in some cases a nominal amount of funds to pay three months' expenses). A person may not have more than two QPRTs, and one of them must be for her *principal* residence. Therefore, a vacation home can be transferred to a QPRT, provided the grantor uses it at least fourteen days each year. A married couple could actually have *three* QPRTs: one for the principal residence, one for the husband's vacation home, and one for the wife's vacation home. If they had separate principal residences or wanted to split their joint residence into two QPRTs, then the couple could have four QPRTs. In practice, there are seldom more than two.

The residence must continue to be used as the grantor's personal residence throughout the term of the QPRT. There is a special exception if the grantor is institutionalized (i.e., hospitalized or in a nursing home), but otherwise, ceasing to use it as a residence causes the QPRT to become disqualified. Nevertheless, if the residence is destroyed or damaged an exception applies, and if the residence is sold, the proceeds should be used to purchase another residence within two years. If the proceeds are not used for another residence, there is a complicated rule that requires the QPRT to convert to a GRAT, and that the GRAT begin making annual payments to the grantor based on the original value of the residence when it was placed in the QPRT, for the remainder of the QPRT term.

A condo could be used in a QPRT, as could shares in a cooperative. Even a houseboat could be used if it is your principal residence. Problems or questions arise where the residence consists of something more than a house, such as a house, several barns, cottages, and one hundred acres of land. Can all this be placed in one QPRT if it is your "personal residence"? The rule is not entirely clear and is constantly being examined by the IRS, but the approach seems to be that appurtenant buildings used by the grantor for residential purposes and land that is reasonably appropriate for the particular residence's size and location would be approved.

Putting a mortgaged residence in a QPRT is generally a bad idea since the part of each payment that constitutes principal will be an additional gift to the remainder beneficiaries.

For a while, advisors were recommending that the grantor who established a QPRT *purchase* the residence back from the QPRT just prior to the end of the term. This would have produced an almost-too-good-to-be true result, which the IRS quickly squashed by issuing tax regulations that require a QPRT to state in its terms that the grantor (and the grantor's spouse) is prohibited from purchasing the residence from the QPRT.

At the end of the term, the residence belongs to the beneficiaries, or to the trust if the trust is to continue. The grantor and his spouse no longer own the home and no longer have the legal right to live there. Not to worry. The QPRT can contain a provision that requires the trustee to lease the residence to you (at fair market rent, of course) for reasonable periods of time, with extensions, etc. In other words, occupancy by the grantor and spouse can be protected for as long as they like. Alter the term, and the residence can be sold (if not leased by the grantor), but the grantor, since he is not a beneficiary of the trust, would get no benefit from the sale.

During the term, the QPRT is structured as a grantor trust and so all income and gains are taxed to the grantor. If the principal residence is sold from the QPRT during the term, the gain will be eligible for the $250,000 capital gain exclusion (or $500,000 if married, even though only one spouse is the grantor). But remember the rules stated above where the trust ceases to be a QPRT.

After the term, the grantor is typically no longer the owner for tax purposes, so all income is taxed to the trust, or to the beneficiaries if distributed, depending on the terms of the trust. If the residence is sold, the trust or the beneficiaries will have a capital gain since their cost basis is equal to that of the grantor. This is, perhaps, somewhat of a downside to the QPRT, but it must be compared with the considerable estate tax savings likely to result if the grantor outlives the term of the trust.

Here is an illustration of the potential tax costs of a QPRT. Ray transfers his home to a ten-year QPRT. The home is worth $300,000 and the IRS tables indicate that Ray has made a gift to his children (the remaindermen) in the amount of $51,000. Ray's cost basis in the home is $40,000. Ten years pass, and now the home belongs to the children. Ray begins to rent the home from the children at a fair rental of $1,800 per month. The rent payments are income to the children, less expenses, taxes, etc., and depreciation based on $40,000 minus the cost of the land. In year fourteen Ray dies, and the value of the home is $700,000. Only the $51,000 gift is included in Ray's estate as an "adjusted taxable gift"; the balance (in value) of $649,000 is free of estate taxes, for a savings of as much as $325,000. The children then sell the home for $700,000 after expenses. They will have a capital gain of about $660,000 (that is, $700,000 sale proceeds less their cost basis of $40,000—actually the $40,000 will be further reduced by the depreciation deductions taken during the rental period). The federal capital gains tax will be about $165,000 (25 percent of $660,000).

In this illustration, the net savings to the children was $325,000 less $165,000 or $160,000, a substantial amount. However, there may be other factors to consider that would materially change the picture. For instance, if Ray did not have a large estate to begin with, the estate taxes may in fact be *less* than the capital gains taxes, and it would be better to *keep* the residence. Thus, before a QPRT is employed, your advisor should make a careful comparison of the projected results with it and without it.

Personal residence trust (PRT). This is a seldom-used alternative to the QPRT and basically must follow all of the same rules discussed above except for one major difference: with the personal residence trust (PRT), the home may *not* be sold during the term. Since this "locks in" the grantor, the PRT is not used very often.

Irrevocable life insurance trust (ILIT). Sometimes referred to (especially by the authors) as "the last meaningful estate tax loophole," the irrevocable life insurance trust (ILIT) provides an accessible means of producing estate-tax-free dollars that is without equal in terms of the potential savings measured against what the grantor has to give up in return.

Before we talk about the incredible benefits of ILITs, however, it is important to understand the basics of how life insurance proceeds may be subject to estate tax. Estate taxation of life insurance proceeds centers around ownership of the policy and payment of the proceeds. If the proceeds of a policy are paid to the insured person's "estate," then they will be fully subject to tax on the insured person's death, regardless of ownership. The term *estate* in this context includes the executor of the estate, creditors of the estate, or any other beneficiary arrangement that requires the proceeds to be used to pay a debt, claim, expense, or tax, liability of the insured person's estate. For instance, it is not unusual for an insurance policy to be taken out on a person, either by the person's creditor or by the person himself at the request of the creditor, to cover payment of the person's debt should he die before the debt is paid off. If that happens and the policy proceeds are used to pay the debt, they will be subject to estate tax in the person's estate, *regardless* of who owns the policy.

This does not mean that proceeds of a life insurance policy cannot ever be used to pay the deceased person's estate taxes, as in fact, they often are. It *does* mean that if there is an *obligation* to use the proceeds for that purpose, they will be subject to a tax. However, if a beneficiary other than the "estate" receives the proceeds and decides to loan them to the estate for taxes, or if the beneficiary of the insurance policy has inherited other assets and doesn't want to sell them, certainly she can instead decide to use the insurance proceeds to pay the taxes, as long as there is no obligation to do so.

The other cause of estate taxation of life insurance is *ownership* of the policy. Many (if not most) people confuse owner with beneficiary. The beneficiary of a policy is *not* necessarily the owner. The owner is the one who has the right to borrow against the policy, the right to name or change the beneficiary, the right to cancel or surrender the policy, the right to exchange the policy, etc. The tax code and regulations make it clear that if the insured person holds *any* of these "incidents" of ownership, the *full* policy proceeds will be included in his estate. And this can be the case even if the incidents of ownership are held by an entity that the insured *controls,* such as a corporation or a trust.

Note, however, that this does not automatically mean the proceeds will actually produce a tax. There could be other factors that would reduce or eliminate the taxes. For instance, if a person owns a policy on her own life under which her spouse is named as beneficiary, the proceeds are fully included in her estate on death, but there will be no tax on the proceeds because the receipt of funds by the spouse qualifies for the unlimited estate tax marital deduction. The problem in that event is the inclusion of those funds in the estate of the surviving spouse, to the extent of those funds remaining at death. This is where the ILIT can save the day . . . and the taxes.

The ILIT should be irrevocable because we don't want anyone treated as the owner of the trust, as will be seen later. The purpose of this is to offer the opportunity of escaping taxes not just in one estate but in several. The

ILIT is typically a trust for the benefit of the spouse and/or children and is a very common part of the estate plans of families whose estates exceed the "tax-free" amount, whether state or federal, or where liquidity (cash) will be needed on the insured's death.

If the individual already has a life insurance policy, ownership of the policy can be *assigned* (transferred) to the ILIT. This is done by signing an "irrevocable assignment form" available from the insurance company or from the agent. Proper completion of the form will indicate that the ILIT will be the new owner *and* the beneficiary. It would be a serious mistake to name a beneficiary other than the ILIT. When an existing policy is transferred to an ILIT (or to anyone, for that matter), the tax code provides that if the insured/transferor dies within three years of the date the policy is transferred, then the proceeds of the policy will be included in his estate for tax purposes—no exceptions, no leeway. Note that this does not mean the beneficiary will not receive the money; it merely means that the deceased insured's estate tax return will report the proceeds as part of the estate in computing the tax.

For this reason, where the insured has a spouse, and the policy is transferred to an ILIT, the ILIT will usually contain a "fail-safe" clause, providing that if the insured/transferor dies within three years of the transfer of any policy to the ILIT, then the proceeds of such policies will be held separately under the ILIT and administered for the surviving spouse in a way that will qualify for the estate tax marital deduction. This arrangement will render those proceeds tax free if the insured dies within three years and is survived by his spouse. The trade-off is that whatever is left of these proceeds will then be included in the estate of the surviving spouse. If the insured dies after the crucial three-year period, the fail-safe clause would not apply, and the entire trust could provide for the family (grandchildren can be included), free of the estate taxes in the insured's estate. The three-year concern is completely avoided if the policy is purchased at the outset by the trustee of the ILIT. This way there is *no* policy transfer, so no three-year period to worry about. (It is not unusual for an ILIT to contain both new policies and transferred polices.)

Because the estate tax marital deduction can and usually does produce a zero estate tax on the first spouse's death but results in a large estate tax on the surviving spouse's death, a need (and a huge market) arose for a product that would accommodate this problem. Without hesitation, the insurance industry offered a special type of policy that would insure any two people and pay off on the second death (i.e., on the death of the survivor of the two insureds). What's more, the second-to-die policy usually would be much cheaper than a single life policy, since, effectively, the risk is spread out. As a result, many ILITs hold one or more of these "second-to-die" or "joint-life" insurance policies. In some cases the provisions of the trust would not change, but in others, a second ILIT should be created to hold these policies. Unfortunately, no general rule can be stated except to get the best expert advice.

Once the policies are in the trust, the premiums have to be paid. Ideally, they should be paid by the trustee of the trust, who typically receives the money from the settlor of the trust (usually the insured person). In order for the transfers to the trust to be free of gift taxes, the trust must be structured so that transfers to the trust are considered to be gifts to the beneficiaries of the trust; this is accomplished by giving the beneficiaries the power to *withdraw* the transferred amounts. This power of withdrawal (called a Crummey power after the name of a case that decided the issue, as discussed earlier in this chapter) is usually limited to the tax-free gift equal to the "annual exclusion amount" per beneficiary per year. In addition, the beneficiaries are given only a short time to withdraw (a "window"), typically thirty days, after they receive written notice by the trustee that a contribution has been made to the trust. They then will have thirty days after receipt of the letter to withdraw their share of the contribution. It is very important for tax purposes that these notices are sent and records are kept accordingly. Also, if the ILIT is designed as a GST trust, careful thought must be given to the application of the GST exemption allocation rules, and more often than not contributions to a GST ILIT require the filing of a gift tax return to allocate GST exemption whenever a transfer is made to the trust to pay premiums.

Hopefully (and typically), the beneficiaries will not withdraw, as they ultimately will inherit much more if the policy stays in place, and at the expiration of the window the trustee can use the funds to pay the premium of the life insurance policy. If a beneficiary did withdraw his share, it is likely that the settlor would reconsider continuation of his contributions and, without these, the policy would lapse. He might also reconsider the share of that beneficiary in the rest of his estate; in the usual case, wise beneficiaries will not exercise their right of withdrawal. It is also possible to provide that each year the settlor, in making a contribution, may designate the donees who will have the withdrawal power on that year's gift.

How does the ILIT operate? The ILIT generally does not accumulate or hold many assets other than the life insurance policies during the life of the insured, so the only trust administration consists of receiving the contributions, sending out withdrawal notices, and paying the policy premiums when due. When the insured dies, however, the picture changes considerably. At that time the trustee will collect, perhaps, hundreds of thousands and in not a few cases millions of dollars, and the ILIT shifts into gear.

As noted above, an ILIT may be designed to continue for many lives or it may be designed to end shortly after the death of the insured. The first objective for estate tax purposes is that the proceeds be excluded from the estate of the insured, and that is accomplished as stated earlier in this section. Thereafter, the specific provisions of how the proceeds will be administered and how long the trust will last are up to the settlor and her advisors. Often, the ILIT will provide benefits for the surviving spouse and the children (and grandchildren if designed as a GST ILIT), at the discretion of the trustee, for the life of the surviving spouse. On the death of the surviving spouse, the remaining assets could be divided among the children equally, either outright or when they reach certain ages. If there are grandchildren, the trust could continue to provide benefits to the children for their lives, then to the grandchildren for their lives, and then the assets would be paid out to great-grandchildren some years later, all *without estate taxes* in any preceding estate. This is a generation-skipping trust and involves some very careful drafting and planning.

As a good general rule, the trustee of the ILIT should be an "independent" trustee, that is, someone (or some institution such as a bank or trust company) who is not a beneficiary of the trust and not subordinate to or controlled by the settlor. This allows the trust to have considerably greater flexibility in its operation. It is permissible for family members or beneficiaries, and in some cases even the settlor, to have the power to remove and replace trustees, but this is a delicate area and should be approved by expert advisors.

S corporation trusts. An "S corporation" is a corporation that qualifies for and has made (along with its shareholders) the special federal tax election under subchapter S of the tax code to bypass the tax at the corporate level and be taxed only at the shareholder level. In effect, a qualifying S corporation (S corp.) pays no tax on its income. Instead, the shareholders pay the tax on the corporate taxable income in proportion to the percentage of shares they own in the corporation, similar to partners of a partnership. (A number of states allow a corporation to elect this treatment for state income tax purposes.) That is, a 15 percent shareholder of an S corporation will pay a tax on 15 percent of the corporate taxable income, whether or not it is distributed to her.

There are a number of requirements that must be met before a corporation can qualify as an S corp., and the one pertinent to this discussion is that only certain types of trusts may be shareholders of an S corp. If the trusts do not meet the strict requirements, the S corp. could *lose* its qualification (which sometimes inadvertently happens), and the results can be extremely costly in additional taxes, as well as an inability to reinstate the election for a number of years.

Only four types of trust will qualify as S corp. shareholders: a grantor trust, a qualified subchapter S trust (QSST), an electing small business trust (ESBT), and a voting trust.

The *grantor trust* qualification is relatively easy, since any trust that qualifies as a grantor trust will be eligible to hold S corp. stock. It does not matter what the terms of the trust may be, and no election needs to be made, so long as the trust is a grantor trust and the grantor is a U.S. citizen or resident. If you recall, a grantor trust is one where the grantor (settlor) is treated as the owner of the trust for federal income tax purposes, and so there is no tax at the trust level: all income and losses are passed through to the grantor. For S corp. purposes, then, every revocable trust can hold S corp. stock, as can grantor retained interest trusts (GRITs), grantor retained annuity trusts and unitrusts (GRATs and GRUTs)—at least during the grantor's term—and defective irrevocable grantor trusts.

The QSST exception is quite different from the grantor trust exception in that the terms of the trust itself must meet certain requirements, and the beneficiary of the trust must join in making the S corp. election for tax purposes. To qualify, a QSST can only have one current income beneficiary, except that in certain circumstances spouses can be co-beneficiaries of the income of a QSST. Except where spouses are concerned, the QSST may only have *one* current income beneficiary, as noted, and in any event *all* of the trust income *must* be distributed to the current income beneficiary. Furthermore, during that beneficiary's lifetime, if any *principal* distributions are made from the QSST, they may *only* be made to the income beneficiary. No other beneficiary may receive principal during the income beneficiary's lifetime. On the income beneficiary's death, however, the trust may provide that the principal will pass to other beneficiaries. If the trust continues after the beneficiary's death and continues to hold S corp. stock, it must qualify again as either a

QSST, a grantor trust, or an ESBT (described below); otherwise the S corp. could lose its election.

The QSST may also be drafted to last for a period of years rather than for the lifetime of the income beneficiary, but in this case the principal must pass to the income beneficiary at the end of the term. It cannot pass to another unless the income beneficiary dies before the end of the term.

Trusts that may not have originally been intended specifically as QSSTs may nevertheless qualify as QSSTs and therefore may hold S corp. stock provided they meet the income distribution requirements. For instance, a QTIP trust will qualify because of the mandatory distribution of income.

One of the planning drawbacks to the QSST is the inability to provide for several beneficiaries in a single trust, giving the trustee the power to distribute or not distribute the income among those beneficiaries at its discretion. A trust that overcomes this drawback, but not without a cost, is the "electing small business trust" (ESBT).

The ESBT is the only trust that may hold S corp. stock, have more than one beneficiary, and allow the trustee discretion over distributions, without causing a loss of the S corp. election. Since it is regarded as a "tax break" by Congress and the IRS, the ESBT must meet special, strict requirements.

First, all beneficiaries must be qualified S corp. shareholders—that is, where individual beneficiaries are concerned. Next, the trustee of the trust must elect to have the trust treated as an ESBT. Next, the portion of the trust attributable to S corp. stock is treated as a *separate trust* for income tax purposes, and taxed separately at the *highest* income tax rate. This separate tax treatment for some but not all trust income, with the required separate accounts and computations, can make an ESBT an accountant's nightmare (or dream, depending on how you look at it). And the issue of paying the highest tax on all S corp. income in the ESBT will be an additional cost, but in cases where the income and distributions are large to begin with (i.e., already in the highest tax bracket), it won't matter. The bottom line seems to be that if large amounts of income can regularly be paid on S corp. stock, and if the settlor wants one trust to benefit a number of beneficiaries with discretion to treat them unequally, and if other estate-planning considerations favor the use of the ESBT, then it could be the best way to hold the S corp. stock—but there are a lot of "ifs" here.

Generation-skipping transfer tax trusts. As discussed earlier, the basic concept of estate taxation centers around ownership of assets at death and the retention of control and enjoyment over assets that the deceased person has transferred before death. In other words, if Dad transferred assets to a trust that provided for you for your lifetime and then for your children for their lifetimes, and then perhaps for your grandchildren, and after that, for your great-grandchildren, no one of you would ever have owned those assets, nor would any of you have transferred any of the assets. Therefore, there would be no estate tax on those assets on your death, or on your children's death, or grandchildren's deaths, or when your great-grandchildren received them. Depending upon how much Dad originally placed in the trust, the savings could easily run into the *millions* of dollars. Can this be done?

The answer is yes, and it is called "generation skipping." Although there are certain limitations placed on generation-skipping transfers (GST) because of extensive use (or abuse, in the eyes of Congress and the IRS) by the mega-rich from the 1930s to the 1970s, opportunities still remain to save huge amounts of federal and state estate taxes under present law. Before we begin the discussion, however, it is appropriate to warn you that the GST rules and regulations are among the most complex and intricate areas of the tax code. Lengthy legal texts have been written on the subject, and it is impossible to review the details and numerous considerations in a discussion of this type. Therefore, what follows is a brief overview of its workings to give you an idea of how you might use GST planning.

The basic concept of GST planning is to provide a trust for the benefit of younger-generation individuals (let's assume they are lineal descendants, specifically, children, grandchildren, great-grandchildren, etc., although they need not be) in such a way that those individuals can enjoy all the benefits of the trust assets without owning them for tax purposes. The GST trust is sheltered from the GST tax by use of the GST tax exemption. The estate tax implications of the GST trust skip generations, but the enjoyment of the trust property skips no generation. In other words, the trust assets will not be taxed in the estates of the successive generations so long as these assets remain in trust.

To illustrate, in her will, Christine leaves $3 million to an irrevocable GST trust for the benefit of her two children and three grandchildren and shelters the GST trust from the GST tax by allocating GST exemption to the trust on a timely filed gift tax return. Such a trust would normally provide that the trustee, in its discretion, can distribute any amounts of income and/or principal for the benefit of any or all of the five beneficiaries. The distributions need not be equal. The trustee could arrange to make regular payments of income to children, or they could pay tuition for the grandchildren or for vacations, insurance, house painting, car, mortgage, or anything else the trustee decides is appropriate. On the other hand, there could be periods where the trustee makes no distributions. If drafted properly, a child could even serve as trustee of the GST trust without triggering adverse estate tax consequences.

Let's say the funds are invested wisely. Over the years they grow to $6 million, and then the two children die of "old age." There would be no estate taxes generated by the GST trust and no probate on the children's deaths, and the GST trust could continue, on the same basis, for the lives of the grandchildren. Over the years, the grandchildren have married and have children (Christine's great-grandchildren), and as the great-grandchildren are born, they automatically become beneficiaries of this GST trust. In most states, a number of (usually twenty-one) years after the death of the last surviving grandchild, the trust will end and the remaining balance will be distributed to the great-grandchildren, presumably in equal shares. There will be no estate tax or probate on the trust assets on the death of the grandchildren or on the distribution to the great-grandchildren. In all, the trust will have run about one hundred years with no estate taxes after the first tax on Christine's death, and no probate throughout that time. (There could be probate and/or tax on the estates of the great-grandchildren if they failed to plan, but even this could be avoided using what is called a GST super trust.)

The reason Christine chose to fund her GST trust with $3 million is because that happens to be under the GST tax exemption each person is allowed in 2020 under the federal tax code—$10 million indexed for inflation to $11.58 million. (Sound familiar?) Like the gift tax and estate tax allowances, the GST exemption amount is indexed for inflation, and is the same amount as the gift and estate tax allowances (which has not always been the case).

If Christine had funded the GST trust with more than her available GST tax exemption, the trust would have been forever "tainted" in part with perpetual exposure to the high GST tax (40 percent in 2020), unless she had a spouse who agreed to "split the gift" and use a part or all of his GST and gift tax exemptions. Furthermore, it should be noted that the GST exemption is an exemption from the GST tax and *not* from the gift or estate tax.

It is also important to understand that the generation-skipping transfer tax is a special tax *separate* from the gift and estate tax, and it is imposed when certain transfers are made to persons who are two or more generations younger than the person who makes the transfer (e.g., a person who makes a gift to grandchildren or great-grandchildren) or to an unrelated person that is more than about thirty-seven and a half years younger than the person making the transfer. The GST tax can be almost confiscatory since it is imposed on top of an estate or gift tax. For a dramatic example, say that Christine has a second trust with $10 million in it, and on her death, instead of passing to her children, it passes to her three grandchildren, and the estate tax rate and the GST tax rate are each 40 percent. Since Christine had made a total of $13 million of transfers ($3 million lifetime gift plus $10 million trust passing at her death), her estate would be subject to a 40 percent estate tax and a 40 percent GST tax on the excess above her tax-free exemption amounts. *Both* taxes are applied!

The GST exemption may be used just about any way the transferor wishes—such as by outright gift or in a GST trust. Whatever is not used during lifetime or at death is lost—it cannot be used by a surviving spouse (although the spouse will have her own GST exemption to use). There is no portability of the GST exemption. As illustrated above, a GST trust is clearly the most sensible way to use it since it can continue for more than two generations. While some states have the "rule against perpetuities" limit of about one hundred years, some states have abolished this rule, such as Delaware, New Hampshire, and South Dakota, and would permit a GST trust to last virtually forever. Gifts that qualify as "tax-free" gifts under the tax code (i.e., the annual exclusion gifts and qualifying gifts for medical expenses and tuition) are additionally exempt in most instances but not all (beyond the GST exemption), so grandparents in high estate tax brackets employ these exemptions often.

Another benefit of the GST trust is that it can be designed to protect the GST trust assets from a beneficiary's creditors. If the GST trust is fully discretionary, in that the trustee alone makes distribution decisions, and if the trustee is "disinterested" (i.e., not a beneficiary), then not only will the GST trust grow without reduction for estate taxes, but it will also grow without reduction by creditors, including in most states the ex-spouse of a GST trust beneficiary. Where asset protection is a goal, the GST trust should not contain Crummey powers, and if a beneficiary is to be granted a "power of appointment," it must be carefully drafted (or not included at all). Lastly, it is always a good idea to include a "spendthrift" clause, prohibiting assignment or attachment of a beneficiary's share.

We'd like to turn now to a trust we call the GST super trust. Huge leverage can be realized on the GST exemption through the use of life insurance. For instance, Karen creates a GST trust and contributes $1 million cash to it at a time when her available GST exemption exceeds $1 million. The trustee of the trust uses the $1 million to purchase $10 million of insurance on Karen's life. Since the trust was funded with an amount that did not exceed Karen's GST tax exemption, and assuming the GST exemption was allocated to the insurance trust on a timely filed gift tax return, the full $10 million *and whatever it grows to in the future* can be forever exempt from GST taxes *and* from estate taxes. When the numbers move into this neighborhood, the question arises as to whether such a huge amount even ought to be handed over to beneficiaries. As suggested by the illustration in Christine's case, the extended GST trust often lasts about one hundred years (but can last longer in states that have abolished the rule of perpetuities, discussed briefly above and in more detail below). If funds are wisely invested and not lavishly distributed, the balance could easily grow into $100 million or $500 million or more! This is often referred to as a "dynasty" trust, sort of a GST super trust.

The term of one hundred years is a carryover from the English common law and based on the concept that while it is all right to keep property in trust, somebody must own the property sometime. Otherwise, carrying it to the extreme, so much property would end up in trust where it would never be sold or passed along for other generations to sell that it would hinder the normal growth and development of communities. It was thought, then, that a rule ought to be made that prohibits perpetual trusts except where charities are involved, and that a long-enough trust period for anyone's purposes should be measured by the duration of the life of an individual (any individual) called "a life in being," plus an additional twenty-one years. Under favorable circumstances this would add up to about one hundred years. Therefore, every trust (except those where the funds go to or are held for charity or trusts established in states that have extended the allowable period) must terminate by then, or a court will order it terminated. This is called "the rule against perpetuities."

But times change, at least in some places. Although every state in this country had adopted some version of the rule against perpetuities, a growing number of states decided, for reasons unnecessary to explore, that it would *not* be harmful to the particular state's communities to allow a private (non-charitable) trust to last more than one hundred years; in fact, they could last *forever*, which, as one comedian was reputed to have said, can be a really long time, especially when you get to the end. Thus a number of states have abolished the rule against perpetuities for trusts created and governed under the laws of that state.

In other words, in the illustration above, Karen could establish her trust in, say, South Dakota by naming a South Dakota trustee and having the trust administered there. Getting off to a healthy $10 million tax-free start on Karen's death, the trust could provide estate-tax-free distributions and accumulations forever, regardless of where the beneficiaries might live (and the group of beneficiaries could be quite a large group one hundred years from now). This can produce a pretty impressive result. How impressive? If after annual distributions and administration fees the trust netted only a 5 percent after-tax return, it would grow to about *$20 billion* in 160 years! This kind of money would certainly provide handsomely for Karen's children, grandchildren, great-grandchildren, great-great-grandchildren, great-great-great . . . wait a second! Karen has two children and two grandchildren. What if that's the end of the line? What if the trust does grow to $20 billion in 160 years and there are only one or two beneficiaries? Or none? What if South Dakota sinks?

One of the most difficult and abstract aspects of truly long-term trusts is deciding on provisions for beneficiaries and situations so remote as to be almost impossible to imagine. For this reason, experienced drafters build in a great deal of flexibility to allow for totally unforeseeable circumstances, including changes in the law. It is not uncommon in a long-term trust to see provisions that allow changing the location and governing law of the trust, amending the trust, even terminating the trust if its purposes can't be met. Nevertheless, even with all the expert advice, it is at best a complicated, thought-provoking, and often expensive exercise with few if any "right" answers.

Structured settlement trust. In many personal injury settlements, the injured party will be advised to receive the settlement over a period of years instead of in a lump sum. This is called a "structured settlement." For instance, say that Lew, the injured party, may be offered the choice of a lump-sum payment of $1.3 million, or $75,000 per year for the rest of his life, with a guarantee of payments over forty years. (In other words, if Lew died in nine years, his family or other named beneficiaries could receive the payments for the thirty-one-year balance of the guaranteed term.)

One of the reasons this option may be chosen (although it should *not* be the only reason) is that the tax code provides that payments received on account of personal injuries or sickness are *free* of income taxes, whether received in a lump sum or over a period of time. This is so even though a part of the structured settlement payments are actually interest on the lump sum.

Accordingly, if the structured settlement payments are made to a trust established by the injured party, the payments will still be tax free. If, however, after the payments are received by the trust, they are invested and earn income, then, of course, the income earned on such investments will be currently taxable (typically under the grantor trust rules), as described above.

The *trap* that accompanies structured settlements is not related to income taxes but *estate* taxes, as we have discussed earlier.

Spousal limited access trust (SLAT). Sometimes spouses understand the estate tax advantage of making a lifetime gift, but they hesitate to make a gift due to the uncertainty of life. Will there be enough funds to take care of themselves during their lifetime if they make a large gift now? In the right situation, a "spousal limited access trust" or SLAT can be the perfect planning vehicle, obtaining the tax advantage and eliminating the fear at the same time. In a SLAT, one spouse makes a large gift into an irrevocable trust for the benefit of the other spouse. The SLAT is not designed as a marital deduction trust, as one goal is for the SLAT's assets to escape the estate tax in both spouses' estates, and as stated above, a true marital deduction trust is taxed in the surviving spouse's estate. With a SLAT, the beneficiary spouse can be the trustee as long as distributions to himself are limited to "health, education, maintenance, and support," with broader distribution authority in the hands of an independent trustee (either a co-trustee or one that can be appointed at a later time). A SLAT is a grantor trust to the settlor (and funding) spouse, so the settlor must understand that the income tax obligations of the trust will remain with her, even if the spouses later divorce (a new tax rule as of 2018). The divorce issue can be addressed either in the trust or in a divorce separation agreement, and sometimes a couple will each settle and fund a SLAT for the other, not as reciprocal (identical) trusts but as trusts, in the similar vein with the same goals. Note that there is no gift tax advantage to a SLAT. The donor must apply his lifetime exemption to the amount transferred to the SLAT.

Keep This in Mind

If you have gotten this far, you now know more about trusts than everyone around you. But there's just a bit more you need to complete the picture—the tax treatment of trusts, and the important differences between trusts and probate and probate and taxes. We have attempted to explain these in a simple way, but the bottom line is: avoiding probate does *not* mean avoiding taxes, and the tax rules relating to the many different types of trust can be quite complicated, so be sure your advisor is knowledgeable in taxation of trusts.

14

Dealing with Lawyers

To employ an attorney I ne'er was inclined; They are pests to society, the sharks of mankind; To avoid that base tribe my own will I now draw; May I ever escape coming under their paw.

—from the will of William Ruffell

We believe it can be safely said that as a class we lawyers do not enjoy the highest regard of the public. And unfortunately, this disregard goes way back. Lawyers are unaffectionately referred to in a biblical passage by Luke, which begins, "Woe unto you also, ye lawyers!" And who hasn't heard, at least ten times, Shakespeare's unfortunately famous line from *Henry VI, Part 2,* "The first thing we do, let's kill all the lawyers"? (Although, in fact, Shakespeare's rebel, Jack Cade, calls for the death not only of lawyers but of all scholars and gentlemen. In that regard, at least, we got some respect.)

But what is the first thing we do when we have a will problem, an estate problem, or a trust problem? We call our lawyers and ask for their help. Many people are fortunate enough to have an excellent and trusting relationship with their lawyers, while others use them only when and if they have absolutely no other choice. Many are fortunate enough to find a good, competent lawyer who does a thorough and efficient job for a (believe it or not) fair fee, while others have the misfortune to hire an incompetent who is paid far more than he is worth. Worse yet, the problem often in the latter case is that neither the client nor the lawyer realizes he is incompetent until it's too late.

Perhaps the first rule to learn, if you want to find a good lawyer, is not to prejudge the attorney. *Don't* assume all lawyers are alike or are of equal competence or incompetence, and, above all, don't start off the relationship with an attitude of mistrust. Just as a tip, we can tell you that we don't trust clients who don't trust us. If a client comes in with a major chip on his shoulder, assuming that we're going to cheat him or give him minimum representation with maximum fee, then we suggest he find another attorney.

To make a lawyer-client relationship work best for both, there must be, at least until it is otherwise indicated, a relationship of *mutual* trust and confidence. But this does not mean that you will never have a disagreement or that your lawyer will never make a mistake or that you are stuck with each other forever. As we will explain, as objectively as we can (since we have been clients as well as lawyers), when it comes to dealing with lawyers, there is a time to speak and a time to listen, a time to pay and a time to be paid, a time to hire and a time to fire.

Hiring an Estate-Planning Lawyer

Just about everyone thinks that just about every lawyer can draft a will. Basically this is true, but whether the will is well drafted and achieves the client's wishes in the best way is another question. Furthermore, as we have explained, *a will is not an estate plan*. Therefore, to develop the best estate plan for your family, you need a lawyer who is competent at estate planning, not just at drafting wills. And remember also that you should not be the person to decide that all you need is a simple will. In most cases, we have found that clients are led to this decision more by a desire to spend less on legal fees than by an informed judgment.

Finding an estate-planning lawyer is somewhat less difficult than finding an estate-settlement lawyer (discussed later in this chapter), because estate planning is more of an acknowledged specialty among lawyers. There are numerous estate-planning organizations and most of them have lawyer-referral services, which are a bit more reliable than the general lawyer-referral services offered by most bar associations. Before you resort to the bar association, a good way to begin is to investigate whether your city has an "estate-planning council." These organizations are made up of professionals who specialize in estate planning, and most have their own lawyer-referral services. Call the one closest to you and get the names of two or three lawyers in your area you can interview. In addition, or as an alternative if you cannot locate the estate-planning council, you can contact the trust department at one or two local banks and ask them to give you the names of local lawyers they would recommend to prepare your estate plan. Compare the two or three lists you get from these various sources to see if there are any names that are common to all of them. If so, it is likely that those lawyers do a good deal of estate planning. It is always a good idea to go to the attorney's website and investigate the lawyer's credentials. Is the lawyer active in the local estate-planning bar association, which indicates a desire to stay current with developments? Has the lawyer lectured or written on issues of concern in estate planning? How experienced is the lawyer? In any event, set up interviews with two or three of these lawyers and tell them ahead of time that you are *interviewing* lawyers to do your estate plan.

Be respectful of the free time they may give you and prepare your questions beforehand. Your questions should include: (1) What's your feeling about avoiding probate? (2) What are your general recommendations on choosing a personal representative? (3) Do you recommend that I act as trustee of my own living trust? (4) Can you advise me on how to transfer assets to my living trust? (5) Can you give me an idea of a range of what your fees will be? (6) Will I be billed periodically so I can see the cost versus the progress?

The answers you receive to these questions should give you a rough idea of how comfortable and knowledgeable the lawyer is in the field of estate planning. If he gets defensive about avoiding probate, for instance, he may be one of those lawyers whose attitude about probate is, "What's all the fuss about?" (Meaning: "You'll be dead. What should you care about the delays and extra costs?") And if he suggests that he should be the personal representative of your estate, or that you can't be trustee of your own revocable trust, politely cut the meeting short and go on to your next interview.

As for legal fees for your plan, try to understand that it is usually not possible for a lawyer to provide a fee until the lawyer knows what your plan will involve. That is like asking a realtor how much a house costs. Will the estate plan be a will and a trust? Or two trusts? Preparation of one deed? Or four deeds? Special provisions for a child? Parent? Stepchildren? If a lawyer gives you a fee quote based on a short informational interview, that's another reason to skip to the next interview.

One note of caution as you interview lawyers. In many states the lawyer-client privilege does not attach until a formal legal engagement is undertaken. If your matter involves sensitive information, be careful what you say until you actually engage the lawyer and establish the privileged relationship.

After you have made your selection, be frank and open with the lawyer: Tell him your concerns and make your objectives clear. Don't be afraid to ask questions throughout the relationship, but be prepared to pay for the time he spends answering them. Finally, if you intend to get a second opinion on your plan, tell him so, and don't be upset if the second opinion turns up some suggested changes. So long as they are not major, you should stick with your initial selection. If the changes are major, the lawyer himself should then have some explaining (or perhaps refunding) to do.

Hiring an Estate-Settlement Lawyer

When someone in your family or someone close to you dies and you are responsible for settling the estate, one of the first things you do is seek the advice of an estate lawyer, if for no other reason than to find out just what you are supposed to do. (See the Personal Representative's Checklist in the appendix for an idea of what needs to be done.) Do you pay all the deceased's bills? File his tax return? Collect on his life insurance? How do you locate all of his property? Can you withdraw the funds from his joint bank account? How do you sell his car? Can you do all this on your own without a lawyer?

DO YOU NEED A LAWYER AT ALL?

Even in the smallest estates, there are often questions that arise that require at least the consultation of an experienced lawyer to prevent you from doing the wrong thing, which could lead to trouble and more legal fees later. Quite often, however, particularly in small to medium-sized (in relation to the tax laws) nonprobate estates, it may not be necessary to hire a lawyer to settle the estate. You may only need a few hours of consultation to guide you through the necessary steps. And in some cases, particularly where there are no disputes or other problems, you may not need a lawyer at all.

For instance, Mom and Pop have sold their home and live in a retirement community. Their only assets consist of two joint bank accounts totaling $65,000. On Pop's death, assuming he died of natural causes, there is nothing for Mom to do to settle his estate. It is not necessary to probate his will, there will be no estate or inheritance tax, and, assuming no lawsuits, Mom has free access to the bank accounts without the need for legal action.

Even where there is a probate estate, if the size of the probate estate is small (the allowable amount varies from state to state, ranging from $5,000 to $100,000) and the family situation is simple (a spouse and/or children), then, as discussed in chapter 7, most states have simplified probate procedures. In such cases, these procedures allow for the settlement of the estate with the mere filing of one or two forms, which the clerk of the court will usually help you complete. Probate clerks are the unsung heroes of estate administration! And many probate courts also have "Lawyer for the Day" programs where volunteer lawyers will assist you at no cost in the filing of simple probate forms.

For larger estates, however, where more formal probate is required by law, or where the estate distribution may be more complicated, or where a contest takes place (or might take place), you would be foolish to attempt to handle the matter without an experienced estate attorney. In which case, how do you determine if you need one, and where do you find one?

In general, if you find yourself with the responsibility of settling an estate, it is a good idea to consult with an estate attorney to have him advise you on just what your responsibilities are and whether he feels you can handle them on your own. It may sound silly to suggest going to an attorney to ask if you need an attorney, but, aside from books like this and online "do-it-yourself" software, there is nowhere else to go, except to the probate court itself. The clerk of the court will certainly listen to you and try to help you evaluate your case, and if you know the forms you wish to file he will be very helpful in assisting you in what needs to be done, but the clerk does not offer legal advice, and we have found that, except in the simplest of cases, the clerks usually play it safe and direct you to an attorney.

I suggest you pick the best estate attorney you can find rather than someone who looks like he needs work and will do the job cheaply, and be prepared to pay for the time and advice she gives you. Be frank about why you are there. Don't give her the impression that you don't trust her, but rather that you wish to do as much as you can on your own, and that you recognize the value of competent professional assistance. If you *think* you have a small and simple estate, but the attorney still tells you it's complicated and will require a lot of work, get a second opinion. Better to pay for two or even three consultations than to hire someone whose advice you question from the very beginning. If it turns out that you *do* need an attorney, which in many cases you can figure out for yourself without the need for a consultation, then get the best the estate can afford.

WHERE TO FIND AN ESTATE-SETTLEMENT LAWYER

They may be everywhere, but they are tough to find. It's not at all difficult to find one who would be quite pleased to help you settle the estate, but will he do it well? Many people suggest asking friends and neighbors if they know of a good estate lawyer you can use, and this is one route you may take, although not a very reliable one, in my opinion, unless your friend or neighbor is in a position to be able to compare the particular attorney's work with others.

The next-best resource, though again, in our opinion, not a solidly reliable one, is that of the local bar association or better, as noted earlier, the local estate-planning council. Bar associations have lawyer-referral services that provide names of attorneys in specified areas of the law to anyone who asks. For instance, you can call the local bar association's lawyer-referral service and ask for the names of one or two lawyers or law firms that handle the settlement of estates, and they will supply you with referrals.

The problem is that aside from having the attorneys complete a brief questionnaire, the bar associations do nothing to ascertain whether or not the attorneys to whom they refer you are true specialists or even of above-average competence in the particular area of law. In fact, if an attorney decides that he wants to receive referrals in a particular area of the law—settling estates, for example—he simply registers with the local bar association lawyer-referral service and represents that he has extensive experience in that area. He is then placed on their list of "estate-settlement lawyers," and, depending on where he is on the list, his name is given to callers who ask to be referred to estate lawyers. A lawyer would not normally seek referrals in an area with which he is not familiar or experienced, particularly in light of the dramatically increased tendency to sue lawyers for malpractice; therefore, a referral from the bar association ought to lead you to a lawyer who has some experience in the requested field. However, under the typical bar association referral system, there is no assurance that the lawyer referred to you is outstanding or even particularly competent in the applicable area.

Larger, successful law firms almost always have specialists in every area, including estate settlement. Just search the web for the top one hundred largest law firms in the United States to find one near you. Each of these firms has hundreds, some thousands, of lawyers, specialists in every known field, and no job is too big or too small, *provided* you have the money. In firms like these, if the size of the estate matches the size of the law firm, you'll probably get competent advice and service—but you'll pay for it. So where does that leave all of the in-between estates and estates where a giant law firm is not desirable for some reason?

Perhaps the best source of referrals to good lawyers is lawyers themselves. They know who is at the top of their profession, who wins the most will contests, who is consulted by their brethren on complicated trust *and estate* tax matters, who lectures, teaches, and is published in the field, who is called in as an expert witness to interpret trust law or a will question, and who *they* use to handle their *own* estates. We know of no outside resource that can match this. So rather than going to an unknown estate lawyer (unless of course you know of one already), find a lawyer that you or a friend or neighbor has used in the past or are familiar with now and ask him who the best estate lawyer in the area is. This referral is far more likely to bring you to an acknowledged specialist than any of the other sources.

Once you have the names of at least two estate lawyers, you should consider interviewing them before reaching a decision. Unfortunately, as discussed earlier, this interview is more to get an overall impression of the attorney and her firm than it is to see if she gives you the right answers to your questions. Short of having another lawyer do the interviewing, there is little way to tell whether she knows how to settle estates, except for her own assurances to you that she can do it.

There have been occasions where lawyers have, before the fact, hired (or attempted to hire) *themselves* as attorneys for the estate. Every so often you will see a provision in a will that says something like, "I direct my executor to engage the law firm of Tadpole and Snodgrass to act as attorneys for my estate." Aside from the question of ethics in attempting to preclude the personal representative from hiring the lawyer of his choice, such a provision is *not* binding on the personal representative, and he is under *no* obligation to employ the lawyer as "directed" by the testator. For the drafting lawyer to add this type of instruction is considered to be unprofessional and in poor taste, and in some cases it can lead to trouble.

In one estate, for instance, the testator's will instructed his personal representative to "select Ralph Moody as the attorney for the personal representative of the will and as attorney for the estate." (Ralph also drafted the will.) When the testator died, his personal representative followed his instructions and engaged Ralph to handle the estate.

Shortly thereafter, however, she became quite dissatisfied with his services. She asked him to withdraw from the case and offered to pay for his services to date, hiring another lawyer to continue. Ralph *refused* to withdraw and sued the estate for breach of contract, claiming that it was obliged to continue using his services as lawyer for the estate. The executrix was then forced to petition the court to order Ralph's removal and instruct him not to interfere with estate settlement. The court quickly approved the discharging of Ralph, stating,

> Because of the special relation of attorney and client, the law permits the termination of that relationship in a manner not recognized with respect to other contracts. The client has the absolute right to discharge the attorney and terminate the relation at any time with or without cause, no matter how arbitrary his action may seem. The provision in the will directing the personal representative to hire the lawyer is not binding. It is merely advisory, even though the language used frequently sounds mandatory. The personal representative is not bound to accept an attorney whom he does not select.

Note that this type of provision is quite different from one selecting the lawyer as personal representative of your estate. As discussed earlier, this is quite acceptable, assuming it is *your* decision, and in such cases it is likely that the lawyer, as personal representative, will hire himself or his law firm as lawyer for the estate, which is not a problem so long as they do a good job. If, however, you have named someone else as personal representative, and your lawyer adds a provision in your will requiring that he or his firm should be the lawyers for your estate, I would ask him to remove the provision, at *his firm's* expense.

If the relationship you have with your lawyer or law firm is such that you really wish your personal representative and trustee to continue to work with them, you should consider a personal note to them stating that and requesting they honor your wish in that regard, but remember, it is not binding on them. If you want to be sure the lawyer or the firm stays in the picture to help administer the estate, you may name them as personal representative and trustee, or co–personal representative and co-trustee.

Lawyers' Fees—Planning Estates

The easiest estates to settle are those that are well planned during the *lifetime* of the deceased. To most people, an "estate plan" means having a will. In fact, if your estate is properly planned, the will is only a small part of your estate plan, and if you haven't already learned from reading this book, passing your estate through your will is the most vulnerable, time-consuming, and expensive way to pass your estate. Therefore, money spent on a good estate plan to simplify estate settlement, save taxes, and avoid probate is money well spent—as long as you don't overspend in proportion to the value of your estate.

The story is told of the woman who walked into the lawyer's office, telling him that she wanted him to plan her estate. He said he would be glad to, but he required a $5,000 retainer. She made out the check, handed it to him, then he said, "Thank you. Now, tell me about your estate," to which she replied, "You just took it!"

It's one thing to declare how valuable a good estate plan may be, but it's another to pay for it. If the cost is disproportionate to the value or size of the estate, then the client has been done a disservice.

Fees for estate planning are as varied and as volatile as the winds, and there are no "standard" guidelines. For many years, lawyers would draft wills as "loss leaders," charging token amounts such as $500 or $750 for the will, in the hopes of attracting other business or in the hopes of being able to handle the estate of the person when he died. And if the lawyer was allowed to handle the estate, the loss leader usually paid off, since a $750 will was in most cases hardly adequate to deal with the complexities in settling an estate. Then along came the living trust and the realization that with competent and expert advice a family could avoid probate and save thousands in estate taxes as well. This is what we call "estate planning."

Because every estate and family situation is different, it is difficult to standardize estate-planning fees. In embarrassing contrast to the $750 will, we have seen lawyers charge as much as $5,000 for a will and $25,000 for a trust. And some lawyers, without justification, charge a percentage of the estate to *prepare* the estate plan documents. A typical revocable estate-planning trust, by itself, should not cost $25,000 or a will (unless it contains a trust) $5,000, except in complicated circumstances that involve a special case or an extraordinary amount of time and expertise. As to charging a percentage of the estate, we cannot see how this bears any relation to the work done, except that in some cases, larger, more complicated estates do involve more time and expertise. In such cases, we believe it would be fair to agree to a fee based on the time the lawyers must spend on the plan, together with a premium if some particular expertise is effectively employed, but *not* a fee based on the size of the estate.

There have been cases where instead of charging an immediate fee, a lawyer will accept a share of the estate. This arrangement raises ethical questions to say the least, and it is likely that the attorney would *not* be entitled to a share of the estate, although he would be entitled to be paid fairly for the services he performed. There are also situations where the testator thinks so highly of the lawyer that in addition to the fee for preparing the plan, he wants to give him a bequest under the estate. Here, the lawyer may be entitled to the testator's bequest, depending on the circumstances (such as where the lawyer was related to the testator), but even in the most honest of cases, a bequest to the lawyer who prepares the will raises strong suspicions of fraud or undue influence, in addition to the serious ethical questions involved. As a general rule, lawyers agree and ethical rules *require* that in such cases the will should be prepared by another lawyer, with the possible exception of cases where the lawyer receiving the bequest may be closely related to the testator, such as a child, sibling, niece, nephew, etc. Otherwise, it is not at all unusual for the court to void the bequest to the lawyer who drafted the will, while leaving the remaining provisions intact.

This statement may confuse you if you have seen or heard of a situation where the lawyer who drafted the will received a bequest without incident. This is quite possible. Remember that unless it was informed, the court normally would have no way of knowing that one of the beneficiaries was also the lawyer who prepared the will. Therefore, if no one objects, the lawyer will receive the bequest. And also remember that the *only* ones who can object, as pointed out in chapter 10, are those people who would stand to benefit if their objections are successful. Note that in these cases, even though a person does not have standing to object to the will, if she feels that fraud or undue influence has been committed, she can nevertheless report the matter to the local agency governing the professional behavior of lawyers.

Before you engage an attorney to do your plan, get at least an estimate, if not a fixed fee, for the work to be done. A fair way to approach the problem (which we have used with great success) is to have an initial conference to review your family and financial situation and to determine your objectives in setting up an estate plan. After this review, a letter of recommendation is prepared and sent to you, describing the work to be done and an estimate of the fees the lawyer will charge to complete it. The conference and letter are paid for separately, so that if for some reason you wish to stop at that point or have the work done elsewhere, you are free to do so, and you still have the benefit of the conference and recommendations. The letter of recommendation is also quite useful if you wish to show it to another lawyer to get a second opinion.

You should be aware that in order to get through this first step of analysis of your existing situation and recommendations of a plan, you must disclose to the lawyer *all* of the details of your family and financial situation. Occasionally, we find that some clients are reluctant to tell us everything they have for fear that we might charge them more. As noted, estate-planning attorneys generally do *not* base their fees on the size of your estate. The estate plan for a $500,000 estate may well cost the same amount as the estate plan for a $2 million estate, depending on the family circumstances and objectives. And speaking of objectives, these are the *most* important things to communicate to your estate lawyer, since this will determine the basic structure of your plan. What good would it be if your lawyer creates a trust for you but the provisions of your trust do not accomplish your wishes?

Lawyers' Fees—Settling Estates

Lawyers love estates. Especially probate estates. And most especially, large probate estates. The bigger the probate estate, the bigger the fee—it stands to reason. There is much more work for the lawyer to do and much more responsibility to take on than there is for nonprobate estates. But is this the lawyer's fault? We have a tendency to criticize lawyers for charging so much to settle an estate, but, in fact, the more costly estates, from the standpoint of legal fees, are the result of a poor estate plan or no plan and are generally not the fault of the lawyers.

Regardless of where the fault lies, however, what is a fair fee to settle an estate? As with personal representative's fees, the underlying rule a probate court applies when deciding on contested legal fees is, "What is reasonable under the circumstances, taking into consideration the nature, extent, and complexity of the services performed?" Although a fee of 1 percent of an estate may be unreasonable in one case, a 10 percent fee may be quite reasonable in another. And a number of states have pre-established fees that an attorney may charge in settling a probate estate, with rates similar in fashion to those of a personal representative's fee—for instance, 5 percent of the first $5,000, 4 percent of the next $20,000, 3 percent of the next $75,000, etc. Most states, however, simply adhere to the test of reasonableness and look at each case on its own. Since attorneys' fees to administer a probate estate might be subject to approval by the probate court before payment, a beneficiary or personal representative who thinks the attorney is charging too much can file an objection with the court to the amount of the fee, and the court will review it.

When the court reviews a contested attorney's fee, it will look carefully at the size and nature of the estate, then examine the attorney's report of what was done and how much time it took, and it will also consider whether the amount of time the lawyer claims to have spent on the case was reasonable under the circumstances. In one case, a lawyer, in defending his fee, claimed to have spent "a great deal of time and considerable difficulty" in selling some stock represented by forty-eight certificates in fourteen different corporations. The court's inquiry revealed, however, that the securities were sold through a stockbroker and the lawyer's time primarily consisted of making copies of the certificates and talking to the broker. The court cut the lawyer's requested fee by two-thirds. In another case, however, a lawyer spent nearly one thousand hours of his time over a nine-year period on estate matters. He produced a detailed time log, itemizing all of his activities on behalf of the estate, and this was corroborated by other evidence. The court allowed him the full fee of $85,000.

In many cases, the lawyer will, in the course of representing the estate, perform services that are outside the normal course of estate representation, and this will often warrant an additional fee. For instance, if the estate is sued by a creditor, or if there is a will contest, this will require considerable additional legal time. Other examples would include the sale of estate property or the running of a business. A classic example of additional fees for business-related matters is illustrated in the Saperstein estate.

Abe Saperstein was the founder and owner of the world-famous Harlem Globetrotters basketball team. Saperstein owned the team as a sole proprietorship (meaning it was in his name alone), and on his death the personal representative had the obligation of managing the team. Since the objective was ultimately to sell the team, one of the first things done to facilitate a sale was to form a corporation to hold ownership of the team. Because of the nature of the estate and the complexity of the laws regarding sports teams, incorporating involved extensive legal work. In addition, Saperstein never bothered to have any of the key players sign contracts; this posed a serious impediment to a sale. The personal representative and the attorneys then negotiated with the "star players"—Meadowlark Lemon, Fred Neal, Robert Hall, and Hubert Ausbie—and were successful in getting them to sign favorable contracts. The lawyers and personal representative continued to improve the operation of the team to a point where it began to show a profit, and it was ultimately sold to the Potter Palmer Group for $3.71 million. The lawyers received a fee of $123,000 for the incorporation and other business work, and they asked for an additional fee of $140,000 for estate services. Saperstein's beneficiaries objected.

At the trial, the beneficiaries pointed out that it was the personal representative and not the lawyers who did most of the work and that the lawyers submitted no time records to substantiate any work that they did do. The court noted, however, that it was established that the lawyers had material involvement in the weekly operations of the Globetrotter team business, that they negotiated the contracts with the key players, that they were instrumental in developing the profitability and ultimately the sale of the team at a price almost double that of the value on the date of Saperstein's death. "This was," the court said, "an unusual and unique estate, requiring extraordinary and broad-ranging legal and nonlegal services." The fee was considered reasonable under all the circumstances and allowed.

In discussing the matter of fees with your estate lawyer, you should be sure that you *both* understand just what the fee arrangement will be and, at least in general terms, what it will include. Most states require the final fee arrangement to be reduced to writing and signed by you and the lawyer (often called an "engagement letter") before the work is begun. As explained earlier, the fee would normally cover all matters routinely settling the estate, including the filing of necessary forms to probate the will, assisting in the preparation and filing of inventory and accounts, assistance in collection of estate assets, and other routine matters. What is usually *not* included is negotiation and sale of estate assets (unless the transaction is nominal), handling of will contests or objections to accounts by beneficiaries, and handling of suits brought by creditors. Some lawyers, especially tax lawyers, will also handle the preparation and filing of the estate tax returns as part of their representation.

Depending on the state in which the estate is being administered, you may be required to pay a fixed fee according to the state's schedule of allowable fees, or you may agree on a percentage of the estate, or you may simply arrange to pay an hourly fee for routine matters and a negotiated fee for additional ordinary work (which we feel is best and the fairest for both parties). If you do agree upon an hourly fee, ask the lawyer to send you a detailed monthly statement showing the time spent to date and who performed the work, so you can keep abreast of your costs.

Remember, these fee arrangements are on behalf of the estate. If you are on the "other side," acting *against* the estate, there are no state-regulated fees, and it is up to you and your lawyer to reach an agreement. In a will contest, for instance, your lawyer may ask for a nonreturnable retainer against a percentage (one-third to one-half) of the recovery he wins for you. On the other hand, if you are simply objecting to an accounting, the fee will normally be on an hourly basis.

Whether you are for or against the estate, however, and whatever fee arrangement you agree upon, as stated above, make sure you ask your lawyer to explain it in a letter to you. We guarantee that this will come in handy for both of you because, when it comes to money, we all have a tendency to be "forgetful."

Firing an Estate Lawyer

At some point between the petition for probate of the will and the allowance of the final account of the personal representative, you may decide that you are unhappy with your lawyer and you want to fire him. But is it that easy? Can the lawyer obstruct the settlement of the estate if he refuses to be fired? And what if he won't return the estate files and papers to you?

Before you even think about firing the lawyer you hired to handle the estate, you should first be sure of your reasons for firing him. If it is simply a lack of communication, of which many lawyers are guilty, this by itself is not a good reason, since, despite it, he may be doing a superb job in settling the estate. If there has been no communication, put the pressure on him to bring you up to date immediately. If he neglects your calls and letters, show up at his office and demand to see someone regarding the status of the estate. If this doesn't work, maybe it's more than a lack of communication and you should consider changing lawyers.

If communication is not a problem and you are receiving regular reports, but you are nevertheless dissatisfied with your lawyer's performance, once again you should try to identify the problems. We find that if clients are not made aware of the amount of time it takes to settle an estate, they think that any delays are the lawyer's fault, no matter how efficient the lawyer may be. If it is something other than the delays that bothers you, before you do fire your lawyer, get a second opinion on his performance. Consult with another estate lawyer, describing the situation as best you can; you might even give the second lawyer the authorization to call or write to your lawyer for additional information to help him evaluate the situation. We have seen a number of situations where just a call or a letter from another lawyer investigating the matter will snap the first lawyer into action.

If it turns out that your first lawyer is simply incompetent and is not handling the estate properly, one of two things can happen on inquiry from your "new" lawyer (after you have told the first he has been fired). One, he may recognize the fact that he can't handle the estate and gladly turn over the files, provided you pay him for work he has done to date. If you feel this is fair, you can pay; otherwise, you can fight it, but he still has to turn over the files—he cannot keep them as hostage for payment. If you do decide to challenge the fees, most local bar associations have a low-cost or free so-called "fee arbitration board," and after the parties agree to be bound by the board's decision, it will listen to both sides and render a judgment.

The second possibility is that your original lawyer will ignore the fact that you are firing him and simply continue to do work on the estate, asserting that he has some sort of "right" to continue. This is improper. Remember that as a client, you have the *absolute right* to discharge your attorney at any time with or without cause, no matter how arbitrary your decision may seem. The only stipulation the court makes is that you may be required to pay a fair fee for the work done to the date of the discharge.

If the lawyer ignores your instructions or refuses to return the estate files and records to you, then you may have to resort to filing a complaint with the disciplinary committee of the local bar board. Before you do this, though, you should understand that it will necessitate some time and involvement on your part, and you should review your record-keeping to make sure you have the "evidence" to back up your claims. Bar associations are quite responsive to a client's complaint, but they don't automatically prejudge the lawyer to be wrong or the client to be right. Usually they'll ask each party (the client and the lawyer) to detail his or her side of the story, and then they will reach a decision. The process could require you to take the time to respond to subsequent inquiries by the board, and in some cases you may be required to attend a hearing, although a hearing would be unlikely in the simple case of a refusal to return files. In short, you should use a complaint only as a last resort; bringing a formal complaint to the bar board, however, will usually motivate all but the most cantankerous lawyers to cooperate, since the board has the power to recommend suspension or even disbarment for professional misbehavior.

Before you make the move to fire your lawyer, be sure you have a new lawyer ready to take over the handling of the estate. The procedure for finding the new lawyer will presumably be no different from that for finding the first, and don't be discouraged if you find that you have to change lawyers partway through the settlement of the estate. It is not unusual to use more than one attorney in estate settlements. This is because despite the initial screening or interviewing process, it is sometimes difficult to tell whether the attorney you initially choose will be able to do the job. It may only later become apparent that he is not adequately familiar with handling estates or that he simply does not have the time to work on your case. In either event, as soon as you realize that you would be better off changing lawyers, you should start looking for another. Be prepared to explain in some detail why you are making the change, as lawyers are often wary of a client who jumps from lawyer to lawyer, complaining all the way. In any event, the longer you wait, the longer it will take to settle the estate, and the greater the exposure to interest and penalties for late payment of taxes or other expenses. Remember, you are not obliged to keep a lawyer, only to pay him the fair value for the services rendered.

Often the problem, or at least a part of the problem, is not the lawyer but the estate itself. That is, a poorly planned estate can make a reasonably good lawyer, who may have had no trouble with a well-planned estate, look bad. And if the lawyer is of marginal competence to begin with, a poorly planned estate will simply make matters worse. But regardless of the competence of the lawyer, when estate complications arise, legal fees go up, it takes more time to settle the estate, and clients often get mad at the lawyer because of it. The good news is that much of this can be avoided by having a well-planned estate.

Estate settlement can be made extremely smooth and legal fees kept to a minimum by having your own estate plan in good order, keeping in mind that although you should always have a will, a will is *not* by itself an estate plan. In most instances, your estate plan will include a will, a durable power of attorney, and at least one living trust, with the important understanding that ownership of your assets must be coordinated with these documents or your plan will fail.

When all of this is done, you can feel as Ishmael did in the novel *Moby-Dick,* when he said, after signing his will,

> I felt all the easier: a stone was rolled away from my heart. Besides, all the days I should now live would be as good as the days that Lazarus lived. . . . I survived myself.

Keep This in Mind

If we had to tell you which chapter of our book is the most important, it might be this one. This is because whatever it is that is being done, such as drafting a will or a trust, engaging in a contest, settling a dispute, or settling an estate, it is the lawyer you selected who will be the key to resolving any of these in the right or best way. Thus, do not rush to choose, and *do* interview and investigate before you decide. Remember, you are dealing with issues relating to life and death.

Appendix:
Personal Representative's Checklist

NOTE: With the exception of the deadline for filing the estate tax returns, the time periods indicated on the following checklist in which the items should be begun or completed are offered *only* as general guides, and meeting these time periods is normally possible only under the best of circumstances. Often, the key family members are too distraught over the loss of a loved one to act promptly, or the required information is not immediately available. Nevertheless, it is always a good idea to engage the estate attorney as promptly as possible after a person's death, because, in many instances, the attorney can proceed to take some or all of the steps outlined below, thereby taking the pressure off the family members.

I. WITHIN THE FIRST WEEK AFTER DECEDENT'S DEATH

A. Arrange a conference with decedent's immediate family and gather all available information as to decedent's assets, debts, location of personal financial and business financial data, and estate plan documents.

B. Guard against identity theft by notifying the major credit reporting agencies of the decedent's death.

C. Meet with decedent's attorney, or the attorney you select to handle the estate, and:

1. Bring an inventory of all assets that you are able to locate, in which decedent held sole ownership of or held a joint interest.
2. Bring an inventory of all decedent's debts outstanding at the time of death.
3. Bring all decedent's legal documents that you can find: wills, trusts, contracts, buy-sell agreements, partnership agreements, employment contracts, leases, corporate record books.
4. Bring all decedent's personal income tax returns for the three years preceding death, and business tax returns for the five years preceding death.
5. Ask your attorney to outline briefly for you the steps to be taken during the administration/settlement of the estate.
6. Ask your attorney to explain his fees in representing the estate. Have him confirm the arrangement in a letter.

D. Compile and review decedent's most recent (past six months to one year) personal and financial statements.

E. If decedent owned a bank safe-deposit box, arrange to have it opened, and then inventory all the contents.

F. After inventory of safe-deposit box is completed, remove those documents from the safe-deposit box that require immediate action to be taken (stocks, bonds, other paper representation of passive investments, leases, notes, etc.).

G. If decedent left a surviving spouse, arrange with the spouse to prepare a monthly budget of her expenses.

H. If decedent left surviving dependents, determine all sources of income that can be applied for their immediate benefit.

I. After consulting with the estate's attorney, determine whether you will need to open probate proceedings in the probate court (this is a matter of the amount of probate assets and the statutory monetary threshold for filing probate proceedings in the particular state the decedent was domiciled in at the time of his death). If probate is necessary, complete and have signed the required court papers in order to commence probate proceedings.

J. If there are no members of decedent's family living in decedent's home at time of death, or if decedent did not leave a surviving spouse, then immediately arrange to seal decedent's home. (After the home has been sealed, do not enter it alone until a complete inventory and appraisal of the contents has been completed.)

K. Contact or meet with decedent's accountant: the accountant will be able to provide you with critical information about decedent's financial arrangements, business investments, and tax filings.

L. Contact or meet with decedent's wealth manager: the wealth manager will be able to provide you with critical information about decedent's portfolio, passive investments, etc.

   1. It is often necessary to take immediate action with regard to certain types of passive investments that are risky and need to be watched closely, such as puts, calls, or commodity contracts. Often personal representatives will need to sell such assets and reinvest in more stable investments in order to ensure the preservation of the estate's assets.
   2. Cancel open orders on brokerage accounts.
   3. Check all investments to see whether any have short deadlines for exercising any rights: stock options, warrants, purchase rights, and pension plans.

M. Determine whether the decedent had casualty policies and assets that need to be insured.

   1. Reevaluate the coverage, and if it is not adequate to protect the value of the estate assets, increase the coverage. Also determine whether you want to change insurance companies.
   2. Determine who the new owner of the policy should be (it will be either the surviving joint owner of the asset, the trustee of the trust in which the asset is now held, or the administrator/personal representative of the estate) and arrange to have new endorsements on the policies.
   3. Review the homeowner's policy, especially if the home is now vacant and a new policy needs to be issued. Arrange, if not already

the case, to have the policy insure the contents of the home for the replacement value, not the fair market value.

N. If decedent owned a car at time of death, change the automobile registration and insurance coverage over to the new owner's name. (Depending on the state's statutes, this might be done outside the probate court. Further, some states allow the surviving spouse to continue to operate the car under the same policy for the duration of the policy period.)
O. Discuss with family members and estate's attorney all possible issues and areas in which the estate might be subject to liability. Take all necessary steps to reduce or eliminate the estate's exposure to such liability.
P. If decedent owned an interest in a closely held business, go to the business's headquarters and review all physical assets on-site (you might want to arrange for an immediate inventory in order to prevent any losses of such assets). Also, make the necessary arrangements to see that the business is continued, or terminated if appropriate, in an orderly fashion.
Q. Inspect all real estate parcels decedent owned at time of his death.
R. File (or arrange for funeral home to file) on behalf of widow for Social Security death benefits, survivor's benefits, and Veteran's Administration death benefits.
S. Secure several certified copies of death certificate, which you will need for court filings, insurance policies, etc.

II. WITHIN TWO WEEKS AFTER DEATH

A. Complete the following probate administrative proceedings:
    1. File petition for letters testamentary (i.e., probate of will).
    2. If necessary, arrange for witnesses to the will to testify as to proper execution of the will.
    3. Publish creditors' notices in accordance with the court rules or state statutes.
    4. If appropriate, obtain heirs' assents or file proper notices of the filing of the will to all heirs. Heirs and beneficiaries should be sent a copy of the will.
B. Apply for widow's allowances and dependents' allowances or awards, where necessary and appropriate.

C. Apply for a federal tax identification number for the estate and any revocable trust that is now irrevocable.
D. Arrange with the surviving spouse to recover all decedent's mail, or, alternatively, arrange to have all mail delivered to your address or held for your pickup.
E. Apply to recover from or have benefits issued to appropriate beneficiaries of all decedent's life insurance policies, and at that time notify every insurance company to forward the form 712 to yourself or to the estate's attorney. (Note: a form 712 [or the equivalent] must be filed with the estate tax returns for *each* policy on the life of the decedent.)
F. If decedent's death resulted from accident, determine whether the estate should file any claims pursuant to accidental death, life insurance policies, disability claims, health insurance policies, or job-related claims.
G. Review decedent's credit card agreements to:
    1. Determine whether there is any available life insurance coverage on any of the cards' loans or balances.
    2. Cancel all credit cards, or change title to the name of the surviving spouse, where appropriate.
H. If decedent owned an interest in a closely held business that was subject to a buy-sell agreement, commence such proceedings (to sell his share of the business) in accordance with the terms of the agreement.
I. Open an estate account (consider whether to open only a checking account, or a combined checking/savings or money market account).
J. Arrange with health insurance carriers to continue coverage of surviving spouse and dependents, where possible.

III. WITHIN ONE MONTH AFTER DEATH

A. Arrange for appraisals on all real estate and personal property and businesses.
    1. Enter into a written agreement with the appraiser; the agreement should contain the deadline when the appraisal will be due, a date on which you will forward the appraiser a written remainder, and a provision allowing you to hire another appraiser if the appraisal is not delivered as promised, and that you will not be obligated to reimburse the appraiser for his services unless and until the appraisal report is completed and delivered.

2. When hiring an appraiser for real estate and closely held businesses, hire someone who has a well-developed reputation for making such appraisals and is known by the state's revenue department, or has at least handled substantial estate appraisals and knows how to conduct himself before a tax audit.
3. Appraisals must be obtained on all real estate, closely held businesses, personal property items of value (refer to your state's statutes on the threshold for requiring an appraisal on an item of tangible personal property; some states set the limit at $3,000), rare coins, antiques, jewelry, paintings, other collections, oil and gas interests, interests in partnerships, real estate ventures.
4. Obtain values of all passive investments such as stocks, bonds, etc. This can usually be obtained through a broker. Review with the estate's attorney the figure the IRS and state taxing authorities want to receive. (Often it is the mean fair market value selling price on the day of the decedent's death, but there are some intricacies involved in this analysis. Your broker can usually supply you with this information at no charge.)

B. Determine whether the estate is a party to any lawsuits, whether already existing or pending, and if so, determine whether the estate is plaintiff or defendant. Review the proceedings with the attorney handling the lawsuit.

C. Begin to estimate available cash sources to the estate and amounts of estate taxes and administration expenses.

D. Arrange for or collect decedent's ongoing accounts receivable such as rents, royalties, loan payments.

E. Review with the estate's attorney and heirs whether any postmortem (after-death) estate planning is advisable (this usually consists of making disclaimers to achieve estate tax savings in the estates of the heirs, in particular the decedent's surviving spouse). Disclaimers have very strict time requirements and often complicated filing requirements, so review this early on, as it often takes some time for the heirs to reach a decision on such matters.

F. Obtain copies of all gift tax returns that decedent filed during his life. Usually, the estate's attorney will want copies of these as well.

G. Determine what the state requires to be done in order for you to obtain inheritance or death tax releases on the estate assets. This varies, and in some states this step can take place at the time you file the state estate or inheritance tax return.

H. If anyone owned a life insurance policy on the decedent's life that you intend to claim is excludable from the estate, arrange with the insurance company to receive the original policy once the proceeds are paid to the beneficiary. You will need to submit the policy (or the insurance company form 712) with the federal estate tax return in order to establish that no tax is due from the estate on that policy. (Note the distinction between owner and beneficiary. If the deceased *owned* the policy, the proceeds will be counted in his estate for estate tax purposes.)

IV. WITHIN THREE MONTHS AFTER DEATH

A. Review and assess with the estate's attorney whether any of decedent's closely held corporate stock can be redeemed and the proceeds used to pay federal estate taxes and administration expenses.

B. Pay the decedent's funeral bills and the expenses of decedent's last illness, if any. Make an effort to determine and locate the decedent's creditors and notify them of his death.

C. Determine whether it is advisable to make an early withdrawal of any certificate of deposits held by decedent.

D. File state and federal *income* tax returns, if necessary, for the last taxable year of decedent's life.

E. Where decedent did not make specific bequests of his personal property, proceed to distribute the personal property items in accordance with the decedent's will.

F. Make an inventory of all gifts the decedent made within three years of death. This information will be necessary for filing the federal estate tax return. Most states will require the same information for either the three years or the two years preceding death, depending on the state's tax regulations.

G. Confer with the estate's attorney or tax advisor to determine whether the estate's accumulated income should be accumulated or distributed.

H. Confer with the estate's attorney or accountant to determine whether the estate should elect a fiscal or annual tax year.

I. If decedent owned real estate in other states at the time of his death, arrange for ancillary probate proceedings in those jurisdictions.

V. SIX TO NINE MONTHS AFTER DEATH (OR MORE, DEPENDING ON TAX OR LEGAL DELAYS)

A. This is the time period in which you will be working with the estate's attorney and possibly an accountant in preparing the estate's federal and state estate tax returns. (The return is due nine months after death; there are many guidelines and booklets available on this, including from the IRS, that review and explain how these returns must be completed.)

B. Thoroughly document the backup material for each schedule of the estate tax return; this will assist you in the event the estate is audited.

C. If there are more than adequate funds in the estate to cover any increased taxes or expenses on account of audits or other foreseeable costs, make distribution of the specific bequests in the will, after obtaining signed releases from the beneficiaries of those bequests.

D. Upon the completion of the estate administration, and after payment and filing of estate and fiduciary tax returns, and upon completion of any tax audit, prepare and file the final account with the court (if a probate estate), sending a copy to each beneficiary together with a release for the beneficiary to sign. After signed releases are received, have your final account allowed by the court and, at the same time, make distribution of the balance of the estate to the beneficiaries. If a trust is a beneficiary, that share should be given to the trustee of the trust.

E. Record tax releases on real estate, where necessary.

F. Ask the estate's attorney to review the surviving spouse's estate plan to determine whether any immediate changes need to be made to that plan, such as a new will, a living trust, a durable power of attorney, a gift-giving plan, etc.

Glossary

529 Plan. Also known as a "qualified tuition plan" after a provision in the Internal Revenue Code allowing for the income and growth on contributions to such a plan to be tax free if used for the beneficiary's qualifying educational expenses. Contributions are considered gifts for gift tax purposes but would normally qualify for the $15,000 (for 2020) annual gift-tax-free exclusion. The exclusion can be taken up to five years in advance ($75,000), but requires the filing of a gift tax return to do so. Traditionally limited to college tuition expenses, in 2018 it was expanded to include K–12 elementary and secondary school tuition for public, private, and religious schools (with a $10,000 limitation), and in 2020 was expanded to include the repayment of education loans (also with a $10,000 limitation).

Abatement. The forced reduction of shares or bequests when the testator's estate has insufficient assets to pay all debts, expenses, and bequests in full.

Accounting. The financial statement submitted to the court and to the beneficiaries by the personal representative (or trustee, in the case of a trust), showing all probate (or trust) assets in the estate (or trust) and all transactions affecting or arising from those assets, from the time the personal representative (or trustee) was appointed. Accountings are usually filed on an annual basis.

Ademption. When an item of property that was mentioned in the will is subsequently sold or otherwise disposed of before death, thereby preventing the beneficiary from inheriting the item.

Administration. The management of the estate of a deceased person.

Administration Expenses. All the expenses connected with settling an estate, including personal representative's fees, attorney's and accountant's fees, court fees, and the expenses related to estate property.

Administrator. A person named by a court to handle the settlement of the estate of a person who dies without a will, or for a deceased who had a will but no named personal representative.

Administrator CTA (Cum Testamento Annexo). When there is a will but no personal representative named in the will, or the ones named decline or are unavailable, then an administrator is appointed "with the will annexed."

Administrator De Bonis Non. An administrator appointed to succeed a previous administrator and settle the remainder of the estate.

Advancement. An amount given to an heir by the deceased during his lifetime intended as an "advance" against the heir's share under the will.

Ancillary Administration. Additional probate proceedings that must be carried out when the deceased owned property in a state or states other than that where he had his principal residence.

Applicable Exclusion Amount. Formerly referred to as the unified credit, it is the tax credit allowed under the federal tax code that is applied cumulatively to gift or estate taxes that may be due.

ART Child. A child who is born through the use of artificial reproductive technology. Local law must be consulted regarding an ART child's ability to inherit, especially if the child is conceived after the death of a parent. Careful drafting of estate plan documents can easily make sure ART children are provided for (if that is the intent of the testator).

Ascertainable Standard. A provision typically included in a discretionary trust intended to guide the trustee in exercising its discretion. The commonly used standard is "health, education, maintenance, and support." Use of this standard can allow a spouse or other beneficiary to act as trustee without exposing the trust assets to inclusion in the trustee's estate for tax purposes.

Asset Protection Trust. A trust, domestic or offshore, that is designed to protect the assets of the settlor while at the same time allowing the settlor to be a beneficiary.

Attestation Clause. A statement at the end of the will saying that the witness saw the testator sign, in their presence, and that they then signed in his presence and in each other's presence.

Attorney-in-Fact. Under a power of attorney (durable or otherwise), the person named to act as legal agent for the person who gives the power of attorney.

Beneficiary. A person who is entitled to receive benefits (usually money or other property) from a trust or an estate.

Bequest. A gift of money or other property under a will or trust.

Charitable Lead Trust (CLT). An irrevocable trust where the income of the trust is paid to a charity for a specified term of years, and the remainder passes to beneficiaries (usually family) specified by the grantor. Virtually the opposite of a charitable remainder trust.

Charitable Remainder Trust (CRT). An irrevocable trust where the grantor retains an income for life and the remainder passes to a qualified charity. The CRT is tax exempt, and it may sell the grantor's appreciated assets and pay no capital gains tax. In addition, the grantor is usually entitled to a present income tax deduction for the future gift to charity.

Codicil. An amendment to a previous will, but executed with the same formalities as a will.

Common Disaster. Where two or more people, including the testator and a beneficiary, die in the same accident and it is impossible to tell who died first. Also referred to as a "simultaneous death."

Common Property. Property that is held by two or more parties under one of the forms of co-ownership, i.e., joint tenancy, tenancy in common, tenancy by the entirety, or community property.

Community Property. In the states of Arizona, California, Idaho, Louisiana, Nevada, New Mexico, Texas, Washington, and, to a certain extent,

Wisconsin, property that is acquired by spouses during their marriage. (In most of these states, gifts and inheritances are excluded.) Spouses each have a one-half interest in their community property and therefore only one-half of such property can be disposed of by will. Some states, such as Alaska, permit spouses to choose the community property regime.

Convenience Account. An account—usually a bank account—that has been opened in joint names but only for the convenience of one of the joint owners and not with the intent that the noncontributing owner receive the balance in the account. As a result, the account could be part of a deceased owner's probate estate.

Corporate Trustee. An organization such as a bank or a trust company that receives, holds, and manages money and other property for a fee from members of the public under a trust agreement.

Co-Tenancy. When two or more parties own the same property at the same time and the property remains undivided.

Co-Tenant. One of the owners under a co-tenancy.

Co-Trustee. Another person, often a family member, who serves with the trustee in helping to make decisions concerning the trust.

Crummey Power. A provision, typically in a trust, where a beneficiary is given the power, which usually lasts thirty to sixty days, to withdraw his share of a contribution made to the trust by the settlor or some other party. The purpose of the power is to cause the contribution to the trust to qualify as a tax-free "annual exclusion" gift to the beneficiary or beneficiaries.

Crummey Trust. A trust that contains Crummey powers, though otherwise it could be any type of trust.

Decanting. The act of transferring assets (often all assets) of one trust into a new trust with more favorable provisions. Decanting is formally recognized in the majority of U.S. states.

Devise. A gift of real estate under a will.

Directed Trust. Providing in the terms of a trust that the trustee must follow the direction of a named trust "advisor" or trust "director" as to certain functions of the trust, such as investments of the trust assets or distributions to trust beneficiaries. Except in the case of fraud or intentional wrongdoing, a trustee who follows such direction will not be held liable in the case of losses or other claims resulting from the direction. The majority of states have statutes governing directed trusts.

Disclaimer. When a beneficiary or heir under a will, an estate, or a trust does not wish to accept the bequest, he may disclaim it without tax consequences if he does so in writing within a certain time, usually nine months, after he becomes entitled to the bequest.

Discretionary Trust. A trust that allows the trustee to decide "in its discretion" how much to distribute to the beneficiaries from time to time.

Divided Trust. Bifurcating a trust so that each separate part is administered separately, as if it were an independent trust, typically with different trustees.

Domicile. The place where a person permanently resides, even though he may not spend all or even a majority of his time there.

Donee. A person who receives a gift.

Donor. A person who makes a gift; sometimes one who creates a trust (see **Settlor**).

Durable Power of Attorney. (See also **Power of Attorney.**) If a power of attorney is a "durable" power, it must be in writing, and unlike a power that is not a durable power, the right to act under a durable power continues even though the person giving the power has become legally incompetent. A power of attorney, whether durable or not, expires on the giver's death. (It's not *that* durable!)

Dynasty Trust. An irrevocable trust intended to last (and grow) for several generations after the settlor (in some states, forever), bypassing estate taxes in each successive generation. (See **Generation-Skipping Trust** and **Rule Against Perpetuities.**)

Escheat. If a person has no will and no heirs, his property returns (escheats) to the state, after payment of debts and expenses.

Estate Tax Return. Internal Revenue Service form (706) that must be filed within nine months of a person's death if the person's total estate consisted of more than a specified amount of assets ($11.58 million for deaths in 2020). Some states impose their own estate tax (or inheritance tax) and have a separate filing threshold and form.

Executor. A person (or organization) named in a will to handle the settlement of the estate according to the will. Under modern laws (and as used in this book) now called a "personal representative."

Family Trust. In common usage, a trust agreement that provides for a certain portion of the estate or trust to be set aside in a separate trust to operate for the benefit of the family (spouse, children, relatives, or any combination thereof).

Fiduciary. Anyone responsible for the custody or management of property belonging to others, such as a personal representative, trustee, guardian, or conservator.

Fiduciary Duty. The high degree of trust, responsibility, and objectiveness required of anyone acting as a fiduciary.

Fraudulent Conveyance or Transfer or Voidable Transaction. A transfer that is deemed to have been made with the intent (express or implied) to defeat or prejudice the claim of a known or future creditor, and which may therefore cause the transferred property to be considered available to satisfy the claim of the creditor.

Funding. The transfer of property to a trust.

Generation-Skipping Trust. A trust that is designed to provide benefits for two or more successive generations after that of the grantor without being exposed to estate tax from generation to generation, and as well to avoid the generation-skipping transfer tax (GST) imposed when a person attempts to provide for someone two or more generations younger than himself. The younger generations may (but need not) be lineal descendants of the settlor/grantor. There is a GST exemption of $1 million per grantor. (See **Dynasty Trust** and **Rule Against Perpetuities.**)

Gift. The transfer of any type of property from one individual to another without consideration (payment).

Gift Tax. The federal (and sometimes state) tax levied on the act of making a taxable gift, usually charged to the donor.

Gift Tax Exclusion (Annual). The amount of a gift that is not subject to a gift tax, measured or allowed on an annual basis. The amount is indexed for inflation and changes from time to time.

Gift Tax Return. An Internal Revenue Service form (709) that is required to be filed with the donor's income tax return to report annual gifts of over $15,000 per donee or of any amount if the gift does not qualify as a "present interest." The gift tax return would show gifts occurring in the previous calendar year.

Grantor. A person who creates a trust—also called donor or settlor.

Grantor Retained Annuity Trust (GRAT). An irrevocable trust for a specified term of years, during which the grantor will receive a specified annual sum (an annuity) and after which the remaining trust assets belong to the remainder beneficiaries, outside the grantor's estate.

Grantor Retained Interest Trust (GRIT). Similar to the GRAT, except that the annual payments to the grantor may be tied to the actual income of the trust. Close family members may not be remainder beneficiaries of a GRIT.

Grantor Trust. A trust that, for income tax purposes, is treated as owned by the grantor and that results in all income of the trust being taxed to him.

Guardian ad Litem. A representative (usually an attorney) appointed by the court to represent the interest of a minor or incompetent person.

Heir. The person or persons who will inherit probate property according to the laws of a state when a person dies without a will.

Holographic Will. A will that is completely handwritten by the testator and signed and dated by him, with or without witnesses. An unwitnessed holographic will is valid in only a few states.

Incapacitated Person. A person who has been legally declared by a court to be unable to handle his own affairs.

Intangible Personal Property. Property other than real estate and other than property that can be "touched." Examples of intangible property: stocks, bonds, bank accounts, copyrights, patents, etc., as they all merely represent the right to receive something of value.

In Terrorem Clause. A statement in a will or trust providing that any beneficiary who contests the document or in any way interferes with its operation will forfeit his share. Binding in most states.

Inter Vivos Trust. A trust created while the creator of it is alive—a "living" trust.

Intestate. When a person dies without a will, he dies intestate.

Inventory. A list of all the estate assets that come into the hands of the personal representative of the estate. The inventory must be filed with the court within a prescribed period after the fiduciary is appointed.

Irrevocable Life Insurance Trust (ILIT). An irrevocable trust that holds (as owner and beneficiary) one or more life insurance policies on the settlor's life and is typically designed to produce estate-tax-free benefits, which would include the proceeds of the life insurance, for the settlor's family or others.

Irrevocable Trust. A trust that cannot be changed or revoked by the person who created it.

Issue. Lineal descendants of a person, e.g., children, grandchildren, great-grandchildren, etc. Modern statutes no longer use the term "issue" and use "descendants" instead.

Joint Ownership. When two or more people own the same property at the same time, generally in equal shares, with the understanding that on the death of any one, the survivor(s) will own the whole.

Joint Property. Any property in joint ownership form (not just real estate).

Joint Tenancy. Same as joint ownership.

Joint Tenant. One of the joint owners in a joint ownership or a joint tenancy.

Joint Trust. A trust with two settlors, both of whom contribute assets to the trust, but with one set of trust provisions, commonly benefiting both settlors for their lives and then other family members. Although the concept may appear simple and more economical than having two trusts, drafting such trusts can be very tricky, and the perceived savings are quickly obscured by the complicated legal and tax confusion that typically results from such trusts. It should also be noted that, despite the foregoing, joint trusts are often used in community property states where certain laws override the provisions of the trust.

Joint Will. One will that is declared to be the will of two persons, usually husband and wife, signed by both and witnessed as a regular will. Joint wills are generally a bad idea.

Kiddie Tax. The income tax imposed on the unearned income (dividends, interest) in excess of an annual exemption on a child under age eighteen, and under certain conditions to age twenty-four. The tax on the excess income is levied at the tax rate imposed on trusts, which is a very high rate.

Lapsed Gift. A gift or bequest that is not paid to the named beneficiary because he or she is deceased and the will did not provide for the bequest to be paid to another.

Letters of Administration. The official document given by the court authorizing the personal representative to act. Also known as "letters testamentary."

Life Estate. The right to the use of property during one's lifetime only, after which the property belongs to the "remaindermen" outright.

Life Tenant. A person who has a life estate.

Living Trust. A trust created during the lifetime of the person who created it.

Living Will. Not a will at all but a legal declaration (signed and witnessed like a will) stating that in the event of a catastrophic illness, the person does not (or does) wish to be kept alive by artificial means or heroic measures. A few states do not formally recognize living wills.

Marital Deduction. A deduction for estate and gift tax purposes for the amount of property that passes to a spouse from the other spouse.

Marital Deduction Trust. A trust established to receive an amount on behalf of the surviving spouse that qualifies for the marital deduction.

Miller Trust. A "safe harbor" trust under the Medicaid rules, allowing a trust to be funded with the *income* of a Medicaid beneficiary in an "income-cap" state, so that the beneficiary may qualify for Medicaid. Also called a "qualified income trust."

Nominee Trust. A special purpose trust originally designed to hold real estate, and thus sometimes called a "realty trust," where the identity of the beneficiaries is contained in a document *separate* from the rest of the trust, called a "schedule of beneficial interest" or "SBI."

Noncontest Clause. See **In Terrorem Clause.**

Noncupative Will. An oral will, allowed only in extreme cases (and not in all states) such as where the testator faces imminent death.

Nonprobate Property. Property owned or partially owned by the deceased but which does not pass through his probate estate, such as jointly held property, property with a beneficiary designation (like a retirement account), or property in a living trust.

Offshore Trust. A trust that is settled and governed by the laws of a jurisdiction other than the United States. In the vernacular, it is generally one that is literally offshore, such as those found in places like Gibraltar, the Cook Islands, the Bahamas, etc., and generally used for asset protection purposes. (See **Asset Protection Trusts.**)

Partition. The right of a co-tenant and in some cases a life tenant to have the commonly held property divided by court order. Where real estate is concerned, this usually means a court-ordered sale of the property and division of the net proceeds.

Per Capita. When a distribution or share is given equally to each person in a group (as opposed to **Per Stirpes**). For example, if a trust terminates, and the trust states that the trust assets are to be distributed to all then-living beneficiaries "per capita," then each then-living beneficiary receives an equal share.

Per Capita at Each Generation. Commonly referenced as "equally near, equally dear," per capita at each generation treats the individuals at each generational level equally. For example, say that at the date of the decedent's death, the decedent had two (2) living daughters, a predeceased son leaving three (3) living children of his own, and a predeceased daughter leaving two (2) living children of her own. Under this example, each living daughter would receive 25 percent of the estate and the five (5) grandchildren would equally share the predeceased children's combined 50 percent, thereby each receiving 10 percent of the estate.

Personal Property. Any property other than real estate.

Personal Representative. A person (or organization) appointed by the court to handle the settlement of an estate. Formerly called the **Executor.**

Personal Residence Trust (PRT). An irrevocable trust to which a grantor may transfer a personal residence (one per trust, maximum two trusts) and retain the right to live there for a specified term of years, after which, if the grantor survives the term, the residence escapes tax in the grantor's estate.

Per Stirpes. When a distribution or share is given by right of a person's ancestor. For instance, if the testator leaves his estate to his two sons "or their descendants, per stirpes," and both sons are deceased, son A leaving one child, son B leaving four children, then A's child will take one-half the estate and B's children will share the other half. Per stirpes is also referred to as "right of representation."

Pooled Trust. A "safe harbor" trust under the Medicaid rules allowing a trust established by a charitable organization to receive and pool funding from individuals eligible to receive Medicaid. Assets contributed to such a trust are ignored for Medicaid eligibility purposes if on the individual's death any trust distributions from the individual's account are used first to reimburse the state for benefits paid to or for the individual.

Portability. Where the deceased is survived by a spouse, and where the value of the deceased's estate is less than the allowable exclusion ($11.58 million in 2020), the personal representative of the deceased's estate may elect to preserve ("port") the amount of the unused exclusion of the deceased's estate over to the (future) estate of the surviving spouse, thereby increasing the allowable exclusion for the surviving spouse's estate. This is done by filing a federal estate tax return (form 706).

Pourover Provision. A provision in a will that usually gives the bulk of the estate to a living trust created by the testator before or at the time the will is signed.

Power of Appointment. The power to dispose of property held under someone else's will or trust, although a person could transfer property and *retain* a power of appointment for himself.

Power of Attorney. A document (or verbal instruction) giving someone the right, which can be broad or very limited, to legally act for the person giving the power, typically with respect to administrative and financial matters. If a power of attorney is a "durable" power, it must be in writing, and unlike a power that is not a durable power, the right to act under a durable power continues even though the person giving the power has become legally incompetent. A power of attorney, whether durable or not, expires on the giver's death.

Pretermitted Heir. A child or other lineal descendant who has been improperly omitted from the will.

Private Family Foundation. For estate-planning purposes, this generally means a noncharitable entity similar in some respects to a trust established for the benefit of a family. The private (family) foundation originated in foreign civil law jurisdictions where trusts are not recognized and characteristically would provide benefits for family members over generations. In traditional private foundations, the beneficiaries may not have the same rights as beneficiaries of a trust. Today, most civil law countries (e.g., those in Europe and South America), as well as virtually all of the Caribbean jurisdictions, have private foundation laws, and just recently, New Hampshire and Wyoming became the first U.S. states to allow them, although they may not offer the same benefits as the foreign foundation.

Probate. The procedure in each state required to settle legally the estate of a deceased person and transfer his "probate property."

Probate Property. Property that may be transferred only through the probate procedure and would therefore include property or proceeds payable to the estate of the deceased, as well as property titled in the deceased's name alone or as a tenant in common.

Protector. A person or entity other than a trustee who is given certain powers over the trust, such as the power to veto trust distributions, change trustees, etc. The protector, unlike a trustee, does not have legal title to the trust property. A protector is sometimes referred to as a "Trust Advisor."

Purpose Trust. A trust that is established for a purpose (e.g., furtherance of a business, maintenance of a building, care of a pet) rather than for specified beneficiaries. Some states such as Oregon and South Dakota have specific purpose trust laws, and the Uniform Trust Code, enacted by many states, has a section regarding purpose trusts. A purpose trust is recognized in most offshore jurisdictions.

Qualified Domestic Trust (QDOT). A trust that is used if the surviving spouse is not a U.S. citizen. If a QDOT is not used in such a case, the marital deduction is lost.

Qualified Income Trust. See **Miller Trust.**

Qualified Personal Residence Trust (QPRT). The same as a PRT, except that in a QPRT the residence may be sold without losing the tax benefits of the trust.

Qualified Terminable Interest Trust (QTIP Trust). A trust leaving mandatory income to a spouse and optionally principal at the discretion of a trustee, where the spouse can be given no control over the disposition of the remaining trust principal at her death. The QTIP trust can qualify for the estate tax marital deduction.

Realty Trust. See **Nominee Trust.**

Release. The document that the personal representative or trustee will ask the beneficiaries to sign before receiving their bequest, releasing the estate or trust from further liability.

Remainderman. The person(s) designated to receive what is left when a trust or estate terminates.

Residuary Estate. Whatever remains of the estate after payment of debts, expenses, taxes, and specific bequests. In a "pourover" will, the residuary estate is left to a living trust.

Retained Interest. Typically in a trust, whether revocable or irrevocable, where the settlor has retained some part or interest, such as an income stream, in the property transferred to the trust.

Revocable Trust. A trust that may at any time be altered, amended, or revoked by the creator.

Right of Severance. The right of a co-tenant to separate or divide commonly held property under a joint tenancy or a tenancy in common.

Right of Survivorship. The right of a joint tenant (but not a tenant in common) to take the whole of the jointly held property if he survives the other joint tenant(s).

Rule Against Perpetuities. A rule of trust law providing that a family-type (i.e., noncharitable) trust must terminate at a certain future time. In general, it works out to ninety to one hundred years after the transfer becomes irrevocable. Many states have abolished or revised the rule and allow such trusts to continue without limitation or decades past the one-hundred-year rule.

Self-Settled Trust. A trust where the person creating the trust (the settlor) is also the beneficiary or one of the beneficiaries of that trust.

Settlor. A person who creates a trust.

Severance. The act of dividing commonly held property (see **Partition**).

Special Needs Trust (SNT). A trust naming a person with disabilities as beneficiary, established by another person, providing the trustee with complete discretion to make (or not to make) distributions to or for the beneficiary, having in mind both the beneficiary's special needs and benefits that may be available to the beneficiary outside the trust.

Spendthrift Provision. The provision in a trust agreement that allows the donor to place the share of the beneficiary out of reach of the beneficiary's creditors. The funds of this particular beneficiary (other than the donor) while in the trust cannot be attached or recovered by someone suing the beneficiary. (See also **Asset Protection Trust.**)

Spousal Lifetime Access Trust (SLAT). Also sometimes referred to as a spousal limited access trust, the SLAT is an irrevocable trust created and funded by one spouse, using that spouse's own funds, for the benefit of the other spouse, and also if desired for children and grandchildren. Use of a SLAT can provide estate tax savings and asset protection for the family.

Spray Provision. A provision in a trust giving the trustee the discretion to make unequal distributions among the beneficiaries. Also known as a "sprinkle provision."

Stepped-Up Cost Basis. An increased (usually) tax cost in property that takes effect when that property is received as the result of a person's death and included in the person's estate for estate tax purposes. If the property decreased in value in the hands of the decedent, then the cost basis has a "step-down" at death.

Street-Name Securities. Stocks or bonds of a customer that are held in the name of the brokerage house for ease of transfer.

Structured Settlement Trust. A trust that is funded with payments to be received over a period of time as the result of a settlement in a personal injury lawsuit.

Successor Personal Representative. A person named in a will to replace the first-named personal representative if he is not able to serve for any reason.

Successor Trustee. A person appointed to replace the original trustee when the original trustee ceases to serve for any reason.

Supplemental Needs Trust. A special trust established for a person who is receiving or who may be receiving benefits under a welfare benefit program where the trust provides benefits that are over and above (supplemental) to the person's basic needs for food, clothing, and shelter. The assets in a properly drafted supplemental needs trust will not affect the person's eligibility for government benefits. This type of trust may or may not be the same as a special needs trust, depending on the respective terms.

Tangible Personal Property. Property other than real estate that has inherent value and can be touched, such as jewelry, furniture, clothing, automobiles, boats, machinery, etc.

Tenancy by the Entirety (T by E). A special form of joint tenancy in which only spouses can be co-tenants and neither (alone) can cause a division of the property. T by E is not available in all states.

Tenancy in Common. When two or more parties own the same property at the same time, but not necessarily in equal shares, and there is no right of survivorship, so that a deceased co-tenant's share passes through his estate. Any co-tenant can cause a division of the property (see partition).

Testamentary. By or under a will.

Testamentary Trust. A trust created under the terms of a will, and therefore only effective through the probate process. A testamentary trust also requires the filing of annual accountings to the probate court, whereas a living trust only requires accountings to the beneficiaries.

Testate. Dying with a will.

Testator. The person who makes a will.

Transferee. One who receives transferred property.

Transferor. One who transfers property.

Trust. A relationship in which one person (the trustee) is the holder of the legal title to property (the trust property) to keep or use for the benefit of another person (the beneficiary), although in some cases a person can be a trustee and also a beneficiary of the same trust.

Trust Advisor. Typically a party appointed in the terms of the trust and given the authority to direct the trustee as to certain matters, such as investments of trust assets or distributions to beneficiaries. A trust may also have a party designated as "trust advisor" whose advice may be sought by the trustee but not necessarily followed. See also **Protector** and **Trust Director.**

Trust Director. See **Trust Advisor.**

Trustee. An individual or professional organization that holds the legal title to property and manages it for the benefit of another person or persons. It is also possible for a person to be trustee of a trust in which she is also a beneficiary.

Under-65 Trust. A "safe harbor" trust under the Medicaid laws, allowing a discretionary trust to be established for a person who is under the age of sixty-five and allowing the assets in such a trust to be ignored for Medicaid eligibility purposes, if the trust provides for reimbursement to the state on the death of the beneficiary.

Undivided Interest. A share of property that has not been physically set aside or divided, such as a joint interest in a home or a tenancy in common in stocks.

Undue Influence. Persuading a person to change his will in a way he would not have done on his own.

Unified Credit. A tax credit, allowed by the federal government, that may be applied toward either gift or estate taxes that may be due.

Index

Simutaneous deaths 191

196

Durable Power of Attorney & 198

Ceases upon death

352 - gets his estate plan attorney